Napoleon is supposed to have said, 'glory is fleeting, but obscurity is forever', but this collection of essays both revisits some of the most glorious episodes of the Napoleonic Wars and rescues from obscurity some fascinating but overlooked episodes For over 20 years the Napoleon Series website and forum have functioned as a major hub for the international community of Napoleonic scholars. This book was commissioned with the support of then-editor of the Napoleon Series, distinguished Napoleonic scholar Robert Burnham, and the writing team are all contributors to the website. There is material here on the armies of France, Britain, Prussia, and Austria as well as some of the smaller German states, and the chapters range across the span of the European conflict from 1805 to 1814.

Andrew Bamford is editor of the From Reason to Revolution series and has written extensively on the wars of the eighteenth century and Napoleonic era.

# Glory is Fleeting

## New Scholarship on the Napoleonic Wars

Edited by Andrew Bamford

Foreword by Robert Burnham

Helion & Company Limited

Helion & Company Limited
Unit 8 Amherst Business Centre
Budbrooke Road
Warwick
CV34 5WE
England
Tel. 01926 499619
Email: info@helion.co.uk
Website: www.helion.co.uk
Twitter: @helionbooks
blog.helion.co.uk/

Published by Helion & Company 2021
Designed and typeset by Mach 3 Solutions Ltd (www.mach3solutions.co.uk)
Cover designed by Paul Hewitt, Battlefield Design (www.battlefield-design.co.uk)



Cover: Detail from 'Bataille près d'Eggmuhl: le 22 Avril 1809', aquatint by and after Johann Lorenz Rugendas II (Anne S.K. Brown Collection).



ISBN 978-1-912866-69-4

British Library Cataloguing-in-Publication Data.
A catalogue record for this book is available from the British Library.



For details of other military history titles published by Helion & Company Limited, contact the above address, or visit our website: http://www.helion.co.uk

We always welcome receiving book proposals from prospective authors.

# Contents

# List of Plates

# List of Maps

# List of Contributors

**Daniel Clarke** holds a Masters in Conflict Studies from the University of Wolverhampton and currently works for the children's charity NSPCC. A version of his Masters thesis, 'Why Englishmen Fought in the American Civil War', was published in the magazine *History Today*. He has since delved deeper into the varied history of the Napoleonic Wars, which led to writing a handful of articles for the Napoleon Series website and this chapter. Daniel is currently working on a book of biographies about Austrian officers who participated in the Napoleonic Wars.

**Guy Dempsey** is a lawyer by profession, but his avocation is the use of primary sources for the study of Napoleonic military history. He has written four books and numerous articles on First Empire topics, preferring to explore less familiar territory. Guy has an abiding interest in the military uniforms of the period and considers his ultimate goal to be the compilation of a definitive list of first-hand sources for research in that area. His next work will be a translation of a book of uniform prints by Carle and Horace Vernet and Eugène Lami that was published in 1822.

**John H. Gill (Jack)** is an adjunct professor at the Near East–South Asia Center for Strategic Studies, affiliated with the National Defense University in Washington DC. Specializing in military history of the Napoleonic period, his publications include *Thunder on the Danube*, *With Eagles to Glory*, and *A Soldier for Napoleon* (editor), as well as chapters, articles and papers presented to the Society for Military History, the Consortium on the Revolutionary Era and the German Studies Association. His most recent book is *The Battle of Znaim: Napoleon, the Habsburgs and End of the War of 1809* (2020). A former US Army South Asia Foreign Area Officer, his other publications include an Atlas of the 1971 India-Pakistan War, chapters on current Indian and Pakistani political-military affairs, US-Indian relations, and India-Pakistan crisis behaviour.

**David Hollins** was born in Aberdeen, Scotland, in 1962. After graduating from University College London, he trained as a maritime solicitor and began his career in commercial shipping. He is a frequent contributor to specialist Napoleonic magazines and has written a number of books related to the Austrian army and its battles.

**Kevin F. Kiley** is a retired US Marine Corps artillery officer who, among other assignments, served in the First Gulf War and the liberation of Kuwait. He is a graduate of the United States Military Academy at West Point and holds a master's degree in military history from Norwich University. He is the author of four books on Napoleonic period as well as three books on military uniforms as either author or co-author. He is an avid collector of toy and model soldiers and he lives with his wife and son in Jacksonville, North Carolina.

**Hans-Karl Weiss** was born in the mid-1950s in a small town in Southern Germany. From childhood on he had a strong interest in history. After graduating from university as physician he worked, amongst places, for three years in the NHS from 1987 to 1990. Back in Germany he settled as a general practitioner. The main interests on the military historical side are the French Revolution and early Napoleonic Wars. He published numerus articles in periodicals such as *Depesche*, *Circulaire*, *Der Sammlerbrief* and others.

**Garry Wills** was born in Kingston upon Thames, UK. After working for Mars Incorporated for 28 years, he has been pursuing a lifelong interest in the Napoleonic Wars, which began in 1973, when he started wargaming the period. In 2009 Garry had an article on Denis Davidov published in *First Empire* magazine and then self-published his first book in 2011, *Wellington's First Battle*, about the Battle of Boxtel in 1794. Based on this research Garry also had a series of articles published in the *Smoothbore Ordnance Journal* relating to British artillery in Flanders 1793-5. In 2018, Garry also published a small booklet summarising three years of research into the 24 men recorded on the First World War memorial in his village. In 2020, Helion published Garry's latest book, *Wellington at Bay: The Battle of Villamuriel, 25 October 1812*.

# Foreword

In 1995, Fons Libert created a website known as the Napoleon Series. It quickly grew into an international meeting place for Napoleonic scholars and enthusiasts. Ideas and opinions were freely exchanged, and people began submitting papers for publication on the site. No longer was having an article or a book published just the purview of academicians. Weekend historians and gifted amateurs were encouraged to share their research and a Napoleonic history renaissance began! In its first 25 years over 21,000 articles, maps, images, and reviews were added to the website. At the last count, 200 individuals had written articles and contributed material. The effort is international in scope with contributors from 25 countries and every continent. And this was just the research section of the website. The Napoleon Series also hosted a bulletin board, called the History Forum. On its people could pose questions, give opinions, and discuss Napoleonic history. It soon grew into a large, vibrant community of over 1,000 registered members. In 20 years they posted 195,000 questions, answers, items of interest, and news on the Forum.

Many authors will tell you writing their first book was the hardest and that it gets easier with subsequent volumes. The Napoleon Series was the place where many of the historians who write for Helion and other publishers got their start. It was on its History Forum that a new author could pitch his idea for a book and be encouraged by those who have been published already. It was also a place that a writer, regardless if he was a first-time author or one who had written many books, could go for help when he had reached an impasse and was looking for an answer to what seemed like an impossible question. No query was too hard for the experts who were part of the History Forum community.

Dr Andrew Bamford, the editor of Helion's 'From Reason to Revolution 1721-1815 Series' approached me with an idea that would build on the Napoleon Series' success as a starting place for new authors. He wanted to commission a book that would focus on a specific aspect of the Napoleonic Wars. The idea was to use the book as a vehicle to encourage individuals to try their hand at writing, without having to commit to a full-length book. At the same he wanted to give previously-published authors the opportunity to have published articles that were stand-alone pieces published, but could not because they were too short for a book.

*Glory is Fleeting* is the result of this ground-breaking idea. There are three new authors as well as four well known individuals. All but one of the articles are about the wars in central Europe between 1805 and 1813, and one is on a French division at Salamanca in 1812. Their research brings to light new information on topics that have been too long ignored! Enjoy!

Robert Burnham
Editor (Retired)
The Napoleon Series

# Introduction

In 2008, the Napoleon Series website published my first 'serious' article on the Napoleonic Wars. I had written pieces for popular magazines before, but this was the first time that I had submitted anything for publication that was based on primary source archival research, and its acceptance was a huge confidence boost as I worked to complete my doctoral studies. In those same studies, I was able to use the Napoleon Series Discussion Forum to obtain support, advice, and recommendations from fellow scholars, and also to tap into the vast array of scholarship represented by twenty-odd years' worth of past articles. As my own research continued, I was able to add more of my own contributions to the site – including a complete reworking of my original article, the ability to do that being one of the great advantages of an online platform over a print journal – and in due course Napoleon Series editor Bob Burnham and his team were kind enough to review my own first published work and, later, the Napoleonic titles that I was able to commission for the From Reason to Revolution book series of which this volume forms a part.

One of the first things that I did, when tasked by Helion with setting up From Reason to Revolution, was to invite book submissions from the contributors to the Napoleon Series Discussion Forum, and this has led to a number of full-length titles by authors such as Steve Brown, Paul Demet, and Gareth Glover. However, it also struck me that here was an opportunity for other contributors, perhaps those starting out as I had been back in 2008, to gain experience of publishing by submitting a shorter piece as part of an edited collection, or to share a piece of research that might not, on its own, be sufficient to form the basis of a full-length book. Had I known how lengthy a process putting together such a volume was going to be, I might have thought twice before suggesting it – apart from the inevitable delays caused by the global Coronavirus pandemic, personal reasons meant that two of the original eight contributors were unable to write the chapters that they had planned, with Garry Wills gallantly stepping up to fill the gap with a new contribution and bring the total back up to seven. I am pleased to say that amongst those seven contributors we have a mixture of relatively new authors (experts, nevertheless, in their own fields) and established 'names' who will be familiar to readers of Napoleonic history.

My other goal with this project was to try and help move the Napoleonic focus away from the English-language publishing industry's apparent obsession with Wellington and Waterloo, and in this I am pleased to say that the contents of the seven chapters speak for themselves. Daniel Clarke's chapter on the Anhalt Duchies discusses a topic that I, for one, have never seen analysed in such detail in an English-language publication before, and much the same can be said for Hans-Karl Weiss's detailed account of Prussia's light infantry arm in the campaign of 1806. Kevin Kiley also takes that campaign as his focus, but looks at it primarily from the French perspective to draw out the operational lessons of the devastatingly-successful French pursuit of the defeated Prussians. Less decisive in its results than Jena-Auerstadt was the Battle of Caldiero, but David Hollins gives us a detailed account of the pivotal point in the 1805 Italian campaign and reminds us that Napoleon's Ulm-Austerlitz operations were not the only land fighting in that dramatic year.

Anyone familiar with the 1809 campaign will be aware of Jack Gill's incredible depth of work on this topic, which now stretches over five different books. Nevertheless, he is able to offer us something new with a detailed account of the Franco-Italian operations in the southern and eastern Tyrol – less well-known than the actions fought by Napoleon's Bavarian allies further north, but no less interesting. Our one trip to the Peninsula does discuss one of Wellington's battles, but the focus is on the French side where Garry Wills provides a convincing reassessment of the role of Maucune's division at Salamanca and also sheds some light on the vexed and emotive question of captured trophies. Lastly, Guy Dempsey takes us to the Battle of the Nations – Leipzig, 1813 – to explore the role of the one British unit to make it to that crowded field – Captain Bogue's Rocket Troop.

As the chapters came in and the work of putting this book together began, I was repeatedly impressed with the quality of the work that has gone into these chapters, and I hope that readers will likewise be favourably impressed. In closing this introduction, then, I would like to take the opportunity to thank all seven contributors again – both for their work, and for their patience with the unusually-lengthy gestation period of this volume – and, most of all, to thank Bob Burnham for all his work as editor of the Napoleon Series, for the support and encouragement that he gave to my own work, and for kindly agreeing to furnish this volume with a Foreword.

Andrew Bamford
January 2021

# 1

# 'We Endured a Lot, Suffered a Lot': The Anhalt Duchies during the Napoleonic Wars 1804–1814[1]

Daniel Clarke

At the beginning of Napoleon's reign as Emperor of France, there were four small principalities along the River Elbe ruled by branches of the same family.[2] These were Anhalt-Dessau, Anhalt-Bernburg, Anhalt-Köthen, and Anhalt-Bernburg-Schaumburg-Hoym, with a combined population of close to 120,000 people. The senior line was that of Anhalt-Dessau, ruled by Herzog Leopold III (1740–1817) since 1751; followed by Anhalt-Bernburg and Fürst Alexius Friedrich Christian (1767–1834); Anhalt-Köthen with Fürst August Christian Friedrich (1769–1812); and Fürst Karl Ludwig (1723–1806) who ruled Anhalt-Bernburg-Schaumburg Hoym.[3] On 20 August 1806 Fürst Karl Ludwig von Anhalt-Bernburg-Schaumburg-Hoym died, and his eldest son from his second marriage, Fürst Victor II (1767–1812), became the (disputed) ruler of the principality.

The Anhalt houses were not natural supporters of Napoleon or of France. Throughout the preceding century they had allied themselves with Austria and

1 During the course of my research Dr Wilma A. Hofmann, PhD, of Buffalo, New York, of *German Script Translations* (https://germanscripttranslations.com), helped me with a number of translations of reports from the Landesarchiv Sachsen-Anhalt. I have credited her in the following footnotes when I have used quotes and other information from her translations.

2 In 1804 there were actually five principalities, the one not mentioned here is Anhalt-Köthen-Pleß, which was created in 1765 based upon lands in Prussian Silesia.

3 Daniel Clarke, 'Officers of the Anhalt Duchies who Fought in the French Revolutionary and Napoleonic Wars, 1789–1815', *Napoleon Series* (June–November 2017) <http://www.napoleon-series.org/research/biographies/Anhalt/c_AnhaltBiographies.html> (accessed 30 March 2019); Peter H. Wilson, *From Reich to Revolution: German History, 1558-1806* (London: Palgrave Macmillan, 2004), p.376.

Prussia during any outbreak of conflict within Europe. With the destabilising French Revolution and the resulting wars of the 1790s, a number of family members of the Anhalt houses fought in the armies of their allies. Prinz Wilhelm Ludwig von Anhalt-Bernburg-Schaumburg-Hoym (1771–1799), the son of Fürst Karl Ludwig, commanded the Austrian Infanterie Regiment Kaiser Nr.1 at the Battle of Stockach in March 1799 where he was killed. Fürst August Christian Friedrich von Anhalt-Köthen gained the rank of *Feldmarschall-Leutnant* in the Austrian army and was badly wounded at the Battle of Wattignies in 1793, where he was unhorsed during a cavalry charge in which he was bayoneted several times and taken prisoner. Other members of the Anhalt houses held general officer rank and regimental command in the Prussian and Dutch armies as well.[4]

During France's 1806 war with Prussia the Anhalt houses remained neutral. However, they had sympathy for those nations wishing to rid Europe of Napoleon. This was particularly so for the newly created Herzog Leopold III von Anhalt-Dessau, who, in 1803, was given this title by Kaiser Franz II of the Holy Roman Empire, if he promised to support Austria in future conflicts. Since then Austria had been defeated by Napoleon in 1805, Franz II had been demoted to Franz I von Austria, and the Holy Roman Empire had been dissolved. Due to the promise of support for Austria the Anhalt houses did not join the *Rheinbund*—Confederation of the Rhine—created by Napoleon in July 1806. It was only in late 1806, when they saw the ease with which the Grande Armée had swept the Prussian army aside, the houses agreed that Herzog Leopold III should travel to Paris and negotiate their own entry into the *Rheinbund*. The price he exacted was quite generous, as in return for them providing a battalion-sized, 800-man infantry contingent for the *Rheinbund*, the ruling families were made Herzöge and were promised that the men of their battalion would not serve outside of Central or Northern Europe during future wars. The Anhalt Duchies officially became part of the *Rheinbund* on 11 April 1807.[5]

After entering the *Rheinbund* preparations began immediately in the newly elevated duchies to raise the required number of troops promised to Napoleon. In Dessau Herzog Leopold III issued a proclamation dated 23 May 1807,[6] calling

4 Clarke, 'Officers of the Anhalt Duchies', <http://www.napoleon-series.org/research/biographies/Anhalt/c_AnhaltBiographies.html> (accessed 30 March 2019); August von Witzleben, *Prinz Friedrich Josias von Coburg-Saalfeld, Herzog zu Sachsen* (Berlin: R. Decker, 1859), Vol.II, p.323.

5 Wilson, *From Reich to Revolution* (London: Palgrave Macmillan, 2004), p.338–342; W.J. Rawkins, *CB6, Armies of the Confederation of the Rhine, The Rheinbund Contingents 1806-1813, Part 2: Anhalt, Lippe, Reus, Schwarzburg, Waldeck, Mecklenburg-Schwerin, Oldenburg and Frankfurt* (Norwich: The History Book Man, 2015), pp.5–12; Michael Frisch, *Anhalt-Dessaus Freiheitskämpfer 1813 bis 1815 und der opferreiche Gang anhaltischer Bataillone für und gegen Napoleon in der Zeit von 1807 bis 1815* (Dessau-Großkühnau: Eigenverlag FFW Dessau-Kühnau, 2015), p.13.

6 Landesarchiv Sachsen-Anhalt (LASA), Z 44, C 16c 5 Nr. 42: Publicandum (öffentliche Bekanntmachung) wegen Stellung eines Kontingents zur Rheinbundsarmee vom 23. Mai 1807 und einzelne das Kontingent

for 350 men to join his contingent, which was to form part of the newly raised Bataillon Anhalt.[7] The Herzöge of Bernburg (240 men) and Köthen (210 men) put in place similar measures to raise their quotas as well. Anhalt-Bernburg-Schaumburg-Hoym did not contribute materially to the formation of the Bataillon Anhalt, as its population was so small: even today Hoym, the former principality's capital, has a population of only around 2,500 people. Many of the smaller German principalities that joined the *Rheinbund* did not have any form of standing military units—apart from perhaps a few palace guards—but in the case of the Anhalt Duchies, they could form their contingent upon the foundation of Anhalt-Dessau's small Jäger Korps. It was decided by the Herzöge that their battalion should contain five fusilier companies. Chosen to command the battalion was *Oberst* Friedrich Ernst von Chambaud (1757–1814) of Dessau. In 1791 he had been serving in the Prussian infantry as a *Hauptmann*, like his father before him,[8] when the then Fürst Leopold III of Anhalt–Dessau enticed him into the service of his home state to become the commander of the Dessau garrison with the rank of *Major*. Chambaud later began to organise the Jäger Korps, of which he became commander in 1795. As Anhalt-Dessau had not taken part in the fighting of the French Revolutionary Wars, Chambaud had not seen active service for over a decade by 1807. Finding suitable company officers to expand the Jäger Korps into a battalion proved difficult. Chambaud had to resort to promoting *unteroffiziere* to the rank of *Leutnant*—including an *unteroffizier* named Georg Hoppe (1783–1833),[9] who we shall read more about later—and employing *hauptmann* who had no ties, or had lost their connection, with the duchies. The former included a *Hauptmann* Hohnstein, who only months before had been an officer in one of the Brunswick infantry regiments, which had fought alongside the Prussian army at Jena and Auerstadt; while the latter included newly

betreffende Sachen, 1807–1809, 1821–1822, 'Proclamation of Herzog Leopold III of Anhalt-Dessau dated 23 May 1807'.

7 The battalion was also sometimes titled the 'Infanterie-Bataillon der Herzogtümer Anhalt', but in official returns and reports the title 'Bataillon Anhalt', or 'Bataillon von Anhalt' is commonly used. For economy of space I have used 'Bataillon Anhalt'.

8 Chambaud's father was Alexander von Chambaud who attained the rank of *Oberstleutnant* in the Prussian army. Chambaud also had two brothers, Alexander Friedrich Wilhelm and Maximilian Rudolph Theophilus. They too served in the Prussian army and both were killed in 1806 fighting against Napoleon.

9 Hoppe was born on 8 April 1783 in Zehmigkau, Anhalt-Dessau and enlisted in the Anhalt-Dessau Jäger Korps in 1802. He later became an *unteroffizier* and was promoted to *Leutnant* in 1807. In 1810–1811 in Spain he was the Bataillon Anhalt's *quartiermeister*, before being promoted to *Hauptmann* in 1811 and given command of the battalion when it was reorganised. In February 1812 he was promoted to *Oberstleutnant* and led the battalion in Russia and during the Siege of Danzig in 1813. In January 1814 he was promoted to *Oberst* and led the Anhalt contingent in Belgium, and also in 1815 when Napoleon escaped from Elba and returned to France, taking part in the sieges of Méziéres and Charleville. He died on 6 April 1833.

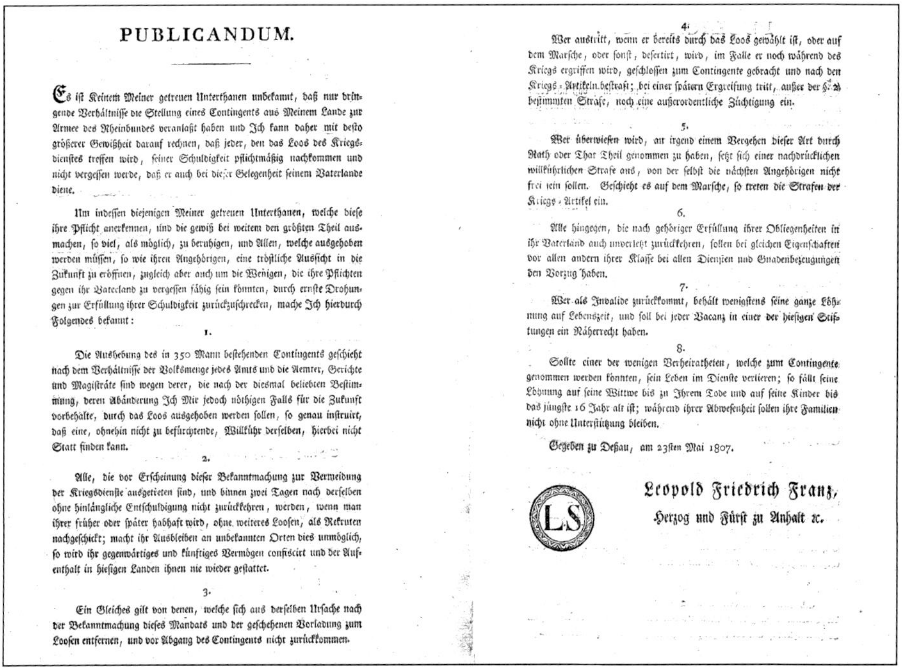

PUBLICANDUM.

Es ist Keinem Meiner getreuen Unterthanen unbekannt, daß nur dringende Verhältnisse die Stellung eines Contingents aus Meinem Lande zur Armee des Rheinbundes veranlaßt haben und Ich kann daher mit desto größerer Gewißheit darauf rechnen, daß jeder, den das Loos des Kriegsdienstes treffen wird, seiner Schuldigkeit pflichtmäßig nachkommen und nicht vergessen werde, daß er auch bei dieser Gelegenheit seinem Vaterlande diene.

Um indessen diejenigen Meiner getreuen Unterthanen, welche diese ihre Pflicht anerkennen, und die gewiß bei weitem den größten Theil ausmachen, so viel, als möglich, zu beruhigen, und Allen, welche ausgehoben werden müssen, so wie ihren Angehörigen, eine tröstliche Aussicht in die Zukunft zu eröffnen, zugleich aber auch um die Wenigen, die ihre Pflichten gegen ihr Vaterland zu vergessen fähig sein könnten, durch ernste Drohungen zur Erfüllung ihrer Schuldigkeit zurückzuschrecken, mache Ich hierdurch Folgendes bekannt:

1.

Die Aushebung des in 350 Mann bestehenden Contingents geschieht nach dem Verhältnisse der Volksmenge jedes Amts und die Aemter, Gerichte und Magisträte sind wegen derer, die nach der diesmal beliebten Bestimmung, deren Abänderung Ich Mir jedoch nöthigen Falls für die Zukunft vorbehalte, durch das Loos ausgehoben werden sollen, so genau instruirt, daß eine, ohnehin nicht zu befürchtende, Willkühr derselben, hierbei nicht Statt finden kann.

2.

Alle, die vor Erscheinung dieser Bekanntmachung zur Vermeidung der Kriegsdienste ausgetreten sind, und binnen zwei Tagen nach derselben ohne hinlängliche Entschuldigung nicht zurückkehren, werden, wenn man ihrer früher oder später habhaft wird, ohne weiteres Loosen, als Rekruten nachgeschickt; macht ihr Ausbleiben an unbekannten Orten dies unmöglich, so wird ihr gegenwärtiges und künftiges Vermögen confiscirt und der Aufenthalt in hiesigen Landen ihnen nie wieder gestattet.

3.

Ein Gleiches gilt von denen, welche sich aus derselben Ursache nach der Bekanntmachung dieses Mandats und der geschehenen Vorladung zum Loosen entfernen, und vor Abgang des Contingents nicht zurückkommen.

4.

Wer austritt, wenn er bereits durch das Loos gewählt ist, oder auf dem Marsche, oder sonst, desertirt, wird, im Falle er noch während des Kriegs ergriffen wird, geschlossen zum Contingente gebracht und nach den Kriegs-Artikeln bestraft; bei einer spätern Ergreifung tritt, außer der §. 2. bestimmten Strafe, noch eine außerordentliche Züchtigung ein.

5.

Wer überwiesen wird, an irgend einem Vergehen dieser Art durch Rath oder That Theil genommen zu haben, setzt sich einer nachdrücklichen willkührlichen Strafe aus, von der selbst die nächsten Angehörigen nicht frei sein sollen. Geschieht es auf dem Marsche, so treten die Strafen der Kriegs-Artikel ein.

6.

Alle hingegen, die nach gehöriger Erfüllung ihrer Obliegenheiten in ihr Vaterland auch unverletzt zurückkehren, sollen bei gleichen Eigenschaften vor allen andern ihrer Klasse bei allen Diensten und Gnadenbezeugungen den Vorzug haben.

7.

Wer als Invalide zurückkommt, behält wenigstens seine ganze Löhnung auf Lebenszeit, und soll bei jeder Vacanz in einer der hiesigen Stiftungen ein Näherrecht haben.

8.

Sollte einer der wenigen Verheiratheten, welche zum Contingente genommen werden könnten, sein Leben im Dienste verlieren; so fällt seine Löhnung auf seine Wittwe bis zu Ihrem Tode und auf seine Kinder bis das jüngste 16 Jahr alt ist; während ihrer Abwesenheit sollen ihre Familien nicht ohne Unterstützung bleiben.

Gegeben zu Deßau, am 23sten Mai 1807.

L.S.

Leopold Friedrich Franz,
Herzog und Fürst zu Anhalt rc.

Public announcement of Herzog Leopold III von Anhalt–Dessau from 23 May 1807, requesting volunteers to enlist in the Bataillon Anhalt. (Landesarchiv Sachsen–Anhalt: Z 44, C 16c 5 Nr. 42)

promoted *Hauptmann* Albrecht von Sonnenberg (1777–1827), who had been born in Bernburg, had joined Saxony's hussar regiment at the age of 15 in 1792, and who, in 1803, became a *Leutnant* in the Bavarian cavalry.[10]

When the Bataillon Anhalt was forming, it was agreed between the three herzöge that they would each finance their own contingent.[11] The companies of the battalion were therefore divided accordingly: Dessau provided men for the 1st and 2nd companies, Köthen the 3rd company, Bernburg the 4th company, while the

10 George F. Nafziger, *The Armies of Germany and the Confederation of the Rhine*, 1792–1815 (Privately Published, 1993), Vol.I, pp.1–2; Frisch, *Anhalt-Dessaus Freiheitskämpfer 1813 bis 1815*, p.13; L. Zeidler, *Der Spanische Feldzug des Bataillons Anhalt im Jahre 1810* (Zerbst: Friedrich Römer, 1844), pp.1–4; Ferdinand Siebigk, 'Georg Hoppe', in Historische Kommission bei der Bayerischen Akademie der Wissenschaften (ed.), *Allgemeine Deutsche Biographie* (Leipzig: Duncker & Hunblot, 1881) , Band XIII, pp.114–115; Andreas Gottfried Schmidt, *Anhalt'sches Schriftsteller-Lexikon, oder historisch-literarische Nachrichten über Schriftsteller, welche in Anhalt gebohren sind oder gewirkt haben* (Bernburg: Friedrich Wilhelm Gröning, 1830), p.403; Clarke, 'Officers of the Anhalt Duchies', <http://www.napoleon-series.org/research/biographies/Anhalt/c_AnhaltBiographies.html> (accessed 30 March 2019).

11 LASA: Z 18, C 16c 5 Nr. 45, *Verschiedene das Bataillon angehende Sachen, Berichte des Obersten von Chambaud aus Tirol, Wien usw., 1809*, 'Report of *Oberst* Chambaud, dated 3 October 1809, Vienna', Translated by Dr Wilma A. Hofmann, PhD.

5th company contained a mixture of men—80 from Bernburg, 50 from Köthen, and 23 from Dessau. Each company contained 157 officers and men giving the battalion a strength of around 785 men. The herzöge also decided that their contingents should wear the same uniform as each other. This design was a coat of dark, or forest, green—the traditional German uniform colour of light infantry such as *jägers*—with a collar of rose-pink. In 1809 there was a slight change when the turnbacks of the coat were also faced rose-pink, instead of being left as forest green. The headwear was a French-style shako—with commissioned officers wearing a bicorn, which was later replaced in 1812 by a shako—and grey breeches with black gaiters. Needing to arm and equip the battalion quickly, liberal use was made of Prussian equipment, with the men being armed with Prussian pattern muskets. However, in 1809 there was a change when the battalion was issued French muskets just prior to the campaign against Austria.[12]

After the call for volunteers in May, Chambaud and his officers did not have much time to train their men, as *Général de Division* Henri-Jacques-Guillaume Clarke (1765–1818), Governor of Berlin, arrived in Dessau on 23 June to inspect the progress of the battalion's organisation. Only two weeks later, Chambaud received orders to march to the fortress at Glogau (Glogów) in Silesia. At 3:00 a.m. on 4 July the Bataillon Anhalt assembled itself in Dessau's marketplace, and at 4:00 a.m. Herzog Leopold III entered. He offered his soldiers words of encouragement, telling them to remember their homelands and to complete their duty with 'zeal and honour'. After these regal words the battalion marched out of Dessau northward followed by a crowd of citizens.[13]

The battalion reached Berlin on 8 July, where it was ordered to assemble in the Lustgarten the next day, so that Clarke could inspect it. He was pleased with the appearance of the officers and men—some of who had been supplied with any missing equipment at Zehlendorf, just outside of the city—but he noted that the ranks of the battalion were thinner than he had seen in Dessau. After resting, the battalion left Berlin on 11 July and crossed the River Oder before reaching Glogau on 19 July. Even though the battalion had seen no combat, and had left Dessau just two weeks previously, the desertion rate amongst the soldiers and *unteroffiziere* had been vast. From a starting strength of nearly 800 men the battalion had dwindled to 280 men. *Quartiermeister* Schröder—whose short history of his time with the battalion the events of 1807 are taken from—believed that the large

12 Nafziger, *The Armies of Germany and the Confederation of the Rhine*, Vol.I, pp.1–2; Rawkins, *CB6, Armies of the Confederation of the Rhine*, pp.2 and 20–38; Zeidler, *Der Spanische Feldzug des Bataillons Anhalt*, pp.1–4.

13 LASA: Z 44, C 16c 5 Nr. 51a, Geschichtliche Darstellung der Entstehung und der Schicksale des von Anhalt-Dessau zur Armee des Rheinbundes gestellten Kontingents, Beschreibung der Märsche desselben von dem im Juli 1807 erfolgten Ausmarsch bis zum Einmarsch in Spanien am 6. Mai 1810, verfasst vom Regierungsrat Schröder, 1807–1810, subsequently referred to as 'Schröder's Bataillon Geschichte, 1807–1810'; Frisch, *Anhalt-Dessaus Freiheitskämpfer 1813 bis 1815*, pp.13–14.

number of desertions had five causes. Firstly, the battalion was mostly composed of raw recruits who had a dislike for soldiering, as they had been taken from their 'peaceful duties' at home; secondly, the march had been 'arduous' in the heat of summer with heavy equipment; thirdly, the military discipline imposed on the recruits made a poor impression upon them, because they were not used to it; fourthly, they were afraid of what their future held, having passed several convoys of wounded; and fifthly, while marching through Prussian territory, recruits had been persuaded to desert so as not fight against their countrymen and former allies.[14]

The Anhalters began their duties as part of the Glogau garrison on 21 July. Due to the amount of desertion, officers and men had be on duty every other day. This left limited time for the officers to adequately train their men, or for them to learn their own role. However, the battalion's duties in Glogau did not last long, as on 28 July the governor of the fortress inspected it and told Chambaud that he was to move the battalion to the village of Quilitz (Kwielice), several miles to the south. The village was too small to accommodate even the remaining 280 men, and surrounding villages were used to house the battalion as well. These villages remained the men's home until September, when they marched back to Dessau the way they had come.[15]

While cantoned in and around Quilitz, Chambaud organised a celebration for the birthday of Herzog Leopold III on 10 August. He had two run-down huts decorated in a suitably patriotic manner and ordered the men to gather. At 2:00 p.m. the battalion formed in an open space near to the two huts. The village priest from Quilitz then gave a short sermon, after which Chambaud said some words of his own before he led the battalion in giving three cheers for the Herzog 'with great jubilation'. After this the officers were served wine and punch, the soldiers got beer and brandy, while a group of local musicians provided the entertainment that went on until about midnight.[16]

After returning to Dessau on 13 September the battalion was dispersed into its various company depots, where the task was began to rebuild it. This was made a little more difficult in 1808, when an extra sixth company was added to the battalion establishment. Like the 5th Company, the 6th Company was a composite of men from all three duchies. In theory the addition of this company gave the

14 LASA: Z 44, C 16c 5 Nr. 51a, 'Schröder's Bataillon Geschichte, 1807–1810'; Frisch, *Anhalt-Dessaus Freiheitskämpfer 1813 bis 1815*, p.14; Zeidler, *Der Spanische Feldzug des Bataillons Anhalt*, pp.3–4.

15 LASA: Z 44, C 16c 5 Nr. 51a, 'Schröder's Bataillon Geschichte, 1807–1810'; Frisch, *Anhalt-Dessaus Freiheitskämpfer 1813 bis 1815*, p.14.

16 LASA: Z 44, C 16c 5 Nr. 51a, 'Schröder's Bataillon Geschichte, 1807–1810'; Frisch, *Anhalt-Dessaus Freiheitskämpfer 1813 bis 1815*, p.15.

Bataillon Anhalt a strength of 860 officers and men, and was done to conform much more closely with the organisation of French battalions.[17]

Then, in February 1809, Napoleon showed the first signs of trying to break the promise he had made to Herzog Leopold III in 1806, when he had agreed only to use the Bataillon Anhalt in Central and Northern Europe. *Oberst* Chambaud was ordered to take three companies to Boulogne on the coast of northern France; where, in September 1808, Napoleon had gathered companies from other *Rheinbund* contingents and dispatched them to fight in Spain.[18] Chambaud left Dessau on 3 February and arrived in Metz on 5 March. Here his command briefly served in the garrison, before new orders arrived instructing him to march to Strasbourg where he arrived on 13 March. By this time events had been occurring in Central Europe that meant the Bataillon Anhalt was needed to fight a war with France against Austria.[19]

In the meantime, the remaining three companies of the battalion had received orders on 25 March to concentrate with other *Rheinbund* contingents at Würzburg. *Hauptmann* Johann Hartmann (born 1756) led them to the city where they arrived on 6 April. Here a division of four *Rheinbund* infantry regiments was formed under the command of *Général de Division* Marie-François Rouyer (1765–1824), who spoke fluent German having served in the Austrian army before the French Revolution. In Strasbourg Chambaud received more orders on 8 April also telling him to take his detachment to Würzburg, but on 13 April Rouyer marched the division to Donauwörth. Rouyer then received more directions on 19 April to take his men to Ingolstadt. However, as the Bataillon Anhalt was not complete, he left Hartmann and also the battalion formed by the two Lippe principalities behind. At Donauwörth on 25 April Chambaud finally reunited the Bataillon Anhalt.[20]

After Napoleon's defeat of the Austrians at Regensburg on 23 April, Rouyer's division was ordered to concentrate at that city. The Bataillon Anhalt departed Donauwörth on 27 April and arrived in the city on 29 April. When the battalion arrived in Regensburg it had belatedly become part of the 5ème Régiment d'Infanterie du Rhin—the regiment having been officially decreed by Napoleon at the end of 1808—as the 1er Bataillon, while the Lippe contingents formed the 2e Bataillon.[21] To lead the regiment Chambaud was chosen instead of the senior

17 Nafziger, *The Armies of Germany and the Confederation of the Rhine*, Vol.I, p.1–2; Rawkins, *CB6, Armies of the Confederation of the Rhine*, p.13.

18 Zeidler, *Der Spanische Feldzug des Bataillons Anhalt*, p.5; Rawkins, *CB6, Armies of the Confederation of the Rhine*, pp.49–51, and 85–86.

19 John H. Gill, *With Eagles to Glory: Napoleon and his German Allies in the 1809 Campaign* (Barnsley: Frontline Books, an Imprint of Pen & Sword Books, 2011), p.388; Zeidler, *Der Spanische Feldzug des Bataillons Anhalt*, pp.4–5.

20 Gill, *With Eagles to Glory*, pp.388–390; Zeidler, *Der Spanische Feldzug des Bataillons Anhalt*, pp.5–7.

21 Subsequently, unless stated within the text, the Anhalt and Lippe battalions served together. As this work is focussed on the Anhalt contingent, I shall continue to refer to them as the Bataillon Anhalt.

officer from Lippe.[22] Now Napoleon changed his axis of advance, and to protect his right flank Rouyer's division was sent to the city of Passau on the Danube and Inn Rivers, where it arrived between 4–5 May. At Passau Napoleon ordered the construction of redoubts and other fortifications to protect the city and the large magazine there. Any soldier who volunteered for this work was paid extra on top of his daily pay. This supplement helped the Bataillon Anhalt's *Quartiermeister* Schröder, because the finances of the battalion were in a perilous state. So perilous in fact, that Chambaud had to ask Rouyer for a loan of 2,800 Francs to pay for the battalion's necessities. The battalion remained in the city until the end of July 1809, when the division was attached to *Maréchal* François-Joseph Lefebvre's (1755–1820) VII (Bavarian) Corps, which was about to try and subdue the Tyrol.[23]

The Bataillon Anhalt left Passau with Rouyer's division on the morning of 23 July and marched to Salzburg, arriving on 26 July. The summer heat took its toll, with Sonnenberg noting that it caused 'extreme fatigue' amongst his men, with several dropping from the column and then not being able to catch up by the end of the day's march. With little rest the battalion continued onwards to Lofer during the night of 26–27 July, passing through Reichenhall (Bad Reichenhall), where the villagers 'welcomed the troops with cannon fire and music choirs'. From Lofer the column reached Söll on 28 July, 'without being overly bothered by the few insurgents that sporadically appeared from up the mountains'. Passing through Rattenberg on 29 July, there was a short halt near Schwaz, before the column marched at 3:00 a.m. on 30 July to reach Innsbruck, where the battalion was rewarded with a day's rest the following day.[24]

It was on 31 July that Lefebvre ordered Rouyer to take his division through the Brenner (Brennero) Pass, head southward down the valley of the River Eisack (Isarco), and capture Brixen (Bressanone). The Bataillon Anhalt left Innsbruck with Rouyer's division early on 1 August and bivouacked at Matrei (Matrei am Brenner) that night. The next day the column reached the entrance to the Brenner Pass, where no Tyrolean insurgents were found. As Sonnenberg wrote: 'The most important and also well fortified pass on the Brenner had been left unoccupied by the insurgents. Upon demolition of the fortification we continued to advance

22 This officer was *Oberstleutnant* Friedrich Johann Georg von Campe (1749–1819), who was invalided and unable to accompany his battalion in the field.

23 LASA: Z 18, C 16c 5 Nr. 47, *Rapporte vom anhaltischen Kontingent, 1809–1810*, 'Report of *Hauptmann* Sonnenberg, dated 14 May 1809, Passau'; Gill, *With Eagles to Glory*, pp.391–394 and 397; Zeidler, *Der Spanische Feldzug des Bataillons Anhalt*, pp.6–7; Frisch, *Anhalt-Dessaus Freiheitskämpfer 1813 bis 1815*, p.9.

24 LASA: Z 18, C 16c 5 Nr. 47, 'Report of *Hauptmann* Sonnenberg, dated 7 August 1809, Sterzing', Translated by Dr Wilma A. Hofmann, PhD; Gill, *With Eagles to Glory*, pp.397–398. In his report Sonnenberg suggests that the *Bataillon Anhalt* reached its bivouac near Innsbruck at midnight on 30 July.

to Sterzing'.[25] The division reached Sterzing (Vipiteno) in the evening, but had a disturbed night. Some Tyroleans opened floodgates to the fields the 4ème Régiment d'Infanterie du Rhin (Ducal Saxon) was bivouacked in and flooded them. Due to this, the advance on Brixen was delayed until 4 August.[26]

The division departed Sterzing in the early hours of the morning, with the Saxons of the 4ème Régiment d'Infanterie du Rhin leading and the Bataillon Anhalt following. The road leading to Brixen follows the path of the River Eisack on the left, east, bank until the hamlets of Oberau and Unterau (Franzenfeste), where the road crossed a small bridge to the right, west, bank.[27] The valley is very narrow, with steep hills on the left and the fast-flowing river on the right of the road. At Mauls (Mules) the insurgents had placed an obstruction, but the Saxons cleared this quickly. However, at Mittewald (Mezzaselva) there was a sharp skirmish when, 'we encountered a defended fortification. We drove out the enemy, emptied and destroyed the fortification, and advanced up to Unter–Au [sic]'.[28]

After this initial encounter with the insurgents the column continued toward the hamlet of Oberau, where the bridge to cross the river was located. The insurgents knew this and put up strong resistance to the leading battalion of Saxons. This included insurgents, who, located among the steep hillsides, rolled large boulders and logs down into the column causing dozens of casualties. While the Saxons attempted to take Oberau, the insurgents set fire to the bridge and withdrew to Unterau. To capture the bridge before it burnt through completely, some Bavarian cavalry accompanying the division tried to rush across, but the planks were already badly damaged and the weight of the horses broke them, sending the men and horses into the river to drown.[29] Summarising these events Sonnenberg reported later: 'At the bridge, they assembled in larger numbers and were able to withstand our attacks until they had burned down the bridge. The terrain was used well by the enemy … The division was fired upon from the right side and was met with stones rolling down on them on the left side'.[30]

After the collapse of the bridge the Saxons were withdrawn from Oberau to reform. The insurgents renewed their attacks from the hillside, believing that

25 LASA: Z 18, C 16c 5 Nr. 47, 'Report of *Hauptmann* Sonnenberg, dated 7 August 1809, Sterzing', Translated by Dr Wilma A. Hofmann, PhD.

26 LASA: Z 18, C 16c 5 Nr. 45, 'Report of *Oberst* Chambaud, dated 23 August 1809, Mathsee', Translated by Dr Wilma A. Hofmann, PhD; LASA: Z 18, C 16c 5 Nr. 47, 'Report of *Hauptmann* Sonnenberg, dated 7 August 1809, Sterzing', Translated by Dr Wilma A. Hofmann, PhD; Gill, *With Eagles to Glory*, pp.398–399.

27 In 1809 Oberau and Unterau were two small hamlets on each bank of the river consisting of an inn and two houses in the former and four or five houses in the latter, but due to population increases they were combined into the present village, or *comune*, of Franzenfeste.

28 LASA: Z 18, C 16c 5 Nr. 45, 'Report of *Oberst* Chambaud, dated 23 August 1809, Mathsee', Translated by Dr Wilma A. Hofmann, PhD; Gill, *With Eagles to Glory*, p.399.

29 Gill, *With Eagles to Glory*, pp.399–400.

30 LASA: Z 18, C 16c 5 Nr. 47, 'Report of *Hauptmann* Sonnenberg, dated 7 August 1809, Sterzing', Translated by Dr Wilma A. Hofmann, PhD.

this was a retreat. It was now the Bataillon Anhalt's time to come to grips with the Tyroleans: 'Since the 4e Regiment had already suffered great losses, the 5e Regiment was called upon to attack – and while the enemy left the bridge during our forward rush, he also burned the bridge down'.[31] Part of the battalion was sent up the slopes of the hillside along a narrow track.[32] Sonnenberg's company spearheaded this advance, amidst a constant flow of boulders rolling toward them: 'the column advanced rapidly in files four men deep along the steep slope on the left side of the river. The 5e Regiment took the lead during this manoeuvre because the 4e Regiment that had been exposed the most until then, had been rather scattered'.[33] Sonnenberg was nearly crushed by a boulder but managed to save himself, although he injured his ankle and suffered heavy bruising to his left side:

> I only escaped from being crushed by the boulder by throwing myself over this suddenly appearing edge and down a very steep ravine. After tumbling down the mountain, I managed to come to a stop at the foot of the mountain, lying right next to *Leutnant* Schutzay who was already down there.[34]

During the fighting the insurgents were driven back, with some Saxons finding a footbridge over the river, which they crossed single file to attack Unterau. Later the Bataillon Lippe joined this force, while the Bataillon Anhalt and another Saxon battalion spent the night in Oberau. The wounded were looked after in Oberau's inn, amongst who were nine Anhalters, while another two men had been killed.[35]

In the early part of the evening Rouyer felt that he could not remain isolated at Oberau, and decided upon a retreat back to Sterzing. Chambaud dryly noted it was because, 'it became impossible to march to Brixen'.[36] What he did not report was that the retreat was done in a panicked manner, as the march began at 1:00 a.m. on 5 August, while the Saxons were left to defend the hamlet. Once the division had arrived in Sterzing and were resting, in the late afternoon the Saxons also arrived

31 LASA: Z 18, C 16c 5 Nr. 45, 'Report of *Oberst* Chambaud, dated 23 August 1809, Mathsee', Translated by Dr Wilma A. Hofmann, PhD.

32 This was perhaps the current Via Collerena Blasbàühelweg that leads to three modern homes. In his report Sonnenberg reported that when his company reached the end of the track there was a farmstead.

33 LASA: Z 18, C 16c 5 Nr. 47, 'Report of *Hauptmann* Sonnenberg, dated 7 August 1809, Sterzing', Translated by Dr Wilma A. Hofmann, PhD.

34 LASA: Z 18, C 16c 5 Nr. 47, 'Report of *Hauptmann* Sonnenberg, dated 7 August 1809, Sterzing', Translated by Dr Wilma A. Hofmann, PhD.

35 LASA: Z 18, C 16c 5 Nr. 45, 'Report of *Oberst* Chambaud, dated 23 August 1809, Mathsee', Translated by Dr Wilma A. Hofmann, PhD; Gill, *With Eagles to Glory*, p.400.

36 LASA: Z 18, C 16c 5 Nr. 45, 'Report of *Oberst* Chambaud, dated 23 August 1809, Mathsee', Translated by Dr Wilma A. Hofmann, PhD.

after a hounded retreat when their ammunition had run out, suffering about 950 casualties in the fighting to capture Brixen.[37]

The Bataillon Anhalt remained at Sterzing until midnight on 10 August when it marched toward Innsbruck with Lefebvre's corps. At Matrei Rouyer's division took the road to Hall (Hall in Tirol) where it began to arrive around 9:00 p.m. on 11 August, having endured an 18-hour march. At Hall the battalion did not take part in the fighting at Bergisel on 13 August, but the Tyroleans did sporadically skirmish with the outposts. On 14 August Sonnenberg had one such encounter: 'The insurgents approached the 5e Regiment's bivouac … in close-order formation and came into shooting distance. However, after the positions of our outposts were strengthened by the advancement of my … company, the insurgents retreated back into their mountain valleys'.[38] That night Rouyer's division left it's positions and fell in with Lefebvre's corps once again and retreated to Salzburg, arriving on 20 August.[39] Here, 'the men had a rather ragged appearance and many of our knapsacks were lost during the various affairs and the numerous mountain climbing episodes', and orders were given to supply the battalion with new uniforms and equipment.[40]

Remaining in cantonments near to Salzburg, the division received orders on 31 August to march to Vienna on 1 September. The journey was completed in easy stages, now Austria was negotiating a peace treaty, and Vienna was reached on 21 September,[41] with the soldiers of the Bataillon Anhalt being quartered in an old barracks and the officers amongst the Viennese. Early next morning at 8:00 a.m. *Général de Division* Guillaume-Mathieu Dumas (1753–1837) inspected the regiment, noting to Chambaud that there was, 'nothing to criticise, except that the 5e Regiment was missing 2 *Chefs de Bataillon*'. He also told Chambaud that it would be reviewed by Napoleon in person the next day! Chambaud also had other pressing matters to deal with, as the battalion's war chest was empty. To fill this void he borrowed 6,000 Thalers from Prinz Johann Georg von Anhalt-Dessau (1748–1811), who resided in the city, and a further 9,000 Thalers from the Frege banking family of Leipzig.[42]

37 LASA: Z 18, C 16c 5 Nr. 45, 'Report of *Oberst* Chambaud, dated 23 August 1809, Mathsee', Translated by Dr Wilma A. Hofmann, PhD; LASA: Z 18, C 16c 5 Nr. 47, 'Report of *Hauptmann* Sonnenberg, dated 7 August 1809, Sterzing', Translated by Dr Wilma A. Hofmann, PhD; Gill, *With Eagles to Glory*, pp.400–403.

38 LASA: Z 18, C 16c 5 Nr. 47, 'Report of *Hauptmann* Sonnenberg, dated 24 August 1809, Anthering', Translated by Dr Wilma A. Hofmann, PhD.

39 LASA: Z 18, C 16c 5 Nr. 45, 'Report of *Oberst* Chambaud, dated 23 August 1809, Mathsee', Translated by Dr Wilma A. Hofmann, PhD; Gill, *With Eagles to Glory*, pp.402–403.

40 LASA: Z 18, C 16c 5 Nr. 47, 'Report of *Hauptmann* Sonnenberg, dated 24 August 1809, Anthering', Translated by Dr Wilma A. Hofmann, PhD.

41 Gill, *With Eagles to Glory*, pp.402–403.

42 LASA: Z 18, C 16c 5 Nr. 45, 'Report of *Oberst* Chambaud, dated 3 October 1809, Vienna', Translated by Dr Wilma A. Hofmann, PhD.

On the morning on 23 September, which 'was a bright, sunny autumn day', the battalion assembled in the courtyard of the Schönbrunn Palace, where, 'a large crowd had gathered ... to see the Emperor and attend the spectacle of the muster'.[43] Also present were two *Garde Impériale* infantry regiments, the 5e Régiment d'Infanterie de Ligne, a Polish unit and two horse artillery batteries. At about 8:00 a.m. Napoleon appeared with *Maréchal* Louis-Alexandre Berthier (1753–1815) and other officers and walked over to the Bataillon Anhalt. He spent the next hour with the Anhalters and, 'the whole time I myself', wrote Chambaud, 'had to stand next to His Majesty to answer all questions and to confer the orders regarding the military movements the Regiment was supposed to perform'.[44] The battalion firstly performed some drill, before Napoleon pointed to a spot in the courtyard and told Chambaud to advance as if to attack with a bayonet charge. Once this was done, Napoleon pointed to another spot and asked that this be done a second time, and he apparently remarked of the battalion's movements, '*tres bon*'.[45] Chambaud was extremely pleased with this part of the review, as, 'I drilled a lot with the Bataillon von Anhalt and we performed many movements and towards the end also some together with the 2ten Bataillon. Everything worked perfectly'.[46]

However, the observation by Dumas that the regiment was missing two *chefs de bataillon* did not escape Napoleon's attention. After walking along the ranks of the battalion, talking to soldiers whose answers Chambaud translated for him, Napoleon turned to the him and asked who the 'most active and most distinguished company leader' was. Chambaud reported that he answered all of the captains 'are competent, brave, and well informed'. Napoleon then turned to Berthier and said, 'One should appoint *Capitaine* N. N. ... from the 5e Régiment d'Infanterie de Ligne as the *Chef de Bataillon* for Anhalt'. Chambaud, alarmed by this, turned to Rouyer and reported later that, 'even though I was standing very close to His Majesty, that he [Rouyer] should request from His Majesty, to allow the promotion to happen from within the Bataillon Anhalt – the Ducal General immediately did as I asked but received no answer'.[47]

Rouyer received no answer because Napoleon was speaking to *Hauptmann* Hohnstein, who answered his questions in 'a determined and decisive manner

43 LASA: Z 44, C 16c 5 Nr. 51a, 'Schröder's Bataillon Geschichte, 1807–1810'; Frisch, Anhalt-Dessaus *Freiheitskämpfer 1813 bis 1815*, p.24.

44 LASA: Z 18, C 16c 5 Nr. 45, 'Report of *Oberst* Chambaud, dated 3 October 1809, Vienna', Translated by Dr Wilma A. Hofmann, PhD.

45 LASA: Z 44, C 16c 5 Nr. 51a, 'Schröder's Bataillon Geschichte, 1807–1810'; Frisch, Anhalt-Dessaus *Freiheitskämpfer 1813 bis 1815*, p.24.

46 LASA: Z 18, C 16c 5 Nr. 45, 'Report of *Oberst* Chambaud, dated 3 October 1809, Vienna', Translated by Dr Wilma A. Hofmann, PhD.

47 LASA: Z 18, C 16c 5 Nr. 45, 'Report of *Oberst* Chambaud, dated 3 October 1809, Vienna', Translated by Dr Wilma A. Hofmann, PhD.

to the satisfaction of His Majesty', until he was asked in which nation's service he had served before joining the battalion. Unfortunately Hohnstein answered: 'In the service of the Duke of Brunswick'. Napoleon 'immediately terminated the conversation', and spoke to a soldier.[48] Napoleon then spoke to *Hauptmann* Ludwig Barth, Hartmann and Sonnenberg, before he came to *Hauptmann* Anton von Santorini (died 1810). After talking for a short time, Napoleon asked directly if Santorini could lead a battalion, and he 'answered with his own military frankness in the affirmative,'[49] and Napoleon 'immediately appointed him as *Chef de Bataillon* of Anhalt'.[50]

Chambaud was appalled by this, because Santorini was a junior *Hauptmann*, and feared the others would be upset. He turned to Berthier, who was close to him, and asked if the decision could be changed. According to Schröder's history, Berthier replied, 'If the Emperor named him Lieutenant Colonel he will stay!'[51] However, Chambaud reported a slightly different version of events:

> All objections that I dared to make ... all arguments brought forth by the Prince of Neuchâtel couldn't change this matter – and now, the *Hauptleute* Hartmann, Hohstein, and von Sonnenberg feel so miserable and dejected that they wanted to humbly ask for dismissal from service. – I had to use all available means and do everything in my power to finally calm them again. This affects me deeply and unfortunately I recognise that this matter caused a great disadvantage to the Bataillon von Anhalt.[52]

However, Chambaud's efforts did not work, as Sonnenberg soon afterwards requested, and was granted, an extended leave of absence. He did not serve with the battalion again.[53]

48 LASA: Z 18, C 16c 5 Nr. 45, 'Report of *Oberst* Chambaud, dated 3 October 1809, Vienna', Translated by Dr Wilma A. Hofmann, PhD. As noted previously, the Brunswick regiments had served with the Prussians in 1806. However, in 1809 Herzog Friedrich Wilhelm von Brunswick (1771–1815) had raised his Black Legion in Bohemia and marched it across northern Germany to Kassel, embarrassing Napoleon's Dutch and Westphalian soldiers in the process. He then escaped with his men to Britain and fought in Spain and Portugal.

49 LASA: Z 44, C 16c 5 Nr. 51a, 'Schröder's Bataillon Geschichte, 1807–1810'; Frisch, Anhalt-Dessaus *Freiheitskämpfer 1813 bis 1815*, p.25.

50 LASA: Z 18, C 16c 5 Nr. 45, 'Report of *Oberst* Chambaud, dated 3 October 1809, Vienna', Translated by Dr Wilma A. Hofmann, PhD.

51 LASA: Z 44, C 16c 5 Nr. 51a, 'Schröder's Bataillon Geschichte, 1807–1810'; Frisch, Anhalt-Dessaus *Freiheitskämpfer 1813 bis 1815*, p.25.

52 LASA: Z 18, C 16c 5 Nr. 45, 'Report of *Oberst* Chambaud, dated 3 October 1809, Vienna', Translated by Dr Wilma A. Hofmann, PhD.

53 Shortly after Sonnenberg effectively resigned as a company commander, *Hauptmann* Hohnstein also departed the battalion.

Later that evening Chambaud received an aide to Napoleon at his quarters and was presented with his *Legion d'Honneur*.[54] He perhaps deserved this for the work he now had to do to reorganise the battalion's structure. Instead of six companies of fusiliers, Chambaud had to make it conform to French battalion organisation with four companies of fusiliers and one each of grenadiers and *voltigeurs*. He reported: 'These changes in organisation will also greatly affect the foundation upon which the Ducal Serene Highness of Anhalt assembled the 6 companies'. This was because the contingents provided by the three duchies would now be intermixed, particularly in the grenadier and *voltigeur* companies. Another consequence was, 'the Grenadiers will entail a greater expense than the *Voltigeur*; the *Voltigeurs* on the other hand will entail a greater expense than the Fusilier'. With the battalion's finances stretched already, Chambaud suggested a new funding system to deal with these changes, whereby each herzog contributed equally to a war chest of 100,000 Thalers.[55]

After several months of campaigning the Anhalters expected to be sent back to their homes; but Napoleon needed men in Spain. Therefore, on 15 November orders were issued to send them there with Rouyer's division. Instead of a Christmas with their families, the Anhalters spent the months of December 1809–February 1810 marching through southern Germany and France. They crossed the Pyrenees at the end of February 1810 and arrived in the city of Gerona on 12 March 1810, where *Maréchal* Pierre Augereau (1757–1816) inspected them the next day, in preparation for his march to Barcelona escorting 1,000 carts of supplies for the blockaded garrison. With the departure of both Sonnenberg and Hohnstein and the promotion of Santorini, new company commanders had been appointed during the winter months. They were *Hauptmann* Christian Kitzinger, Friedrich Wachler (died 1811), and Franz van der Horst.[56]

On 14 March Augereau's convoy departed Gerona, and along the road south Spanish guerrillas attacked it constantly. The Bataillon Anhalt reached Barcelona a few days later, before it was put into quarters in the village of Saria (Sarriá). Later *Général de Brigade* François Xavier Schwarz (1762–1826) with Rouyer's 1er Brigade was sent to the village of Manresa, north-west of Barcelona, when Augereau took part of his corps to capture Tarragona. Schwarz's brigade was soon surrounded and running out of supplies, and a relief column was sent to him on 25 March, which also became trapped. A second force was organised on 2 April,

54 LASA: Z 44, C 16c 5 Nr. 51a, 'Schröder's Bataillon Geschichte, 1807–1810'; Frisch, Anhalt-Dessaus *Freiheitskämpfer 1813 bis 1815*, p.25.

55 LASA: Z 18, C 16c 5 Nr. 45, 'Report of *Oberst* Chambaud, dated 3 October 1809, Vienna', Translated by Dr Wilma A. Hofmann, PhD.

56 Zeidler, *Der Spanische Feldzug des Bataillons Anhalt*, pp.13–18, 27, 84; Frisch, *Anhalt-Dessaus Freiheitskämpfer 1813 bis 1815*, p.28; Digby Smith, *Napoleon's German Division in Spain* (Huntington: Ken Trotman Publishing, 2014), Vol.II, pp.170–171; Sir Charles Oman, *A History of the Peninsular War*, (London: Greenhill Books, Lionel Leventhal Limited, 1996), Vol.III, pp.290–291.

which included a detachment of 150 men from the Bataillon Anhalt led by van der Horst. The Spanish caught this column between the villages of Esparreguera and Matorell. Outnumbered, the column broke and fled back to Barcelona, with 80 of the Anhalt detachment being lost.[57]

Augereau failed to capture Tarragona and ordered a retreat back to Gerona, which began on 11 April. Gerona was now overcrowded with nearly 20,000 soldiers, and the battalion was given quarters in Pont Major in a half-destroyed convent. Here disease spread rapidly amongst the men, who spent their days escorting supply trains in and out of the city. This lasted until 2 August when the battalion was sent to garrison the region along the coast from La Pera through La Bisbal, Palamós, Calonge, and Sant Feliu de Guixols, as part of a brigade led by Schwarz—who had managed to break out of Manresa, and re-join Augereau's corps before it retreated back to Gerona. The battalion's duties included hunting guerrillas and stopping communication between the Spanish and the British Royal Navy. Sickness had taken its toll, and instead of over 860 men the battalion had barely 325 effectives. The rest were at the battalion's depot in Gerona convalescing or in hospital. Others were dead, including Santorini who died on 23 August. *Hauptmann* Hartmann was promoted to replace him.[58] Chambaud was also very sick and he was invalided home to Dessau on 27 August.[59]

*Teniente General* Enrique O'Donnell (1769–1834) had marched his Spanish division across Catalonia in early September 1810, in order to surprise the scattered garrisons around Gerona in concert with the Royal Navy. On 14 September O'Donnell swept down onto Schwarz's forces around La Bisbal, while the Royal Navy captured the garrisons along the coast. The whole of Schwarz's brigade was captured, including the 345 men of the Bataillon Anhalt led by Hartmann.[60] The standard of the battalion was destroyed when it was realised there was no hope of escape, with the staff's finial being hidden in Hartmann's uniform.[61] The Anhalters

57 Zeidler, *Der Spanische Feldzug des Bataillons Anhalt*, pp.30–55; Frisch, *Anhalt-Dessaus Freiheitskämpfer 1813 bis 1815*, p.28; Smith, *Napoleon's German Division in Spain*, Vol.II, p.172–177; Oman, *A History of the Peninsular War*, Vol.III, p.294–295.

58 LASA: Z 18, C 16c 5 Nr. 47, 'Report of *Hauptmann* Kitzinger, dated 30 August 1810, La Bisbal', Translated by Dr Wilma A. Hofmann, PhD; 'Report of *Hauptmann* Wachler, dated 1 August 1810, Pont Major', 'Report of *Leutnant* Hermann, dated 24 August 1810, Gerona'; Zeidler, *Der Spanische Feldzug des Bataillons Anhalt*, pp.66–96; Frisch, *Anhalt-Dessaus Freiheitskämpfer 1813 bis 1815*, p.29; Smith, *Napoleon's German Division in Spain*, Vol.II, pp.187–188, 191; Oman, *A History of the Peninsular War*, Vol.III, p.297.

59 *Oberst* Chambaud died on 3 December 1814 in Dessau, never recovering from his illness. It seems that he had started to become ill in December 1809 and was offered a yearly pension to retire then, but he refused to do so. Frisch, *Anhalt-Dessaus Freiheitskämpfer 1813 bis 1815*, p.8.

60 Zeidler, *Der Spanische Feldzug des Bataillons Anhalt*, p.96–110; Frisch, Anhalt-Dessaus *Freiheitskämpfer 1813 bis 1815*, p.30; Smith, *Napoleon's German Division in Spain*, Vol.II, pp.187–192; Oman, *A History of the Peninsular War*, Vol.III, pp.297–298.

61 Smith, *Napoleon's German Division in Spain*, Vol.II, pp.192–193.

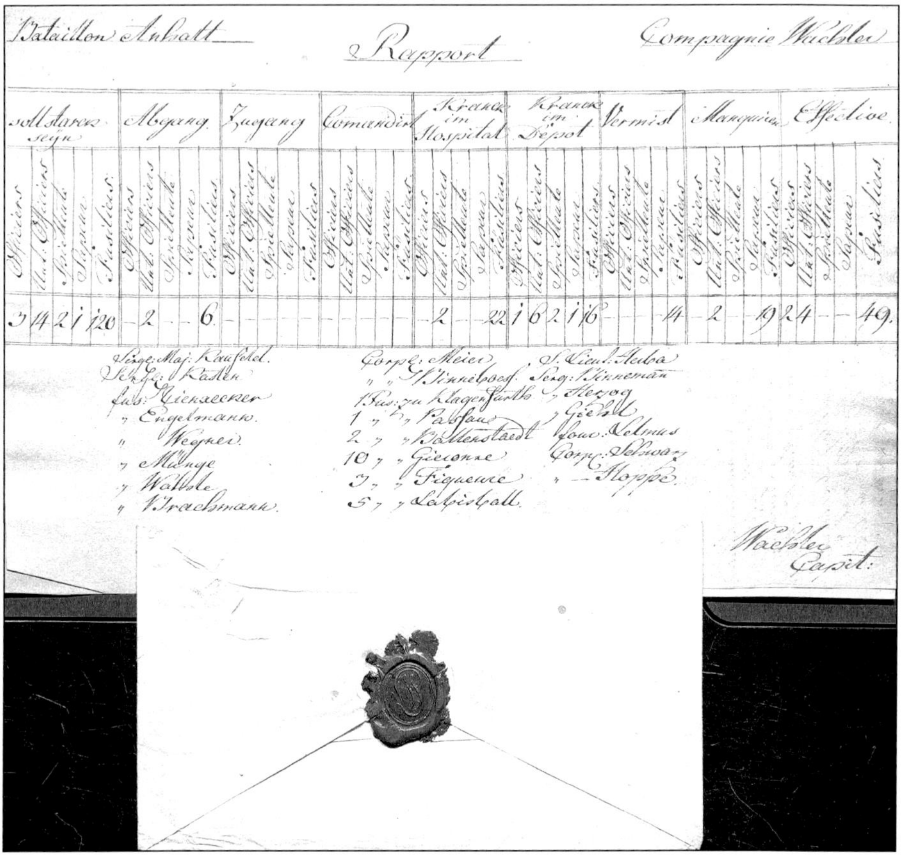


A return report written by *Hauptmann* Friedrich Wachler on 9 August 1810, with the envelope it was sent to Dessau in with a wax seal. (Landesarchiv Sachsen-Anhalt: Z 18, C 16c 5 Nr. 47)

were taken aboard Royal Navy ships near Palamós and taken to Tarragona, where they were held in deplorable conditions until January 1811. By this time, due to the conditions they were held in, 135 men had been recruited into the British service. A handful of others had been released due to their invalidity, including *Leutnant* Georg Hoppe who made his way to Gerona, while others had died of sickness, *Hauptmann* Wachler among them.[62]

In January 1811 the officers, including Hartmann and Kitzinger, were taken to Bellver Castle on the island of Mallorca, while the remaining 134 soldiers and

62 LASA: Z 18 C 16c 5 Nr. 51, 'Report of *Oberstleutnant* Hartmann, dated 16 June 1811, Belvedera [Bellver Castle, Mallorca, Spain]', Translated by Dr Wilma A. Hofmann, PhD; Zeidler, *Der Spanische Feldzug des Bataillons Anhalt*, pp.125–142; Frisch, *Anhalt-Dessaus Freiheitskämpfer 1813 bis 1815*, p.30.

*unteroffiziere* were shipped to the prison island of Cabrera. Conditions here were such that 29 men soon died of sickness and the remaining 105 sought service with the British to avoid the same fate.[63] Hartmann and Kitzinger—along with officers from the other *Rheinbund* contingents captured at La Bisbal—were later taken by ship to Britain in October 1811. As a more senior officer Hartmann was taken ashore at Portsmouth and taken to the small town of Thame in Oxfordshire, where he spent the remainder of the war keeping the Bataillon Anhalt's finial safe. Kitzinger, meanwhile, was taken up the coast to Scotland, surviving a shipwreck along the way, before reaching Edinburgh, where he remained as a prisoner of war. They were both released in April 1814 after the abdication of Napoleon.[64]

The men who escaped capture on 14 September, because they were convalescing in Gerona, were organised into two companies commanded by *Hauptmann* Barth, and the 5e and 6e Régiments d'Infanterie du Rhin were later amalgamated under the command of *Oberst* Heeringen of Waldeck-Pyrmont. They remained in Gerona, wasting away of disease, until January 1811, when orders were received stating that they would be returning to their garrisons in Germany. On 25 January 1811 the Anhalters and their comrades from Lippe and the 6e Régiment d'Infanterie du Rhin began their journey home. When the men reached Perpignan, they were distributed to several coastal towns where the men convalesced for two months. After this rest the Anhalters went to Metz, arriving on 17 May, and then travelled through Mainz and Frankfurt, before they arrived at their garrisons in the first week of June 1811. Including officers, only 54 men of the Bataillon Anhalt made it back to their families.[65]

Throughout the summer and autumn of 1811, the Bataillon Anhalt was rebuilt, including contingents of 378 men from Dessau, 259 men from Bernburg, and 226 men from Köthen. The most senior officer remaining was Barth, but he was quickly superseded by the newly promoted *Hauptmann* Hoppe, who was later promoted to *Oberstleutnant* in February 1812 and given command of the rebuilt Bataillon Anhalt. A whole new slate of company commanders was needed, and to fill this void *Leutnants* Gottlieb Birkner, Wilhelm Löwe and Friedrich Herrmann were promoted to *Hauptmann*, with Löwe leading the grenadiers and Herrmann the *voltigeurs*. These men were very experienced, having served in 1809 in Austria and Spain in 1810. Two new officers joined the battalion in the form of *Hauptmann*

63 Zeidler, *Der Spanische Feldzug des Bataillons Anhalt*, pp.142–155, 183–207; Frisch, *Anhalt-Dessaus Freiheitskämpfer 1813 bis 1815*, p.30. For a good description of the conditions endured by prisoners of war on Cabrera see, Georges Blond (Trans. Marshall May), *La Grande Armée* (Edison: Castle Books, A division of Book Sales Inc., 2005), pp.291–295.

64 LASA: Z 18 C 16c 5 Nr. 51, 'Letter of *Oberstleutnant* Hartmann, dated 28 January 1812, Thame [Oxfordshire]', Translated by Dr Wilma A. Hofmann, PhD; Zeidler, *Der Spanische Feldzug des Bataillons Anhalt*, pp.209–223.

65 Zeidler, *Der Spanische Feldzug des Bataillons Anhalt*, pp.145–154; Smith, *Napoleon's German Division in Spain*, Vol.II, p.194.

Carl Marcks and Friedrich Klaette. By January 1812 the Bataillon Anhalt was ready for service once more, and orders arrived for Hoppe to assemble it in Dessau.[66]

The battalion left Dessau travelling in wagons heading for Hamburg on 23 February 1812, as their marching orders had been late to arrive. However, this was countermanded and the battalion travelled to Varel on the north coast of Germany, where they remained in garrison until April. On 30 April they moved to Oldenburg and onto Bremen the following day, where the Bataillon Lippe was met and the 5e Régiment d'Infanterie du Rhin was resurrected, with Hoppe receiving overall command. In Bremen the battalion became part of the 34e Division and was ordered to Berlin on 10 May, entering the city on 18 May. After a handful of days new orders directed the battalion to Danzig (Gdańsk) where it arrived on 18 June, with the loss of four men to desertion. Ominously, Napoleon later issued orders in July directing that each battalion should have transport for 20 days of supplies. To comply with this directive Hoppe and the battalion's new *quartiermeister*, Leopold von Morgenstern (1790–1864), purchased four wagons and 16 horses to pull them.[67]

Unexpectedly, after months of mundane garrison service, the Bataillon Anhalt received orders on 5 October to march the next day for the city of Smolensk—this was the first sign for the battalion that the tide of war in Russia had turned against Napoleon. The battalion marched as directed and had reached Georgenburg (Jurbarkas) by 17 October. However, it was ordered to retrace its steps to Tilsit (Sovetsk) that night, arriving on 19 October. From here the battalion was directed to Königsberg (Kaliningrad), where it arrived on 28 October. In the city the battalion once again became part of the 34e Division commanded by *Général de Division* Louis Henri Loison (1771–1816), which was composed of new, young conscripts.[68]

On 9 November the division was ordered to march to Vilna (Vilnius), but the 5e Régiment d'Infanterie du Rhin, along with the regiment from the Grand Duchy of Frankfurt, remained behind. It was only on 16 November that the Bataillon Anhalt received directions to go to Kovno (Kaunas), to escort supplies for the divisional artillery. The march was done in cold weather and the three to four feet

66 LASA: Z 44, C 16c 5 Nr. 66, '*Kurzer Abriss der Geschichte des Bataillons Anhalt, welches im Jahr 1811 von den durchlauchtigsten Herzögen zu Anhalt als Mitglieder des Rheinbundes gestellt wurde, vom Ausmarsch bis zur Rückkehr nach Dessau am 6. Februar 1814 vom Regierungsrat Dr. Morgenstern, Bd. I–II, 1811–1814*', subsequently referred to as 'Morgenstern's Bataillon Geschichte Bd. I–II, 1811–1814'; Frisch, Anhalt-Dessaus *Freiheitskämpfer 1813 bis 1815*, p.34; Zeidler, *Der Spanische Feldzug des Bataillons Anhalt*, pp.84, 153.

67 LASA: Z 18, C 16c 5 Nr. 56, *Rapporte von dem Bataillon aus Danzig, 1812*, 'Reports of *Hauptmann* Klaette, dated 30 March, 1812, Varell [sic]; 1 May 1812, Bremen; 20 June 1812, Danzig; and 7 August 1812, Danzig'; LASA: Z 44, C 16c 5 Nr. 66, '*Morgenstern's Bataillon Geschichte Bd. I–II, 1811–1814*'; Frisch, *Anhalt-Dessaus Freiheitskämpfer 1813 bis 1815*, pp.34–35.

68 LASA: Z 44, C 16c 5 Nr. 66, 'Morgenstern's Bataillon Geschichte Bd. I–II, 1811–1814'; Frisch, Anhalt-Dessaus Freiheitskämpfer 1813 bis 1815, p.35; Adam Zamoyski, *1812: Napoleon's Fatal March on Moscow* (London: Harper Perennial, 2005), p.504.

of snow that fell during 21 November. The men also began to see soldiers of the Grande Armée travelling in the opposite direction to them. Once at Kovno more orders were received to join the division in Vilna and the battalion started its march on 28 November. The landscape was desolate, with burnt-out houses and the carcasses of horses at the sides of the snow- and ice-covered road. The battalion also saw ragged, individual soldiers, 'who, haggard, covered with dirt, barely able to drag himself away, was to the thoughtful a picture of the sorrow that made him suspect his own future'. In the dark evening of 29 November, the battalion reached the village of Wiewe (Vievis), where some houses, 'were stuffed with [the] dead bodies of solidified soldiers'. The battalion reached Vilna on 1 December.[69]

A print by Richard Knötel showing an officer and infantryman of the *Bataillon Anhalt* in 1812. (New York Public Library, Vinkhuijzen Collection)

69 LASA: Z 44, C 16c 5 Nr. 66, 'Morgenstern's Bataillon Geschichte Bd. I–II, 1811–1814'; Frisch, Anhalt-Dessaus *Freiheitskämpfer 1813 bis 1815*, pp.35–36.

In Vilna the battalion was split into four commands: Hoppe and two companies remained in the city; *Leutnant* Koseritz's company was sent to Miedniki (Medininkai); Birkner and his company was sent to meet a supply train and escort it; while Klaette's and Marcks' companies were supposed to escort *Quartiermeister* Morgenstern to Rzkontz with the battalion's wagon train, but they were not allowed to leave the city until the morning of 10 December.[70] Koseritz's men came back to Vilna unscathed, but Birkner lost eight men to Cossacks and the weather when the temperature dropped to -27°C. However, the battalion at least avoided the fate of the rest of Loison's division. It was sent to the town of Oshmiana (Ashmyany) on 5 December and the next night temperatures dropped to -37.5°C. When the division accompanied the retreating Grande Armée into Vilna on 9 December hardly any men were left, with evidence that 8,000 of the division's 10,000 men died between 6–7 December. On the evening of 9 December, the Bataillon Anhalt was ordered to Oshmiana to strengthen what was left of the rearguard, and at 10:00 a.m. on 10 December the Russian advance guard closed in on the town.[71]

At about the same time, at 9:00 a.m., *Quartiermeister* Morgenstern had finally been given permission to take the battalion's supply train out of Vilna to Kovno. However, near the village of Ponary (Paneriai) the road to Kovno ascended low hills, and with the freezing night-time temperatures this had become icy. Even before Morgenstern and *Wagenmeister* Beyer reached this incline wagons, caissons and cannon were blocking the road. When Morgenstern reached Ponary with his train *Maréchal* Michel Ney (1769–1815) was ordering that all wagons should be pushed off the road and burned. Morgenstern, Beyer and the wagon teams unhitched their 16 horses and loaded them down with as much of the wagons' contents as they could. Morgenstern then sent some of the men to find another road. They quickly found a side road and the convoy reached Kovno in the evening of 11 December. A few hours after these events, the Bataillon Anhalt with the rearguard reached Ponary and found the road 'obstructed by abandoned equipment and carts'. It was here that the pursuing Cossacks attacked. Supported by horse artillery the Cossacks closed in on the rearguard, which meant its 'organisation fell into disarray'. During the skirmishing *Hauptmann* Löwe of the grenadier company was killed, when his 'face was shattered by a cannon ball'.[72]

70 It has proven impossible to find any modern name for Rzkontz, although it could be the village of Rykantai, on the main highway between Vilnius and Kaunas.

71 LASA: Z 44, C 16c 5 Nr. 66, '*Morgenstern's Bataillon Geschichte Bd. I–II, 1811–1814*'; LASA: Z 18, C 16c 5 Nr. 63, *Rapporte vom Bataillon in Danzig, 1813*, 'Report of *Hauptmann* Klaette, dated 25 December 1813 [1812], Königsberg', Translated by Dr Wilma A. Hofmann, PhD; Frisch, *Anhalt-Dessaus Freiheitskämpfer 1813 bis 1815*, pp.37–38; Zamoyski, *1812: Napoleon's Fatal March on Moscow*, pp.504–507, 510–511.

72 LASA: Z 44, C 16c 5 Nr. 66, '*Morgenstern's Bataillon Geschichte Bd. I–II, 1811–1814*'; LASA: Z 18, C 16c 5 Nr. 63, 'Report of *Hauptmann* Klaette, dated 25 December 1813 [1812], Königsberg', Translated by Dr Wilma A. Hofmann, PhD; Frisch, *Anhalt-Dessaus Freiheitskämpfer 1813 bis 1815*, pp.38–39; Zamoyski, *1812: Napoleon's Fatal March on Moscow*, pp.512–514.

By the time Hoppe reached Kovno with the Bataillon Anhalt, he could muster only 40 of the 380 men who had been in Vilna in the first week of December. Of these 30 men had been left in a hospital in Vilna and taken prisoner, a further 20 men had been killed in skirmishing, while, '*Korporal* Kühn and *Füsilier* Günther burned to death in a fire that broke out at night in the house that they were staying in'.[73] The rest had been scattered during the retreat. However, those who remained could still fight. Ney formed a rearguard outside of Kovno on 13 December to let as many stragglers catch up as possible, but Cossacks soon appeared. They used their horse artillery to good effect once again, and *Hauptmann* Berckhausen of the Bataillon Lippe was killed. According to Klaette, 'a howitzer grenade shattered his left foot after which he pleaded with his men to shoot him. Since nobody could be found to do so, he took one of the two pistols he always carried with him, put it into his mouth and shattered his head'. This broke the will of both battalions and they retreated from the fighting, leaving Ney with a few French troops. The remnant of the battalion made its way to Königsberg and arrived during 20 December.[74]

At Königsberg Hoppe posted an officer at the main gate to direct stragglers to the battalion's quarters. By Christmas Day the battalion had gone from 80 men to 23 officers and 404 men. However, 150 of these had typhoid fever or had been disabled by frostbite during the retreat from Vilna. Of the officers only Hoppe and Marcks escaped illness, with Barth, Herba and Klaette suffering from typhoid fever. Klaette reported overall that: 'The extreme cold during this campaign was too much for the human nature to bivouac unscathed. *Leutnant* von Schiller ... went to the hospital in Tapian where he remains in a pitiable condition having suffered severe frostbite to face, hands, and feet'.[75] But the battalion could not remain in the city, as the Russians were driving southward threatening to cut it off, so in the evening of 4 January 1813 the battalion received orders to march to Frauenburg (Frombork). The men of the battalion who were too ill to march could not be transported, as the wagons had been abandoned at Ponary, and they were left in Königsberg with Barth. The Prussians took prisoner those men left in Königsberg when they broke their alliance with France and allied with Russia. When the battalion reached Frauenburg it mustered barely 250 officers and men, as the 'forced marches cost

73 LASA: Z 18, C 16c 5 Nr. 63, 'Report of *Hauptmann* Klaette, dated 25 December 1813 [1812], Königsberg', Translated by Dr Wilma A. Hofmann, PhD.

74 LASA: Z 18, C 16c 5 Nr. 63, 'Report of *Hauptmann* Klaette, dated 3 January 1813, Königsberg', Translated by Dr Wilma A. Hofmann, PhD; LASA: Z 44, C 16c 5 Nr. 66, '*Morgenstern's Bataillon Geschichte Bd. I–II, 1811–1814*'; Frisch, *Anhalt-Dessaus Freiheitskämpfer 1813 bis 1815*, p.38–39; Zamoyski, *1812: Napoleon's Fatal March on Moscow*, pp.518–519.

75 LASA: Z 18, C 16c 5 Nr. 63, 'Report of *Hauptmann* Klaette, dated 3 January 1813, Königsberg', Translated by Dr Wilma A. Hofmann, PhD.

us further losses because our soldiers could not keep up due to injuries to their feet, or because they became indisposed otherwise'.[76]

From Frauenburg the Bataillon Anhalt entered Danzig (Gdańsk) on 14 January. Here the Anhalters endured a 10-month siege defined by two elements: poor sanitary conditions and supplies of food, which caused disease to spread rapidly; and, secondly, long hours of outpost duty punctuated by short periods of intense fighting. The former necessitated an immediate change in organisation of the *Rheinbund* regiments in the garrison, because their strength had been decimated. The contingents were combined into a single, two-battalion regiment commanded by *Oberst* August Karl, Freiherr von Egloffstein (1771–1834) of Saxe-Weimar, with Hoppe and Heeringen leading a battalion each. The Anhalters formed two companies in this 10-company regiment.[77]

Disease killed men as soon as the siege began and continued unabated until April. According to *Général de Division* Jean Rapp (1771–1821), governor of Danzig, 50 men died each day in January and this rose to 130 from February. The number of dead was overwhelming, and Hoppe reported that soldiers were left in the houses where they died for days, before they were thrown into the River Mottlau (Motlawa), 'where they served the fish for food'.[78] To combat the spread of disease Rapp ordered each battalion to create a hospital. When Hoppe complied with this order 90 Anhalters were admitted, which rose to 120 in March. However, the main problem was a lack of food supplies. This meant the sick could not recover and soon half of the 30,000-man garrison were dead or dying. Quite early on horsemeat was being eaten and, after the granaries were destroyed by fire in October and November, the need became desperate. Hoppe and Morgenstern had managed to keep 11 of the battalion's train horses alive, but by November they were too weak to work. Therefore, Hoppe had them bayoneted and the carcases dragged to a slaughterhouse so they could be butchered.[79] Summarising these events, Klaette wrote:

76 LASA: Z 18, C 16c 5 Nr. 63, 'Report of *Hauptmann* Klaette, dated 20 January 1813, Danzig', Translated by Dr Wilma A. Hofmann, PhD; LASA: Z 44, C 16c 5 Nr. 66, *'Morgenstern's Bataillon Geschichte Bd. I–II, 1811–1814'*; Frisch, *Anhalt-Dessaus Freiheitskämpfer 1813 bis 1815*, pp.39–40; Michael V. Leggiere, *Napoleon and the Struggle for Germany: The Franco-Prussian War of 1813* (Cambridge: Cambridge University Press, 2015), Vol.I, pp.72–75.

77 LASA: Z 18, C 16c 5 Nr. 63, 'Report of *Hauptmann* Klaette, dated 20 January 1813, Danzig', Translated by Dr Wilma A. Hofmann, PhD; Nafziger, *The Armies of Germany and the Confederation of the Rhine*, Vol.I, p.3; Rawkins, *CB6, Armies of the Confederation of the Rhine*, pp.15–16.

78 LASA: Z 44, C 16c 5 Nr. 66, 'Morgenstern's Bataillon Geschichte Bd. I–II, 1811–1814'; Frisch, *Anhalt-Dessaus Freiheitskämpfer 1813 bis 1815*, p.43.

79 LASA: Z 44, C 16c 5 Nr. 66, 'Morgenstern's Bataillon Geschichte Bd. I–II, 1811–1814'; Frisch, *Anhalt-Dessaus Freiheitskämpfer 1813 bis 1815*, pp.43–46, 49; Jean Rapp, *Memoirs of General Count Rapp, First Aide-de-Camp to Napoleon* (London: Henry Colburn and Co, 1823), pp.258–259, 265, 272–277, 323.

> [M]any soldiers perished here in the local field hospitals. Unfortunately, the reason is that in the months of February, March, and April infectious diseases were rampant ... and about half of the garrison that originally counted some 30,000 men, fell victim to these. Added to this was the fact that ... we only received half-sized portions and furthermore had to live ... on horse meat, a most indigestible and unhealthy food.[80]

The fighting at Danzig occurred in four phases. On 5 March the Russians launched an attack on the suburbs of Langfuhr and Alt Schottland. In Alt Schottland the Anhalters of Klaette's company came under repeated attack from 3:00 a.m.:

> [A]lmost every single soldier from our Battalion fired about one hundred to one hundred and twenty bullets. We were also forced to retake an old entrenchment ... where Russian riflemen had taken a hold. We were successful in our initial attempt to retake this entrenchment by storm. We lost this position again after we ran out of munition and the Russian forces started an attack driven by a bayonet run. We were able to retaliate and retake this post finally when a Bavarian Battalion came to our assistance.[81]

In the fighting Hoppe was bruised by a spent musket ball—and later received his *Legion d'Honneur*—while *Feldwebel* Biermonitz died when his leg was shattered, but *Füsilier* Lorenz was shot through both legs by a musket ball and survived. Apart from outpost skirmishing and a sortie in April to gather supplies, the siege lines remained quiet until 9 June, when Rapp launched a large-scale sortie along the whole line. Rapp reported the sortie was a success, forcing the Russians from Schoenfeld, Wonneberg and Pitzkendorf, with a loss of 1,800 men.[82] Klaette, however, reported a different outcome: 'Unfortunately, this time these [positions] were too strong, and we had to retreat back to the city in the evening without having gained any advantage'.[83]

During the afternoon of 10 June, a courier arrived with the news of the armistice agreed between Napoleon and the allies. It was during the armistice that Rapp paraded the garrison in front of the Russian positions. Hoppe reported that 6,000

80 LASA: Z 18, C 16c 5 Nr. 63, 'Report of *Hauptmann* Klaette, dated 20 November 1813, Danzig', Translated by Dr Wilma A. Hofmann, PhD.

81 LASA: Z 18, C 16c 5 Nr. 63, 'Report of *Hauptmann* Klaette, dated 20 November 1813, Danzig', Translated by Dr Wilma A. Hofmann, PhD.

82 LASA: Z 44, C 16c 5 Nr. 66, 'Morgenstern's Bataillon Geschichte Bd. I–II, 1811–1814'; Frisch, *Anhalt-Dessaus Freiheitskämpfer 1813 bis 1815*, pp.45–46; Rapp, *Memoirs of General Count Rapp*, pp.265–271, 287–290.

83 LASA: Z 18, C 16c 5 Nr. 63, 'Report of *Hauptmann* Klaette, dated 20 November 1813, Danzig', Translated by Dr Wilma A. Hofmann, PhD.

men took part with a further 3,000 watching, 'so that one could conclude from this the strength of the garrison'.[84] The cordiality between the forces did not last long, and shortly after the armistice ended the besiegers attacked the suburbs of Ohra and Langfuhr. In the fighting Langfuhr changed hands a number of times. At this time Prussian forces had strengthened the Russian besiegers, and Klaette commented that his company, 'engaged in a hard-fought battle with the Prussian fighters. One has to do them justice and admit that they are extremely courageous fighters that are far superior when compared to the Russians'.[85] Realising that they could not take Danzig by storm, the Russians and Prussians took advantage of their naval forces blockading the harbour. In the first days of September these bombarded the city, but 'caused minimal damage'. However, a similar bombardment during the night of 18–19 October caused a large fire that destroyed Danzig's warehouses and granaries, which included the remaining food supplies. This loss meant Rapp could not defend Danzig effectively and the suburbs of Ohra and Schidlitz were allowed to burn when fires broke out. Rapp opened negotiations for Danzig's surrender in mid-November and on 29 November terms had been agreed with the Russians and Prussians.[86]

In the 10-month siege 89 men of the battalion were killed or had died of sickness and 44 men had been wounded. Fourteen officers and 143 men survived. They found also that the Anhalt Duchies had turned against Napoleon and joined the allies. In Article 6 of the surrender terms this change was recognised, and it was stated that the *Rheinbund* contingents should receive instructions from their governments as to what they should do. These were received on 10 December, but Hoppe and others were worried that by marching home they would be breaking the terms of their surrender. They wrote to Rapp and he assured them that they would not be and that they could return to their homelands. However, when the contingents went to *Major* Hacke of the allied staff to get their orders and marching route, he refused and the Bataillon Anhalt was sent to quarters in the village of Mielenz (Miłoradz). Finally, on 31 December, the confusion was cleared up and the battalion began its march to Dessau on 11 January 1814. At Soldin (Myślibórz) Hoppe was ordered to take as many officers as he could in advance to Dessau, and he arrived there on 28 January, while the battalion followed on 6 February.[87]

84 LASA: Z 44, C 16c 5 Nr. 66, 'Morgenstern's Bataillon Geschichte Bd. I–II, 1811–1814'; Frisch, Anhalt-Dessaus *Freiheitskämpfer 1813 bis 1815*, p.46.

85 LASA: Z 18, C 16c 5 Nr. 63, 'Report of *Hauptmann* Klaette, dated 20 November 1813, Danzig', Translated by Dr Wilma A. Hofmann, PhD.

86 LASA: Z 44, C 16c 5 Nr. 66, '*Morgenstern's Bataillon Geschichte Bd. I–II, 1811–1814*'; Frisch, *Anhalt-Dessaus Freiheitskämpfer 1813 bis 1815*, pp.47–50; LASA: Z 18, C 16c 5 Nr. 63, 'Report of *Hauptmann* Klaette, dated 20 November 1813, Danzig', Translated by Dr Wilma A. Hofmann, PhD; Rapp, *Memoirs of General Count Rapp*, pp.303–327.

87 LASA: Z 44, C 16c 5 Nr. 66, 'Morgenstern's Bataillon Geschichte Bd. I–II, 1811–1814'; Frisch, *Anhalt-Dessaus Freiheitskämpfer 1813 bis 1815*, pp.50–51.

While the Bataillon Anhalt was besieged in Danzig, Herzog Leopold III had been treading a tightrope with the allies on one side and Napoleon on the other. On 2 April 1813 advance elements of General of Cavalry Ludwig Adolf Wittgenstein's (1769–1843) Russian army entered Dessau and Köthen, after the French had retreated to the River Saale. Wittgenstein told Leopold III that he was requested to raise a battalion for Russian service. Leopold insisted that the Anhalt Duchies wished to be considered neutral territory, but was told that if he was 'not inclined to his request, the land was to be treated as hostile'. On 13 April Leopold III agreed to the formation of a battalion and recruitment began for the Anhalt-Dessau-Köthen Jäger Bataillon, which was to consist of four companies totalling 602 officers and men. It was uniformed in a dark green *überrock* tunic, with rose-pink collar patches with a white cross in the centre. It was raised on a voluntary basis and the first volunteers were the sons of government officials, who had been promised commissions. *Major* Waldemar Krohne (1774–1829) was chosen to command the battalion. He was not from Anhalt but was a German in the Russian service.[88]

Training of the Jäger Bataillon began on 19 April for nine to 10 hours each day. However, the battalion was moved to Rosslau (Roßlau) on 1 May to guard the bridges there. When the allied army retreated across the River Elbe after their defeat at Lützen, the Jäger Bataillon was moved to Dömitz, and later to Laueburg on 20 May, when Hamburg became threatened. On 29 May it was moved to the Vierlande area and the island of Ochsenwerder to guard pontoon bridges across the river. Here it lost one *korporal* wounded and a soldier captured. When the French captured Hamburg on 30 May the Allies evacuated the area, but the Jäger Bataillon remained with a rearguard at Boizenburg. However, the corps commander, *Generalleutnant* Ludwig George Thedel, Graf von Wallmoden-Gimborn (1769–1862), realised that the Jäger Bataillon was only partly trained and the battalion was marched to Crivitz, arriving on 5 June. After the summer armistice was announced the battalion spent June and July shuffling between encampments at Dömitz, Grabow, and Crivitz.[89]

After the allies withdrew and the armistice came into effect, the Anhalt Duchies were once again occupied by French forces. On 20 June Napoleon demanded that the duchies raise a battalion of infantry and a regiment of cavalry. Herzog Leopold

88 LASA: Z 44, C 16c 5 Nr. 209, '*Kurzer Abriss der Geschichte des im April 1813 von Anhalt-Dessau und Anhalt-Köthen gestellten Bataillons unter dem Befehl des Kaiserlich Russischen Majors von Krone, verfasst vom Oberleutnant Ackermann, 1813*', subsequently referred to as '*Ackermann's Bataillon Geschichte 1813*'; Frisch, *Anhalt-Dessaus Freiheitskämpfer 1813 bis 1815*, pp.66–67; Nafziger, *The Armies of Germany and the Confederation of the Rhine*, Vol.I, p.3; Rawkins, *CB6, Armies of the Confederation of the Rhine*, pp.16, 22, 24; Leggiere, *Napoleon and the Struggle for Germany*, Vol.I, pp.155–156.

89 LASA: Z 44, C 16c 5 Nr. 209, '*Ackermann's Bataillon Geschichte 1813*'; Frisch, *Anhalt-Dessaus Freiheitskämpfer 1813 bis 1815*, pp.67–69; Leggiere, *Napoleon and the Struggle for Germany*, Vol.I, pp.268–293.

III resisted these calls, with men now in Danzig and with the allies, but any objections were dismissed. At a meeting on 23 June the herzöge agreed to create the two-squadron Anhaltische Regiment Jäger zu Pferde consisting of 500 men. The regiment was to be formed at the expense of the duchies, with the French supplying only the weapons. To raise the necessary funds the herzöge raised 10,000 Thalers through new taxes and 7,500 Thalers in a special tax on Jewish families. The first conscripts arrived in Dessau on 27 June, with Dessau providing 219 officers and men, Bernburg 150 and Köthen 131. Chosen to lead the regiment was *Major* Leopold Bürkner (1784–1865), who had previously served in the Prussian hussars, but more recently had been a merchant in Dessau. Bürkner was one of the few who had ridden a horse before, and to help train the conscripts several non-commissioned officers from the French 9e Régiment de Chevau-Legers-Lanciers were used. As the regiment was hurriedly raised it was dressed in the same uniform as the Bataillon Anhalt.[90]

However, while training of the cavalry was progressing, the herzöge sent an agent named Sternegg to Vienna in June to speak with Klemens, Fürst von Metternich-Winneburg zu Beilstein (1773–1859), about what plans Austria had to enter the war. By mid-July the herzöge had their answer, as Sternegg sent a letter dated 9 July to Leopold III's *Regierungsrat* (Councilor), and had also been in communication with their advisor *Geheimrat* August von Rode (1751–1837). Sternegg advised that all the allied representatives were gathered in Prague and that he was travelling with Metternich there before returning to Dessau. Sternegg was quite positive Austria would enter the war, writing: 'It will take a great deal of effort to counter the might of Austria that strongly insists on finalising a lasting peace treaty'. In fact Sternegg seems to have been willing Austria to enter the war: 'Our dear Anhalt has suffered terribly but now it shall – and will be different, soon'. Sternegg got his wish on 9 August when Austria declared war on France.[91]

Once Austria entered the war with the Allies, the Anhaltische Regiment Jäger zu Pferde was assigned to *Général de Brigade* Martin-Charles Gobrecht's (1772–1845) brigade of *Général de Division* Dominique Vandamme's (1770–1830) I Corps. Having moved to Bernburg on 25 July, Bürkner was ordered to move with the corps to Dresden on 14 August; but he found time to visit his new wife in

90 Gärtner, Markus and Wager, Edmund, 'Das Chasseur-Regiment der Anhaltinschen Herzogtümer in Jahr 1813', *Depesche: Uniformen und Heere vergangener Zeiten*, 28 (December 1996), pp.15–21, <http://www.napoleon-online.de/quellen_depesche.html> (accessed 16 March 2019); Wittich, Karl-Heinz, 'Das Anhaltische Chasseur–Regiment 1813', *Salzlandkreis* (January 2013), <https://www.salzlandkreis.de/media/6134/wittich_anhaltisches-chasseur-regiment-1813.pdf> (accessed 16 March 2019); Nafziger, *The Armies of Germany and the Confederation of the Rhine*, Vol.I, p.8; Rawkins, *CB6, Armies of the Confederation of the Rhine*, pp.39–43; Frisch, *Anhalt-Dessaus Freiheitskämpfer 1813 bis 1815*, p.11.

91 LASA: Z 44, C 16c 5 Nr. 83, *Die Mission des Herrn von Sternegg nach Prag und Wien, 1813*, 'Letter of Sternegg dated 9 July 1813, Vienna', Translated by Dr Wilma A. Hofmann, PhD; Leggiere, *Napoleon and the Struggle for Germany*, Vol.II (Cambridge: Cambridge University Press, 2015), pp.22–64.

The Anhaltische Regiment Jäger zu Pferde, 1813. A print by Richard Knotel showing two troopers and an officer (with white plume) of this hastily organised regiment, which was destroyed at the Battle of Kulm on 29–30 August 1813. (New York Public Library, Vinkhuijzen Collection)

Oranienbaum. When he returned to the regiment at Raguhn he found it in chaos: *Rittmeister* Koch had deserted, taking several men with him, and new horseshoes and saddles had not arrived as promised. Writing about what he found on 17 August, he pleaded:

> Please forgive me, I have only ever received your consideration and never blame; I am trying whatever I can to better relegate and organise. But I can promise, for I have seen it while we were working through the night, my officers are getting better, or I will come after them like the devil himself!

However, Bürkner's efforts to make the regiment more efficient failed, and desertion had become such a problem that on the eve of the deciding day of the Battle of Kulm on 29–30 August, the regiment was reduced to a single squadron of 250 officers and men.[92]

On the morning of 30 August Bürkner and his men were drawn up near to the village of Kulm (Chlumec) in reserve. From here they watched the attacks of the Austrians and Russians that began at 7:00 a.m. At about 11:30 a.m. they heard the sound of cannon to their rear, which announced the arrival of a Prussian corps descending on the French flank. After 1:30 p.m. the French infantry brigade sent to delay the Prussian advance could no longer do so, and Gobrecht's cavalry were sent to support them. Immediately they engaged a Prussian hussar regiment, with the Anhalters attacking them in front and the 9e Régiment de Chevau-Legers-Lanciers in the flank, forcing them to retreat. This exposed an artillery battery that had three cannons captured before it escaped. By 2:00 p.m. the pressure from the Austrians and Russians in front, and the newly arriving Prussians in the flank, was too much for the French infantry which began to break. At this point a Prussian battery deployed across the road leading from Kulm supported by the 10. Schlesisches Landwehr Regiment. To clear the road Gobrecht's brigade charged into the still-forming infantry and broke them. The commander of the Prussian regiment was *Major* Christian Friedrich von Anhalt-Köthen-Pleß (1780–1813) who was killed.[93]

92 LASA: Z 44, C 16c 5 Nr. 211, *Korrespondenz mit dem Groß-Major Bürkner, 1813*, 'Report of *Major* Bürkner dated 17 August 1813, Raguhn', Translated by Dr Wilma A. Hofmann, PhD; Gärtner and Wager, 'Das Chasseur-Regiment der Anhaltinschen Herzogtümer', p.17-18, <http://www.napoleon-online.de/quellen_depesche.html> (accessed 16 March 2019); Wittich, 'Das Anhaltische Chasseur-Regiment 1813', <https://www.salzlandkreis.de/media/6134/wittich_anhaltisches-chasseur-regiment-1813.pdf> (accessed 16 March 2019).

93 Graham J. Morris, 'The Battle of Kulm, 29th–30th August 1813', *Battlefield Anomalies* (September 2016), <https://battlefieldanomalies.com/the-battle-of-kulm/> (accessed 16 March 2019); Wittich, 'Das Anhaltische Chasseur–Regiment 1813', <https://www.salzlandkreis.de/media/6134/wittich_anhaltisches-chasseur-regiment-1813.pdf> (accessed 16 March 2019); Clarke, 'Officers of the Anhalt Duchies', <http://www.napoleon-series.org/research/biographies/Anhalt/c_AnhaltBiographies.html> (accessed 30 March 2019).

The allied forces continued to close their trap around Vandamme's troops, who either surrendered or escaped from the battlefield. Caught in the trap were Bürkner and his regiment. In the confusion only 30 men escaped and Bürkner with 80 men was captured by Austrians. Those who escaped were amalgamated with the 9e Régiment de Chevau-Legers-Lanciers, while Bürkner and the others were sent to Lugos (Lugoj) in the Banat, Romania, where, 'neither nature nor people can please the eye or lighten the mood', and held as prisoners until March 1814. At Lugos the bubbling issue of German nationalism and concern for his men occupied Bürkner's thoughts: 'Oh God, I wish I still had my Regiment so that we could unite with all Germans. But no, for me only the sorrow remains that tears at my soul. The worries about my dear regiment. How many have survived and where are they?'[94]

Having left the Anhalt-Dessau-Köthen Jäger Bataillon in Crivitz, they later took part in the corps review at Goldberg on 20–21 July. Here the *quartiermeister* informed Krohne that the battalion's funds had run out, and as a temporary measure the Jäger Bataillon was given 1,000 Thalers from the British subsidy that funded Wallmoden's corps. An officer was sent to Dessau, but he only reached Zerbst and he then went to Berlin where no funds could be found. It was then suggested the Jäger Bataillon could be paid directly from the British fund. The officers supported this proposed arrangement and negotiations with Lieutenant General Charles Stewart (1778–1854)—the British Military Commissioner with the allied armies—began, with an agreement signed on 27 July. However, the next evening orders arrived directing the Jäger Bataillon to Rostock, a port on the German coast. This made many *unteroffiziere* and soldiers suspicious, with some accusing the officers of signing the agreement so that the men could be sent to Canada to fight with British forces against the United States, while they remained in Europe. A large group from the battalion gathered at the officers' quarters to voice their concerns. One of the company commanders addressed them, after the men had refused to march the next day. This calmed the men and orders from Wallmoden came stating the battalion would march to Neustadt (Neustadt-Glewe) instead. The men then dispersed, but the next day it was found 19 of them had deserted during the night.[95]

After the armistice ended the Jäger Bataillon marched to the Stecknitz, a tributary of the Elbe, on 14 August, having been attached to *Oberstleutnant* David

94 LASA: Z 44, C 16c 5 Nr. 211, 'Letter of *Major* Bürkner dated 17 November 1813, Lugos', Translated by Dr Wilma A. Hofmann, PhD; Wittich, 'Das Anhaltische Chasseur–Regiment 1813', <https://www.salzlandkreis.de/media/6134/wittich_anhaltisches-chasseur-regiment-1813.pdf> (accessed 16 March 2019); Gärtner and Wager, 'Das Chasseur-Regiment der Anhaltinschen Herzogtümer', p.18, <http://www.napoleon-online.de/quellen_depesche.html> (accessed 16 March 2019); Morris, 'The Battle of Kulm, 29th–30th August 1813', <https://battlefieldanomalies.com/the-battle-of-kulm/> (accessed 16 March 2019).

95 LASA: Z 44, C 16c 5 Nr. 209, '*Ackermann's Bataillon Geschichte 1813*'; Frisch, Anhalt-Dessaus *Freiheitskämpfer 1813 bis 1815*, pp.69–70.

August Martin's (1764–1829) Hanoverian brigade. However, on the night of 22 August *Maréchal* Louis-Nicolas Davout's (1770–1823) corps, which was defending Hamburg, bypassed Wallmoden's flank and reached Schwerin on 24 August. Wallmoden ordered a withdrawal but news of the allied victory at Großbeeren a few days earlier arrived, and he sent Martin's brigade to Grabow. Here the two corps faced each other until Davout withdrew during the night of 2–3 September to the Stecknitz. On 10 September the Jäger Bataillon went with Martin's brigade to probe Davout's positions. On 12 September the battalion was probing between Molin (Mölln) and Ratzeburg, when the small Swedish force of *Generalmajor* Eberhard von Vegesack (1763–1818) supporting Wallmoden was attacked, which uncovered Martin's right flank who ordered a withdrawal to Wittenburg.[96]

A few days later Wallmoden received intelligence that Davout was sending part of *Général de Division* Marc Pécheux's (1769–1831) division to Magdeburg, to open communication between there and Hamburg. Wallmoden made plans to intercept this force and moved his corps to Dannenberg on 15 September. The next day Pécheux's division was found near the Göhrde forest in Oldendorf and Eichdorf. After sending two columns through the forest to turn both French flanks, Wallmoden formed two columns of infantry, including the Jäger Bataillon, in the forest to attack Pécheux frontally. At 4:00 p.m. the two columns moved forward, driving in the French outposts. The French were formed on a ridge, and when Pécheux saw the columns debouch from the wood he ordered his left flank to retreat and formed his right into three columns as a rearguard. These became squares when cavalry from one of the outflanking forces attacked. The Jäger Bataillon was formed behind two Hanoverian battalions and when they arrived at the ridge Pécheux's men were already routing, as they were being attacked from all sides. In the attack the Jäger Bataillon lost 10 men wounded and received a captured ammunition wagon as a reward for its service.[97]

After sleeping on the battlefield, the battalion marched to Dömitz with the corps, remaining in cantonments until 4 October, when it was attached to a force commanded by *Generalmajor* Wilhelm von Dörnberg (1768–1850). In the night of 5–6 October the Jäger Bataillon marched to Vellahn to be able to capture the bridge at Büchen the next day. However, the French had built two redoubts to

96 LASA: Z 44, C 16c 5 Nr. 209, '*Ackermann's Bataillon Geschichte 1813*'; Frisch, Anhalt-Dessaus *Freiheitskämpfer 1813 bis 1815*, pp.70–72; Stephen Summerfield, *Brazen Cross of Courage: Russian Militia, Partizans, Volunteers and the Russo-German Legion during the Napoleonic Wars* (London: Partizan Press, 2007), pp.97–99.

97 LASA: Z 44, C 16c 5 Nr. 209, '*Ackermann's Bataillon Geschichte 1813*'; Frisch, *Anhalt-Dessaus Freiheitskämpfer 1813 bis 1815*, pp.72–74; North Ludlow Beamish, *History of the King's German Legion* (London: Thomas and William Boone, 1837), Vol.II, pp.186–198; *Generalleutnant* Ludwig George Thedel Graf von Wallmoden-Gimborn, 'Dispatch Dated 20 September, 1813, Domitz', in *The London Gazette Extraordinary*, Thursday 7 October 1813, Issue 16784. <https://www.thegazette.co.uk/London/issue/16784/page/1975> (accessed 12 March 2019).

protect the bridge, and Dörnberg tried to force a crossing anyway, costing the Jäger Bataillon two dead and five wounded men. After this failure Dörnberg withdrew to Zarrentin (Zarrentin am Schaalsee), remaining there to watch Davout's positions until 1 December.[98]

On 1 December Davout evacuated his Stecknitz positions, withdrawing closer to Hamburg. He also advised the corps of his Danish allies to retreat into Holstein. The Jäger Bataillon, with Dörnberg's force, followed the Danes on 2 December, catching their rearguard at Steinhorst and Siebenbäumen on 4 December, and in a sharp engagement to capture the villages the battalion lost four officers and 26 men wounded and eight dead. The Danes withdrew toward Rendsburg and to try and encircle them Wallmoden-Gimborn moved his corps to Bovenau by 8 December. Dörnberg and the Jäger Bataillon crossed the Eider Canal, but while Dörnberg marched to Haby and Groß Wittensee, two companies of the battalion were left at Sehested (Sehestedt) and the other two guarded the crossing at Kluvensiek. On 10 December the Danes attacked Dörnberg's dispersed forces and advanced on Sehested. Here the Danes threw out the garrison, including the two companies of the Jäger Bataillon, which lost six officers and 150 men captured, at around 11:00 a.m., but part of the Russo-German Legion soon recaptured the village. However, they advanced too far beyond Sehested and were surprised and routed by Danish cavalry. The Danes did not take advantage of this success, content with desultory skirmishing until the late afternoon when they withdrew. During the afternoon the Jäger Bataillon garrisoned Sehested once again. Overall the battalion lost 50 men dead and wounded, and of the 150 men who were captured 42 managed to escape, most likely during the counterattack of the Russo-German Legion.[99]

Following the Battle of Sehested the Jäger Bataillon were given orders to assemble in Neumünster, where the battalion gathered between 11–13 December. On 14 December more orders arrived for the battalion instructing it to march to Hildesheim to reorganise, and they reached the city on 3 January 1814. On 6 January instructions from Herzog Leopold III were received for the battalion to return home to Dessau. The Jäger Bataillon arrived in Dessau on 14 January, where Leopold III had been labouring to organise a coherent force to serve with the allies.[100]

98 LASA: Z 44, C 16c 5 Nr. 209, '*Ackermann's Bataillon Geschichte 1813*'; Frisch, *Anhalt-Dessaus Freiheitskämpfer 1813 bis 1815*, pp.74–76.

99 LASA: Z 44, C 16c 5 Nr. 209, '*Ackermann's Bataillon Geschichte 1813*'; Frisch, Anhalt-Dessaus *Freiheitskämpfer 1813 bis 1815*, p.77; Beamish, *History of the King's German Legion*, Vol.II, pp.204–218.

100 LASA: Z 44, C 16c 5 Nr. 209, '*Ackermann's Bataillon Geschichte 1813*'; LASA: Z 44, C 16c 5 Nr. 219, 'Kurzer Abriss der Geschichte des im Jahr 1814 von Anhalt-Dessau zu den Heeren der gegen Frankreich verbündeten hohen Mächte mit Anhalt-Köthen gemeinschaftlich gestellten Regimentes vom Regierungsrat Morgenstern, 1814', subsequently referred to as '*Morgenstern's 1814 Bataillon Geschichte*'; Frisch, *Anhalt-Dessaus Freiheitskämpfer 1813 bis 1815*, pp.78, 80–82.

When Napoleon was defeated at Leipzig between 16–19 October 1813, he retreated to France with the remnant of the Grande Armée. At the end of October the former *Rheinbund* members fell under the administrative control of the allies, who, like Napoleon, set about trying to organise the forces into something they could use for their war effort. Leopold III sent letters to the allies in November declaring that Dessau and Köthen were ready to raise forces in support of the allies,[101] and he was directed to finalise his ideas with the Governor General of Saxony, Major General Nikolay Grigorievich Repnin-Volkonsky (1778–1845). It was concluded that the Anhalt Duchies should provide a line battalion of 1,000 men and a *landwehr* battalion of 1,600 men. However, Leopold III had not included Herzog Alexius Friedrich Christian von Anhalt-Bernburg in his negotiations, and on 7 December he replied to a letter from Leopold that he believed each duchy was acting independently, which meant he was already raising his own contingent.[102]

As we know, the Bataillon Anhalt besieged in Danzig and the Anhalt-Dessau-Köthen Jäger Bataillon were ordered to Dessau in December, where they arrived between January and February 1814. To create the combined Anhalt-Dessau-Köthen Linen Infanterie Bataillon these two formations were merged and organised into four companies, with Hoppe being promoted to the rank of *Oberst* to command it. The Anhalt-Dessau-Köthen Landwehr Bataillon was also four companies strong and command was given to *Hauptmann* Christoph Möbes. However, the two battalions never attained their targeted establishment and both could only field around 550 men each. Attached to the line battalion was the small 50-man Freiwilliger Jäger Korps led by *Leutnant* Harsleben. It was a volunteer unit in which the men had to purchase their own uniforms and equipment. Meanwhile, in Bernburg, the Anhalt-Bernburg Jäger Bataillon had been raised. There is evidence that the battalion had begun as a *freiwilliger* unit in Frankfurt in the summer of 1813, organised by one *Major* Sonnenberg. When it was called to Bernburg, its two regular companies were augmented by two more of *landwehr*, giving it an establishment of four companies of around 450 men. These were the forces put into the field for the allies in 1814 by the Anhalt Duchies.[103]

101 In May 1812 Herzog Augustus Christian Friedrich von Anhalt-Köthen had died, and his underage nephew, Ludwig Augustus Karl Friedrich Emil, succeeded him, but Herzog Leopold III von Anhalt-Dessau acted as his regent until 1817.

102 LASA: Z 44, C 16c 5 Nr. 212, Verhandlungen wegen der von den verbündeten Mächten begehrten Augmentation (Vermehrung) des stehenden Kontingents und Organisation der Landwehr, 1813–1814, 'Letter of Major General Repnin-Volkonsky, dated 10 November 1813, Leipzig'; LASA: Z 44, C 16c 5 Nr. 219, 'Morgenstern's 1814 Bataillon Geschichte'; Frisch, *Anhalt-Dessaus Freiheitskämpfer 1813 bis 1815*, pp.80–81.

103 LASA: Z 44, C 16c 5 Nr. 219,'Morgenstern's 1814 Bataillon Geschichte'; Frisch, *Anhalt-Dessaus Freiheitskämpfer 1813 bis 1815*, pp.81–82; Nafziger, *The Armies of Germany and the Confederation of the Rhine*, Vol.I, pp.3–5; Rawkins, CB6, Armies of the Confederation of the Rhine, pp.16–18; Clarke, 'Officers of the Anhalt Duchies', <http://www.napoleon-series.org/research/biographies/Anhalt/c_AnhaltBiographies.html> (accessed 30 March 2019).

Once these forces were assembled in Köthen on 3 February they were ordered to march to Kassel, where they would be become part of Major General Paul Karl Friedrich August, Prinz von Wurttemberg's (1785–1852) brigade of German contingents, and they arrived on 16 February. However, the prinz had already left the city and after marching to Unna on 23 February, Hoppe was informed

The Freiwilliger Jäger Korps and Landwehr Bataillon of Anhalt Dessau-Kothen in 1813–1814. A print by Richard Knotel depicting these two units, which were raised at the end of 1813 and into the spring of 1814; both units fought in Belgium in March before returning to the Anhalt Duchies after Napoleon's abdication. (New York Public Library, Vinkhuijzen Collection)

his battalions would form part of *Generalleutnant* Johann Adolf, Freiherr von Thielmann's (1765–1824) Saxon division instead. The Anhalters reached Tournai in Belgium on 15 March. When they were inspected by the corps commander, General of Cavalry Karl August, Großherzog von Saxe-Weimar-Eisenach (1757–1828), he remarked to Thielmann: 'There are still people who look like soldiers', perhaps having heard from his own contingent's commander, Egloffstein, about the Anhalters' service in Danzig. At Tournai Hoppe's regiment, consisting of the line and *landwehr* battalions and Harsleben's Jäger Korps, were assigned outpost duties in the villages of Rume (Rumes), Taintignies and Villeman (Willemeau). Sonnenberg's battalion meanwhile was assigned to Prinz Paul's brigade and were quartered in Tournai itself.[104]

On 26 March the French commander in the Low Countries, *Général de Division* Nicolas Joseph Maison (1771–1840), advanced from Lille and captured Ghent. Thielmann planned to cut Maison off from Lille by advancing north from Tournai, but realised that his division was dispersed and concentrated it at Audenarde (Oudenaarde) instead. To garrison Tournai in his absence he left the Ducal Saxon contingent of Egloffstein and Hoppe's battalions. However, he demanded that Harsleben's Jäger Korps be attached to Sonnenberg's battalion but Hoppe was conscious of the tensions between the herzöge of Dessau and Bernburg, and suggested that Harsleben could be assigned to *Generalmajor* Friedrich von Brause's (1769–1836) brigade, which Thielmann accepted. Then, on 30 March, Maison withdrew from Ghent and occupied Courtrai (Kortrijk) with the intention of retreating back into France.[105]

Thielmann quickly realised in the early morning of 31 March that Maison had withdrawn, and set off after what he thought would be the French rearguard. Brause's brigade, with Harsleben's Jäger Korps, reached Sweveghem (Zwevegem) at 6:00 a.m., drove out the French outposts and formed on a ridge overlooking Courtrai—where the three divisions of Maison's corps could be seen, not just a rearguard. Prinz Paul's brigade was then deployed in three columns in front of Sweveghem, with Sonnenberg's men as a reserve behind part of the Saxon 3. Landwehr Regiment. When he found Thielmann was isolated, Maison attacked his line with his divisions and the untrained Saxon *landwehr* quickly began to rout. Thielmann ordered the Saxon Kürassier Regiment to charge the French, but they were brushed aside by the 2e Chasseurs-à-Cheval de la Garde Impériale,[106]

104 LASA: Z 44, C 16c 5 Nr. 219,'Morgenstern's 1814 Bataillon Geschichte'; Frisch, *Anhalt-Dessaus Freiheitskämpfer 1813 bis 1815*, pp.82–83.

105 LASA: Z 44, C 16c 5 Nr. 219, 'Morgenstern's 1814 Bataillon Geschichte'; Frisch, *Anhalt-Dessaus Freiheitskämpfer 1813 bis 1815*, p.83; George F. Nafziger, *The End of Empire: Napoleon's 1814 Campaign* (Solihull: Helion & Co., 2015), pp.358–365.

106 This regiment was raised in 1813 as the 6e–9e escadrons of the Chasseurs-à-Cheval de la Garde Impériale. However, it operated as a separate regiment and was part of the Young Guard. It should not be confused with a newly raised regiment of the same name in 1815, which was considered part of the Old Guard.

who rode to the spot where Harsleben's men were deployed. In the ensuing confusion Harsleben was wounded in the shoulder and *Jäger* De Marees was captured by one the troopers. However, before the trooper could take him to the rear, *Jäger* Koeselitz shot and killed the cavalryman allowing De Marees to escape. Sonnenberg's battalion was also caught in the rout, but no casualty details exist. Thielmann was left to regroup his division at Audenarde that afternoon.[107]

To cover the retreat of his baggage train into France, Maison went with two of his divisions and some artillery to Tournai. In Tournai were Hoppe and Egloffstein with their battalions, some Saxon hussars and four cannon, excluding the heavy guns of the town's defences. During the early evening Maison's divisions approached the town and skirmishers were sent forward to pick off men from the walls. This does not seem to have been productive, as Morgenstern suggests only one Anhalter was killed and two others were wounded during the whole engagement. When this failed Maison used his cannon to bombard the walls, with Egloffstein directing the town's guns to reply. The cannon fire died down at around 10:00 p.m. During the night Maison received reports that Tournai's garrison had received reinforcements, and he retreated to Lille on the morning of 1 April.[108]

Thielmann's division regrouped at Tournai on 1 April, with Hoppe's battalions being assigned outpost duty in Eze (Ere) and St. Mauer (Saint–Maur). On 4 April news that Paris had surrendered to the allied army on 31 March was received, and 'was proclaimed by the sound of the bells [of Tournai]'. A week later on 9 April hostilities in Belgium came to an end, and Harsleben's Jäger Korps and Möbes' *landwehr* battalion were given permission to return to Dessau on 30 April, where they arrived on 3 June. Hoppe and the line battalion were moved to quarters in Lille, before marching to Maastricht. From here the battalion went to Eisenach and returned to Dessau on 16 July, their war now ended.[109]

Throughout the period 1804–1814, the leaders of the Anhalt Duchies faced many of the same problems that their contemporary rulers did in the other small principalities and duchies, which joined the *Rheinbund* in 1806 and 1807. One of the main concerns was how to create a viable military formation out of the limited resources and manpower available. In the Anhalt Duchies, the Anhalt-Dessau Jäger Korps was used in 1807 as the nucleus around which the Bataillon Anhalt was built. However, like other small *Rheinbund* members, some officer positions had to be filled by men who had no connection with the duchies. This included *Hauptmann* Hohnstein, who had served in the forces of Brunswick, and, in 1808, *Hauptmann* von Santorini, who was born in Mainz. However, unlike the Reus

107 LASA: Z 44, C 16c 5 Nr. 219, 'Morgenstern's 1814 Bataillon Geschichte'; Frisch, *Anhalt-Dessaus Freiheitskämpfer 1813 bis 1815*, pp.83–84; Nafziger, *The End of Empire*, pp.365–367.

108 LASA: Z 44, C 16c 5 Nr. 219, 'Morgenstern's 1814 Bataillon Geschichte'; Frisch, *Anhalt-Dessaus Freiheitskämpfer 1813 bis 1815*, p.84; Nafziger, *The End of Empire*, pp.368–369.

109 LASA: Z 44, C 16c 5 Nr. 219, 'Morgenstern's 1814 Bataillon Geschichte'; Frisch, *Anhalt-Dessaus Freiheitskämpfer 1813 bis 1815*, pp.84–85.

principalities for example, where three quarters of the officers were 'foreign',[110] in the Bataillon Anhalt *unteroffiziere* of the original Anhalt-Dessau Jäger Korps were promoted instead to fill gaps. This included Hartmann who was promoted from *leutnant* to *hauptmann* in 1807, and Hoppe who was promoted to *leutnant* from *korporal*. Native officers who had left the duchies and were serving in the military forces of other states were also encouraged to join the battalion; an example here would be *Hauptmann* von Sonnenberg, who was born in Bernburg but who had firstly joined the Saxon and later the Bavarian army, becoming a *leutnant* of cavalry in the latter.

A second concern throughout the period was unit cohesion and morale, particularly when a high percentage of the recruits were conscripts who did not want to perform military service. This showed itself in 1807, when the battalion was reduced to 280 men from an establishment strength of 785 men just weeks after leaving Dessau. However, after the Bataillon Anhalt was rebuilt in 1808, during the campaign against Austria in 1809 the cohesion of the battalion had improved markedly, with very few reports of desertion. At the beginning of 1809 the battalion contained 862 officers and men, while at the end of the campaign this was 725. Of this discrepancy, Chambaud's report of 3 October 1809 in Vienna states that 82 officers and men could be accounted for as being sick in hospital, while he listed only 13 as missing, presumably having deserted.[111] If the 82 sick men were added to the 725 who were present for duty, this would give the battalion a strength of 807 officers and men; nowhere near the huge losses of 1807.

However, much of the progress made during 1808–1809 was destroyed when the battalion was sent to Spain in 1810. Here disease took about half of the officers and men from the active duty list, particularly during the summer of 1810, and confined them to the hospitals or battalion depot in Gerona. On 14 September those garrisoning La Bisbal and other villages on the Spanish east coast were taken prisoner, including most of the senior officers. All of this meant that only 54 officers and men returned to the Anhalt Duchies in June 1811, which necessitated the rebuilding of the Bataillon Anhalt. This time, however, the core of officers and men from the Anhalt-Dessau Jäger Korps was no longer available to build upon, and junior officers were promoted to senior positions—such as Georg Hoppe, who went from *leutnant* to *oberstleutnant* within the space of a few months in 1811. With the large number of conscripts, and officers promoted above their potential talents, desertion became a more prevalent problem in 1812, which is why—combined with the severe winter weather—only 380 officers and men of the battalion were present for duty in Vilna at the beginning of December. However, on a more positive note, when the battalion had time to gather itself in Königsberg after its retreat at the

110 Gill, *With Eagles to Glory*, p.386.

111 LASA: Z 18, C 16c 5 Nr. 45, 'Report of *Oberst* Chambaud, dated 3 October 1809, Vienna', Translated by Dr Wilma A. Hofmann, PhD.

end of the month, its strength rose to over 400 men, while many veteran French regiments could barely count 200.[112] This number, though, dropped to around 250 effectives when disease and frostbite was taken into account.

During the Siege of Danzig in 1813 it is widely stated that the *Rheinbund* contingents had to be combined into a single regiment, because of losses suffered mainly through desertion, but also disease.[113] Looking at the reports of the officers written at the end of the siege, there is hardly any mention of acts of desertion, but disease, partly caused by the lack of food supplies, is frequently commented upon. Hoppe reported that in March 1813 120 Anhalters were convalescing in the battalion hospital, which was essentially half of the Bataillon Anhalt's remaining effective strength.[114] In his report at the end of the 10-month siege *Hauptmann* Klaette reported that only six soldiers of the Bernburg contingent had deserted during the period, although suggests that the contingent from Dessau lost more men than this to the same cause.[115] Overall, it seems that disease took more *Rheinbund* soldiers from the ranks compared to desertion, and that they may have been treated somewhat unfairly by history to this point.

Those formations raised in 1813, the Anhaltische Regiment Jäger zu Pferde and the Anhalt-Dessau-Köthen Jäger Bataillon, were built hurriedly and suffered as a result. The cavalry regiment was filled with conscripts, the majority of who had never ridden a horse, while the officers, like *Major* Bürkner, had never commanded large bodies of men before. Therefore, desertion and inefficiency was high, reducing the regiment from 500 to 250 men after a handful of weeks' service, before it was captured *en masse* on 30 August at Kulm. The Jäger Bataillon was much more reliable, being led by a professional officer in the service of Russia, although many of the junior officers, along with the soldiers, were volunteers. The combination of professional leadership and the enthusiasm of young, patriotic volunteer officers created a steady unit, which endured quite substantial losses in a handful of minor engagements but never panicked or routed. The same could also be said of the units created in February 1814. Here veterans of Danzig and the somewhat experienced men of the Jäger Bataillon steadied the new volunteers and conscripts. The officers were now also seasoned campaigners from the original Bataillon Anhalt or the Anhalt-Dessau-Köthen Jäger Bataillon, and meant the new Anhalt-Dessau-Köthen Linen Infanterie Bataillon was reasonably well led.

Overall, the Anhalt Duchies created quite an efficient fighting force in the period 1809 to 1814, which for the most part performed admirably in battle. After

112 Bowden, Scott, *Napoleon's Grande Armée of 1813* (Chicago: The Emperor's Press, 1990), pp.16–17.

113 Nafziger, *The Armies of Germany and the Confederation of the Rhine*, Vol.I, p.3; Rawkins, *CB6, Armies of the Confederation of the Rhine*, p.15.

114 LASA: Z 44, C 16c 5 Nr. 66, 'Morgenstern's Bataillon Geschichte Bd. I–II, 1811–1814'; Frisch, *Anhalt-Dessaus Freiheitskämpfer 1813 bis 1815*, pp.43–46.

115 LASA: Z 18, C 16c 5 Nr. 63, 'Report of *Hauptmann* Klaette, dated 20 November 1813, Danzig', Translated by Dr Wilma A. Hofmann, Ph.D.

the losses suffered in Spain the Bataillon Anhalt never attained the unit cohesion of 1809, garnered through hours of training in 1808. However, the battalion nevertheless remained effective through to the end of the Siege of Danzig. The same cannot be said for the Anhaltische Regiment Jäger zu Pferde, hastily raised as it was with barely four weeks of training before it was sent to the front. Yet as Chambaud wrote in 1809: 'We endured a lot, suffered a lot, but even in this moment, the spirit of the Battalion could not be better and we are all alert and ready to march forward again'.[116]

## Bibliography

***Bibliographical Note***

I have to thank a couple of people who have helped me to complete this project. They are Dr Wilma A. Hofmann, PhD, of Buffalo, New York, of *German Script Translations* (https://germanscripttranslations.com), who has completed many of the transcriptions and translations used in this chapter. As I am not a native German reader or speaker, she has helped me greatly to understand the various reports I have used. The other two people are Dr Andreas Erb and Anke Boeck of the Landesarchiv Sachsen-Anhalt in Dessau, who prepared the collections when I visited and were very patient with me, given the language difficulties we encountered.

***Archival Sources***

*Landesarchiv Sachsen-Anhalt, Abteilung Dessau (LASA)*

LASA, Z 18, C 16c 5 Nr. 45, *Verschiedene das Bataillon angehende Sachen, Berichte des Obersten von Chambaud aus Tirol, Wien usw., 1809.*

LASA, Z 18, C 16c 5 Nr. 47, *Rapporte vom anhaltischen Kontingent, 1809–1810.*

LASA, Z 18, C 16c 5 Nr. 50, *Verschiedene das Bataillon Anhalt in Spanien angehende Sachen, Katastrophe von Labisbal, 1810.*

LASA, Z 18, C 16c 5 Nr. 51, *Verschiedene Kontingentssachen, die Konferenz zu Dessau wegen der Reorganisation des Kontingentes, dessen Ausmarsch nach Varel, Berichte des Kommandeurs Hoppe, 1811–1812.*

LASA, Z 18, C 16c 5 Nr. 56, *Rapporte von dem Bataillon aus Danzig, 1812.*

LASA, Z 18, C 16c 5 Nr. 61, *Das anhaltische Chasseurregiment, seine Stellung und anderes darauf bezügliches, 1813.*

LASA, Z 18, C 16c 5 Nr. 63, *Rapporte vom Bataillon in Danzig, 1813.*

116 LASA: Z 18, C 16c 5 Nr. 45, 'Report of *Oberst* Chambaud, dated 23 August, Mathsee', Translated by Dr Wilma A. Hofmann, Ph.D.

LASA, Z 44, C 16c 5 Nr. 42, *Publicandum (öffentliche Bekanntmachung) wegen Stellung eines Kontingents zur Rheinbundsarmee vom 23. Mai 1807 und einzelne das Kontingent betreffende Sachen, 1807–1809, 1821–1822.*

LASA, Z 44, C 16c 5 Nr. 51a, *Geschichtliche Darstellung der Entstehung und der Schicksale des von Anhalt-Dessau zur Armee des Rheinbundes gestellten Kontingents, Beschreibung der Märsche desselben von dem im Juli 1807 erfolgten Ausmarsch bis zum Einmarsch in Spanien am 6. Mai 1810, verfasst vom Regierungsrat Schröder, 1807–1810.*

LASA, Z 44, C 16c 5 Nr. 66, *Kurzer Abriss der Geschichte des Bataillons Anhalt, welches im Jahr 1811 von den durchlauchtigsten Herzögen zu Anhalt als Mitglieder des Rheinbundes gestellt wurde, vom Ausmarsch bis zur Rückkehr nach Dessau am 6. Februar 1814 vom Regierungsrat Dr. Morgenstern, Bd. I–II, 1811–1814.*

LASA, Z 44, C 16c 5 Nr. 83, *Die Mission des Herrn von Sternegg nach Prag und Wien, 1813.*

LASA, Z 44, C 16c 5 Nr. 84, *Die Missionen des Grafen von Waldersee zu den verbündeten Herrschern, 1813–1814.*

LASA, Z 44, C 16c 5 Nr. 209, *Kurzer Abriss der Geschichte des im April 1813 von Anhalt-Dessau und Anhalt-Köthen gestellten Bataillons unter dem Befehl des Kaiserlich Russischen Majors von Krone, verfasst vom Oberleutnant Ackermann, 1813.*

LASA, Z 44, C 16c 5 Nr. 210, *Geschichte der Entstehung und der Auflösung des Anhaltischen Jägerregiments zu Pferde im Jahr 1813, vom Major L. Bürkner, 1833.*

LASA, Z 44, C 16c 5 Nr. 211, *Korrespondenz mit dem Groß-Major Bürkner, 1813.*

LASA, Z 44, C 16c 5 Nr. 212, *Verhandlungen wegen der von den verbündeten Mächten begehrten Augmentation (Vermehrung) des stehenden Kontingents und Organisation der Landwehr, 1813–1814.*

LASA, Z 44, C 16c 5 Nr. 219, *Kurzer Abriss der Geschichte des im Jahr 1814 von Anhalt-Dessau zu den Heeren der gegen Frankreich verbündeten hohen Mächte mit Anhalt-Köthen gemeinschaftlich gestellten Regimentes vom Regierungsrat Morgenstern, 1814.*

***Published Sources***

Aster, Karl Heinrich, *Die Kriegsereignisse zwischen Peterwald, Pirna, Königstein und Priesten im August 1813 und die Schlacht bei Kulm* (Dresden: Adler und Dietze, 1845).

Beamish, North Ludlow, *History of the King's German Legion* (London: Thomas and William Boone, 1837).

Beaulieu-Marconnay, Carl Freiherr von, 'August Freiherr von und zu Egloffstein', Historische Kommission bei der Bayerischen Akademie der Wissenschaften (ed.), *Allgemeine Deutsche Biographie, Band V* (Leipzig: Duncker & Hunblot, 1877).

Blond, Georges (Trans. Marshall May), *La Grande Armée* (Edison: Castle Books, A division of Book Sales Inc., 2005).

Bowden, Scott, *Napoleon's Grande Armée of 1813* (Chicago: The Emperor's Press, 1990).

Broughton, Tony, 'Generals Who Served in the French Army during the Period 1789–1815', *Napoleon Series* , <http://www.napoleon-series.org/research/c_frenchgenerals.html>

Bucher, Ludwig Ferdinand, *Der Feldzug des Dritten Deutschen Armee–Corps in Flandern* (Leipzig: Hermann Costenoble, 1854).

Clarke, Daniel, 'Officers of the Anhalt Duchies who Fought in the French Revolutionary and Napoleonic Wars, 1789–1815', *Napoleon Series*, <http://www.napoleon-series.org/research/biographies/Anhalt/c_AnhaltBiographies.html>

Frisch, Michael, *Anhalt-Dessaus Freiheitskämpfer 1813 bis 1815 und der opferreiche Gang anhaltischer Bataillone für und gegen Napoleon in der Zeit von 1807 bis 1815* (Dessau-Großkühnau: Eigenverlag FFW Dessau-Kühnau, 2015).

Gärtner, Markus and Wager, Edmund, 'Das Chasseur–Regiment der Anhaltinschen Herzogtümer in Jahr 1813', *Depesche: Uniformen und Heere vergangener Zeiten*, 28 (December 1996), pp. 15–21, <http://www.napoleon-online.de/quellen_depesche.html>

Gill, John H., *With Eagles to Glory: Napoleon and his German Allies in the 1809 Campaign* (Barnsley: Frontline Books, an Imprint of Pen & Sword Books, 2011).

Leggiere, Michael V., *Napoleon and the Struggle for Germany: The Franco–Prussian War of 1813* (Cambridge: Cambridge University Press, 2015).

Lehmann, Gustaf, *Die Ritter des Ordens Pour le Mérite, Zweiter Band: 1812–1913* (Berlin: Ernst Siegfried Mittler und Sohn, 1913).

Morris, Graham J., 'The Battle of Kulm, 29th–30th August 1813', *Battlefield Anomalies*, <https://battlefieldanomalies.com/the-battle-of-kulm/>

Mikaberidze, Alexander, *The Russian Officer Corps in the Revolutionary and Napoleonic Wars, 1792–1815* (New York: Savas Beatie LLC, 2005).

Nafziger, George F., *The Armies of Germany and the Confederation of the Rhine, 1792–1815* (Privately Published, 1993).

Nafziger, George F., *The End of Empire: Napoleon's 1814 Campaign* (Solihull: Helion & Co., 2015).

Oman, Sir Charles, *A History of the Peninsular War* (London: Greenhill Books, Lionel Leventhal Limited, 1996).

Rapp, Jean, *Memoirs of General Count Rapp, First Aide-de-Camp to Napoleon* (London: Henry Colburn and Co, 1823).

Rawkins, W. J., *CB6, Armies of the Confederation of the Rhine, The Rheinbund Contingents 1806–1813, Part 2: Anhalt, Lippe, Reus, Schwarzburg, Waldeck,*

*Mecklenburg-Schwerin, Oldenburg and Frankfurt* (Norwich: The History Book Man, 2015).

Sañudo Bayón, Juan José, 'Anhalt–Lippe Infanteria Regimento No 5, #1,116', *Base de Datos sobre las Unidades Militares en la Guerra de la Independencia Española* (Madrid: Instituto de Historia y Cultura Militar, 2007).

Schmidt, Andreas Gottfried, *Anhalt'sches Schriftsteller-Lexikon, oder historisch-literarische Nachrichten über Schriftsteller, welche in Anhalt gebohren sind oder gewirkt haben* (Bernburg: Friedrich Wilhelm Gröning, 1830).

Schwertseger, Bernhard, *Geschichte der Königlich Deutschen Legion 1803–1816, Band II* (Hannover and Leipzig: Hahn'sche Buchhandlung, 1907).

Siebigk, Ferdinand, 'Georg Hoppe', in *Historische Kommission bei der Bayerischen Akademie der Wissenschaften (ed.), Allgemeine Deutsche Biographie, Band XIII* (Leipzig: Duncker & Hunblot, 1881).

Six, Georges, *Dictionnaire Biographique des Les Generaux de la Revolution et de l'Empire (1792–1814), Tome I A–J* (Paris: Librairie Historique et Nobiliaire Georges Saffroy, 1934).

Six, Georges, *Dictionnaire Biographique des Les Generaux de la Revolution et de l'Empire (1792–1814), Tome II K–Z* (Paris: Librairie Historique et Nobiliaire Georges Saffroy, 1934).

Smith, Digby, *Napoleon's German Division in Spain Volume II: The Germans in Catalonia 1808–1813* (Huntington: Ken Trotman Publishing, 2014)

Summerfield, Stephen, *Brazen Cross of Courage: Russian Militia, Partizans, Volunteers and the Russo-German Legion during the Napoleonic Wars* (London: Partizan Press, 2007).

Wilson, Peter H., *From Reich to Revolution: German History, 1558–1806* (London: Palgrave Macmillan, 2004).

Wittich, Karl-Heinz, 'Das Anhaltische Chasseur-Regiment 1813', *Salzlandkreis* (January 2013), <https://www.salzlandkreis.de/media/6134/wittich_anhaltisches-chasseur-regiment-1813.pdf>

Witzleben, August von, *Prinz Friedrich Josias von Coburg-Saalfeld, Herzog zu Sachsen,* (Berlin: R. Decker, 1859).

Zamoyski, Adam, *1812: Napoleon's Fatal March on Moscow* (London: Harper Perennial, 2005).

Zeidler, L., *Der Spanische Feldzug des Bataillons Anhalt im Jahre 1810* (Zerbst: Friedrich Römer, 1844).

2

# That Other Battle in 1805: Second Caldiero

David Hollins

Overshadowed by Napoleon's victory at Austerlitz, the Italian campaign of 1805 represents a more even fight as the main Austrian army under Archduke Charles took on the French Armée d'Italie under *Maréchal* Masséna. On 31 August 1805, the Archduke was appointed commander of the Italienarmee, which was intended to comprise 94,000 troops by 16 October. Directing operations, planning, and intelligence was the chief of staff, *Feldmarschalleutnant* Zach, best known for his travails at Marengo in 1800. To the north in the Tyrol was *Feldmarschalleutnant* Hiller with another 10,000 men. The army had been reorganised in line with Mack's order of 1 August 1805: each infantry regiment now comprised one grenadier battalion and four fusilier battalions, each composed of four companies. The Archduke thought that this change had advantages, but felt that its hasty introduction meant the units would lose cohesion. The lack of local horses meant the Italienarmee only had full teams for the four 6-pounder cavalry batteries.[1] The interim commander, *General der Kavallerie* Bellegarde, had organised some exercises in spring 1805, albeit line infantry had to perform the role of the grenzers, who were still on the Military Border sowing crops.

The original allied plan called for an advance into northern Italy, but as Napoleon's intentions became clear, the Archduke was ordered to send five battalions to the Tyrol on 25 September followed by 25 battalions and 16 squadrons to reinforce the army in Germany two days later. On 5 October, Kaiser Franz II wrote to Charles, then in his headquarters at San Stefano, that his instructions were now only to operate in line with the army in Germany.[2] The Archduke could only await events as hostilities commenced.

1 Moritz von Angeli, *Erzherzog Carl von Österreich als Feldherr und Heeresorganisator* (Vienna: Braumüller, 1896), Vol.III, p.58.

2 Angeli, *Erzherzog Carl*, Vol.III, p.70.

The Treaty of Luneville in 1801 had confirmed Austrian rule over most of the former Venetian Republic. Its border now ran along the Adige, the largest river in north-east Italy. To the west was the new Kingdom of Italy, which included the city of Verona. The Austrians held the walled suburb of Veronetta on the east bank. The Austrian right wing under *General der Kavallerie* Bellegarde comprised the advance-guard under *Feldmarschalleutnant* Vukassovich, manning Veronetta and outposts along the river, and *Feldmarschalleutnant* Simbchen's division around Caldiero. Based around San Gregorio, the centre under *Feldmarschalleutnant* Argenteau comprised divisions under *Feldmarschalleutnante* Lindenau, Vogelsang, and Reuss-Plauen. The left wing under *Feldmarschalleutnant* Davidovich comprised divisions under *Feldmarschalleutnant* Rosenberg in Montagnana and *Generalmajor* Lowenberg in Solesino.[3] However, on 16 October, *Generalmajor* Mittrowsky was ordered to take half of his men plus a brigade from Simbchen and two of Vukassovich's grenzer battalions to reinforce Hiller in the Tyrol.

Now Emperor and King of Italy, Napoleon recalled Masséna from semi-retirement to replace *Maréchal* Jourdan as commander of the Armée d'Italie on 30 August 1805. At his headquarters at Alpo, Masséna was instructed to contain the Austrian forces, while Napoleon advanced into Germany. His army of about 42,850 men,[4] comprised six infantry divisions under Verdier, Gardanne, Duhesme, Serras, Molitor, and Partouneaux and three cavalry divisions under d'Espagne, Pully, and Mermet, composed of 13 infantry regiments, 10 cavalry regiments and 72 guns, which held Verona and the west bank of the Adige. Masséna's men were poorly equipped and only a third were veterans, but his artillery wanted for nothing.[5]

## The Battle of Verona: 18 October 1805

Masséna was empowered by Napoleon to take any measures to protect against a surprise attack. So, a temporary armistice, which required six days' notice before hostilities, was agreed in Verona on 29 September. Having fortified Castel-Vecchio and Legnano, the French erected their own barricades across the bridges. Masséna had focused his attention on the eastern suburb of San Giorgio, but at the same time, he reinforced the observation cordon between Zevio and Legnano to the south to draw Austrian attention from his true target. Receiving news of Napoleon's advance, Masséna terminated the agreement on 8 October, so that hostilities would commence on 14 October.

On the same day, Charles ordered his troops into their camps on the flat ground on the east side of the Adige. *Feldmarschalleutnant* Vukassovich's lines extended

3 Angeli, *Erzherzog Carl*, Vol.III, pp.74-77.
4 Jean Koch, *Memoires de Masséna* (Paris: Paulin et Lechevalier, 1850), Vol.V, Annex 6.
5 Koch, *Memoires de Masséna*, Vol.V, p.50.

north from Veronetta 37 kilometres up the Adige through Volargne to Ossenigo, maintaining contact with Hiller. The main crossing from Verona was over the stone Ponte di Castelvecchio bridge, which the Austrians blocked with a wall across the middle. There were three other crossings, which were obstructed by thick earth banks, on each of which was a single cannon. Beyond lay the Campagnola, a large expanse of trees and ditches under the guns in the Castel Vecchio and the Zeno bastion on the Verona side. About 800 metres from Castel Vecchio, the Austrians had constructed defensive works held by two companies of IR37 Auffenburg: a closed redoubt close to the river and three *flêches* (arrowhead-shaped earthwork) positioned towards the suburb of San Giorgio in a semicircle, which extended round to the walls of Veronetta to close off the Campagnola. A company of 2. Banal Grenzer and a battalion of IR37 Auffenburg occupied San Giorgio. The rest of IR37 and a squadron of HR3 Erzherzog Ferdinand held Avesa and Quinzano, 15 minutes away. Veronetta had been fortified and garrisoned by IR22 Coburg, while Parona was occupied by a 2. Banal Grenzer company.

Believing that the Austrians had mined the furthest arch of the Castelvecchio bridge, Masséna thought that surprise and speed would be prerequisites to success.[6] So, he massed 24 *voltiguer* (light infantry) companies from battalions in the divisions under Gardanne and Duhesme to form his assault column under *Général de Brigade* Camus, supported by 3e Sappeurs and a light artillery company. From Gardanne's division, 22e Légère, 29e Ligne and 52e Ligne, together with 23e Chasseurs à Cheval plus two companies each of foot and horse artillery, would follow. The rest of Gardanne's division was joined by Duhesme's division in reserve. The other three bridges were guarded by 101e Ligne. Verdier's division, positioned between Perzacco and Roverchiara, was to mount a diversion downstream and most of the light cavalry was around Zevio on the lower Adige, while Serras' division held the upper Adige. The remaining forces stood in reserve behind Verona.

At 3:00 a.m., Masséna arrived and led his column silently on to the bridge. As the sappers set charges in the Austrian wall, 25 voltigeurs crossed the Adige in a boat. At 4:00 a.m., the charges were blown and the voltigeurs attacked the Austrian outpost, chasing its defenders off. *Général de Brigade* Solignac rushed forward at the head of 3e Sappeurs and all the sappers in the rest of Gardanne's division, but they soon discovered that the Austrians had not mined the bridge. Led by the voltigeur companies under *Colonel* Campi, the French column surged forward as their artillery opened up from the castle. Despite fog hanging in the air and the difficult terrain, the voltigeurs deployed on the Campagnola and headed for the Austrian earthworks, chasing the outposts back towards San Giorgio. In the meantime, the IR37 Auffenberg troops holding the entrenchments were joined by a battalion of their comrades on the higher ground behind.

6 Koch, *Memoires de Masséna*, Vol.V, p.86.

As he had planned, *Feldmarschalleutnant* Vukassovich hastened the other two battalions and a squadron of HR3 Erzherzog Ferdinand forward from Avesa to secure the San Leonardo hills. Under fire from Veronetta into their right flank, but otherwise facing little resistance, the French continued to advance in closed columns, led by 22e Légère and 52e Ligne with 29e Ligne in support, until the artillery fire and musketry from the earthworks brought them to a halt. The French captured two Austrian cannon, but Vukassovich had now arrived and assailed the French left, driving them back. The French re-formed and the assault was renewed. Vukassovich threw HR3 Erzherzog Ferdinand into the fray and they initially were successful in cutting down the French skirmishers. However, the French formed squares and, aided by artillery fire across the river, drove off the Austrian cavalry. Their attack had stalled, but in the meantime, *Général de Brigade* Compère was advancing his six battalions led by 29e Ligne. Several attempts were now made to seize the earthworks, but failed in the face of stiff resistance. Then a squadron of 23e Chasseurs à Cheval and three light cannon joined the fray until, eventually, the Austrian troops were forced to abandon the earthworks and retreat north towards the hills around Avesa. Abandoned by their comrades, the IR37 troops holding the redoubt could only surrender. With their communications secured, the French fanned out north of Verona. By 3:00 p.m., a lively artillery duel had broken out with the defenders of the San Giorgio suburb and during the afternoon, Gardanne's division drove Vukassovich's troops from their positions on the high ground round Avesa. Despite fierce fighting, by 5:00 p.m., they had chased the remains of IR37 Auffenburg out of San Leonardo and occupied the hills around Ca Albertini.

The Austrians regrouped: around 4:00 p.m., *General der Kavallerie* Bellegarde had directed a 6. St. Georger Grenzer battalion on to the ridges between Ca Albertini and San Felice to help Vukassovich. *Generalmajor* Sommariva directed *Oberst* Keller with a battalion of 2. Banal Grenzer to advance on Quinzano, where he joined the infantry companies and a cavalry detachment holding Parona in falling on the French left to cover Vukassovich's withdrawal up the valley. The lead units of O'Reilly's and Simbchen's divisions marched on the hamlet of San Felice in the Val Pantena, northeast of Verona. As darkness fell and fatigue set in, the French made a hasty withdrawal and the fighting petered out. Austrian losses totalled around 400, plus seven guns lost in the flight into the hills. IR37 Auffenburg had suffered a heavy toll, so they had to be replaced by four battalions of IR34 Davidovich on 20 October. French casualties were similar, but the 29e and 52e Ligne had suffered badly.[7]

7 Koch, *Memoires de Masséna*, Vol.V, p.89; Edouard Gachot, *Le troisième campagne d'Italie* (Paris: Plon-Nourrit, 1911), p.46; Friedrich Spanoghe, 'Der Feldzug 1805 in Italien', *Österreichische Militärische Zeitschrift*, II (1823) pp.12-13.

At dawn, around 7:30 a.m., French cannon had opened fire from Verona to Legnano, joined by musketry from the outposts in between. Ordered to mount a diversion in the north, Serras left part of his division at Rivoli and demonstrated in front of Pescantina, 11 kilometres north-west of Verona, pinning down half of Vukassovich's division. Around 8:00 a.m., the first reports reached Charles's headquarters that the French had 'thrown a bridge at Beccacivetta [south of Verona] and crossed the Adige in force and were advancing on the eastern bank'.[8] Later and more accurate reports confirmed that 'At dawn, the enemy effected a crossing over the Castelvecchio bridge, took the high ground at San Leonardo and forced *Feldmarschalleutnant* Vukassovich to retreat towards Monte Tondo'. However, 'In the meantime, Veronetta remains under (Austrian) control'.[9] French efforts to break the gates of San Giorgio with heavy artillery and mortar rounds continued without success, despite the additional fire from five cannon on the Campagnola.

By 10:00 a.m., the French activity around Beccacivetta had ceased, but Verdier was still busy. His division had assembled all the floating mills along the lower Adige and built a bridge near Albaredo, 25 kilometres south-east of Verona. At noon, two battalions of the 23e Légère crossed and quickly broke through *Generalmajor* Radetzky's outpost line. Another French crossing was attempted at Legnano, but was driven off by Austrian outposts. By 2:00 p.m., reports reached Austrian headquarters that 'the enemy is advancing in two columns, one towards Albaredo and the other towards Minerbe'.[10] Believing this was the real French attack, heading for the rear of the Caldiero position, Archduke Charles sent three columns against Verdier around 5:00 p.m.: *Generalmajor* Nordmann (six battalions and eight squadrons) marched from Arcole towards the Zerpan bridge along the Fossa Serego channel towards Albaredo; *Feldmarschalleutnant* Argenteau (17 grenadier battalions and eight squadrons) headed through Desmonte and Canevera; *Feldmarschalleutnant* Reuss-Plauen (16 battalions and eight squadrons) marched towards Cucca. As the Austrian columns approached, *Colonel* Deriot knew his 23e Légère had completed its task and withdrew it across the river. That night, the Austrians encamped between Albaredo and Ca de Sette in two *Treffen* (battle lines). The grenadier battalions of IR7 and IR56 were pushed forward to secure the left flank around Michelorie, while cavalry detachments held it and Miega. Patrols were despatched towards Bonavigo and Minerbe during the night, but found no sign of the French.

Nightfall brought Charles reassuring news that French attempts against Veronetta had been beaten off, which encouraged his belief that their real attack would come downriver. The next morning, 19 October, he continued his advance: *Generalmajor* Nordmann marched on Bonavigo, while Reuss-Plauen

8 Spanoghe, 'Der Feldzug', p.6.
9 Spanoghe, 'Der Feldzug', p.6.
10 Spanoghe, 'Der Feldzug', p.7.

and Argenteau headed for Minerbe, followed by *Feldmarschalleutnant* Davidovich with eight-and-a-half battalions and 14 squadrons marching from Bevilaqua. However, it soon became clear from patrol reports that at the first sign of the Austrian advance the previous evening, the French had withdrawn and taken up the bridge at Beccacivetta. Verdier had run a successful diversion and the Austrian troops could only trudge back to their camp at San Gregorio.

## A Brief Pause

Masséna had failed to capture Veronetta but had secured the bridgehead through Castelvecchio on to the hills northeast of Verona. Over the next 10 days, the bridgehead was fortified and manned by Gardanne and Duhesme's divisions, while the whole area along the Adige was reconnoitred. On 26 October, after travelling through Austrian lines, the spy Jouraud reported signs of a retreat being prepared, although he exaggerated Austrian numbers.[11]

The Austrian right wing under *General der Kavallerie* Bellegarde comprised 42 battalions and 24 squadrons, of which 24 battalions and 16 squadrons held the entrenched position at Caldiero. The remainder were deployed partly as the advance-guard along the Adige and garrison of Veronetta, with the rest securing the Monto Lessini hills and communications with Hiller along the upper Adige. Angry that Vukassovich had failed to position enough troops near the Adige to repel Masséna's attack, Archduke Charles dismissed him. *Feldmarschalleutnant* Rosenberg took command of the advance-guard, but limited himself to holding Veronetta, placing *Generalmajor* Frimont's troops down the *chaussee* (main road) at San Michele, while keeping his main force in the Pantena valley. The centre under *Feldmarschalleutnant* Argenteau consisted of 22 grenadier and 16 fusilier battalions, plus 24 squadrons camped at San Gregorio. An advance-guard of six grenzer battalions and eight squadrons was positioned at Arcole with outposts watching the Adige. The left wing under *Feldmarschalleutnant* Davidovich, comprising 11 battalions and six squadrons, was camped at Bevilaqua. An outpost line manned by six grenzer battalions and 10 squadrons extended further to the mouth of the Adige.[12]

On 2 August, while still Minister of War, Charles had ordered the interim commander in Italy, *General der Kavallerie* Bellegarde, to start construction of defences. In the north, a redoubt (enclosed earthwork) with four cannon and a howitzer was constructed on Monte Nanfari with another lower down on the northern side for two cannon and one howitzer to cover the Bocca di Scalucz saddle. Down the steep slope from Monte Nanfari was the village of Colognola. At

11 Gachot, *La troisième campagne*, p.34.
12 Angeli, *Erzherzog Carl*, Vol.III, pp.114-116.

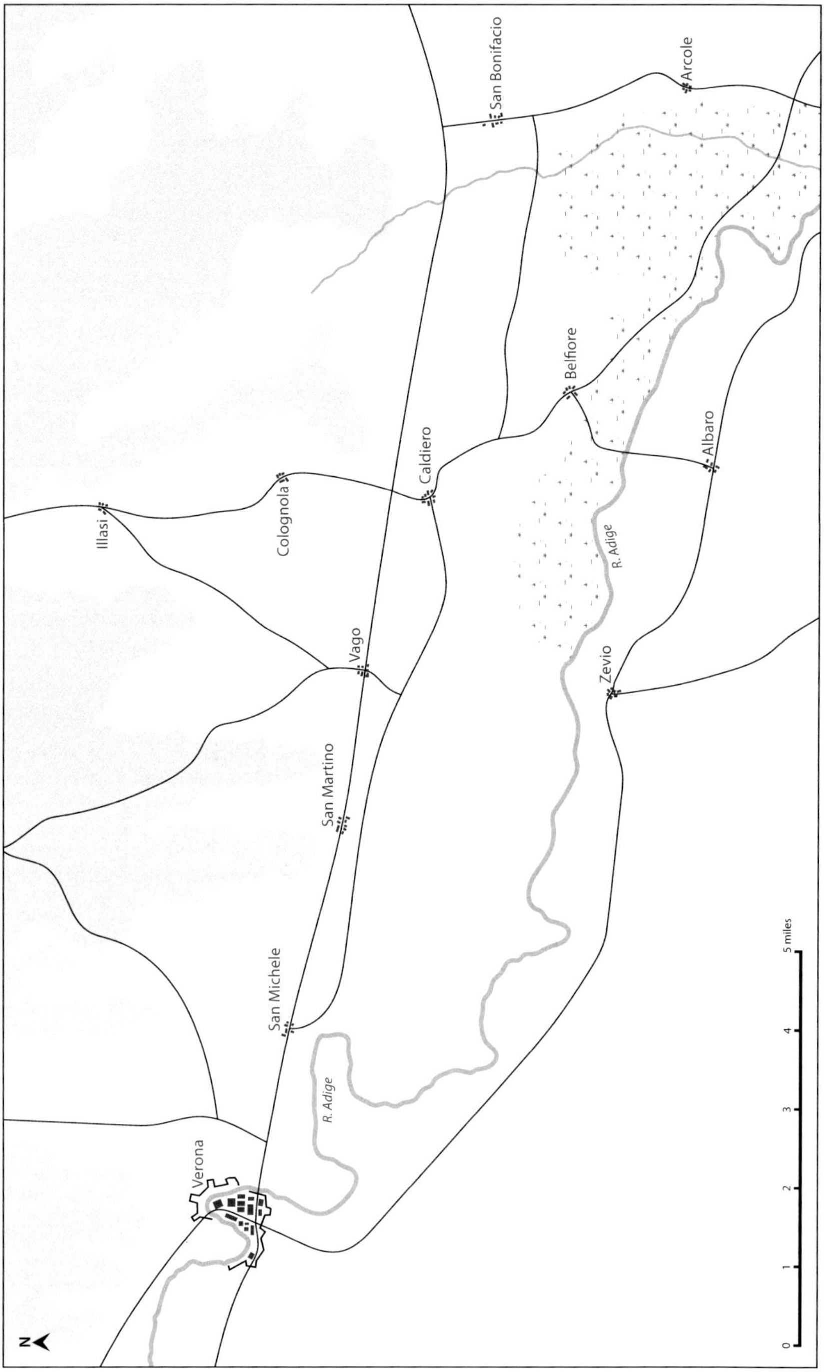


Area of Operations, Caldiero Campaign. (Map by George Anderson © Helion and Company)

its northern end stood the church surrounded by a 1.8-metre-high stone wall, and further south, a redoubt for two cannon. Immediately to its south was the Villa Peverelli mansion with its open garden to the east, facing on to the village piazza. From there, 25 houses ran south down the ridge, about 40 metre above the lower village, and on to the slopes to the east. Slits had been cut in village walls. Two redoubts were built on the highpoints of Monte il Torre for two cannon and one howitzer each, commanding the roads leading up from the lower village, which were barricaded.[13] Below the southern redoubt were two cannon in a flêche on the spur. Three redoubts guarded the key chokepoint on the *chaussee* from Verona to the east: one on Monte Zovo with four cannon and one howitzer; to the south behind Caldiero village were redoubts, each with two cannon and one howitzer, on Monte San Mattia and Monte Rocca. A *flêche* west of Monte Zovo carried two cannon, which would create a crossfire on the approach to Caldiero. Additional infantry trenches ran south from the *chaussee*. The flat ground there was suitable for cavalry, as only the roads from Stra to Gombion and Caldiero had side-ditches. These roads were covered by a *flêche* at Chiavighetto and a redoubt at Ponterotto. A chain of entrenchments extended to the ricefields around Chiavicca del Christo, where a large redoubt stood near the Adige dyke. Several stone buildings would provide defensive strongpoints.[14]

On 22 October, news reached the Archduke's headquarters of Augereau's advance towards the Tyrol and the first report of Mack's surrender at Ulm arrived during the night of 24/25 October. The next morning, Charles reviewed his situation in *Betrachtungen über die Lage der k. auch k.u.k. Armee in Italien* (Observations about the position of the Imperial Army in Italy): 'the army in Germany has suffered the fate, which unfortunately was all too predictable … Perhaps this army is the only force left to the Austrian monarchy'.[15]

Preparations for a withdrawal began, but in order to escape and to raise morale, Charles knew a battle was still necessary. Adopting a defensive posture, he would face the same dilemma as at Aspern-Essling in 1809: which way would the real French attack cross the major river? An attack through Veronetta was relatively easy as the French controlled the bridge. However, crossing at Bevilaqua presented the opportunity to outflank the Austrian positions from the south. So, using his wings as the initial line of resistance, Charles would then mass his troops from the centre against whichever was the main axis of the enemy assault. Masséna was indeed planning a second attempt to seize Veronetta. From there, he would force Charles back to his positions around Caldiero. This battle would be the second of four major actions fought there during the Napoleonic Wars.

13 The sites of several of these redoubts are still marked by clumps of trees.
14 Spanoghe, 'Der Feldzug', pp.17-19.
15 Angeli, *Erzherzog Carl*, Vol.III, pp.98-99.

## Battle Renewed: 29 October 1805

After receiving news of Ulm on 26 October, Masséna decided to attack the Austrian positions.[16] Around 6:00 a.m. on 29 October, the French marched across the Castelvecchio bridge. Under cover of artillery, the divisions of Duhesme and Gardanne deployed on the Campagnola and moved to the north of Veronetta without facing opposition. Austrian light troops fell back on Ca Albertini, covered by three battalions of IR34 Davidovich. Once the French reached San Giorgio at 10:00 a.m., the small Austrian garrison abandoned the suburb and fighting erupted along the outpost lines. Thinking it had a large garrison, the French circumvented San Leonardo, intending to cut it off from the Austrian forces. At the foot of Monte Lessini, they divided into two columns: Duhesme headed for Tagliaferro; Gardanne marched along the defile running between Veronetta and San Leonardo, reuniting at San Mattia. After plenty of skirmishing, it was here that the real fighting began. The two columns attacked the Austrian positions at San Dionigio but were initially repelled. However, descending from the valley of Avesa, voltigeurs from Duhesme's division in two columns drove the 2. Banal Grenzer battalion back towards Negra, exposing the right flank of *Feldmarschalleutnant* Rosenberg's position (IR34 Davidovich). After steady resistance, Rosenberg withdrew his men into the Marzana hills to secure the higher ground.[17]

To the north, at 4:00 a.m., six large vessels began ferrying *Gênêral de Division* Serras's division across the river at Pescantina, 12 kilometres upriver from Verona, and under cover from artillery at Arce, they constructed a bridge at Polo. *Generalmajor* Sommariva's outposts withdrew. Serras intended to bottle up Sommariva around San Ambrogio, using three columns marching towards Mazurega, San Ambrogio and Cavalo, but Sommariva escaped towards San Giovanni to join *Feldmarschalleutnant* Rosenberg. Serras halted at Cavalo and observed the nearby valleys to secure the French left flank.

Unsure of French intentions, the Archduke ordered his centre to prepare for action and sent eight battalions from the reserve towards Villanuova to reinforce the right wing. The Archduke moved his headquarters to the more central San Bonifacio, where he intended to observe French activity until their intentions became clear. They repeated the previous diversion: A report from *Feldmarschalleutnant* Davidovich arrived at 3:00 p.m., stating that:

16 Gachot, *La troisième campagne*, p.52.

17 The regiment had four 3-pounder cannon and 49 crew. Total losses were 28 dead, 104 wounded, 127 prisoners and 52 missing. *Feldmarschalleutnant* Rosenberg's report singled out the leadership of *Major* d'Assante and *Hauptmann* Schwellay. See Gustav Wust, *Geschichte des k.k. Linien-Infanterie-Regiments 34 Prinz Regent von Preussen* (Vienna: K-k Hof- und Staatsdrückerei, 1860), pp.202-203.

> [T]he enemy began a heavy artillery barrage even before dawn at Legnano, but it only lasted a short time, following which they made some half-hearted attempts to cross the river… The enemy outposts have significantly during the night and all the signs are that large reinforcements are moving upstream to Verona.[18]

Meanwhile, despite sustaining heavy losses, the French left had driven Rosenberg's right on to the ridges of Monte Tondo. The heavily-wooded terrain made it difficult for the Austrians to judge the enemy strength and it was now only possible to maintain communications with Rosenberg through patrols moving along difficult paths across the steep hills.

Once the French had secured San Leonardo and reached the Pantena valley, Masséna demanded the surrender of Veronetta. The Austrian garrison conceded, while allowing themselves time to escape. The French promptly ripped up the bridge defences and, towards noon, the divisions under Molitor, Partouneaux, d'Espagne, and Mermet crossed the Adige. Deploying outside the Vicenza gate, they immediately set off towards San Michele, driving back the former defenders of Veronetta. With his left anchored on San Michele, *Generalmajor* Frimont drew his advance-guard up in two *Treffen* (battle lines) with artillery in front. Massena sent d'Espagne's chasseurs and some of Partouneaux's grenadier battalions forward, but steady short-range Austrian fire foiled their attacks until French voltigeurs stormed San Michele. Driven back by superior numbers, Frimont fought a second delaying action around San Martino for an hour before withdrawing further down the *chaussee*.

It was now 4:00 p.m. and Masséna decided to delay his assault until the following morning. However, to prevent an Austrian withdrawal, he would use the available daylight to launch probing attacks and reconnoitre the enemy positions himself. As the Austrians fell back, Molitor's division attacked their rearguards.[19] Assaulting Vago, the French right flank came under attack from IR29 Lindenau, which had crossed the Vago torrent. After a steady display, the regiment was driven off by *Général de Brigade* Valory at the head of 60e Ligne and two squadrons of 24e Chasseurs à Cheval, losing two cannon. The villages of Ca dell'Ara and Stra then changed hands several times amid fierce fighting and as twilight fell, Massena even broke through Caldiero to reach the first trenches behind the village. Only a steady mix of artillery and musketry fire from the entrenched positions halted the French advance. Later, the French withdrew from Caldiero, but Masséna had forced the Archduke to fight a major engagement, preventing a withdrawal. The Archduke was now in no doubt that Masséna was intent on a serious attack,

18 Spanoghe, 'Der Feldzug', p.22.

19 Koch, *Memoires de Masséna*, Vol.V, Annex 9 (Molitor's report).

confirmed by the steady stream of reports from the south of French troops evacuating their positions, leaving only cavalry vedettes along the western riverbank.

## Similar Plans: 30 October 1805

In his headquarters in Vago, Masséna prepared his next assault. In a plan typical of Napoleonic warfare, he would outflank the Austrians to the south, then smash through the centre to cut off the Austrian left, throwing it into the marshy ground around Arcole. Supported by *Général de Brigade* Pully's cavalry at Oppeano, *Général de Division* Verdier's division would cross the Adige at dawn on 30 October at Perzacco. Seizing the causeways to Arcole, he would fight his way into the rear of the Austrian left around Villanuova. Massena's main force was deployed on the right bank of the Progno d'Illasi torrent, holding Ca dell'Ara, Ca Rizzi, Calderin and Stra with the divisions of Duhesme to the right, Gardanne in the centre and Molitor on the left. Deploying in front of Vago, they would launch attacks as the battle developed. *Général de Brigade* Mermet's cavalry was to move up the road through Gombion and Pantera to reconnoitre the area and support Verdier's advance. Partouneaux's Grenadier Division and the remaining cavalry stood in reserve. To the north, Serras would deploy Mallet's brigade to watch the tracks from Monte Baldo, the main route to *Feldmarschalleutnant* Hiller in the Tyrol. The brigades under Gilly and Guillet would cover the army's left and anchor its flank on the upper Adige.

In the Lessini mountains, *Feldmarschalleutnant* Rosenberg's troops had remained around San Giovanni Baptista, but their patrols, sent as far as Dolce and Parona, found no trace of the enemy. It was clear the French were concentrating against Caldiero, so having received definitive news of Ulm and reduced to about 49,200 men,[20] the Archduke decided on a similar plan: an advance against both French wings to facilitate his main advance in the centre down the *chaussee* towards Stra, prior to breaking clear of the French. In the north, *Feldmarschalleutnant* Simbchen (10-and-a-half battalions, four squadrons of HR8) would march through lower Colognola, climb the San Giacomo hills and fall on the French left. In the centre, *General der Kavallerie* Bellegarde (18 battalions, 14 squadrons) would advance down the *chaussee* towards Vago. The eight battalions from the reserve had reached Villanuova and were directed out in front of the main position, followed by *Feldmarschalleutnant* Vogelsang with ten grenadier battalions and two cavalry regiments.

At the same time, *Feldmarschalleutnant* Reuss-Plauen, with the remaining eight fusilier battalions from the San Gregorio camp plus two grenzer battalions already posted along the Adige and UR3 Erzherzog Karl, was ordered to cross the Zerpan

20 Spanoghe, 'Der Feldzug', p.25.

bridge and march to Porcile. They were followed by *Generalmajor* Nordmann with three battalions of grenzers from the advance-guard at Arcole, together with five grenadier battalions and two squadrons of hussars. Reuss-Plauen was then to head to Gombion and Calderin, while Nordmann marched along the side road through Chiavicca del Cristo to tackle the French flank around Sabbionara. The flank columns were to take their alignment with Bellegarde's column on the *chaussee*. *Feldmarschalleutnant* Argenteau remained in San Gregorio with *Generalmajor* Koller's seven battalions and HR10 Stipicz. To the south, *Feldmarschalleutnant* Davidovich was ordered to assemble all available boats to transport large raiding parties across the river to pin down Verdier.

The Austrian troops were in position by dawn, but thick fog delayed the attack until 11:00 a.m. The Archduke concluded that insufficient time remained to achieve a decisive victory and allow him to retreat. Nevertheless, under cover of the fog, *Feldmarschalleutnant* Simbchen had gone through lower Colognola and reached the Progno d'Illasi, taking the French advance troops around Ca dell'Ara in the left flank. The French counterattacked and, after receiving orders to withdraw around 8.30 a.m., Simbchen fell back on Colognola by 10:00 a.m.[21]

## The Fog Lifts

Fighting broke out to the south, but not as Masséna hoped. Promised 25 boats and bridging materials by the French chief of engineers *Général de Division* Chasseloup-Laubat, together with *Général de Brigade* Lecour's cavalry brigade from Partouneaux, Verdier was actually left with 11 boats and inadequate materials.[22] Frantic searches through the riverside villages located some beams and boards, but the construction effort was hampered by a well-positioned Austrian battery. Although there had been exchanges of outpost fire since dawn, it was relatively quiet, but Nordmann became concerned at reports from *Oberst* Siegenfeld, who commanded the outpost line down to Albaredo, of French troops moving upriver. The threat to the Austrian left prompted Nordmann to take the offensive against Masséna's right north of the Adige. At 8:00 a.m., he marched with five grenadier battalions, two companies of 8. Gradiska Grenzer, some artillery, and HR9 Erdödy. Leaving two grenadier battalions in reserve, he headed along the Fossa Balhi river channel towards Sabbionara. The remaining grenzer battalions manned the southern earthworks.[23]

21 Angeli, *Erzherzog Carl*, Vol.III, p.117.

22 Gachot, *La troisième campagne*, p.65; Koch, *Memoires de Masséna*, Vol.V, p.99 .

23 Franz Vaniček, *Specialgeschichte der Militärgrenze* (Vienna: K-k Hof- und Staatsdrückerei, 1875), Vol. II, p.170. At Ca Goana was 5. Warasdin-Kreuzer Grenzer battalion, at Chiavighetto was 6. Warasdin-St. Georg battalion and at Chiavicca was half of 8. Gradiska battalion.

Taking his men fifty at a time by boat at Zevio, *Général de Brigade* Brun had crossed the river with the 56e and 62e Ligne and as the fog lifted, drove off some outposts. Intending to cover Verdier's bridging operation, Brun set off down the narrow, raised road towards the Porcile causeway. As fighting broke out at Gombion, they encountered the Pantenau channel, but had no bridging materials. Towards 2:00 p.m., in front of the Pantenau farm, the 62e Ligne's advance-guard came under fire from Nordmann's troops, who then attacked the French column. Brun rapidly turned the 62e, with 56e Ligne advancing in support, partly on 62e's left, against their opponents. Twice, the French were repulsed as the 62e Ligne was driven back on their comrades. Some of Reuss-Plauen's troops at Gombion opened fire on the French. Seeing a battalion break up, Brun rallied them and threw them back into action, but he fell, mortally wounded, replaced by *Colonel* Boutroue. Under fire on both flanks, the French fell back under the trees edging the open ground, where they awaited Verdier's crossing. Believing he had fallen into an ambush, Nordmann did not push his advantage. However, the rest of Verdier's division and Pully's cavalry would remain on the southern bank of the Adige that day. As dusk fell, Verdier set up his headquarters downstream at the Persago customs post.

Masséna had arrived at Vago at dawn around 7:00 a.m., where he promptly ordered Molitor to march across the open ground through Ca dell'Ara towards Colognola. The increasing sound of gunfire from the south made him believe that Verdier was on the move and he decided to resume the offensive. In the centre, Gardanne was ordered to advance down the *chaussee* from Vago towards la Rotta, where he was to deploy into two lines to assault the Austrian centre around Stra, before marching to join Verdier at Villanuova. South, on his right, was Duhesme. Flanked by his cavalry further south, Duhesme was to drive the Austrians out of Caldiero and extend his right towards Gombion. Together with Partouneaux, d'Espagne's cavalry would form the reserve. Around 8:00 a.m., Gardanne's voltigeurs and chasseurs à cheval began to engage the Austrian outposts, which they soon drove out of Ca dell'Ara and Stra.

The Archduke had also decided to advance down the *chaussee* with *General der Kavallerie* Bellegarde's troops. At the front under *Feldmarschalleutnant* O'Reilly was *Generalmjaor* Wetzel's brigade (four battalions each from IR2 and IR53). They were led by CLR1 Kaiser and a grenzer battalion, which quickly drove the French advance-guard out of Stra. Bellegarde was advancing cautiously as Reuss-Plauen was not moving to cover his left. At noon, Bellegarde faced Gardanne's main body advancing from Calderin. Gardanne's 1er Brigade was south of the *chaussee* among the mulberry trees and bushes; preceded by 150 voltigeurs, the 2e Brigade was to its north.[24] Gardanne's cavalry were echeloned to the south with artillery in the centre.

24 Gachot, *La troisième campagne*, p.72.

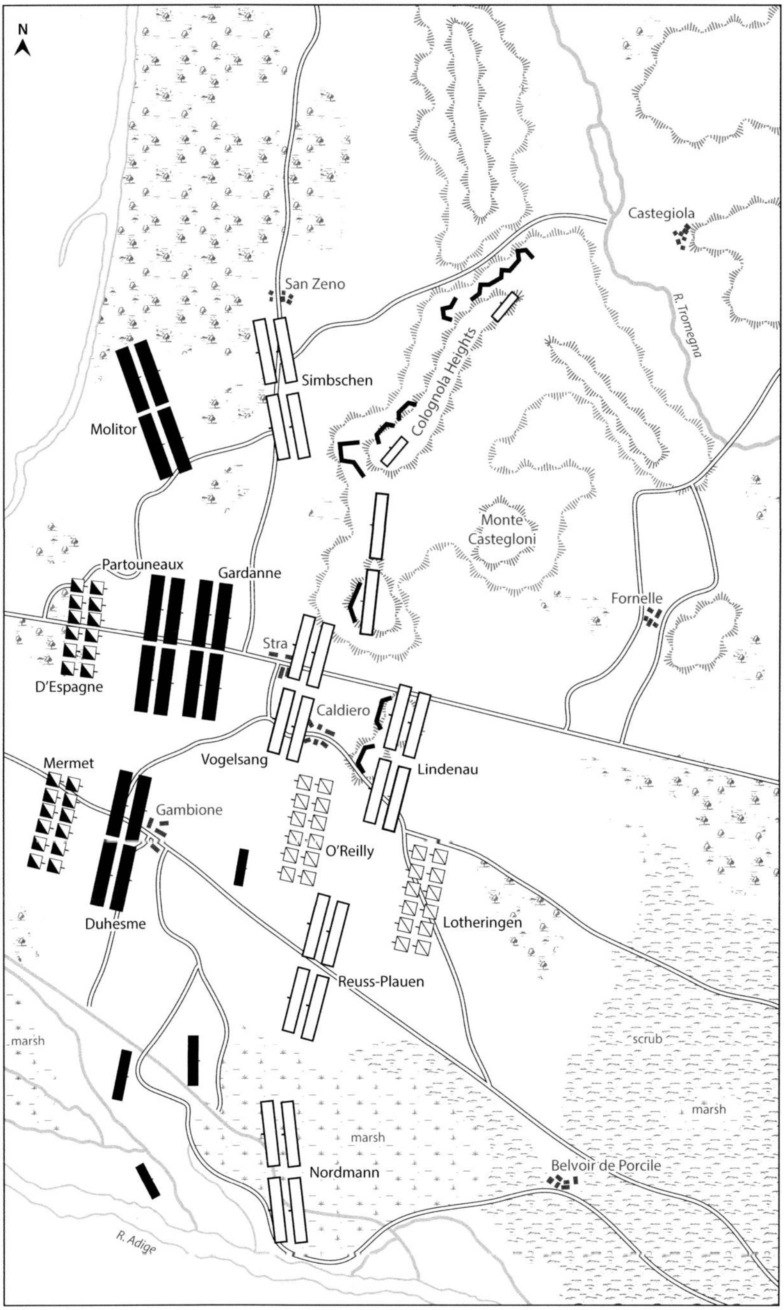


Battle of Caldiero, showing general positions of opposing troops.
(Map by George Anderson © Helion and Company)

*Generalmajor* Wetzel steadily gained the upper hand and drove Gardanne back on La Rotta. Under a hail of musket balls, but supported by 22e Légère, 52e Ligne stood immobile with drums beating as *Chef de Bataillon* Charpentier directed the 1er Battaillon in repelling three Austrian attacks in open ground. Unfortunately, the rest of Gardanne's first line buckled, turned around, and ran back towards the second line, which, fearing the worst, beat the retreat. Seeing Gardanne's predicament, Masséna left Molitor and galloped over to order an artillery detachment into action against Bellegarde's column, but then made his decisive error: he directed *Général de Brigade* Valory to turn the 79e Ligne, which formed Molitor's main reserve, south and attack Bellegarde. Part of Wetzel's brigade wheeled right as the 79e Ligne advanced *en potence*,[25] taking advantage of the bushy terrain, farm buildings, mountain streams and woods to the north of Ca dell'Ara. As many officers soon found their clothing full of musket balls,[26] *Colonel* Roch Godart led his 14 companies in firing a volley at 150 paces into the right flank of the second Austrian line before charging with bayonets lowered.[27] An Austrian hussar regiment moving forward to attack them was driven off by volleys from six companies in a nearby village. The 79e Ligne was engaged for about an hour, gaining time for Gardanne to steady his lines.

On the *chaussee*, Gardanne quickly positioned a battery to block it, the gunners spraying their opponents with canister at 60 paces. Tired and low on ammunition, the Austrians halted. Nine cannon and two howitzers opened up from the French right and aided by d' Espagne, Masséna managed to reorder five battalions, which he formed *en echelon*. Gardanne was ordered to hold his positions either side of the *chaussee* with steady volleys. Gardanne now returned to the offensive, placing his grenadier companies at the front. Rising casualties had forced *Generalmajor* Wetzel to dissolve most of his battalions into open order and skirmish lines. Under rolling fire from the French infantry supported by showers of artillery canister, Wetzel's brigade buckled and was soon being driven back by the closed French formations in disorder.

By 2:00 p.m., La Posta (the post station) and the Ca Rizzi farmhouse had been retaken by the French. One Austrian square held steady and fired on the closed French infantry, at which Masséna dismounted to assemble his scattered voltigeurs into a small unit, which was even able to force its way into the square. Bellegarde despatched a grenzer battalion towards the French artillery, but it was soon in trouble: a young officer was offering his sword to a French sergeant when he fell under six bayonets, along with about 170 of his men. Stra was once again in

25 Flank of the line echeloned forward or back.

26 Anon, *Extrait de l'historique du 79e régiment d'infanterie* (Nancy: Berger-Levrault, 1904), p.12. The regiment suffered 127 casualties.

27 Jean-Baptiste Antoine, *Mémoires du général Bon Roch Godart (1792-1815)* (Paris: Ernest Flammarion, 1896), pp.91-92, 315-321.

French hands. Just beyond, on the north side of the *chaussee*, *Oberstleutnant* Graf Hardegg-Glatz gathered up his scattered division (two squadrons) of CLR1 Kaiser, together with squadrons from HR8 Kienmayer and HR10 Stipicz. They waded into the action as much as the terrain allowed and took some prisoners.[28]

As the fog lifted around 11:00 a.m., Masséna's aide de camp, *Chef d'Escadron* Sibuet, had brought the order to Duhesme to advance on Caldiero in line with Gardanne.[29] He planned to anchor his right on Gambion, expecting to join Verdier there. Led by chasseurs à cheval and six platoons of voltigeurs, Duhesme put his troops in battalion columns *en echelon*, except the 14e Légère, which deployed in front, east of Calderin. Reaching Ca Rizzi, the French 25e Chasseurs à Cheval drove off Austrian cavalry, and some horse artillery fired on Reuss-Plauen's column south of Caldiero. Meanwhile, 300 voltigeurs, commanded by *Colonel* Cassan of the 20e Ligne, were directed to Gombion to establish what was happening in the south. They soon drove an Austrian grenzer outpost out of the village and began cutting loopholes in the walls.

*Feldmarschalleutnant* Reuss-Plauen had reached Madonna di Stra around 9:00 a.m. and awaited events to his flanks. On receiving outpost reports that Duhesme's column was heading towards Gambion to threaten *Generalmajor* Nordmann's line of retreat, Reuss-Plauen decided to act: Led by 6. Warasdin-St. Georg Grenzer under *Oberst* Hermann, three battalions of IR52 Franz Carl and a detachment of UR3 Erzherzog Karl marched up the Porcile causeway, while IR48 Vukassovich marched through Ca Goara, just south of Caldiero, followed by 2/IR29 Lindenau.[30]

Around 2:00 p.m., Reuss-Plauen's men reached Gombion, where they linked up with Nordmann. With its musicians playing, *Général de Brigade* Goulos with the 1er Ligne and some chasseurs à cheval had gone to the aid of Cassan's 200 voltigeurs. Three guns stood on the causeway. After initial resistance, they fell back and were reinforced by *Général de Brigade* Solignac with a grenadier battalion. Reuss-Plauen advanced his column, muskets upright, towards the farm, planning a bayonet attack. As they approached the grenadier battalion, the French unmasked some cannon, which fired into the head of the Austrian column. From the cover of trees and ditches, Austrian skirmishers inflicted significant casualties on the French, but a volley halted the Austrians, who were running low on ammunition. Before they could recover, a French battalion cold-bloodedly marched at them with bayonets lowered. The leading Austrian infantry rushed to the sides of the causeway and the French headed towards the Austrian artillery, which were pouring canister into them. The French reached the guns, which were only saved by the prompt

28 Jaromir Hirtenfeld, *Der Militär-Maria-Theresien-Orden und seine Mitglieder* (Vienna: K-k Hof- und Staatsdrückerei, 1857), Vol.II, p.787.

29 Koch, *Memoires de Masséna*, Vol.V, Annex 10 (Duhesme's report).

30 3 and 4/IR29 were between Monte Rocca and Monte Mattia; three companies of 1/IR29 were in the ditches at Chiavicca under *Oberstleutnant* Seethal. Rudolf von Hödl, *Geschichte des k. und k. Infanterieregiments Nr. 29* (Temesvar: Published by the regiment, 1906), p.239.

intervention of General Staff *Hauptmann* O'Brien with a 31-strong *Zug* (quarter-squadron) of UR3.[31] Driving the French back, the uhlans tried to pursue them, but were severely restricted by the ground either side of the causeway, which was covered in ditches, hedges and bushes, amongst which French skirmishers were hidden.

As the Austrians withdrew towards Caldiero, Goulus tentatively moved down the Porcile causeway. At Chiavighetto, *Major* Mihailjevic noticed that French troops had occupied a hillock, which commanded the causeway, so he attacked the position with his 6. Warasdin-St. Georg battalion. French reinforcements drove the grenzers off after courageous resistance, but *Generalmajor* Colloredo moved a reserve grenadier battalion up and the Austrians held their ground. After a cunning strike by Mihailjevic had forced the French infantry to withdraw, Goulus enfiladed Madonna del Stra with two cannon until the fighting died away.

Reuss-Plauen's right-hand column (IR 48 and 2/IR29) encountered *Général de Brigade* Camus at the head of the 14e Légère about 300 paces from Calderin. The French horns blew and were followed by a volley. Partly broken up *en tirailleur* and with some troops helping the wounded, the 14e had to fall back in good order. Marching up the causeway from Gambion, Austrian infantry reached the first houses in Calderin. Duhesme's voltigeurs and chasseurs moved up, so the 14e halted and turned about. At the head of the regiment, Camus chased off the Austrian skirmishers.

Assured that Goullus was holding Gambion, Duhesme resumed his advance round 4:00 p.m., pushing the 14e Légère down the tree-lined roads towards Caldiero, where ten houses were already burning. Dominated by its church, the village stood on raised ground on the left bank of the Barbiera torrent, split in two by an east-west road. On the west side, some single-storey houses formed a rampart. Duhesme arrived with the 102e Ligne, who had marched at the *pas de charge* to fall into the Austrian left. The voltigeurs chased them back into the streets of Caldiero, throwing Austrian troops out of windows and taking no prisoners. Reuss-Plauen's troops were pushed out, but Camus could not advance further, as the 14e was coming under sustained fire from the cannon just beyond on Monte Rocca.

Reuss-Plauen regrouped his nine battalions together with several cavalry squadrons. Outflanked to the left, the 102e Ligne took heavy casualties. Gathering some voltigeurs, Duhesme tried to control his men, shouting '*Au drapeau, mes camarades*',[32] but two battalions broke up and fled, refusing to obey their officers. Some did not re-form until they reached Calderin; others occupied nearby *casinas* (large farmhouses), from which they were evicted at bayonet-point and the rest reinforced the 14e Légère. The remaining battalion formed square and fell back towards Gambion.

31 Erzherzog Karl von Oesterreich, *Relation über die Schlacht bei Caldiero am 30sten October 1805* (Adelsberg: Austrian General Staff, 17 November 1805), p.3.

32 Gachot, *La troisième campagne*, p.68.

## The Battle for Colognola

Encouraged by his advance in the centre, Masséna made his move to outflank the Austrian position by seizing its fortifications, especially the redoubt on Monte Zovo with its five guns which could be turned against the Austrian centre. On 12 November 1796, Massena had fought at First Caldiero, leading the French left to seize the key village of Colognola. So, he ordered Molitor to move against the same village, albeit now it was fortified with redoubts. Molitor's division had left Vago around 11:00 a.m. Having ordered a renewed assault on the Austrian centre, Masséna led Molitor's division himself as far as the hills. Around noon, two howitzers opened up against Redoubt 10 to the south-west of the village, where *Feldmarschalleutnant* Simbchen was positioned and which guarded the village and its main road from the church down towards Monte Zovo. Step by step, the French climbed the vineyard- and tree-covered slopes in the face of dogged Austrian resistance. Under flanking fire from the Austrian troops and guns on Monte il Torre, Molitor led the 60e Ligne forward in an attempt to storm Redoubt 10. Led by their voltigeurs, the three battalions reached the edge of the ditch before the earthworks and some troops fought their way into the village houses, which a lack of time had prevented the Austrians from fortifying.

To the north, *Général de Brigade* Launay's brigade of 5e and 23e Ligne with four cannon advanced along the main road and then made a more circuitous approach, flanked by 100 dragoons. The rest of the 29e Dragons moved up the Ilasi valley towards San Zeno to guard the left wing. Surreptitiously, the 23e Ligne marched up the road through a gully obscured by vineyards on the western slopes to the north of the church and soon, a lively fusillade at the edge of the church wall announced that *Général de Brigade* Launay was in the village on Molitor's left.[33] Voltigeurs climbed the walls surrounding the church and the infantry engaged Austrian infantry around the northern redoubt. In the centre, the 5e Ligne was sprayed with artillery, but, under cover of the trees, its voltigeurs managed to make their way as far as the Villa Peverelli. Behind them, the infantry in an assault column then began to cross the Count's unwalled garden, attempting to reach the redoubt beyond in a combined assault with the 60e Ligne. Now up at the church, *Feldmarschalleutnant* Simbchen faced a dangerous pincer movement. Two companies of IR7 Schroeder, which had been rallied and re-formed by the church, attacked the head of the column, supported by two companies of IR26 Hohenlohe-Bartenstein, which were already in the garden. The other two companies from the IR7 battalion assailed the French column from the right, while a battalion of IR51 led by Baron Splenyi outflanked its left. Overwhelmed, 1/5e Ligne stalled, lost its

33 Gachot, *La troisième campagne*, p.78; Koch, *Memoires de Masséna*, Vol.V, p.102.

eagle to IR7 and was largely destroyed.[34] Molitor dismounted near a brook, which ran the length of the park and whose waters were given to the already numerous wounded. Followed by two officers, he turned the other battalions of the 5e towards the houses, but at the crossroads between the stone walls surrounding the vineyards, their attack stalled as they came under heavy fire and took nearly 50 minutes to cross some open ground.

Simbchen threw his reserves – a battalion each from IR7 Schroeder and IR51 Splenyi[35] – forward, with steady volleys and bayonets lowered, through the gaps in the entrenchments at the 60e Ligne, which fell back. Launay organised a volley, which prompted the Austrians to withdraw back to the village, but with its left exposed and under fire from the nearby redoubts, 60e Ligne fell back in some disorder. Molitor and his staff were in one of the last houses in the village and were in danger of being cut off, when *Général de Brigade* Herbin made one last effort and fought his way through to save them.[36]

Although fully involved in directing the centre, news of Molitor's advance prompted Charles to despatch IR23 Erzherzog Ferdinand's grenadier battalion to shore up the flank. *General der Kavallerie* Bellegarde was directed to take personal charge of the fight for this key position, although neither would ultimately participate.

After the failure of the first French assault, Molitor gathered the remains of the 5e and 60e Ligne at the foot of the hills around lower Colognola with his reserve of 4/60e Ligne and a squadron of 29e Chasseurs à Cheval and led them in a renewed assault. *Colonel* Teste led the remains of the 5e Ligne back up the slopes to assault Redoubt 13 from the south. Built partly on rocky and partly on pebbly ground, the redoubt only had a low breastwork and shallow trench. At the southern end, the gun was guarded by three companies of IR7, mostly positioned on a hastily built platform behind. One 5e Ligne company reached the ditch and tried to climb the rough walls of the breastworks but were flattened by artillery, although those uninjured tried again. Just at the moment when the gun was recoiling, French infantry rushed through the *embrasure*,[37] as others scaled the breastwork. Briefly, amidst hand-to-hand fighting, a French flag fluttered at the top of the parapet, but its eagle was smashed by canister and the *porte-drapeau* (standard bearer) killed while trying to collect the debris.[38] The French commander was felled and as *Hauptmann* Marinowsky led his men forward with bayonets lowered, the remains of the 5e Ligne were driven back

34 Charrie, Pierre, *Drapeaux et étendards de la Révolution et de l'Empire* (Paris: Copernic, 1982), p.204; Spanoghe, 'Der Feldzug', p.34.

35 1/IR51 guarded the redoubt on Monte Zevo.

36 Angeli, *Erzherzog Carl*, Vol.III, p.126.

37 A gap in the earthwork through which the cannon fired.

38 Koch, *Memoires de Masséna*, Vol.V, Annex 9 (Molitor's report); Henri Demiau, *Historique du 5e régiment d'infanterie de ligne* (Paris: Brulfert, 1890), p.152.

into the ditches, 2/5e losing its flag (but not its eagle) to *Feldwebel* (sergeant-major) Schwarzer and *Gemeiner* (private) Kremsa.[39]

The 60e re-formed and at the *pas de charge* headed for the southern Redoubt 10. They secured the communication trenches, but again failed to enter the redoubt. On a nearby slope, *Hauptmann* Novak of IR26 Hohenlohe-Bartenstein saw the French advance. Leaving one company, he immediately led his other with bayonets lowered into the French rear to aid the two IR26 companies defending the redoubt. As Novak's company cleared the last French from the forward trench, the rest of the regiment moved down the slope to cut the road, making the 60e Ligne's withdrawal more difficult.[40]

On the northern side of the village, 23e Ligne had become bogged down engaging the '*Legion Infernale*', IR51 Splenyi.[41] *Hauptmann* Karove of 1/IR51 sneakily led his 3. Kompanie to the left and round the church, where a French battalion was re-forming. He directed 4. Kompanie to engage the French to their front and other flank. Surprised by the move and speed of the Austrian attack, the French broke up in disorder.[42] Two companies from 2/IR51 moved towards Monte Nanfari and outflanked the French left. As the sun set and fog descended from Monte Nanfari, Molitor was informed that 23e had not been able to capture the northern redoubt. As Gardanne fell back he was in danger of being cut off, so after two hours trying to take the earthworks, Molitor withdrew, leaving the isolated 23e Ligne to make its own escape. The Austrians then chased them back down the hill, capturing a flag and two drums. The French fell back down the slopes in disorder, leaving 500 dead and prisoners behind. To the north-west, *Oberst* Kerekes led two squadrons of HR8 Kienmayer out of San Zeno to drive off the other 29e Dragon squadrons, chasing them as far as Ca dell'Ara, while another two squadrons engaged the 5e Ligne.

As the star-lit night fell sometime after 5:00 p.m., the French left pulled back. Rather forlornly, Molitor was later to report to Masséna that the 79e Ligne had headed south, apparently to attack Bellegarde's right flank, but had become separated from the division and were not available to participate in this key assault.[43]

39 IR7 received five gold and five silver bravery medals – see Andreas Graf Thürheim, *Gedenkblätter aus der Kriegsgeschichte der K.k. Oesterreichischen Armee* (Vienna: K. Prochaska, 1860) pp.30-34 – and claimed two eagles. French eagles could be unscrewed from the flag.

40 Hirtenfeld, *Der Militär-Maria-Theresien-Orden*, Vol.II, p.789.

41 This nickname had been given to the regiment by the French in previous campaigns.

42 *Feldmarschalleutnant* Simbchen, *Generalmajors* Colloredo and Nordmann, *Oberstleutnant* Hardegg, *Hauptleute* Novak and Karove won the Knight's Cross of the Maria Theresa Order; *Feldmarschalleutnant* O'Reilly was awarded the Commander Cross. Hirtenfeld, *Der Militär-Maria-Theresien-Orden*, Vol.II, pp.788- 817.

43 Gachot, *La troisième campagne*, p.80, footnote 1.

## Decision in the Centre

By 3:00 p.m., the decisive moment had come as the French column threatened to break through. While *Feldmarschalleutnant* O'Reilly and Archduke Maximillian struggled to keep *Generalmajor* Wetzel's brigade in order, Archduke Charles directed IR32 Esterhazy under *Oberst* Weissenwolf forward against the advancing French, while he personally led *Feldmarschalleutnant* Vogelsang's five grenadier battalions (*Generalmajor* Lippa's brigade) in support.

On the south side of the *chaussee*, IR53 broke up into several parts. Bellegarde's cavalry could not halt the Austrian infantry fleeing back down the *chaussee*, chased by the voltigeurs, who made 400 metres in ten minutes. As the opposing infantry became mixed together in the defile, the Austrian artillery in the fortifications on the hills found itself unable to fire effectively. IR32 Esterhazy engaged around Stra, their advance supporting to Reuss-Plauen's right, so he could move forward. Faced with being enveloped after the 102e Ligne's retreat, the 14e Ligne evacuated Caldiero and fell back towards Calderin. Around 4:00 p.m., the Austrians had stabilised their positions in the centre, but the French were preparing a new assault.

Gardanne's troops had abandoned their pursuit of IR53. To the south, d'Espagne assailed the Austrian left with Maurin's brigade led by 24e Chasseurs à Cheval, Masséna's Guides under *Chef d'Escadron* Cheval, forcing part of IR32 Esterhazy between the *chaussee* and Caldiero to fall back *en potence* to protect their left. This allowed Masséna to rotate his troops: from each flank, two of Partouneaux's grenadier battalions moved into the frontline to engage IR32 in a firefight. Duhesme called forward the 20e Ligne, which had been slowly marching down the *chaussee*, and directed them at Reuss-Plauen's advancing troops. Three battalions marched past Calderin in closed column. Reinforced by *Général de Brigade* Girardon with the Italian 2° Linea, a grenadier battalion, and six guns from Partouneaux, Duhesme could see that Reuss-Plauen had halted, so he deployed five battalions. Their first volley felled three ranks of Reuss-Plauen's infantry, but disordered by the fleeing 102e, 2/ and 3/20e Ligne were initially repulsed. Closer to the *chaussee*, 4/20e Ligne under *Chef de Bataillon* Joseph Hugo, had remained in column, to cover against any advance by Bellegarde. Now, they could aid Gardanne by attacking a re-formed part of IR53 on the Austrian left and pushing them back on Caldiero. Through the trees, Hugo could see several Austrian cavalry squadrons preparing to move against him, probably DR5 Savoyen. With bayonets lowered, he advanced against them in closed column across the broken terrain. The Austrian cavalry stopped, and its officers moved to the flanks, but the difficult ground prevented a charge. Duhesme threw in a squadron of 25e Chasseurs à Cheval and together with 4/20e Ligne, now deployed and firing from the cover of a dry torrent bed at 20 paces, forced the Austrian cavalry to withdraw. The battalion was hit by a shell, which felled several drummers, as it came under sustained canister fire from Austrian guns, which swept the *chaussee*. Austrian skirmishers advanced ahead of *Generalmajor* Lippa's grenadiers, whose left battalion engaged Hugo and, as he drew his skirmishers back, pushed him back into the hedges around Caldiero.[44] Amidst the chaos, Austrian General Staff *Oberstleutnant* Franz von Binnenthal found himself riding around so much to deliver the Archduke's verbal orders that his horse expired beneath him.[45]

The Austrian column then turned towards Partouneaux's grenadiers. At that moment, 1/20e Ligne came up in support of 4/20e and, using the cover of the torrent, they attacked the flank of the Austrian column. Lippa was forced to pull his left battalion back, so that his troops formed a hook formation, anchored on the bridge at Caldiero. Parts of IR53 re-formed behind, but took no further part in the fighting.[46] Suddenly, the Austrian cavalry reappeared. Thinking they were headed for Hugo's left, 1/20e Ligne did not close up and took the full force of the Austrian charge, which broke the battalion apart. Meanwhile, the other two 20e Ligne battalions launched a bayonet attack on Reuss-Plauen's infantry. Duhesme had re-formed the 14e Légère and 102e Ligne behind 20e Ligne. Supported by Girardon's three battalions with elements of 14e and 102e fighting *en tirailleur*, they outflanked the Austrian left and drove them back on Caldiero.

On the *chaussee*, under steady and increasing French fire, an exhausted IR32 Esterhazy fell back, forced out of the fight by heavy losses.[47] However, Gardanne's men were not in good order as they arrived north of Caldiero. Four of *Generalmajor* Lippa's grenadier battalions, which had not yet fired a shot, calmly and determinedly marched against the French skirmishers as darkness began to fall. To the south, *Hauptmann* Carl Call, commander of 2/IR29 Lindenau, led a determined defence of Caldiero, aided by *Leutnant* Artis and *Fahnrich* Irschik, as the village changed hands several times amidst fierce fighting.

Carrying his hat on his sabre, Gardanne urged his men to make another assault, during which around 5:00 p.m., the French secured Stra and Caldiero. Intent on pushing on through the area between the *chaussee* and Caldiero village, Masséna was still able to rotate his troops. Lenchantin's re-formed brigade advanced to force a wounded *Generalmajor* Lippa to withdraw his grenadiers to the main Austrian earthworks. Reuss-Plauen's troops were driven back on Monte Rocca, where they were issued with brandy and more cartridges before Charles threw them back into the fight. Under a star-lit night, artillery and musketry fire erupted from the Austrian earthworks. Musketry from the forward trenches was particularly effective in decimating Duhesme's packed columns and his advance stalled. Under fire, IR29's chaplain, Ignaz Drescher, went from one company defending

44 Joseph comte Hugo, *Mémoires du Général Hugo* (Paris: Ladvocat, 1823) pp.115-116.

45 Albrecht Zimburg, *Der Krieg in den Bergen*, (Lenzburg: Merker im Effingerhof, 2008) p.267.

46 16 dead, 71 wounded, 168 prisoners and 7 missing: Anton von Marx, *Geschichte des 53ten ungarischen Linien-Infanterie-Regiments* (Vienna: K-k Hof- und Staats-Aerariel-Drückerei, 1832) p.163.

47 For his leadership of IR32, Weissenwolf was promoted to *Generalmajor* on 6 November.

a trench to the others, urging the troops to fight to the bitter end.[48] Suddenly, the French lines began to waver, as Gardanne's men came under increasing fire from the Austrian earthworks on the San Mattia hill. Gardanne ordered his men to form '*groupes*' (small subunits) to reduce the effects of Austrian artillery, but with limited effect.[49] Masséna had no reserves left, but around 5:00 p.m., Charles had ordered *Feldmarschalleutnant* Hohenlohe-Bartenstein to lead his five Hungarian grenadier battalions up with bands playing. Towards 6:00 p.m., as Archduke Maximillian set about reordering broken units, fresh Austrians troops swept forward into Gardanne's exhausted men.

Hugo fell back on Caldiero, which he held with a mixed force of about 1500 men, preventing Reuss-Plauen from advancing. When one of Masséna's aides de camp arrived, Hugo advised that ammunition was running low. Two caissons were sent forward and he was reinforced to 2,500.[50] As Molitor fell back in the north and without news of Verdier, Masséna had to hurriedly withdraw his central forces. *Feldmarschalleutnant* Hohenlohe-Bartenstein launched a second attack with his grenadiers, which pushed the French back down the *chaussee* through Stra. Well-protected by Chasseurs à Cheval and voltigeurs, the French rearguard stopped an Austrian cavalry attack near Stra, but HR10 Stipicz managed to get amongst them to disorder the French retreat. As CLR1 Kaiser engaged the French rearguard in the growing gloom, they were fired on by Austrian gunners, who thought they were French cavalry.[51] Low on ammunition, Duhesme withdrew from the fire-fight near the entrenchments and evacuated Caldiero at 8:00 p.m. To the south, Girardon's troops came under renewed attack from Reuss-Plauen's infantry especially on their left flank. With some support from Goulus, they managed to beat the Austrians off, but Duhesme was pushed back towards Calderin as the fighting petered out. The Austrian troops remained under arms during the night, the centre holding the entrenchments and the villages of Stra and Caldiero. *Generalmajor* Nordmann had secured Chiavicca del Christo, while *Feldmarschalleutnant* Reuss-Plauen was at Madonna di Stra and Chiavighetto with outposts almost as far as Canova. To the north-west, there had been no activity on the upper Adige.

## The Last Fighting: 31 October 1805

Planning a renewed attack the next morning to cover his withdrawal, Archduke Charles ordered *Feldmarschalleutnant* Argenteau to bring the last reserve,

48 Johann Megerle von Mühlfeld, *Memorabilien des Osterreichischen Kaiserstaates* (Vienna: Sollinger, 1827), p.197

49 Gachot, *La troisième campagne*, p.74.

50 Joseph Hugo, *Mémoires*, pp.114-117.

51 Alexander von Einsiedel, *Der Feldzug der Oesterreicher in Italien im Jahre 1805* (Vienna: Verlag des Geographischen Instituts, 1812), p.38.

seven grenadier battalions, from the San Gregorio camp. Four battalions and 12 squadrons were withdrawn from around Caldiero to form an additional reserve either side of the *chaussee* on a small track between that village and Villanuova. However, dawn revealed the French just standing in position and the only activity was irregular outpost fire. As daylight spread across the battlefield, Charles requested an armistice to bury the dead and tend the wounded, but Masséna only agreed to a four-hour suspension until noon in the area around Caldiero. His plan was to renew the fighting: Leaving 4e and 19e Chasseurs à Cheval to reconnoitre downstream, Verdier was ordered to continue crossing the Adige at Zevio, as Nordmann had most of his troops on the Porcile causeway. A loud exchange of artillery heralded a renewed French effort against the Austrian left. This day, Verdier's division would be able to complete its crossing near the mouth of La Fasetta channel on the bridge, which finally arrived and been assembled by a sappeur company aided by the dismounted dragoons. About 10:00 a.m., Nordmann's patrols reported that French troops were approaching from the north, but the thickly-wooded ground prevented an accurate assessment of their strength. The French were in two columns. Having crossed on boats, *Général de Brigade* Digonet with two regiments was heading down the sideroad to attack the Austrian entrenchments around Chiavicca from the front and left flank. By 10:30 a.m., Brun's brigade had crossed the bridge and was surprised only to encounter Austrian patrols as it headed for Sabbionara.

Aide de camp *sous-lieutenant* Maisonneuve led three companies of voltigeurs to within 500 metres of La Bova. Digonet moved towards the Porcile causeway, but on emerging from the trees ran into Nordmann's troops. As his troops fell into disorder under the heavy and overwhelming crossfire, the Austrian commander raced to the frontline, anxious that the earthworks were only 30 minutes' march behind him and his only line of retreat was down a causeway with little solid ground either side. Nordmann decided against trying to send out flanking detachments as they were likely to be cut off and only weaken his force. The French were on the road, just 50 paces distant, with skirmishers either side.

The Austrians fell back on Casa La Bova, held by the Grenadier battalion of IR61 St. Julien, just 800 paces from Chiavicca del Christo. Nordmann managed to hold his troops together and withdrew to that earthwork, where he posted some troops and put others into the trenches in front. The remainder were kept in reserve or in the communication trenches to *Feldmarschalleutnant* Reuss-Plauen on Nordmann's right. Under fire from the guns of Nordmann and Brusch, Digonet's column followed the road past La Bova and launched a three-pronged attack on the Chiavicca earthwork. Its embrasure was left open, from where the Austrians could fire on the French as they advanced down the causeway. Constantly fired upon by French skirmishers from the ricefields, the Austrian troops on the causeway fell into disorder, which became worse at Chiavicca as there was only one entrance into the earthwork. For the next few hours, Nordmann's men would put up fierce resistance, but Nordmann fell, badly wounded by a musket ball into his shoulder, along with two general staff officers.[52] *Generalmajor* Colloredo took command of the Austrian left wing, aided by staff *Oberstleutnant* Nugent, as the Austrian officers struggled to keep their men in order. Some French grenadiers had advanced along the bank of the Adige supported by artillery on the southern bank, seeking to reach the channel, which protected the Austrian left. Realising their aim, Colloredo sent a grenadier battalion, which arrived just in time to halt them. The French advanced along the causeway, which could only be swept with fire from one open, flat area, but the French directed such fire at it that the Austrians were forced to seek cover. Colloredo rode to the threatened position, gathered the troops together and inspired them to return to the fray. Concentrated French fire had already caused heavy casualties among the artillery crews and two companies of IR29 Lindenau in the nearby trenches had sustained another 200. The 18-year old *Fähnrich* Ehrenstein of IR29 led some of his men in servicing the artillery so effectively that their fire drove the French back and the ditches were held.

To relieve the pressure on Nordmann, Reuss-Plauen sent *Oberst* Brusch with IR48 Vukassovich up the Porcile causeway to threaten Digonet's communications. Leaving one battalion in Porcile, *Oberst* Gajoli with a few hundred grenzers, two battalions of IR52 Franz Karl, and four cannon marched across the rice fields and then used local tracks to assail the French left. Under fire from Colloredo's grenadiers in front and Gajoli's men from the left, Digonet fell back on La Bova. There he left the causeway and took cover in a wood. On the Porcile causeway, Digonet placed two cannon behind an abatis and fired into Brusch's infantry column at 40 paces. Brusch rallied his men and reinforced with grenzers in skirmish order and two companies of IR52 Franz Karl, headed for Gambion. Brun started to withdraw north-east to join Duhesme.

Two French battalions headed for Sabbionara, where they were met at 4:00 p.m. by Solignac' grenadiers with Masséna's order to do nothing more. Austrian troops followed them and attacked the two companies guarding the bridge. To prevent a panicked rush for the bridge as twilight fell, Verdier led some chasseurs à cheval at a half-battalion and drove it back. They were joined Masséna's Guides, including aide de camp *Sous-Lieutenant* Pelet-Clozeau, who was wounded in the head by a bullet. *Général de Division* Verdier was injured when his horse fell, so *Général de Brigade* Digonet took command and on receipt of Masséna's order to re-join Duhesme, withdrew on Pantera late in the evening.

In the south, Austrian raiding parties crossed the Adige by boat and a bridge was thrown at Bonavigo. *Generalmajor* Vincent led two infantry battalions and some grenzer companies, accompanied by hussar detachments, across to the southern bank to seize all the available boats and take prisoners. After

52 Hirtenfeld, *Der Militär-Maria-Theresien-Orden*, Vol.II, p.790-791.

occupying Isola Porcarriza, he harried French positions before withdrawing to the northern bank. That evening, Masséna returned to his headquarters at Vago, where the spy Vicotini informed him that Charles was evacuating his wounded and supplies towards Treviso.[53] As the Archduke contemplated his next move, Graf Bubna's arrival from Vienna brought formal confirmation of the disaster at Ulm. Charles decided on one last attack to enable his army to retreat. During the night, the Archduke issued orders for an attack on the French left from the high ground to the north to force them to withdraw on Verona. *Feldmarschalleutnant* Rosenberg had a difficult march up to Triginago to attack the French flank from the hills above Mezzano, while the Austrian right and centre made a general advance. Dawn brought the realisation that the French had already retreated under cover of a light infantry screen. The Austrians reoccupied the villages along the *chaussee*, but there would be no fighting on 1 November. Austrian dead, wounded, and missing totalled 5,672, including 1,581 prisoners.[54] They claimed about 8,000 French losses, including 1,700 prisoners. French sources have consistently claimed lower figures, but their casualties on 30 October were 3,204, with the three main divisions each losing about 900 men.[55]

At 12.15 p.m. on 1 November, the Austrian retreat began, as the Grande Armée crossed the Inn river. Napoleon's chief of staff, *Maréchal* Berthier, ordered Masséna to: 'pursue the enemy without respite ... so that he is not able to attack us when we find ourselves facing the entire Russian army'.[56] Masséna would harry Charles's army back through Villach (Lublijana). Praised by the Archduke for his knowledge of the terrain and tireless activity in planning the battle, Zach recovered his tarnished reputation by directing the retreat to Komorn on the Danube by 6 December. There news arrived of Austerlitz and the armistice. Napoleon was more critical of Masséna, writing that he 'has behaved indifferently. He made bad dispositions and got himself beaten at Caldiero'.[57]

53 Gachot, *La troisième campagne*, p.87.

54 Spanoghe, 'Der Feldzug', p.41.

55 Gachot, *La troisième campagne*, p.81; A. Martinien, *Tableaux, par corps et par batailles, des officiers tués et blessés pendant les guerres de l'Empire (1805-1815)* (Paris: Henri Charles-Lavauzelle, 1899) lists the following officer casualties from the main battle: 1er 7; 5e 21; 6e 1; 14e 6; 20e 14; 23e 5; 29e 8; 52e 6; 56e 6; 60e 10; 62e 5; 70e 7; 101e 2; 102e 12; 22e Légère 5; 23e Légère 4; 2° Linea (Italian) 3; 29e Dragons 6; 3e Chasseurs à Cheval 2; 14e Chasseurs à Cheval 1; 24e Chasseurs à Cheval 3; 25e Chasseurs à Cheval 1; Staff 2; French artillery 2; Italian artillery 1; Engineers 1

56 Napoléon I, *Correspondance de Napoléon Ier* (Paris: Imprimiere Impériale, 1862), Vol.XI, pp.525-526. (Berthier to Masséna, 22 November 1805).

57 Napoléon I, *The Confidential Correspondence of Napoleon Bonaparte with his brother Joseph* (New York: D. Appleton,1855), Vol.I, p.70 (15 November 1805).

## Orders of Battle

FM = *Feldmarschall*
GdK = *General der Kavallerie*
FML = *Feldmarschalleutnant*
GM = *Generalmajor*
GD = *Général de Division*
GB = *Général de Brigade*

**Austrian Italienarmee (Strengths on 20 September 1805)**[58]
Commander: FM Archduke Charles
Chief of Staff: FML Zach
Artillery Director: FML de Vaux

***Right Wing: FML Rosenberg***

| | | |
|---|---|---|
| GM Sommariva | | |
| 1. (Licca) Grenz Reg (3) | 2,041 | 4x3pdr |
| 2. (Ottocac) Grenz Reg (2. Batt + 1 co) | 788 | 4x3pdr |
| 11. (2nd Banal) Grenz Reg (3) | 1,966 | 4x3pdr |
| 3. Erzherzog Ferdinand Hussars (4) | 466 | |
| GM Hillinger | | |
| IR37 Auffenburg (4) | 1,515 | 4x3pdr |
| IR34 Davidovich (4) | 2,294 | 4x3pdr |

***Advance-Guard: General der Kavallerie H. Graf Bellegarde***

| | | |
|---|---|---|
| Division: FML Simbchen | | |
| GM Frimont | | |
| 6. (Warasdin-St. Georg) Grenz Reg (3) | 2,318 | |
| 3. Erzherzog Ferdinand Hussars (4) | 466 | |
| 1. Kaiser Chevauleger (8) | c.800 | |
| 8. Kienmayer Hussars (8) | c.900 | |
| *Oberst* Soudain | | |
| IR22 Coburg (4) | 1,797 | 4x3pdr |
| IR26 Hohenlohe-Bartenstein (4) | 1,666 | 4x3pdr |
| GM Kottulinsky | | |
| IR29 Lindenau (4) | 2,180 | |
| IR7 Schroeder (4) | 1,959 | |

58 Based on documents in carton: Kriegarchiv, Alte Feldakten 1805 Italie X. The only strength figure is 1805 Italie IX 238 and the reserve artillery is 1805 Italie X 213a; Angeli, *Erzherzog Carl*, Vol.III, pp.74-77.

| | | |
|---|---|---|
| ***Reserve: FML Argenteau*** | | |
| [Grenadier Battalions where (1)] | | |
| GM Nordmann | | |
| 5. (Warasdin-Kreuz) Grenz Reg (3) | 2,395 | |
| 8. (Gradiska) Grenz Reg (3) | c.2,300 | |
| (1 battalion each in reserve at Arcole) | | |
| 9. Erdödy Hussars (8) | c.900 | |
| Division: FML Lindenau | | |
| GM Lippa | | |
| IR10 Ansbach (1) | 508 | |
| IR22 Coburg (1) | 494 | |
| IR26 Hohenlohe-Bartenstein (1) | 440 | |
| IR27 Strassoldo (1) | 427 | |
| 8x3pdr | | |
| GM Hohenlohe-Bartenstein | | |
| IR2 Erzherzog Ferdinand (1) | 433 | |
| IR33 Sztaray (1) | 445 | |
| IR34 Davidovich (1) | 462 | |
| IR37 Auffenburg (1) | 502 | |
| IR53 Jellacic (1) | 476 | 10x3pdr |
| Division: FML Vogelsang | | |
| GM H. Graf von Colloredo-Mansfeld | | |
| IR29 Lindenau (1) | 517 | |
| IR48 Vukassovich (1) | 487 | |
| IR51 Splenyi (1) | 432 | |
| IR52 Erzherzog Franz Karl (1) | 472 | |
| IR61 St. Julien (1) | 436 | 10x3pdr |
| GM Koller | | |
| IR7 Schroeder (1) | 622 | |
| IR13 Reisky (1) | 492 | |
| IR16 Erzherzog Rudolph (1) | 489 | |
| IR44 Bellegarde (1) | 499 | |
| IR45 Latterman (1) | 458 | |
| IR56 W. Colloredo (1) | 494 | |
| IR63 Erzherzog Josef (1) | 489 | 10x3pdr |
| Division: FML O'Reilly | | |
| GM Wetzel | | |
| IR2 Erzherzog Ferdinand (4) | 1,892 | 4x3pdr |
| IR53 Jellacic (4) | 2,130 | 4x3pdr |
| Division: FML Prince Reuss-Plauen | | |
| GM Kalnassy | | |
| IR48 Vukassovich (4) | 2,131 | 4x3pdr |
| IR52 Franz Karl (4) | 2,335 | 4x3pdr |

| | | |
|---|---|---|
| GM Mihailovich | | |
| IR32 Esterhazy (4) | 2,294 | 4x3pdr |
| IR51 Splenyi (4) | 1,797 | 4x3pdr |
| Division: FML Prince Lothringen | | |
| GM Walther | | |
| 3. Erzherzog Karl Uhlans (8) | 981 | |
| 5. Savoyen Dragoons (8) | c.800 | |
| GM Vincent | | |
| 4. Levenehr Dragoons (8)[59] | c.800 | |
| 10. Stipicz Hussars (8) | c.900 | |

***Left Wing: FML Davidovich (At Bevilaqua)***

| | | |
|---|---|---|
| GM Radetzky | | |
| 4. (Szluin) Grenz Reg (3) | 2,104 | 4x3pdr |
| 5. Ott Hussars (8) | 931 | |
| GM Gavisini | | |
| IR16 Erzherzog Rudolph (4) | c.2,100 | |
| IR45 Latterman (3) | c.1,580 | |
| IR13 Reisky (4) | c.2,100 | |
| 2. Erzherzog Josef Hussars (6) | 672 | |
| GM Levenehr | | |
| IR63 Erzherzog Josef (4) | 1,971 | |
| 10. (1. Banal) Grenz Reg (3) | 2,382 | 2x3pdr |
| 2. Erzherzog Josef Hussars (2) | 228 | |

***Reserve Artillery***

Facing Verona:
2 x 3pdr; (with 3. Hussars) 2 x 6pdr, 2 x 7pdr howitzer
At Caldiero:
14x6pdr, 4x12pdr, 2x7pdr howitzer
Centre:
2x12pdr,[60] 4 cavalry batteries (4x6pdr, 2x7pdr howitzer),
Left Wing:
12x6pdr, 6x7pdr howitzer, 2x3pdr
With 5. Hussars:
1xCavalry battery (4x6pdr, 2x7pdr howitzer)

59 On headquarters duty
60 Charles ordered the rest of his 12-pounder cannon to move east to Vicenza on 25 October: Angeli, *Erzherzog Carl*, Vol.III, p.102

**French Armée d'Italie: 23 October 1805**[61]
Commander: *Maréchal* Masséna
Chief of Staff: GD Charpentier
Artillery Commander: GD Lacombe Saint-Michel

| | |
|---|---|
| ***1er Division: GD Gardanne*** | |
| GB Compere | |
| 22e Légère (3) | 1,484 |
| 52e Ligne (3) | 1,335 |
| GB Lenchantin | |
| 29e Ligne (3) | 1,564 |
| 101e Ligne (3) | 1,587 |
| 23e Chasseurs à Cheval (3) | 499 |
| 15/2e Artillerie à Pied | 55 |
| 4/6e Batt bis du train | 64 |
| 8x6pdr, 2x3pdr, 2x5in howitzers | |
| ***2e Division: GD Verdier*** | |
| GB Digonet | |
| 23e Légère (3) | 1,409 |
| 10e Ligne (3) | 1,292 |
| GB Brun | |
| 56e Ligne (3) | 1,090 |
| 62e Ligne (4) | 1,438 |
| *Adjutant Général* Ormancey | |
| 4e Chasseurs à Cheval (4) | 429 |
| 19e Chasseurs à Cheval (4) | 413 |
| Dragons à Pied (1 bn. of detachments from 23e, 24e, 28e, 29e, 30e Dragons) | 324 |
| Grenadiers Réunis (2 bns. from 4e Division) | 981 |
| 17/2e Artillerie à Pied | 59 |
| 3/4e Artillerie à Cheval | 49 |
| 1/, 4/, 6/4e Batt du train | 150 |
| 8x6pdr, 7x5in howitzers | |
| ***3e Division: GD Molitor*** | |
| GB Launay | |
| 5e Ligne (3) | 1,690 |

61 Koch, *Memoires de Masséna*, Vol.V, Annex 6; George Nafziger, The Nafziger Collection of Orders of Battle, 805JBH <https://www.scribd.com/doc/133832396/Nafziger-Collection-of-Orders-of-Battle-Index> (accessed 10 July 2019).

| | |
|---|---|
| 23e Ligne (4) | 1,802 |
| GB Herbin | |
| 60e Ligne (4) | 2,089 |
| GB Valory | |
| 79e Ligne (2) | 1,231 |
| 29e Dragons | 410 |
| 5/4e Artillerie à Cheval | 51 |
| 8/2e Artillerie à Pied | 58 |
| 2/, 4/4e Batt bis du train | 109 |
| 5x6pdr | |

***4e Division: GD Duhesme***

| | |
|---|---|
| GB Goulus | |
| 1er Ligne (3) | 1,578 |
| 102e Ligne (3) | 1,611 |
| GB Le Camus | |
| 14e Légère (3) | 1,571 |
| 20e Ligne (4) | 2,164 |
| 25e Chasseurs à Cheval (3) | 434 |
| 19/2e Artillerie à Pied | 53 |
| 2/, 3/6e Batt (bis) du train | 86 |
| 5x6pdr | |

***5e Division: GD Serras***

| | |
|---|---|
| GB Gilli | |
| Tirailleurs Corses (5 cos) | 484 |
| 8e Légère (2) | 1,062 |
| 53e Ligne (3) | 1,587 |
| GB Guillet | |
| 81e Ligne (2) | 989 |
| 106e Ligne (3) | 1,576 |
| Elite du Bataillon de Pioneers[62] | 300 |
| GB Mallet | |
| 1° Dragoni 'Regina' (Italian) | 495 |
| 13e Légère (2) | 973 |
| GB Schilt | |
| 9e Ligne (3e Batt) | 550 |
| Italian Artillery (1 co) | 60 |
| Italian Artillery train | 64 |
| 2x6pdr, 2x3pdr, 7x5.5in howitzers | |

62 1er and 2 Cies, plus detachment of 3e Cie.

| | |
|---|---|
| ***Cavalry Division: GD d'Espagne***[63] | |
| GB Debelle | |
| 3e Chasseurs à Cheval (4) | 386 |
| 14e Chasseurs à Cheval (4) | 428 |
| GB Maurin | |
| 15e Chasseurs à Cheval (4) | 506 |
| 24e Chasseurs à Cheval (4) | 424 |
| 4/1er Artillerie à Cheval | 46 |
| 1/6e Batt bis du train | 59 |
| 4x6pdr, 7x5in howitzer | |
| | |
| ***Cavalry Division: GD Pully*** | |
| GB Fresia | |
| 4e Cuirassiers (4) | 369 |
| 6e Cuirassiers (4) | 353 |
| *Colonel* Rioult-Davenay | |
| 23e Dragons (4) | 286 |
| | |
| ***Cavalry Division GD Mermet*** | |
| GB Lacour | |
| 24e Dragons (4) | 319 |
| 30e Dragons (3) | 193 |
| *Colonel* d'Offenstein | |
| 7e Cuirassiers (4) | 456 |
| 8e Cuirassiers (4) | 452 |
| 3/1er Artillerie a Cheval | 51 |
| 3/, 5/6e Batt bis du train | 65 |
| 4x6pdr, 7x5in howitzer | |
| | |
| ***Reserve: GD Partouneaux*** | |
| GB Solignac | |
| 1/Grenadiers Réunis | 501 |
| 2/Grenadiers Réunis | 496 |
| 3/Grenadiers Réunis | 498 |
| 4/Grenadiers Réunis | 498 |
| GB Valentin | |
| 5/Grenadiers Réunis | 495 |
| 6/Grenadiers Réunis | 415 |
| 7/Grenadiers Réunis | 416 |
| 8/Grenadiers Réunis | 498 |

63 Cavalry divisions appear not to have been numbered.

| | |
|---|---|
| 2° Linea (Italian) (2) | c.1500 |
| 4/4e Artillerie à Cheval | 64 |
| 1/4e Batt bis du train | 68 |
| 4x6pdr, 2x5in howitzers | |

# Bibliography


***Archival Sources***

Kriegsarchiv Vienna, Alte Feldakten 1805 Italie X.

I should like to thank Michael Wenzel for trawling Cartons IX – XI for unit strengths.

***Published Sources***

Angeli, Moritz von, *Erzherzog Carl von Österreich als Feldherr und Heeresorganisator* (Vienna: Braumüller, 1896).

Anon, *Extrait de l'historique du 79e régiment d'infanterie* (Nancy: Berger-Levrault, 1904).

Antoine, Jean-Baptiste, *Mémoires du général Bon Roch Godart (1792-1815)* (Paris: Ernest Flammarion, 1896).

Charrie, Pierre, *Drapeaux et étendards de la Révolution et de l'Empire* (Paris: Copernic, 1982).

Demiau, Henri, *Historique du 5e régiment d'infanterie de ligne* (Paris: Brulfert, 1890).

Einsiedel, Alexander von, *Der Feldzug der Oesterreicher in Italien im Jahre 1805* (Vienna: Verlag des Geographischen Instituts, 1812).

Fremont Barnes, Gregory, *Armies of the Napoleonic Wars* (Barnsley: Pen & Sword, 2011).

Gachot, Edouard, *Le troisième campagne d'Italie* (Paris: Plon-Nourrit, 1911). He claims to have assembled 517 archival documents.

Hirtenfeld, Jaromir, *Der Militär-Maria-Theresien-Orden und seine Mitglieder* (Vienna: K-k Hof- und Staatsdrückerei, 1857).

Hödl, Rudolf von, *Geschichte des k. und k. Infanterieregiments Nr. 29* (Temesvar: Published by the regiment, 1906).

Hugo, Joseph Comte, *Mémoires du Général Hugo* (Paris: Ladvocat, 1823).

Kagan, Frederick, *The End of the Old Order* (Boston: Da Capo, 2007).

Karl, Erzherzog von Oesterreich, *Relation über die Schlacht bei Caldiero am 30sten October 1805* (Adelsberg: Austrian General Staff, 17 November 1805).

Koch, Jean, *Memoires de Masséna* (Paris: Paulin et Lechevalier, 1850). He drew heavily on the OMZ, but used the Marshal's archive and includes useful '*Pieces justificatives*' (Annexes).

Maendl, Maximilian, *Geschichte des K. und K. Infanterie-regiments nr. 51*, (Klausenburg: Published by the regiment, 1899).

Megerle von Mühlfeld, Johann, *Memorabilien des Osterreichischen Kaiserstaates* (Vienna: Sollinger, 1827).

Martinien, Aristide, *Tableaux, par corps et par batailles, des officiers tués et blessés pendant les guerres de l'Empire (1805-1815)* (Paris: Charles-Lavauzelle, 1899).

Marx, Anton von, *Geschichte des 53ten ungarischen Linien-Infanterie-Regiments* (Vienna: K-k Hof- und Staats-Aerariel-Drückerei (1832).

Nafziger, George, The Nafziger Collection of Orders of Battle <https://www.scribd.com/doc/133832396/Nafziger-Collection-of-Orders-of-Battle-Index> (accessed 10 July 2019).

Napoléon I, *Correspondance de Napoléon Ier* XI (Paris: Imprimiere Impériale, 1862) .

Napoléon I, *The Confidential Correspondence of Napoleon Bonaparte with his brother Joseph* I (New York: D. Appleton,1855).

Rothenberg, Gunther, *Napoleon's Great Adversaries* (London: Batsford 1982).

Rüstow, Wilhelm von, *Der Krieg von 1805 in Deutschland and Italie* (Frauenfeld: Reimann, 1853).

Schneid, Frederick, *Napoleon's Italian Campaigns: 1805–1815* (Westport: Praeger, 2002).

Spanoghe, Friedrich, 'Der Feldzug 1805 in Italien', *Österreichische Militärische Zeitschrift* II (1823) pp.3-43. The Zeitschrift was a military journal written to teach the history of war, based on documents in the Kriegsarchiv.

Thürheim, Andreas Graf: *Gedenkblätter aus der Kriegsgeschichte der K.k. Oesterreichischen Armee* (Vienna: K. Prochaska, 1860).

Vaniček, Franz, *Specialgeschichte der Militärgrenze* (Vienna: K-k Hof- und Staatsdrückerei, 1875).

Wust, Gustav, *Geschichte des k.k. Linien-Infanterie-Regiments 34 Prinz Regent von Preussen* (Vienna: K-k Hof- und Staatsdrückerei, 1860).

Zimburg, Albrecht, *Der Krieg in den Bergen* (Lenzburg: Merker im Effingerhof, 2008).

3

# The Prussian Light Infantry in 1806

Hans-Karl Weiss

---

The Prussian Army, or, rather, a small part of it, fought from 1792 to 1795 against Revolutionary France, not without success. The future General Valentini, who took part in the campaigns at the Rhine as a young officer with the *Jäger*, wrote:

> Do we look at the army, as it is in our most lively memory; it was completely equal to their predecessors, with whom Friedrich II started his first wars in Silesia. Its bravery, good will, strong honour and tactical perfection were second to none against any troops in the world... The hussars and to a certain extend also the *Füsiliere* and *Jäger*, as light troops always at the enemy, enjoyed here the special advantages against the other branches of arms of having more opportunities to distinguish themselves and to learn.[1]

Another Prussian officer wrote after the campaign of 1794 to a friend: 'What especially should delight you as a Prussian is the glory, which our brave warriors claimed again in this campaign... I dare to say even more and to assert, that the Prussian Army due to some very good institutions of today's King is in some regards even better, as it was then'.[2]

Eleven years later, in the campaign of 1806, the Prussian army suffered a crushing defeat. The heirs of Frederick the Great, who still regarded themselves as being the best army, went into the war with high hopes only to find them dashed very soon. It is of popular view and well entrenched, not only in English language, that the Prussian Army of 1806 still adhered to the rigid lines of the Seven Years

1 Curt Jany, *Geschichte der Königlich Preußischen Armee bis zum Jahre 1807* (Berlin: Verlag von Karl Siegismund, 1929), Vol. III, pp.305-306.
2 Jany, *Geschichte*, Vol.III, pp.307-308.

War, that their impeccable battalion volleys fizzled out in the autumn fogs of the battles at the Saale, and that the soldiers stood rigid while shot to pieces by French skirmishers. Nothing is more wrong, however, than to imagine that the Prussian Army did not change in armament and tactics compared to the Seven Years War. It underwent many reforms, starting from the new drill regulations of 1788 to a flood of revision and changes, raising 24 light infantry battalions, introducing *Schützen*, and increasing the strength of the *Jäger*.

## Prussian Regiment of Feldjäger

Already before 1744 ad hoc small *Jäger* units did exist. When raised on 15 June 1744 – the Korps Feldjäger zu Fuß as it was named then, was two companies strong. The name translates as corps of field foot *Jäger*; there was also a small mounted unit, called Jäger zu Pferd.[3] From the beginning the *Jäger* were mainly recruited from gamekeepers by trade, or their sons. They already brought desirable skills into the service, usually good shots, knowing how to stalk game and to lay in ambush, and they were also loyal to the state, which employed them. So they hardly suffered from desertion compared to line infantry units. In contrast to the usual infantry the *Jäger* wore a green coat – a traditional colour of their profession. For a while the *Jäger* corps was four companies strong during the Seven Years War, but was reduced to two after the peace in 1763.

In 1773 Frederick the Great increased the *Jäger* to five companies and during the War of the Bavarian Succession (1778–1779) another was added. As of 1 January 1784, the King ordered the formation of a *Feld-Jäger* regiment and four additional companies were raised. In case hunters by trade could not fill the demand, the Prussians tried to recruit *Jäger* from Hesse Cassel, Hesse Hanau or Ansbach Bayreuth, who had served with great distinction for the British Crown in the American War of Independence.[4] After the Prussian state took over the regency of the former Margrave of Ansbach and Bayreuth in 1792 – in Franconia – they added another two *Jäger* companies from the former Ansbach–Bayreuther *Jäger*.

From 1795 until the beginning of the campaign of 1806 the Feldjäger-Regiment consisted of 12 companies, in three battalions of four companies each.

Since 1800 it had two commanders, the so-called *Chef* or proprietor – who was at least a colonel, and could be a general and a so called *Kommandeur* [commander] usually a *Major* or *Oberstlieutenant*. They would both go into the field and command the larger fractions of the regiment. In 1800 the *Chef* was

3 *Jäger*–literally hunter, singular der *Jäger*, plural die *Jäger*–so not the suffix of an s as often incorrectly used in English-language publications.

4 Carl Friedrich Gumtau, *Die Jäger und Schützen des Preußischen Heeres. Erster Theil. Was Sie waren–Ihre Geschichte* (Berlin: Mittler, 1834), p.70.

*Generallieutenant* von Voß and the *Kommandeur* was *Major* von Yorck, who previously was the chef of a *Füsilier* – light infantry – battalion.

In 1805 von Yorck – now *Oberst*, became *Chef* and *Major* von Witzleben *Kommandeur* – they both were leading the regiment in the fateful campaign of 1806.

The regiment was made up as following:

- 1 *Chef*
- 4 staff officers, one of them *Kommandeur.*
- 7 *Capitaines*
- 12 *Premierlieutenants*
- 24 *Secondelieutenants*
- 3 *Adjudanten*
- 36 *Waldhornisten* [wood hornists, French horn players]
- 120 NCOs
- 1,800 *Jäger*
- 1 regimental surgeon
- 12 company surgeons
- 1 regimental quartermaster
- 1 *Auditor* [a legally educated person for consultation in legal matters]
- 1 rifle maker
- 1 rifle stock maker
- 1 *Profos* [a helper of the military law – he would for example obtain the sticks for running the gauntlet, preserved the chains and locks of the prison rooms, and so forth.]

The allocation for the officers was however fluctuating and the exact officers' organization as well as names can be found in the *Ranglisten* which contain the names of officers of each regiment, structure, short histories, and so forth.[5]

## Armament

The original 60 *Jäger* raised at the start of the Silesian Wars were most likely armed with their own traditional hunting rifles and the *Hirschfänger* (hunting dagger: literally deer catcher, to finish off deer or other game, in case when it could not be shot or when wounded). Soon, however, when the *Jäger* were increased, Frederick the Great ordered 400 rifles to be produced. Though there exist no surviving originals it is most likely that they looked like traditional German

5 Anon. *Rangliste der Königlich Preußischen Armee für das Jahr 1806* (Berlin: Himburgsche Buchhandlung,undated), p.25

hunting rifles, octagon and swamped barrels (the shape of the barrel is not cylindrical but a bit conical at the both end), 7–8 fields and grooves, rear and front sights, large calibre of about 15–16mm, rather short of about 100–110cms overall length. The *Hirschfänger* at this time could not be fixed to the barrel. The *Jäger* rifle was, compared to the musket, an accurate firearm. Instead of being loaded with an issued paper cartridge with undersized ball, the *Jäger* had to pre-measure the powder charge, pour it down the barrel and then place the lead ball on top wrapped in a patch and press this tight-fitting projectile with a loading hammer into the barrel. Then usually a so-called starter of about 3 to 4 inches length was used to drive the projectile further down, and then finally with the ramrod (originally of wood – but in the military re placed by iron) the projectile was run down fully in the barrel to sit on the powder charge. Now the pan of the lock had to be primed, often with a very fine powder to produce a more instant flash, the lock closed and the rifle was ready to be fired. It was a time-consuming process – compared to the musket – but only by this laborious procedure could well aimed shots be achieved.

In the Seven Years War the *Jäger* were annihilated in October 1760: when serving as the rear guard and covering a bridge over the Havel river they were caught by Russian cavalry. Only 26 *Jäger* and some officers escaped. The *Jäger* were raised again one year later.[6] The impression was, that when on their own, without any support and attacked by cavalry the *Jäger* would need a side arm which could be fixed on the rifle. In 1773 the *Jäger* were armed with so called *Bajonettgewehre*. These were carbines with rifled barrel, round at the end, so bayonets could be fixed easily; most Grenadier NCOs carried such a rifled carbine in the Seven Years War. Though they had rifled barrels these guns were loaded with a paper cartridge and by that, though superior compared to the smooth bore musket, were inferior in accurate shooting compared to the *Jäger* rifle. Also, the lock and trigger mechanism was sturdier compared to the delicate *Jäger* rifle locks.[7]

The *Jäger* saw themselves as sharp shooters and regretted this re armament. However, as of 9 June 1779 Frederick the Great ordered that a quarter of the *Jäger* should be again armed with a rifle which had to be mainly loaded with patched balls. In 1787 the new king, Friedrich Wilhelm II, ordered that the Feldjäger-Regiment had to be again completely armed with rifles.

Though Kling stated that no such *Jäger* rifles survive, other than a single Ansbach-Bayreuth example,[8] recently one did surface. It has an overall length of 1005mm, barrel length of 624mm, calibre of 15mm and eight fields and grooves. The tip of the ramrod is made out of brass to preserve the fields and grooves when

6 Großer Generalstab, *Kriegsgeschichtliche Abteilung II, Der Siebenjährige Krieg, 1756 –1763* (Berlin: Mittler und Sohn, 1914) pp 257–258.

7 Constatin Kling, *Geschichte der Bekleidung, Bewaffnung und Ausrüstung des Königlich Preußischen Heers. Dritter Teil. Die leichte Infanterie oder Die Füsilier Bataillone 1787 . 1809 und Die Jäger 1744–1809*, (Weimar: Putze und Hölzer, 1912), p.73.

8 Kling, *Die leichte Infanterie*, caption to an illustration between pp.180 and 181.

loading, the trigger guard, a so-called pistol trigger guard. The trigger itself has a *Stechschloß* – two triggers, with the rear one – the real trigger – pre-triggered so that a slight touch of the front trigger is sufficient to shoot, by that achieving a smoother firing, without jerking the rifle when pulling the trigger. Most likely it is a *Wiener Stechschloß* where one could either pre-trigger or use directly the first trigger – which then has a heavier pull.

Already in 1784 it was considered to fix the *Hirschfänger* to the barrel and in 1796 a new *Jäger* rifle was introduced, which had a simpler lock, no pistol trigger guard any longer, and the *Hirschfänger* could be fixed at the right side of the barrel.[9] An original of the rifle is in the *Museum für Deutsche Geschichte* (formerly *Zeughaus* in Berlin). It has a simple lock, overall length of 1080mm, octagon barrel length of 688mm, calibre of 15 mm, seven fields and grooves, a front side of brass, a rear sight of iron with a flap (for different distances), the stock is made traditionally from walnut wood and the total weight is 3310g. Interestingly – this surviving item did not have the 'sledge' to fix the *Hirschfänger* at the right side of the barrel.[10]

The introduction of the new rifle was only gradually realised; it was a very expensive item and not mass produced. Also, originally the locks should have had the *Wiener Stechschloß* but both von Yorck and von Voß decided to go for the simpler lock system which was improved by a change proposed by von Voß to make the trigger pull easier. Von Yorck complained in 1801 that rifles still existed with the *Wiener Stechschloß* along with the 1796 rifle, with improved and ordinary lock. The change to enable fixing the *Hirschfänger* seemed to be completed then although von Yorck complained that to fix the 'sledge' by soldering damaged the barrels and decreased their accuracy. Von Yorck was discontented with the quality of the rifles which had suffered by wear and tear, and even demanded that the *Jäger* should have rifles for everyday use and should receive new ones just for war.[11]

In 1806 there could well be still a variety of rifles and in each company the moulds to cast the fitting balls were stored so that the *Jäger* could cast them on demand; each company took into the field also a chariot with ammunition, pulled by one horse.

In the Seven Years War and later the *Jäger* used their own *Hirschfänger*. In 1773 when the *Jäger* then were increased to five companies, side arms, so called 104 *Pallasche* were ordered (a straight bladed sword, in this context similar to the artillery *Pallasch*).[12] One cannot be sure if all *Jäger* received at this time a new standardised *Hirschfänger* as Gumtau postulates.

9 Heinrich Müller, *Das Heerwesen in Brandenburg und Preußen von 1640 bis 1806–Die Bewaffnung* (Berlin, Brandenburgisches Verlagshaus, 1991), p.100.

10 Müller, *Die Bewaffnung*, pp.100–101.

11 Kling, *Die leichte Infanterie*, p.74.

12 Gumtau, *Die Jäger*, p.51.

Frederick the Great wanted to abolish them in 1784 but when *Oberst* des Granges, then *Chef* of the *Jäger*, proposed that the *Hirschfänger* should be changed so as to be able to be fixed to the rifle, the King agreed. So already from 1784 onwards the Prussians started to convert existing *Hirschfänger* for allowing them to be fixed, as two original items show.[13]

When it was decided to arm all *Jäger* again with the rifle, more *Hirschfänger* were needed. This so-called M 1787 had still a sabre guard.[14] The overall length (the surviving originals differed) was about 71cm total length, blade length of about 59cm and blade with of about 3.1cm.[15] This old *Hirschfänger* is shown by Thieme in his magnificent picture manuscript of 1792.

1796 a new *Hirschfänger* was introduced; it had no sabre guard and could be fixed to the barrel. Still, existing suitable *Hirschfänger* had to be used as well.[16] Those new *Hirschfänger* were indeed produced – as a bill of 18 September 1801 shows, when the Jäger-Regiment was increased by 360 *Jäger* and 24 *Waldhornisten*.[17] This new model and was sometimes referred as *couteau* (French word for knife): existing originals show as usual always different dimensions, it was about 71cm long, length of blade about 57cm width about 3.3cm.[18]

This *Hirschfänger* of new fashion is well depicted in the excellent series of gouaches by Doepler who shows the *Jäger* in parade dress of 1806, the parrot green coat, the tricorne, the *Jäger* rifle as well as the *Hirschfänger*, all in great detail. There the *Jäger* had no tents and no coats, for field dress in 1805 originally green woollen overalls were introduced, soon replaced by grey ones, as the green ones stained the white woollen ones when worn over them. Both may be possible for 1806.

By and large the bulk of the *Jäger* would have been armed in 1806 with a rifle and a *Hirschfänger* of 1796 pattern.

Though the *Jäger* took part in all campaigns and gained wide experience in the so-called small war, it was usually up to the company commander to instruct his soldiers. This changed only in 1800 when von Yorck was appointed as commander for the regiment. He issued standing orders for the regiment.[19] He introduced drill ground exercise – *Jäger* had to undergo tactical manoeuvres as line infantry, and were much more disciplined than before. Still the traditional role of the *Jäger*, the need for speed covering terrain and being expert shots, was maintained; the local commander had to decide on the spot, due to his tactical aim, terrain and strength of the enemy – how to employ his soldiers, modern *Auftragstaktik*.

13 Bernd A. Windsheimer, *Me Fecit Potzdam* (Bissendorf: Biblio Verlag, 2001), pp 90–91, photos at p.333.

14 Windsheimer, *Me Fecit Potzdam*, pp.91–93

15 Windsheimer, *Me Fecit Potzdam*, pp.91-93, photos at pp.333–334

16 Kling, *Die leichte Infanterie*, p.160

17 Kling, *Die leichte Infanterie*, p.164

18 Windsheimer, *Me Fecit Potzdam*, pp.93–97, photos pp.334-335

19 Gumtau, *Die Jäger*, p.147.

This excellent print by Doepler shows the *Jäger* in parade dress of 1806; note the brighter green of the coat in contrast to the *Füsiliere*. The new *Hirschfänger* without hand guard is well depicted. (Anne S.K. Brown Collection)

> In all cases it is a fixed order, that the *Jäger* is not firing prematurely – instead shoots always with effect. Also it is permanently that two *Jäger* defend always each other – the rear and front man. Those two *Jäger* must regard themselves as a single body, therefore one protects the other, so when one has shoot and is without protection, the other has a loaded rifle and is in a state of defence.[20]

The *Jäger* were trained in skirmishing for the attack, for the advance, on the halt, in the retreat, how to reform quickly in the case of emergency. The aim was to occupy terrain like lightning. The skirmishing lines could be formed from a column as well as from a line, and usually the odd *Züge* advanced while to even ones followed as reserves. A *Zug* is sort of a platoon, a section of a company; plural *Züge*.[21]

Each year the companies of the regiment were united to perform drill and manoeuvres from 1 August to 16 September. From 1-16 August the companies drilled twice a day for the individual *Jäger*. From the 16th to the end of August the line evolutions were performed. From 1-16 September light infantry and field service were performed. The end of this regimental exercise was the autumn manoeuvre at Potsdam – all-arms field manoeuvres of parts of the Prussian Army.

As well as with the exercise for the regiment, the teaching and practicing of shooting was highly individual – up to the company commander – until the new commander von Witzleben issued such an instruction in 1805.[22]

All in all, the influence of von Yorck shaped the Feldjäger-Regiment into a highly-motivated unit which was able to fight efficiently as well as in single companies but also in battalion strength or even bigger, as the campaign of 1806 would prove. The strict disciplinarian von Yorck was not always popular with his men, as one eye witness observed in a rear-guard action in 1806, when von Yorck was riding between the skirmishing lines of his own men and that of the French.

> [O]ur colonel Yorck rode very slowly from the right to the left between our and the enemy's firing line, when he arrived at the end, I could hear very clearly, there I stood at the left flank: "*Jäger*, I did well know that the bullets of the enemy would not hit me, I was certain that I had enemies amongst you, who would send me a bullet now. Finally I see that you are strong brave men and from now on I consider you as my true children".[23]

The *Jäger* were mobilised during the autumn manoeuvre period in 1805. In 1806 four companies were attached to the so-called Main Army of the Duke of

20 Yorcks standing orders according to Gumtau, *Die Jäger*, p.148.

21 Gumtau, *Die Jäger*, pp 145–149.

22 Gumtau, *Die Jäger*, p.150.

23 Gumtau, *Die Jäger*, p.167.

Brunswick, along with them the *Chef* of the regiment, von Yorck. Four other companies belonged to the army of the left wing, the Prince von Hohenlohe, one of the was at Hof, a town now in Northern Bavaria, under *Generalmajor* von Tauentzien, two others with the advance guard of Prince Louis Ferdinand at Saalfeld, in Thuringia, on both banks of the river Saale, and another under *Oberst* von Boguslawsky at Neustadt near Schleiz in Thuringia. Three companies belonged to the corps of von Rüchel, two of them under the special order of *Generallieutenant* von Winning at the advanced position up to the Werra river. Those two companies united on the retreat with those of Yorck and stayed there; one company stayed with *Generalmajor* von Lecoq in Westphalia.

After some small unimportant clashes around Hof and the Saalburg a bigger one ensued on 9 October at Schleiz in which the *Jäger* company von Werner took part. They fought alongside the Füsilierbattalion von Rosen (No. 7), all Saxon *Schützen* (sharpshooters) and Hussars. Part of the *Jäger* defended a chapel and the chapel yard and held a superior number of attacking enemy at bay. The *Jäger* had 14 losses in dead and wounded.[24] That was the beginning of the fateful 1806 campaign. The *Jäger* took part in the battles of Jena and Auerstedt and then were mainly in the rear guard to cover the retreat, they had to undergo numerous clashes. Yorck had six *Jäger* companies and three *Füsilier* battalions under his command.

Despite the myth that the Prussian army collapsed like dust, again and again rear-guard actions were fought, like the celebrated action at Altenzaun (for more see later) – here Yorck and his *Jäger* along with three *Füsiler* battalions held his own against a French advance guard under the French *Maréchal* Soult.

In one of these clashes an anonymous eye witness provides interesting insight of how flexibly the *Jäger* fought.

> At the further retreat of our rear guard a clash ensued with all arm branches. The enemy advanced with columns of infantry with a mass of *Tirailleurs*, in the front of them and artillery. From Wahren [today spelt Waren or Müritz, a small town in Mecklenburg] along through the heath of *Nossentin* up to the town of *Nossentin* a fighting retreat was running. The *Jäger* resisted at first stubbornly in the forest.

Two very reliable eye witnesses may account here the way of the fighting. One reports:

> We *Jäger* were placed, as hidden as possible, in a skirmish line in the forest. After we stood here about one hour, enemy infantry approached, which wasn't aware of us, because we stood in trunk holes or behind tree trunks. We let them approach to about 50 paces [in the foot note, Gumtau doubts

24 Gumtau, *Die Jäger*, p.156.

> that the distance was so close but he did not want to change the figure of the witness – but he concludes that due to the account of the second eye witness the distance was very close.] and opened fire. Each of us had marked his man well and the enemy tumbled in great heaps. The survivors took flight and when we had finished loading, no Frenchman was any longer there. With a burning desire we wanted to fall upon the enemy, so that Yorck could restrain us only with the greatest effort to stop us pursuing. According to his order we stayed at our position and after no longer than half an hour the enemy advanced again in columns. This time we opened up at 150 paces and our bullets caused considerable gaps. The enemy also fired, but due to our good cover this did not do us any damage. Then he rushed at us with levelled bayonets. We let him approach to 30 paces, fired with great success and then fled as fast as possible about 400 paces. Here we took again position and received the enemy identically as in our former post. Now the French did not again rush at us with levelled bayonets, but fired continuously. This time we let them approach to about 120 paces, while all the way firing. Now we retreated slowly in the forest, which was favouring us as there was a lot of undergrowth. The *Jäger* knew how to use this advantageously. And several times individual *Jäger* were running up to 30 paces close to the enemy, marked their man and then retreated again, covered by the dense woods. At last Yorck forbade this strictly, which was necessary, because this act of daring did not always succeed and some *Jäger* had to suffer, after the French were aware of it. At the end of the forest we halted. There was continuous skirmishing with the enemy – who was in a distance of about 400 paces. After about an hour had passed a rapid retreat was signalled with bugles [bugle – also called half-moon, similar to a hunting bugle]. We had to cross a plain, till we arrived at an alley of willows which marked a cattle drift and there were ditches on both sides. Here we took position, in the ditch, behind the willows or single fence posts. The enemy arrived and a standing fire fight ensued at a distance of about 400 paces, where the French lost a lot of men.[25]

In the French Revolutionary Wars, the Prussians fought in that conflict from 1792–1795 the *Jäger* distinguished themselves already – amongst other things they even captured four guns. They kept up their quality and even improved it due to such commanders as von Yorck. Most of the original *Jäger* companies disintegrated during the retreat into East Prussia, but, when the war ended in 1807, 10 companies were already again in existence, created out of the survivors and other suitable manpower. When the so called New Prussian Army was formed in 1808-1809 two units were raised out of them, the Guard *Jäger* battalion and the East Prussian *Jäger* battalion, each of four companies.

25 Gumtau, *Die Jäger*, pp.165-166.

## The *Schützen*

The *Schützen*, also sometimes called *Scharfschützen* (literally translated shooter or sharp shooter; in later times the term *Schütze* was a rank of a private in the infantry), were introduced for the Prussian Army in 1787. Each infantry company of the grenadier, musketeer and *Füsiliere* had 10 *Schützen* each as well as a *Schützen* NCO. These were drawn together in each battalion and lead by a *Schützen* officer and as well as a *Flügelhorn* player to give the signals as with the *Jäger*. They were recruited from the best shots and were armed with the so called *Scharfschützengewehr*, a sort of rifled carbine.

In 1806 a musketeer battalion was five companies strong, a grenadier battalion and a *Füsilier* battalion four. The Prussian Guards had six companies per battalion..

However, there was the plan to increase the number of the *Schützen*. Already in 1803, *Generalmajor* von Pelet, *Chef* of Füsilierbattalion No. 14, a highly distinguished officer, took away the *Schützengewehre* from the 48 NCOs of his battalion – who hardly fired at all – and increased the numbers of his *Schützen* to 88. A cabinet order of 21 January 1804 also approved this increase also for the two other *Füsilier* of the Lower Silesian *Füsilier* Brigade: battalions, No. 13 Rabenau and No. 15 Rühle.[26] The Prussian King ordered that this increase should also be realised for the rest of all Prussian *Füsilier* battalions on 21 July 1806, shortly before the mobilisation.[27] There is some doubt if this order was realised for all *Füsilier* battalions for the campaign of 1806, though the war diary of Füsilierbattalion Boguslawsky (No. 22) referred on 12 October to all 88 *Schützen* of the battalion.[28] The author's opinion is that it is very likely that all *Füsilier* battalions took part in the campaign with the increased establishment of 88 *Schützen*.

Also, the Prussian Guard units in 1805 increased their 10 *Schützen* by adding 10 reserve *Schützen* to each company.

Thus, for the campaign of 1806 a Prussian musketeer battalion would field 50 *Schützen*, a grenadier battalion 40 *Schützen*, and a *Füsilier* battalion 88 *Schützen*. A Guard battalion, minus its wing companies which would form a grenadier battalion, would field 100.

The *Schützen* were to be trained like the *Jäger*. They provided also the pool for NCOs. This was viewed critically by some Prussian officers who lamented that it was not always the case that good shots would provide capable NCOs and that, on the other hand, if a highly trained marksman became an NCO he would hardly shoot at all – or, if in the line infantry, carry an NCO's pike instead of a long-arm.

26 Curt Jany, *Die Gefechtsausbildung der Preußischen Infanterie von 1806. Mit einer Anzahl von Gefechtsberichten* (Berlin: Mittler und Sohn, 1907), p.78.
27 Kling, *Die leichte Infanterie*, page 34, fn.3.
28 Jany, *Gefechtsausbildung*, p.78, fn.

The *Schützen* were armed with a so called *Scharfschützengewehr*, sometimes also called *Büchse*. In the Prussian army the majority of grenadier NCOs were already equipped since 1743 with a rifled carbine. It was built much sturdier than a *Jäger* rifle, had an ordinary lock, and the fields and grooves were not cut as deep as for the rifle. The *Scharfschützengewehr* was developed out of those rifled carbines. The rear third of the barrel was octagonal, the rest round, so a bayonet could be fixed. It had eight field and grooves, a frontal sight of brass and a rear sight which by flipping was adjusted for a shooting distance for 150 or 300 paces (one Prussian pace was 73.22 cm, so 109.93 m and 219.66 m respectively). The stock was varnished in black; the butt had a rest for the cheek, brass fittings. About 10,000 of them were produced.

Out of a total length of 1210mm the barrel length was 822mm, the bayonet blade was 34 cm, giving a total length of about 1.55m. The calibre was 18.5mm – a bit smaller than the usual infantry musket.[29] All those measurements are approximate and they could vary to some degree, as surviving originals show, since all items were hand made. The *Schützen* usually fired with infantry cartridges and these were carried in the usual cartridge box at the rear of the hip; only *Schützen* NCOs had a small belly box. The idea was that by that slightly smaller calibre the usual infantry ball had a tighter fit and that by banging down the ramrod the soft lead was pressed into the fields and by that caused a twist of the ball when the *Scharfschützengewehr* was fired.

By the order of 18 February 1790, a so called *Krückstock* (crutch) was introduced. It was made of hazel and had a forked end. It was fixed by a cord to the left side by a coat button on the lapel. When the *Schützen* had to advance or during manoeuvring it was detached and carried it in the hand. When they wanted to fire in kneeling position it was plunged in front of the body and served as rest. These sticks were still carried in the campaign of 1806 as an order book of the musketeer regiment von Wartensleben, (No. 59), shows.[30]

However, the *Schützen* of those battalions which were equipped with the so called *Nothardtschen Gewehr* received the best of those for their fire arms. This was a smoothbore musket which should have replaced to old M 1780/87; it had a rear and front sight, a much smaller calibre than the usual older muskets of 15.1mm, self-priming pan, cylindrical ramrod, length of 1,470mm, and a long bayonet which gave a total length of 2,157mm. In 1806 Grenadier Bataillon Garde (No. 6), Regiment Garde (No. 15), Regiment König (No. 18) and the Grenadierbataillon Rabiel were armed with this musket.[31]

29 Müller, *Die Bewaffnung*, p.97; Kling, *Die Leichte Infanterie*, p.158.

30 Kling, *Die Leichte Infanterie*, p.34.

31 Jany, *Gefechtsausbildung*, p.80 and p.102 appendix no. 15.

A copy of a contemporary print published in Kling, here Regiment No. 7 in 1790. The so-called crutch is depicted in action. (Collection of Markus Stein)

The *Schützen* wore the uniform of their respective regiments and had as distinction the black and white NCOs plume, or pompom for the *Füsiliere*, and the black and white NCO sabre strap and tassels on their side arm.

Each *Schütze* received 35 balls and cartridge per year for shooting practise. This was specified by the instruction of 12 December 1795. They had to shoot, without any restriction, at distances up to 300 paces, either standing, kneeling, laying down, with or without resting their gun, as well as loading in all stationary positions and when moving. They were also trained how to use the terrain and to judge distances. A special target was introduced, which could be elaborated even to the point of painting human silhouettes on it, and the results were recorded. This target was seven Prussian feet high (2.2 m) and three Prussian feet wide (0.94 m). It was divided in three longitudinal sections, a middle one with three circular targets and two side ones. A hit in the middle part was recorded as a good hit – at

Herbert Knötel shows Prussian Guard infantry in field dress. Despite Jany's statement, he still shows the *Schütze* (left) with the *Scharfschützengewehr* instead of the Nothardtschen musket as can be seen carried by the grenadier (right). The crossed lapels were of a new uniform still not introduced for the infantry in 1806; also, the light grey overalls are dubious as Kling shows more natural unbleached linen, as well as the buttons at the end of the overalls. The grenadier depicts tents pegs – carried by each man of the line infantry units, as well as a field axe which were carried – along with the water bottle – in 1806. (reproduced with kind permission of the *Deutsche Gesellschaft für Heereskunde*)

the side just a hit.[32] The results were recorded for each shooter taking part –. as a surviving shooting record of Regiment von Grevenitz (No. 57) shows that not only *Schützen* but also officers took part in firing at the target.[33]

The *Schützen* of each company were placed in the file closing ranks of the NCOs; a deployment to the front was therefore quite easy. However also there was the alternative, due to tactical demand, to form a *Schützen* platoon out of all *Schützen* of the battalion, which could act fairly independently or be detached for special tasks. If deployed in a skirmish line, they were placed in checker board fashion, two *Schützen* forming a pair like the *Jäger*. The second was placed behind the first one in the intervals at about two paces distance, the *Schützen* were about six to seven paces apart. The *Schützen* of such a pair, or the *Schützen* file, fired alternately, one guarding the other and usually only firing when the other had a loaded gun at the ready.

In case the battalion had to defend a position the *Schützen* were placed about 100 paces in front of the battalion to delay the enemy's advance and to cause disorder. In case a regiment or battalion had to advance against an enemy or a hostile position, they were again placed about 100 paces at the front – also to inflict casualties and to disrupt the enemy if possible. As their battalion closed into firing distance, they were to withdraw to the flanks, reform behind it or cover them. In case they had to skirmish against enemy cavalry they were not to be detached more than 25 or 30 paces.[34] Further duties were to cover the regiment at the march, to patrol, to be on out post duty, secure villages for woods, do reconnaissance.

The 1798 report of the Regiment Grevenitz (No. 57) gives detailed information about training. The new *Schützen* were trained six afternoons to get accustomed to the bugle signals, all *Schützen* were trained five days how to interact with the battalion, then again about the meaning of the signals, how to use the different rear sights of the *Scharfschützengewehr* and how to judge distances, how to occupy a village and conduct patrols, how to dislodge an enemy (portrayed for the purposes of the exercise by fellow Prussian soldiers) from a ravine, how to occupy a mill, how to assault villages, and how to make sorties also against enemy presentation including cavalry.[35]

The battle report of the Regiment Fürst von Hohenlohe, (No. 32) at Jena states:

> Close to the position which was now occupied by the regiment, was at the right side in front of us the widespread forest of Isserstedt, and

32 Jany, *Gefechtsausbildung*, p.81.

33 A.v. Taysen, *Die militärische Thätigkeit Friedrichs des Großen während seines Letzten Jahres* (Berlin: Mittler und Sohn, 1886), Appendix 3, p.131.

34 Jany, *Gefechtsausbildung*, p.82; Friedrich August Herzog von Braunschweig und Lüneburg, *Instruction für mein Regiment um dadurch die hauptsächlichen Vorschriften des Königl. Preuß. Reglements genau und exact befolgen zu können* (Berlin: Unknown Publisher, 1791), pp.238-239.

35 Taysen, *Militärische Thätigkeit*, Appendix 3, pp 132-135.

> at our left some other woods, which were strongly occupied by enemy *Voltigeurs*. From the smaller wood in front of us the enemy was dislodged by the *Schützen* of the regiment, only the forest of Isserstedt couldn't be completely cleared of the enemy because it reached right to his position… The *Schützen*, cheered on by their officers who commanded them, were able to withstand the enemy for a long time preventing him to advance, despite the enemy being covered in for them favourable terrain[36]

The Grenadierbattalion Hahn, which had 609 men in line including the *Schützen*, reported in the same battle: '*Lieutenant* von Zarski, who commanded the *Schützen* of my battalion, was sent against the nearby shrubs, I very soon noticed that he succumbed to the superior numbers. He didn't also return with the *Schützen* to the battalion'.[37] The Regiment Winning (No. 23) observes in the Battle of Jena:

> [T]he commander *Oberstlieutenant* von Rathenow in some instances stopped the regiment, aligned it and placed the *Schützen* in the intervals … the lines of the enemy advanced and sent to us light troops, we made 3 to 4 times front and fired, now our *Schützen* were lacking… [38]

*Capitain* von Boyen, who served in the staff of the Duke of Brunswick, witnessed at the Battle at Auerstedt:

> I detected this line, which mainly belonged to the division of *General* Schmettau, still in good battle order, however not advancing, but stationary, exchanging shoots by the drawn-forth *Schützen*, with the enemy who was positioned nearly always covered behind hedges and ditches. While I was riding close to the front in the direction to the left wing, I saw, approximately at the entrance of Hassenhausen, *Feldmarschall* Möllendorf, who in canter and in the reach of the fire of the enemy's *Tirailleurs*, calmly dressed the line.[39]

At the clash at Halle, after the battle of Jena, Regiment Treskow (No. 17) reported:

> At half past seven the regiment was together at the village Schwittersdorf and started its march to Halle. The *Schützen* of the first battalion formed the advance, those of the second, the rear guard… The regiment performed

36 Jany, *Gefechtsausbildung*, p.124.

37 Jany, *Gefechtsausbildung*, pp.126–127.

38 Jany, *Gefechtsausbildung*, p.131.

39 *Generalfeldmarschall* Hermann v. Boyen, *Denkwürdigkeiten und Erinnerungen, 1771–1813* (Stuttgart, Verlag von Robert Lutz, 1899), Vol.I, pp.158-159.

> their march to the village of Dölen at the right in front. When it arrived at the village it was halted and the regiment formed into sections, while *Lieutenant* von Wussow patrolled the village with his *Schützen*, and when he reported to the general, that there was no enemy, the regiment started to march… The enemy… sent during this time 100 to 200 *Voltigeurs* behind a wall of earth at a house, which was placed in front of the left wing of the 1st battalion, in about 800 to 900 paces distance. As soon as the retreat of the 1st battalion started, the *Voltigeurs*, who had been placed behind the earth wall, attacked; also an attack happened from the hedge, and some pieces of artillery, which the enemy had placed on an elevation, started to play. There our *Schützen* were too weak against those superior number of *Voltigeurs* and *Tirailleurs*, it happened that the general made an appeal at the regiment for volunteers to the front.[40]

At the defence at Lübeck, the after-action report of Regiment Owstien (No. 7) records:

> [T]o dislodge those and to support the *Schützen* of Regiments von Kunheim (No. 1) and von Tschammer (No. 27), our *Schützen* were sent up; these being under pressure, soon thereafter a whole company and then again another 100 volunteers were sent after… Still however he [the enemy] increased in numbers behind the hedges and houses and beat back our *Schützen* and then sent out supporting rank and file, who had to fall back onto the regiment.[41]

After 1807 the *Schützen* were abolished.

## The *Füsiliere*

In 1786 Frederick the Great ordered the raising of three light infantry regiments also called *Freiregimenter* – literally free regiments, in reminiscence of those formed in the Seven Years War – of 10 companies each. They were uniformed like those in the Seven Years War, blue coats and light blue facings. They were armed with captured Austrian muskets which were modified to Prussian standards, namely by employing the cylindrical ramrod. On 27 February 1787 his successor Friedrich Wilhelm II ordered an increase to correct the lack of light infantry calling for the formation on 1 June of 20 so-called *Füsilierbataillone*. They were formed out of the three existing light infantry regiments, five standing grenadier

40 Jany, *Gefechtsausbildung*, pp.134–135.
41 Jany, *Gefechtsausbildung*, p.139

battalions, the 3rd battalion of the Regiment Leipziger (No. 3) and selected companies from garrison regiments.

To name those light infantry battalions *Füsiliere* was a bit peculiar, because *Füsilier* regiments did exist already but were nothing else than line infantry regiments, carrying as distinction a fusilier mitre cap similar to the grenadier ones, in contrast to the musketeer regiments wearing the hat. Those original *Füsiliere* lost their name and cap and were classed like the old musketeer regiments simply as infantry regiments.

For the new units a new uniform colour was introduced, dark green in contrast to the blue of the line or the light green of the Jäger. Also, they received a specific drill regulation in 1788 – *Reglement für die Königl. Preuß. Leichte Infanterie.*

From 1795 onwards the number of the original 20 battalions was increased to eventually 24. They were usually brigaded together according to their geographical location. Finally, in 1800, groups of three battalions were formed into eight brigades, the most senior battalion commander of those was called a *Brigadier* – his rank could be a staff officer up to a general. He had more an administrative and inspecting function, though as seen by Pelet, if he chose to do so he very well could influence training and tactics. Some, like Pelet, took the initiative to introduce innovations – like the increase of the *Schützen* for his brigade to 88, which was finally introduced for all *Füsilier* battalions for the 1806 campaign. The battalions were more or less distributed individually to their allocated army in 1806, regardless of their administrative brigade structure.

The battalions were four companies strong and the *Füsiliere* kept this formation unchanged until 1807. Moreover, they were ranged only in two ranks, in contrast to the three of the line.

In 1806 the battalion strength was:

- 1 *Chef*
- 1 *Major*
- 4 *Captains*
- 1 Adjutant
- 12 Subaltern Officers
- 48 NCOs
- 4 surgeons
- 5 drummers, including one battalion drummer
- 1 *Auditeur*
- 1 Rifle and stock maker
- 8 buglers
- 88 *Schützen*
- 512 rank and file including the supernumeraries
- 8 carpenters

Altogether a battalion was 692 men strong.[42]

So, there were in each company two buglers and one drummer as well. The *Füsiliere*, like the grenadiers, had no colours. Initially the *Füsiliere* did not receive tents, but shortly after their raising a need for a reduced number of tents was acknowledged; however, for the 1806 campaign they were left in the depots. Originally a 3-pounder gun was attached to each battalion and the crew was provided from the artillery regiments. Those battalion guns did not prove of use for the *Füsilere* against Revolutionary France and consequently they were not taken into the field for the 1806 campaign.

Each battalion did, however, have:

- 5 bread and one staff waggon, 6 servants, 24 horses
- 1 ammunition wagon – 4 horses and 2 servants
- 2 servants for the two staff officers
- 4 servants and 8 horses for the tent blankets (these were carried into the field despite having no tents)
- 1 packhorse and 1 riding horse for the 4 captains -8 horses and 8 servants
- 30 horses for the 15 subaltern officers, 30 horses – 15 servants
- 2 horses and 1 servant for the Adjutant
- 1 horse and 1 servant for the battalion surgeon
- 1 horse and 1 servant for the Auditor

Each battalion should also have the suttler's wagon as well.[43]

The *Füsiliere* were designated to fight mainly in the woods, hill, villages, to form advance and rear guards, to protect the flanks, keep the opposing light troops at bay, but also to fight in close order. As already noted, the *Füsilere* formed only two ranks deep. A battalion would form for the firefight eight *Züge* or platoons (to complicate matters a company as such was formed in four *Züge*, which could be also used for manoeuvring).

As for skirmishing the regulation of 1788 provides following instruction:

> When that battalion should execute a swarm attack, while advancing, either when standing or during the advance, the designated signal by the battalion bugler will be given, which will be repeated by the buglers of the first and eighth platoon.
>
> Immediately when the signal is given, of one and all the first and eighth platoon, if not ordered otherwise, run 50 paces to the front and disperse, where it should be observed that although those dispersing people do

42 Jany, *Gefechtsausbildung*, p.26, Anon. *Reglement für die Königlich Preußische Leichte Infanterie* (Berlin: Decker, 1788), pp.2-4.

43 Jany, *Gefechtsausbildung*, pp.100–101.

> not have to observe so strict alignment as those in close order, they still have to maintain an approximate direction, for that the dispersing people should not come apart too far, and nobody has more than four to five paces to separate from his next man. This has to be observed especially in an attack in a wood, where all times everybody must see his next man and to be in alignment with him.
>
> As soon as the attacking platoons are in position they advance with strong steps and the supporting platoons follow in close order.
>
> To commence firing, the signal is given, where then the dispersed people will individually start firing, but keep always advancing and keep an eye on the next men, to keep an alignment. This individual fire in that manner lasts until the signal to cease fire is given and then anyone who fires one shot is to run the gauntlet.[44]

The regulation of 1788 – both for line and light infantry – were however modified during the coming years, especially by the instructions of 1 March 1798 by King Friedrich Wilhelm III, which was in handwriting only. It may be that it was printed for the Regiment Unruh (No. 45). It could be that it is in the British Library and transcriptions of it were translated and are still stored in Whitehall, where John Cook made a faithful copy. The author's opinion is that it is genuine as it echoes the statements by Jany.

To make the dispersal into skirmish order easier, the 1798 instructions observes this:

> The Fusilier Battalions being intended to act both as Regular Infantry in the day of action, and as Light Troops in the advanced posts, they will observe the Rules that have been laid down in the forcgoing instructions for the Regular Infantry, as far as they regard their duty in line.
>
> The elementary part of their regulations as Light Infantry will suffer no alteration, excepting in regard to Skirmishing with the flank Divisions, which is in every respect defective.
>
> First the men run themselves out of breath before they can cover the front: secondly it is very embarrassing for the Commanding Officer who cannot commence platoon firing, until his front is cleared; and lastly the men are blown before they can again reach their posts, by which means the Flanks are deprived of the necessary defence, and are left exposed to the attack of the smallest body of Cavalry.
>
> For these reasons the Divisions will henceforth remain to protect the Flanks, unless circumstances require their being otherwise employed, and in lieu of them, a Section from each Platoon will be sent forward to

44 Anon. *Reglement Leichte Infanterie*, pp.44-45.

> skirmish; and the intervals will be left open for them, thus all these inconveniences will be done away and the front of the Battalion more quickly covered, and more quickly cleared.[45]

This needs some commentary. Originally the flank platoons would swarm out – they had to run a bit to cover the front of the battalion. In 1798 now each section of a platoon, and according to the regulations it was four or five files,[46] could deploy to the front more rapidly.

The signals for skirmishing and how to manoeuvre were usually given by signals, the buglers had so called *Waldhörner*, or *Flügelhörner* (French bugle, or hunting bugles, like the *Jäger* and *Schützen*), also sometimes called half-moons due to their shape.

Initially it was up to the battalion commander to introduce those signals – the Battalion Boguslawsky (No. 22) should have had 70. By the order of 18 June 1801 20 identical signals were introduced for the light infantry.[47]

In the field the usual step was 108 paces a minute which had been gradually introduced during the Seven Years War.

In close order firing the Prussian Army performed a radical change to the dogma of the Seven Years War, when the fire at will, where each soldier would fire and load as quick as he could without waiting for any order, was frowned upon. The regulations of 1788 still had formal firing by platoons, where half of the platoons fired, and when finished loading, the other platoons would fire and so on. The art of firing was revised by Rüchel. An instruction of 6 January 1801 improved the use of sharp cartridges (that is lead ball and powder charge, in contrast to blind ones, which would contain powder only), to prevent the too much hurrying at loading, where cartridges often broke, and also by firing. The soldier no longer brought down the musket after having fired in great haste, but remained in the 'present' position until the command to load was given. By this it was hoped to prevent high air shots. Still the Prussian infantry preserved their dominance of fast firing compared to other nations, due to the conical touch hole which enabled a self-priming pan and the cylindrical ramrod, which did not have to be wielded like the conical ones of the British or French muskets. While the Prussians were firing three times, the Austrians would do twice and the French only once.[48]

The so called *Bataillenfeuer* (battle fire) – as the fire-at-will was fittingly called – was now drilled and exercised. Only the opening of the fire was still under tight control of the officers, the instruction says:

45 Friedrich Wilhelm III, *Instruktion für die Infanterie vom 11. März 1798*, transcription, Whitehall, p.45.

46 Anon., *Reglement leichte Infanterie*, pp.81-82.

47 Jany, *Geschichte*, Vol.III, p.493.

48 Jany, *Geschichte*, Vol.III, p.490.

> Are the lads to be drilled for the so called *Bataillenfeuer*, it will be performed as following. The battalion commander at first command : 'Fire by rank ! – Commence firing !' … Battalion at the ready ! The first rank present ! Fire!' When the first rank finished loading, the same commands for the second rank 'Present !' Fire !' Then when the second rank had loaded each lad of the two front ranks [this is also for the line regiments, of three ranks, the third rank would not fire any longer] would fire for individually without waiting for a command, as long as a long roll call of the drummers provides the signal for stopping the firing. The men have to be made aware to support each other in turns (which has to be explained to the men well), that the man of the second ranks is not firing before the front man of the first rank has not finished loading, and the man of the first ranks, waits till the rear man of the second rank has finished before he fires again.[49]

This kind of fire should have been the predominant kind in 1806, but infantry would still fire by battalion or platoon as well, according to the commander. While battalion volleys were used against infantry, platoon fire was used in squares against cavalry thereby always maintaining a firing reserve.

The original three light infantry regiments raised in 1786 were armed with captured Austrian muskets, which proved to be unsatisfactory. So, when the *Füsilier* battalions were raised they received their own *Füsilier* musket and their the *Schützen* the *Scharfschützengewehr*. The *Füsilier* musket was almost identical with the Prussian Modell M 1780/87 for the line infantry, with the exception that it was shorter by about 12cm. Total length was 1330mm, length of barrel 930mm, the calibre was 19.4mm. It had a brass front sight no rear side; in the tang screw a line should have been filed. It had a conical touch hole and an oblique tang screw as well as a cylindrical ramrod. The shorter musket was introduced due to the fact that the *Füsiliere* should be recruited from smaller men compared to the line regiments. The blade length of the bayonet was 36cm, total length 44cm.

Those two constructions, the cylindrical ramrod and self-priming pan, as for the muskets of the line infantry as well, made loading easier and quicker. After firing the soldiers would close the pan then bring the musket to his left side standing, then he would take a cartridge from the box, tear it open with the teeth, pour the powder into the barrel and then push the lead ball, still in the paper wrapping, into the barrel. Now he would draw the ramrod and insert it without wielding, as for conical ramrods, into the barrel and push the ball down to the end of the barrel by a stroke, due to the conical touch hole this would force some powder directly into the closed pan, after that he would bring the ramrod back into the musket stock, again no wielding necessary. As the ramrod did not have to be wielded it was much

49 Jany, *Gefechtsausbildung*, p.55.

easier to avoid hitting the next men and easier to maintain close order. Due to the fact that by the fairly large touch hole a strong flame jetted out and would hit the right-hand neighbour, a so-called flash guard was introduced in 1790 to block the flames.

To enable better aiming the stock had a curved butt neck; the butt had also a cheek rest. A lot of muskets of the line units had still a straight butt neck, which made aiming very difficult but which should gradually be replaced with the curved one as well. The wood was varnished black for the *Füsiliere.*

A lead ball had a weight of 27.5g and a diameter of 16.7mm – providing quite a big windage compared to the musket calibre, as one has still to account the paper wrapping. By that loading was made easier there the cartridge, which contained 14.6 g of powder, would plunge easier into the barrel. The *Füsilier* carried 60 cartridges in his box.

In contrast to the sabre of the line infantry the *Füsiliere* received a so called *Faschinenmesser*, it had a straight blade which was 46cm long and looks similar to a machete. It was carried in a brown scabbard.[50]

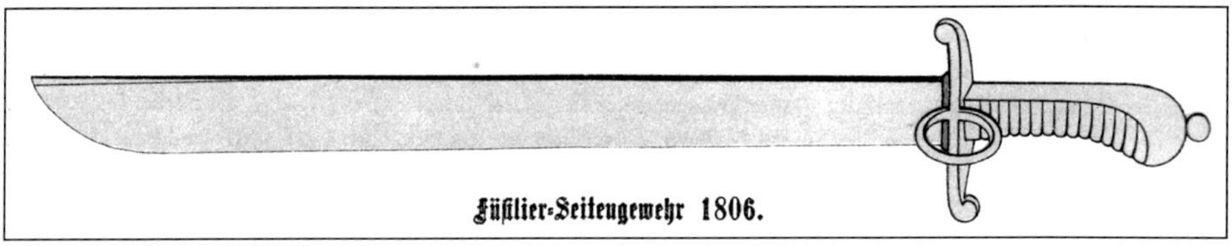


*Faschinenmesser* by Kling. (collection of Markus Stein)

At the end of the reign of Frederick the Great a fast pace of 108 paces per minute came into use, officially sanctioned in the regulations of 1788, it was in general use in 1806.[51]

Already in 1786 it was eventually decided that the light infantry regiments should be clad in green cloth – but this was only realised in 1787 when the *Füsilier* battalions were introduced. In contrast to the bright greenfinch green of the *Jäger* it was dark. From 1801 the shako was introduced as headgear, while the officers retained the hat. The shako was made of black felt and had, with the exception of the visor, no leathern reinforcements. It had an almost cylindrical shape and was only slightly wider in diameter at the top. Around the lower rim was a black woollen lace and around the top a white one. For adornment there was the small flying eagle according to button colour and a pompom either of white, red, or yellow to distinguish the battalions in a brigade.[52] By different facing und button colours, as

50 Kling, *Die leichte Infanterie*, pp.8, 23, Windsheimer, *Me Fecit Potzdam*, pp.30–31, photo at pp.282-283
51 Jany, *Gefechtsausbildung*, p.56.
52 Kling, *Die leichte Infanterie*, p.18.

Another excellent print of Doepler showing the *Füsiliere* in parade dress of 1806. Note the darker green coat in comparison to the *Jäger*, the shorter *Füsilier* musket with red musket sling as for all Prussian infantry regiments, and the red lining of the officers turnbacks. The unit shown is the Füsilierbataillon Borell de Vernay (No. 9). (Anne S.K. Brown Collection)

well as the different pompom colours, the battalions could be distinguished from each other. The officers' coat had long coat tails and red turnbacks.

It is usual a bit of confusion about the allocated numbers for the battalions, while those were given for the *Stammlisten*, they were not allocated in the *Ranglisten*. As said before, three battalions were grouped into an inspection – indicating the location of the garrison. The oldest battalion, the one commanded by the longest-serving commanding officer in that brigade, was usually listed as first and so on. The battalion numbers in brackets are given as in the *Stammlisten*. The pompom colour of the shako creates a bit of confusion – every contemporary picture manuscript shows it differently. Here, Kling has been followed. The spelling of the names is from the *Rangliste* of 1806.

Magdeburg *Füsilierbrigade*
Crimson facings with brass buttons
*Brigadier*: *Generalmajor* von Bila
Bila (No. 7) – white pompom
Graf Wedel (No. 5) – yellow pompom
Kaiserlingk (No. 1) – red pompom

Westphalian *Füsilierbrigade*
Crimson facings with white metal buttons
Brigadier: *Generalmajor* von Ernest
Ernest (No. 19) – white pompom
Ivernois (No. 21) – yellow pompom
Sobbe (No. 18) – red pompom

First East Prussian *Füsilierbrigade*
Light green facings with brass buttons
*Brigadier*: *Generalmajor* von Rembow
Rembow (No. 6) – white pompom
Wakenitz (No. 3) – yellow pompom
Bergen (No. 11) – red pompom

Second East Prussian *Füsilierbrigade*
Light green facings with white metal buttons
*Brigadier*: *Oberst* von Stutterheim
Stutterheim (No. 21) – white pompom
Bülow (No. 24) – yellow pompom
Schachtmeyer (No. 23) – red pompom

First Warsaw *Füsilierbrigade*
Light blue facings with white metal buttons
*Brigadier*: *Generalmajor* von Hinrichs

Hinrichs (No. 17) – white pompom
Borell du Vernay (No. 9) – red pompom
Knorr (No. 12) – yellow pompom

Second Warsaw *Füsilierbrigade*
Light blue facings with brass buttons
*Brigadier*: *Generalmajor* von Oswald
Oswald (No. 16) – yellow pompom
Greiffenberg (No. 4) – red pompom
Kloch (No. 8) – white pompom

Upper Silesian *Füsilierbrigade*
Black facings with brass buttons
*Brigadier*: *Oberst* von Erichsen
Erichsen (No. 10) – white pompom
Rosen (No. 7) – red pompom
Boguslawsky (No. 22) – yellow pompom

Lower Silesian *Füsilierbragde*
Black facings with white metal buttons
*Brigadier*: *Generalmajor* von Pelet
Pelet (No. 14) – white pompom
Rühle (No. 15) – red pompom
Rabenau (No. 13) – yellow pompom[53]

The equipment belts became black in 1797; the musket sling remained red. In 1805 the whole of the Prussian infantry, including foot artillery but with the exception of the *Jäger* (see above), received for the campaign unbleached ticking overalls worn over the white woollen trousers and short gaiters. The *Füsilier* officers wore either green or grey long trousers with a row of small buttons at the side.

The neck stock was black, with the exception of Pelet (No. 14) which was rewarded with a red one for good conduct in the Polish campaign and was allowed to beat the grenadier march; the officers kept the black neck stock. According to Jany, in contrast to Kling, the battalions of both Silesian brigades should have received red neck stocks as well.[54] It has not been possible to verify this by cross checking with contemporary pictures, only Franke shows the complete Lower Silesian Brigade with red neck stocks, as well as Füsilierbataillon Rosen (No. 7) of the Upper Silesian Brigade and strangely also Füsilierbataillon Kloch (No. 8) of the

53 Anon., *Rangliste 1806*, pp.95–105, Kling, *Die leichte Infanterie*, pp 8-9.
54 Jany, *Geschichte*, Vol.III, p.481.

Füsilierbataillon Borrel du Vernay, in campaign dress showing bread bag and calfskin pack. In the rear view is also shown a water bottle (not carried by every soldier); the short queue of 1806 is well depicted, as well as the wide cartridge pouch belt. Kling. (Collection of Markus Stein)

2nd Warsaw Brigade, and by error shows all battalions of the 2nd Warsaw Brigade with black instead of light blue, facings.[55]

In the field a calfskin hip pack – along with a bread bag of natural linen – was worn quite high on the left side of the body. Every fourth to fifth man carried a big water canteen to supply his comrades as well. Already in 1805 the bayonet scabbard was left in the depot.

It is difficult to find battle field reports of Füsilier battalions, but Wilhelm Doering provides some fascinating details in his memoires. He entered the Füsilierbataillon von Boguslawsky (No. 22) as a *Junker* (an officer candidate equipped and doing duty as an NCO).

> There was not a lot of drilling in the companies, because the usual time for exercise was over when I joined the battalion. During a week the battalion exercised about twice – at the most three times. Field service did not happen at all and only the *Schützen* fired at the target. And still the Battalion von Boguslawsky was regarded as the best *Füsilier* battalion in Silesia and had a good reputation in the whole Prussian Army. The reason may have been most likely due to the fact of exercising according to the signals of the *Flügelhorn* was most sophisticated. The colonel had achieved it so far that one or another time he marched out with the battalion, exercised for hours and marched back into town without commanding himself directly. Generally there existed for the all *Füsilier* battalions only few specific ones, I believe only, advancing, retreating, halt, commence firing, stop firing. It was up to the battalion commander to add others – who altogether had a quite independent position... We had a lot of signals... Every signal was identical for all four companies.[56]

Then later, in the days of the 1806 campaign, he gives following accounts:

> It was a beautiful, even hot day; I had placed, to be able to march lightly, my woollen trousers and the waistcoat into the valise, which was on the baggage wagon. I had over the shirt only the rather worn tunic, closed at the front by hooks and eyes and made of military wool, and riding trousers – I did wear such as the officers that is green with a piping of black [facing colour of the battalion] velvet on the side, to be buttoned lengthwise on the sides – over linen underwear.[57]

55 Ludw. Ehrenfr. Franke, *Vorstellung der Koeniglich Preussischen Armee*, 1803, original in Berliner Staatsbibliothek.

56 Wilhelm von Doering, *Erinnerungen aus meinem Leben 1791–1810* (Osnabrück: Biblio Verlag, 1975), pp.31–32.

57 Doering, *Erinnerungen*, pp.47–48.

After first encounters of the advance guards with the French after he met soldiers who had been fighting the French:

> The lads did talk a lot about the dangerous situation they had encountered and survived, about great losses they had suffered and about the bravery of the French. This made a depressing impression on our battalion… At the morning of the 10th [of October] the battalion left the bivouac…
>
> We heard a lively and for hours lasting artillery fire to which we paid exited attention…
>
> Finally we bivouacked, and it was announced that the bread wagons and as well food would arrive shortly… however no wagons appeared. At last the 14th of October [the day of the battle of Jena] was there. An immense fog concealed everything, nevertheless there was already a lot of firing, still however at a great distance from us.…
>
> Our position was such like that we had behind of the very close main road from Jena to Weimar a line of *Schützen* and *Jäger* in front of us. The more the fog was lifting the stronger the firing became. We could recognise steady firing by platoons. The colonel observed the battle, a telescope in front of his eyes, and we along with him, in highest excitement. There were moments in which we regarded it very advantageously for us, and complained, also especially myself, that we probably would not have the opportunity to take part in the victory, there close to us with the Saxons it was still rather quiet. This delusion came soon to an end. It may have been around noon, when even the most predisposed had to concede that the situation had changed to our disadvantage… We still remained spectators.
>
> Along with the Saxons a part of our *Jäger* and *Schützen* was in a fight against the enemy *Tirailleurs* but we also heard battalion volleys. Later we saw units from Weimar advancing to the direction of Capellendorf. It was Rüchel's corps which approached in full haste…
>
> The fight at the Schnecke [a terrain feature of the battle field, where a lot of Saxon troops were placed] became very lively. We took our guns in our hands, a Saxon adjutant handed over the order to advance.… Hardly we were in the act of advancing, the main road to our left, when a lot of Saxons in full flight from the Schnecke came against us, they threw away their guns and some also their haversacks. Now we came into cannon fire. The balls mainly went above us, and I noticed that the *Füsiliere* stooped.
>
> During our short advance Saxon units retreated in full order with music playing and drums beating, at the other side of the main road. Gradually the music and the drums diminished, and the whole mass, partially throwing away their guns, started to run. Now for us the command was shouted: '*En eventail, rechts marschiert auf!*' [to deploy in fan like fashion to the right]. Along with my platoon I still hadn't reached the alignment, when the command: '*Formiert das Carre*!' [form square] was given. I

> still commanded for my platoon '*Kehrt*' [turn about-face] and '*Marsch*' [march]. There I heard the rattling of guns and a whole wave of Saxon infantry threw themselves onto us and I was pressed to the ground...
>
> When I had overcome my momentary bedazzlement, the attack of the enemy, as well as the swarm of fugitives, in which, with few exceptions, also our battalion was involved, had passed by at the other side of the main road. After all that, I didn't unbelievably consider being captured, I saw only white clads [Saxon Infantry] and French cavalry which surrounded the mass...
>
> Only now I noticed a burning pain at my right leg... Meanwhile also French infantry approached and one could not think any longer of escaping...
>
> Now also at the main road a lot of captured Prussians became evident, amongst them also soldiers of the battalion.[58]

The experience of Doering had to be seen in context, as he could only speak of his experience in his battalion. As he correctly observes, the battalion commanders were fairly independent and training could be to some extend different on other battalions. Doering also joined when the annual exercise time was over, held in spring and autumn; here complete field manoeuvres of all arms took place and usually the light infantry received a higher allowance of blanks than the line. For example, on 30 September 1800 the Füsilierbrigade Pelet granted instead of the annual 11 hundredweight of powder for each battalion only nine, and, in place of the remaining two, lead to cast balls so that the usual *Füsiliere* could also be trained to shoot at the target.[59] Also, usually, good officers were allocated, who led Free Corps, or had experience in the American War of Independence, like Gneisenau, and good officers emerged out of them corps commanders of reputation in the campaigns of 1813 to 1815, like Yorck or Bülow, and other such as Müffling, Krauseneck, Thümen, and Dörnberg.

At the reformation of 1808, the *Füsiliere* ceased to exist any longer as independent battalions, but became the third battalion of a line infantry regiment, the other two battalions being musketeers.

## The 3rd Rank and Volunteers

Prince August of Prussia commented in 1807 that the lack of light troops, when they were needed, proved that it was essential to use the third rank as skirmishers.[60]

58 Doering, *Erinnerungen*, pp.50-51, 55-56, 56-59.

59 Jany, *Geschichte*, Vol.III, p.492.

60 Jany, *Gefechtsausbildung*, p.84.

In the later days of Frederick the Great, the Prussian infantry was accustomed to manoeuvre in two ranks only, especially to maintain the usual frontage width when the numbers were short. The Duke of Brunswick, in his instructions for his regiment addresses the third rank.[61] The third rank was used also to form reserve platoons, to cover the flanks or to form a tactical reserve, most likely influenced by the Austrians who did the same when fighting Revolutionary France.

During the Revolutionary Wars, when *Jäger*, *Füsiliere*, or *Schützen* were absent, or too weak, usually volunteers are called to either reinforce the skirmishers or to even form a provisional skirmish line. There is no evidence that the third rank was used as skirmishers.[62] However, on 30 March 1803 a regulation about how to use the third rank as skirmishers was issued by Hohenlohe, of Jena and Prenzlau fame, for the regiments of his Lower Silesian Inspection – Regiments Hohenlohe (No. 32), vac. Grevenitz (No. 57), Treuenfels (No. 29), Strachwitz (No. 43) and Schimonsky (No. 40). He realised that in war it often happened to be advantageous to attack the enemy in skirmish fashion, or to defend oneself against them. This would be the task of the light infantry but in case of absence, or when the own skirmishers were too few; the third rank could be used for this tactical role.

> A, at a signal, for which the at the highest cabinets order of the 18th of June 1801 signal No.5 designated for deploying into skirmish order, could be used, the 3rd rank is drawn forward.
>
> B, the first half of the 3rd rank of each *Zug* (it is assumed that a *Zug* has 18 files) turns right about, the 2nd half left about…
>
> C, the 3rd rank runs forward in such fashion (the lads slope their musket over their shoulder, and grip the cartridge box in the right hand), that the first half runs around the right wind, the second half around the left.[63]

Then about 30 paces in front of the line a skirmish line in chequer board way was formed, the gap one and a half paces and the rear rank three paces behind the first in the interval.[64] Otherwise these skirmishers were to follow the usual practise as described above for the *Schützen*.

It is a great tragedy that those regiments had to realise in 1806 what was neglected in training. Seemingly this order was regarded more or less as a recommendation. There is no evidence that those regiments did use the third rank as skirmishers. However, Ciriacy, who was a *Fähnrich* (NCO officer-candidate, already allowed to wear the officers' sabre strap) in Regiment Zweiffel stated:

61 Braunschweig, *Instruktion 1791*, pp 180-187.

62 Jany, *Gefechtsausbildung*, p.87.

63 Jany, *Gefechtsausbildung*, p.90.

64 Jany, *Gefechtsausbildung*, p.90.

> Of great influence could have been the decree of the year 1806 about the use of the 3rd rank for skirmishing, if there could have been sufficient time to comprehend the true spirit of it and to practise it. The start of the war prevented this. Only few regiments made use at the battle of the Saale of their third rank. Amongst those was namely the Regiment Zweiffel, which was composed mostly of *Einländer* [that is local national Prussians] (Bayreuther).[65]

He also stated that in 1806 a first regulation was issued for the use of the third rank for skirmishing. Jany doubts that – because he could nowhere find any such regulation. To reduce infantry to two ranks was however practised; Rüchel formed his infantry in two ranks, and created out of two-battalion regiments of three ranks, three-battalion regiments of two ranks, two with three companies each and one with fourcompanies.

As can already be seen in the battle reports given above for the *Schützen*, volunteers from musketeer companies or musketeer companies were used to some extent by various regiments. To add a battle report of Infantry Regiment Winning (No. 23) at the Battle of Jena in Rüchel's corps: 'now our *Schützen* were missing, *Oberstlieutenant* v. Hallmann ordered *Premierlieutenant* v. Wobeser, to cover the retreat with the company, this happened as well as the musketeers could do it, *à la débande* [in skirmish order, dispersed]'.[66]

## Conclusion

The Prussian Army of 1806 had the following field battalions:

- 4 Guard Battalions of 6 companies each (in war the wing company of each battalion was used to form a wing company battalion, so there were four Guard battalions of five companies and one wing battalion of four companies in 1806.
- 28 Grenadier battalions of four companies each.
- 112 musketeer battalions of five companies each.
- 24 battalions of *Füsiliere* – light infantry of four companies each.
- 1 Feldjäger-Regiment of three battalions of four companies each.

65 F.v. Ciriacy, *Chronologische Übersicht der Geschichte des Preußischen Heeres* (Berlin and Posen: Mittler, 1820), p.449.

66 Jany, *Gefechtsformen*, p.131.

Out of 171 battalions, 27 consisted of light infantry; one then has to add the *Schützen* of the line infantry and grenadiers, providing another 7,200 men, all trained and specially armed for light infantry duties.

The most popular view in Anglo-Saxon literature was shaped by Petre:

> When in 1806, the precise linear tactics of Frederick came into contact with the more mobile system of the French, they failed absolutely. The Prussians to some extend employed light troops as skirmishers, but they were rarely strong enough to hold back the clouds of skirmishers, constantly relieved and supported by small hand columns, which formed Napoleon's fighting line. Again and again it was proved how impossible it was to carry out, under the fire of skirmishers adept in the art of utilising cover, the solemn deployment and preparation of Frederick's days. The men, incessantly harassed by fire which they could not return with effect during their deployment were already half defeated before they were ready to fight.[67]

Pascal Bressonnet, a French officer employed in the historical section of the French General Staff, comes to an almost completely different view in his tactical study about the battles at Saalfeld, Jena and Auerstedt. Not only did the Prussians fight tenaciously, but also the tactics on the battle field were not that different:

> At Saalfeld, at Auerstedt, and at Jena the French carried the victory. However despite being commanded by men like Lannes, Davout and Napoléon, and even at Jena with superior numbers, this victory was gained other than by a fierce struggle.
>
> The proof of this fierceness is to be found firstly by the numbers of casualties sustained by the *Grande Armée*. Suchet's division for example, suffered on the 14th of October a third of its effective strength as casualties… Finally Davout's corps was reduced by a third at the evening of the same day. Also, secondly, by the length of this struggle; lasting about 10 hours, at Auerstedt and at Jena…
>
> Almost all military historians commit the error to conclude that there existed a big difference in tactics between the French and the Prussians, and saying that the first ones used the *ordre profond* which consisted of columns preceded by *Tirailleurs*. Whilst the second ones still used the linear order.
>
> In reality, study of Saalfeld, Jena and Auerstedt, shows that the French did not use columns other than as formation for preparing the fight and for manoeuvring at the battle field outside of the reach of cannon shot.

67 F. Loraine Petre, *Napoleon's Conquest of Prussia 1806* (London, The Bodley Head 1907), p.22.

> Under artillery fire the columns deployed. Later they deployed when entering the range of the infantry fire, and the fight at the front, in the three battles, shows uniformly the aspect of two lines of battalions, more or less supported by reserves, deployed in musket range and firing at each other for hours.[68]

Bressonnet insisted that the elementary tactics of both armies were not absolutely different but also not identical.

Looking at the light infantry, Jany concludes:

> Also the use of the *Füsilier* battalions did not happen in close interacting with the "heavy" infantry…
>
> The *Füsiliere* very well showed in the Revolutionary Wars as well as in 1806 and 1807, that they were, when engaged, at par with their adversaries, but their more or less weak number and an unlucky distribution meant that not only the light infantry which was available in the army, was missing in the deciding battles for the most part, but also that the *Schützen* were taken off very often, to use those instead of the missing light infantry.[69]

When one is looking at the battlefield reports quoted in this chapter, the absence of the *Schützen*, or their low numbers, is running like a red thread through many reports.

In essence, though having well drilled, well-armed units well versed in the art of the small war, according to eighteenth-century doctrine, the link – the support of skirmishers interacting with their formed units – at the battlefield was at best still in its infancy. Bressonnet devotes several pages in this work to elaborate on this and comparing the French with the Prussian way.[70] He bases his conclusion on the work of Marbot who classes the *tirailleurs* or skirmishers in three classes, the *tirailleurs du marche*, the *tirailleurs de combat* and the *tirailleurs en grande bande*. The *tirailleurs de marche* and *combat* form the light infantry of their parent unit, they protect it during the march but also play a vital part at the battle field, where they shield the proper line and harass the enemy. The *tirailleurs en grande bande*, are nothing else than big units of skirmishers, a battalion and more. At the Battle of Hanau in 1813 supposedly they numbered 5,000 in the woods, and they were also often employed in the French Revolutionary Wars.[71]

68 Pascal Bressonnet, *Études Tactiques sur la Campagne de 1806 (Saalfeld–Iéna–Auerstedt)* (Paris: Libraire Militaire Chapelot, 1909), pp.362, 378.

69 Jany, *Gefechtsausbildung*, p.83.

70 Bressonnet, *Études* Tactiques, pp.369-377.

71 Colonel Marcellin Marbot, *Remarques Critiques sur l'Ouvrage de M. le Lieutenant-Général Rogniat, intitulé : Considérations sur l'Art de la Guerre* (Paris: Anselin et Pochard, 1820), pp.59-66.

The French skirmishers opened fire at quite large distances, Here the observations of the artillery officer von Hiller who commanded the regimental artillery of the Saxon Regiment Churfürst, at the clash at Saalfeld:

> To close a big gap between the Regiments Churfürst and Xavier, the Regiment Churfürst was drawing itself to the right, by that as also in the advance we were always under fire from light infantry. They wounded my men at a distance of 7 to 800 paces, were placed behind hedges and fences, where I could not do any harm with grape shots, which I tried to use with high elevation but did not feel the slightest effect.[72]

Borcke, who was an officer in Rüchel's corps, writes about the same topic at the Battle of Jena at Kapellendorf:

> However [before that he noticed that the enemy artillery was overshooting them] the bullets of enemy *Tirailleurs* reached us from a very great distance, who were placed with advantage in the field bushes and single cover before us, so that we could not see them, that for us in our ignorance it seemed that the bullets came out of the air. To be under such a fire, without seeing the enemy made a bad impression at our soldiers, because, ignorant with that kind of fighting, they lost trust in their own guns and felt immediately the superiority of the enemy. The suffered quickly therefore, in this by all means bad situation in courage, endurance and composure and could not wait for the time to also start shooting, which soon showed to be of our disadvantage.[73]

On the other hand, at the Battle of Auerstedt *Secondelieutenant* von Eberstein of the Regiment Graf Wartensleben (No. 59) states: 'By the fire of the enemy's *Tirailleurs* the 1st battalion of our regiment hardly lost 20 men, there on the other hand amongst them quite a defeat was inflicted by the grape shot of our battalion pieces, which we saw by their dead, when we advanced over their corpses'.[74] Even when the French skirmishers came very close it did not necessarily cause panic or withdrawal, as with this observation from the Grenadierbattalion Hahn: 'The *Tirailleurs* became so audacious, that is was possible that the NCO Steinert of the company of *Capitain* von Grumblow to capture one of them with his NCO's pike'.[75]

72 Jörg Titze, *Die Berichte der sächsischen Truppen aus dem Feldzug 1806 (I) Brigade Bevilaqua* (Norderstedt: Books on Demand gmbh, 2014), p.95.

73 Johann Friedrich Ernst von Borcke, *Kriegerleben des Johann von Borcke 1806–1815* (Berlin: Mittler und Sohn, 1888), pp.30-31.

74 Jany, *Gefechtsausbildung*, p.113.

75 Jany, *Gefechtsausbildung*, p.125.

It is difficult to assess the potential of the Prussian field army which fought the fatal campaign of 1806, especially for the two big battles at Jena and Auerstedt.

The Battle of Jena should not have been fought at all; Hohenlohe should not have accepted the battle. Still, he got drawn into it. The Prussians acted in piecemeal fashion. The forces of Tauentzien, Holtzendorff, and finally Grawert fought on their own, against an increasingly concentrated concentring French army. Rüchel arrived much too late on the battlefield and too low in number, only about 10,000 strong, to be beaten in detail as well.

At Auerstedt, the commander-in-chief the Duke of Brunswick was mortally wounded quite early in the battle, which caused confusion and lack of co-ordination. The command went to the Prussian King, who was not up to the task at all. Brunswick's chief of staff *Oberst* Scharnhorst, instead of advising the King, took over command the Division Schmettau, whose commander was wounded as well. While the infantry fought almost on equal terms, first two, then three, Prussian divisions against those three of Davout – the other two Prussian divisions hardly saw any action at all at the main battle – the massive cavalry superiority of the Prussians gained hardly anything. The famous cavalry charge of Blücher was just 10 squadrons strong, from three different regiments. Clearly the days of decisive cavalry charges in the glory days of Seydlitz were over.

When the King decided to withdraw and to reunite with Hohenlohe and Rüchel, whose fates he did not know; the Prussians were shocked to see the units of Marshal Bernadotte occupying the area around Apolda. This timely arrival of Bernadotte, just as ordered by Napoléon and thus fulfilling completely his operational objective, caused even more confusion in the Prussian retreat and Bernadotte captured nearly the whole Prussian Füsilierbattalion von Kloch (No. 8).

The basic training, and the arms, of the Prussian infantry were adequate as long as they fought in classical light infantry role of the eighteenth century. This can be seen well at the rear-guard action at Altenzaun, where they stood more their ground against the 26e Légère.[76] What was missing was the tactical interaction with formed troops on the battle field. The *Schützen*, who could act as *tirailleurs de combat*, often were absent due being employed away from their parent unit. The Prussians quickly learned from their war experience and by this could model the new Prussian Army in the shortest time for being more tactically adequate at combat, as with giving a permanent *Füsilier* battalion to each regiment of infantry and as well as training the third rank of all line infantry as skirmishers.

In contrast to the fighting style of French Revolution, where the Prussian army fought with distinction, Napoléon by 1806 had revolutionised the operational and tactical art of war. The French army had a much more powerful punch in

76 Eduard von Höpfner, *Der Krieg von 1806 und 1807, Zweiter Theil, der Feldzug von 1806* (Berlin: Simon Schropp und Comp., 1850), Vol.I, pp.95–97, Oscar von Lettow Vorbeck, *Der Krieg von 1806 und 1807* (Berlin, Mittler und Sohn, 1892), Vol.II, pp 309-311.

the attack. Though skirmishers played an important task, good artillery, along with the best infantry in the world at this time, able to fight in a most flexible way, either formed in line or column, was the key for the decision on the battle field. Blaming the Prussian defeat on claims that the rigid lines of Frederick the Great were shot to pieces by the French skirmishers alone, as the well-entrenched view that the army of 1806 fought as in the Seven Years War, reflects poor research rather than reality. Hopefully this chapter shows that the Prussian Army underwent numerous reforms regarding armament, equipment and tactics from the Seven Years War onwards and that the causes of defeat lay elsewhere.

## Bibliography and Note on Sources


Anon. *Rangliste der Königlich Preußischen Armee für das Jahr 1806* (Berlin: Himburgsche Buchhandlung, Undated).

Anon. *Reglement für die Königlich Preußische Leichte Infanterie* (Berlin: Decker, 1788).

Béraud, Stéphane, *La révolution militaire napoléonienne* (Paris: Bernard Giovanangeli Éditeur, 2007, 2013).

Borcke, Johann Friedrich von, *Kriegerleben des Johann von Borcke 1806–1815* (Berlin: Mittler und Sohn, 1888).

Boyen, *Generalfeldmarschall* Herman v., *Denkwürdigkeiten und Erinnerungen, 1771–1813* (Stuttgart, Verlag von Robert Lutz, 1899).

Braunschweig, Friedrich August Herzog von und Lüneburg, *Instruction für mein Regiment um dadurch die hauptsächlichen Vorschriften des Königl. Preuß. Reglements genau und exact befolgen zu können* (Berlin: Unkown Publisher, 1791).

Bressonnet, Pascal, *Études Tactiques sur la Campagne de 1806 (Saalfeld – Iéna – Auerstedt)* (Paris : Libraire Militaire Chapelot, 1909).

Bressonnet, Pascal (Trans. and Annotated by Scott Bowden) *Napoleon's Apogee, Pascal Bressonnet's Tactical Studies 1806, Saalfeld, Jena and Auerstädt* (Berkeley: Military History Press, 2009).

Ciriacy, F.v., *Chronologische Übersicht der Geschichte des Preußischen Heeres* (Berlin and Posen: Mittler, 1820).

Doering, Wilhelm von, *Erinnerungen aus meinem Leben 1791–1810* (Osnabrück: Biblio Verlag, 1975).

Foucart, Paul-Jean, *Campagnes de Prusse et de Pologne (1806–1807), La Campagne de Prusse (Iéna)* (Paris: Berger-Levrault et Cie, 1887).

Franke, Ludw. Ehrenfr., *Vorstellung der Koeniglich Preussischen Armee 1803*, original in Berliner Staatsbibliothek.

Friedrich Wilhelm III, *Instruktion für die Infanterie vom 11. März 1798*, transcription, Whitehall.

Großer Generalstab, Kriegsgeschichtliche Abteilung II, *Der Siebenjährige Krieg, 1756 – 1763*, Band 13: *Torgau* (Berlin: Mittler und Sohn, 1914).

Gumtau, Carl Friedrich, *Die Jäger und Schützen des Preußischen Heeres. Erster Theil. Was Sie waren – Ihre Geschichte* (Berlin: Mittler, 1834).

Höpfner, Eduard von, *Der Krieg von 1806 und 1807, Erster Theil, der Feldzug von 1806* (Berlin: Simon Schropp und Comp., 1850).

Jany, Curt, *Die Gefechtsausbildung der Preußischen Infanterie von 1806. Mit einer Anzahl von Gefechtsberichten* (Berlin: Mittler und Sohn, 1907).

Jany, Curt, *Geschichte der Königlich Preußischen Armee bis zum Jahre 1807* (Berlin: Verlag von Karl Siegismund, 1929).

Kling, Constatin, *Geschichte der Bekleidung, Bewaffnung und Ausrüstung des Königlich Preußischen Heers. Dritter Teil. Die leichte Infanterie oder Die Füsilier Bataillone 1787-1809 und Die Jäger 1744–1809* (Weimar: Putze und Hölzer, 1912).

Lettow Vorbeck, Oscar von, *Der Krieg von 1806 und 1807* (Berlin: Mittler und Sohn, 1891-1892).

Marbot, *Colonel* Marcellin, *Remarques Critiques sur l'Ouvrage de M. le Lieutenant – Général Rogniat, intitulé : Considérations sur l'Art de la Guerre* (Paris: Anselin et Pochard, 1820).

Müller, Heinrich, *Das Heerwesen in Brandenburg und Preußen von 1640 bis 1806 – Die Bewaffnung* (Berlin: Brandenburgisches Verlagshaus, 1991).

Petre, F. Loraine, *Napoleon's Conquest of Prussia 1806* (London: The Bodley Head 1907).

Taysen A. v., *Die militärische Thätigkeit Friedrichs des Großen während seines Letzten Jahres* (Berlin: Mittler und Sohn, 1886).

Titze, Jörg, *Die Berichte der sächsischen Truppen aus dem Feldzug 1806 (I) Brigade Bevilaqua* (Norderstedt, Books on Demand gmbh, 2014)

Windsheimer, Bernd A, *Me Fecit Potzdam*, (Bissendorf: Biblio Verlag, 2001).

Most of those sources listed are available for download at the world wide web, such as the work by Bressonnet, including maps, from Gallica. The best source in English, is the recent translation and annotation of the above-mentioned author, titled *Napoleon's Apogee*. Reading this volume is essential to understand the reasons for the Prussian defeat as well as their and the French's battlefield tactics and operational art of war. This book is more than just a translation of Bressonnet's work, including additional information, numerous illustrations additional to the original work. While in the original work *Auerstedt* was used, Bowden changed it into *Auerstädt*.

Amongst the German sources, Jany's *Gefechtsausbildung* is of equal importance. To understand the development of the operational art of war, the volumes by Stéphane Béraud are one of the best publications about this subject. The classical studies about the campaign are by the German authors Höpfner and von Lettow-Vorbeck and especially the Frenchman Foucart.

To learn more about the outlook of the Prussian Army an excellent source is the website of Markus Stein: <http://uniformenportal.de/>

# 4

# The Pursuit After Jena

Kevin Kiley

> *I must say this to Your Majesty: war shall never be of my doing, for if it were, I should look upon myself as a criminal. Criminal is what I call a sovereign who, for a whim, undertakes a war which the policy of his country does not justify.*
>
> *Napoleon to Friedrich Wilhelm III, King of Prussia, 1806*

Pursuit is defined as a military operation:

> [U]sed to intercept and annihilate a retreating enemy. A pursuit should be conducted when the enemy has lost his ability to operate effectively and attempts to flee. Pursuit requires great energy; the resolution to press on despite fatigue, dwindling supplies, or the approach of darkness; and the proper coordination of all resources, especially highly mobile forces. In addition, commanders must be positioned well forward to provide impetus, encouragement, and timely, proper judgments.[1]

In a successful pursuit, the direct pressure force maintains contact with the enemy main force while an encircling force or blocking force cuts the enemy line of retreat.

## 4:00 p.m. 29 October 1806

Under a flag of truce, the French officer approached the Prussian fortress of Stettin intent on offering terms of surrender for the second time to the garrison.

1 John Alger, *Definitions and Doctrine of the Military Art* (West Point: Department of History, United States Military Academy, 1985), p.17.

The first French offer had been refused: the old Prussian Governor of the fortress, *Generalleutnant* von Romberg, who was 81 years old stoutly determined, at least initially, to defend his post against the French.[2] Halting his horse in front of the fortress for the second time, the French officer again demanded the immediate surrender of the Prussian garrison, warning the Prussian governor that if the fortress was not surrendered in the next 12 hours the French would demand a large indemnity in cash. Further, the garrison commander was informed that there were between 30,000 and 40,000 French troops commanded by *Maréchaux* Murat and Lannes ready to storm the city. The French officer then turned his horse and galloped back to his commander, *Général de Brigade* Antoine Lasalle.

Both the officer who demanded the surrender of the fortress and Lasalle knew that the only French troops in front of Stettin were from Lasalle's light cavalry brigade, with no other French troops known to be in supporting distance. The next morning, however, the Prussian governor of the fortress agreed to surrender. Needless to say, Lasalle and his staff were amazed that they had succeeded in their bluff. Stettin had a garrison of 5,000 well-supplied troops with 100 pieces of artillery.[3] This was the number of artillery pieces that were mounted on the walls of the fortress. In all 281 pieces were captured in the surrender.[4]

The garrison marched out of Stettin to become prisoners of war and undoubtedly were looking for the 30,000 to 40,000 French troops that were supposed to be ready to attack.

Stettin would not be the only Prussian fortress that surrendered to the French without resistance. It would be an indicator of the complete collapse of the Prussian state following the defeats at Jena and Auerstadt and the pursuit that followed. *Maréchal* Jean Lannes would comment that 'The Prussian army is in such a state of panic that the mere appearance of a Frenchman is enough to make it lay down its arms'.[5]

## Preparations

While this short study centres on the pursuit of the defeated Prussian army by the Grande Armée after the shattering defeats at Jena and Auerstadt on 14 October 1806, it is necessary to give some background to the events leading up to that war before the pursuit occurred. The battles of Jena and Auerstadt will not be covered in any depth, but merely mentioned in the timeline of events.

2 Colmar, Freiherr von der Goltz, *Jena to Eylau* (Uckfield: Naval and Military Press, nd), p.57.
3 Von der Goltz, *Jena*, p.57.
4 Von der Goltz, *Jena*, p.57.
5 F. Lorraine Petre, *Napoleon's Conquest of Prussia 1806* (London: Greenhill, 1993), p.253.

*Général de Brigade* Antoine Charles Louis de Lasalle. Engraving by Tavernier after Antoine Gros. (Anne S.K. Brown Collection)

During the French Revolutionary and Napoleonic Wars there is only one example of a relentless pursuit of a decisively defeated enemy that ended with the destruction of that enemy's army and the collapse of that enemy's state. That occurred in October and November of 1806 after the French victories over the Prussian-Saxon army at the battles of Jena and Auerstadt on 14 October 1806. Other armies after other battles had either attempted a pursuit or pursued a defeated enemy, some effectively, most not.

The lengthy Russian pursuit of the French after the 1812 Battle of Maloyaroslavets never brought the French to bay, the French always either eluding Field Marshal Kutusov, commanding the main Russian field army, or fighting through the Russian attempts to stop them. Kutusov finally kept his distance preferring to let General of Cavalry Wittgenstein and Admiral Tshitshagov attempt to destroy the remains of the Grande Armée at the Berezina River in November 1812. Staging an assault river crossing at Studenka, building two trestle bridges in the process, the remnants of the Grande Armée defeated two Russian armies, got across the river, and escaped. Kutusov with the main Russian army failed to appear to assist Wittgenstein and Tshitshagov. Apparently, Kutusov told Lieutenant General Yermelov that it was someone else's turn to fight Napoleon. The French pursuit of the defeated allies after Dresden in August 1813 turned into a disaster for the French when *Maréchal* St Cyr failed to support *Général de Division* Vandamme. The aggressive Vandamme was trapped and defeated at Kulm, half of Vandamme's corps being caught between two allied commands and forced to surrender. Finally, the much-trumpeted Prussian pursuit of the French after Waterloo actually was not well-conducted and did far less damage than is usually acknowledged. Gneisenau, *Generalfeldmarschall* Blücher's chief of staff (who should have been attending to his actual duties instead of trying to be the dashing field commander), led that pursuit and they raised havoc with broken troops and stragglers, but any formed body of troops they wisely left alone as they were still dangerous – ready and willing to fight.

It was only after Jena and Auerstadt that there was an unremitting, savage pursuit of a beaten enemy which resulted in the destruction of the Prussian army in three weeks of manoeuvre, fighting, and relentless pursuit. Only in East Prussia were there any formed Prussian units that survived the 'catastrophe'.[6] These troops under *Generalleutnant* Lestocq were not engaged in the campaign and the French would not encounter them until the Battle of Eylau in February 1807. There the Prussian corps would deliver a decisive attack which may have saved Russian General of Cavalry Bennigsen from a decisive defeat.

6 Clausewitz, Carl (Trans. Conrad Lanza), *Notes on Prussia During the Grand Catastrophe of 1806* (Fort Leavenworth Kansas: Command and General Service School, nd). This was the Prussian term for the disastrous defeat in the 1806 campaign. Clausewitz refers to the term repeatedly throughout his study.

After the more-than-successful Ulm and Austerlitz campaigns, which ended with the near-destruction of the allied army, the Grande Armée was moved to cantonments in southern Germany. Napoleon then began a project to convince the western German states that a mutual defensive alliance with France for collective protection against Prussia and Austria was to their benefit. The new entity created from that alliance was dubbed the Confederation of the Rhine, to which Austria acquiesced but which infuriated Prussia. Prussia also wanted to form an alliance with the northern German states, undoubtedly intended to absorb them at a later time. The creation of the Confederation of the Rhine stopped this idea before it could become a reality, and that only incensed Prussia, especially the Prussian 'war party' headed by Queen Louise, the wife of the Prussian King, Friedrich Wilhelm III.

Prussia had been 'sitting on the fence' internationally and had not been involved in the campaign of 1805. In point of fact, Prussia had not been engaged in the wars against France since 1795. Her generals were supremely confident in their ability to defeat the French, a belief that was not completely shared by the growing group of Prussian reformers headed unofficially by *Oberst* Gerhard von Scharnhorst. Some useful and needed army reforms had been accomplished, such as forming the army into divisions, but it would turn out that this had been too little, too late. These new Prussian divisions, for example, were divisions of 'all arms' which the French had abandoned in 1796-1800, instead favouring homogenous divisions of infantry and cavalry. One prevailing attitude among the Prussian senior military leadership before the Jena campaign disaster was attributed to *Generalfeldmarschall* von Mollendorf: 'This is altogether above my head'.[7]

Prussia was not prepared for war against France, no matter the enthusiasm for it. The example of bravado of Prussian soldiers sharpening their sabres on the steps of the French embassy might be showy and inspiring faith in their ability to defeat the French, but it was bravado only. Fighting the Grande Armée on the ground was another thing entirely. Prussia's king, and nominally the head of the army, Friedrich Wilhelm III 'was simple, brave, and soldierly but weak-willed; his pretty, bossy wife, Louise, had a weakness for feminine versions of various uniforms, and wanted war. There were many elderly generals, with leather lungs and entirely unjustified illusions of infallibility, who insisted on arguing over their orders rather than obeying them'.[8] This type of thinking was at the root of the Prussian problems in 1806.

That level of initiative and training that characterised the Grande Armée and its commanders did not usually exist in the Prussian army of 1806. Thoughtful officers, such as Scharnhorst, recognised this but were not listened to, Frederick the Great's lessons from the Seven Years War taking precedence.

7 Gordon Craig, *The Politics of the Prussian Army* (Oxford: Oxford University Press, 1956), pp.28-29.
8 John Elting, *Swords Around a Throne* (New York: The Free Press, 1988), p.516.

Friedrich Wilhelm III of Prussia. Engraving by Bucchorn after Francois Gérard. (Anne S.K. Brown Collection)

One of the German states that Napoleon invited to join the Confederation of the Rhine was Saxony. This offer angered Prussia, and Prussia 'demanded' that Saxony join Prussia and the proposed League of North German states. Saxony had long been a target of Prussia: Frederick the Great had devastated Saxony during the Seven Years War and forcibly took a good part of the Saxon army into his own service. Further, Napoleon was offering Great Britain Hanover as the beginning of peace negotiations. The French had evacuated Hanover after Austerlitz, which was then occupied by Prussia. Hanover was been the electorate of the Hanoverian kings of Great Britain and their one continental possession. The Prussian government was infuriated that now Napoleon was offering it to Great Britain.[9]

This diplomatic 'manoeuvring' finally led to Prussian mobilisation on 10 August. The Prussians were also trying to 'persuade' Saxony to join her against France. The form of persuasion that the Prussians used was brute force, and Saxony was then allied to Prussia. On 30 August the Prussian army was ordered into Saxon territory and to occupy the country. The Prussian army crossed the Saxon frontier on 6 September and by 12 September the Saxon capital of Dresden was for all intents and purposes taken and occupied by the Prussians.

It is doubtful that Napoleon wanted war with Prussia. He was occupied with the formation and organisation of the Confederation of the Rhine and he undoubtedly realised that if war with Prussia came, Russia would also declare for Prussia. The Tsar had not signed a peace treaty after Austerlitz as the Austrians had done, and were still for all intents and purposes at war with France. Prussia going to war against France would give the Russians an excuse to once again move their armies into central Europe and face off with Napoleon and the Grande Armée. 'Napoleon was extremely careful to avoid actions which might enable the Prussians to accuse him of aggression. His real thoughts remain unknown, but he gave every indication of hoping to prevent this war'.[10]

However, taking all necessary precautions, Napoleon ordered his chief of staff, *Maréchal* Alexandre Berthier, to alert the Grande Armée for impending movement against Saxony and Prussia. The Grande Armée was in cantonments in central Germany, its upkeep being paid by Napoleon's German allies. Berthier was ordered on 5 September to have the army ready to concentrate around Bamberg. The next day the Prussian army crossed the Saxon frontier.

The six corps of the Grande Armée were situated as follows: Bernadotte's I Corps was at Anspach. Davout's III Corps was at Oettingen. Soult's IV Corps was at Passau. Lannes V Corps was at Bischofsheim. Ney's VI Corps was at Memmingen and Augereau's VII Corps was at Frankfort am Main.[11] The Cavalry Reserve

9 Brendan Simms, *The Impact of Napoleon* (Cambridge, Cambridge University Press, 1997), p.230-265.

10 Vincent J. Esposito and John R. Elting, *A Military History and Atlas of the Napoleonic Wars*, Introduction to the Jena Campaign (Greenhill, London, 1999), Map 57.

11 Clausewitz, *Catastrophe of 1806*, p.531.

was commanded by *Maréchal* Murat. The French cavalry were also in southern Germany.

The French *corps d'armée* was an organisation of all arms and its headquarters could control between two and five infantry divisions. Attached to the corps was also either a brigade or a division of light cavalry for scouting and security. Artillery, engineers, and gendarmerie were also attached to the corps. A corps, commanded by either a marshal or a senior general officer, was designed to operate independently and if its commander got into trouble could stand on its own for about 24 hours until help could arrive from other units of the main army.

While the organisation of the *corps d'armée* was the theoretically the same throughout the army, no two corps were identical. Some corps had two infantry divisions, some three, and some even four, but that was determined by the capabilities of the corps commander and to confuse enemy intelligence operations. Napoleon was a skilled user of both intelligence and counterintelligence:

Napoleon also organised a Cavalry Reserve which was composed of all of the army's cavalry except for those assigned and attached to the individual *corps d'armée*. All of the heavy cavalry and dragoon divisions were assigned to the Cavalry Reserve, though sometimes the dragoon divisions might be attached to an infantry corps.

While the corps organisation was permanent, divisions could be detached and attached between corps as necessary. Further, provisional corps could be formed when necessary, such as the one commanded by *Maréchal* Mortier during the campaign. This was a completely flexible system and it, along with the army's sophisticated general staff, gave the French an immense tactical and operational advantage over the Prussians.

The Prussians in 1806 had no organisation similar to the *corps d'armée*. The *corps d'armée* gave flexibility to the Grande Armée both tactically and operationally and it made the chain of command much more easy to handle. Napoleon and the general staff and headquarters only had to issue orders to the corps commanders. It was then the responsibility of the corps commanders and corps headquarters to issue their orders to the attached divisions and other subordinate units.

The Prussian army of 1806 had recently adopted a division organisation, but these were not homogenous divisions of infantry and cavalry, but divisions of all arms. In August 1806 the Prussian Army consisted of the following: 58 infantry regiments, 29 grenadier battalions, 24 fusilier battalions, one regiment of *jägers*, and five battalions of guards. The cavalry consisted of 12 cuirassier regiments, 14 dragoon regiments, 15 uhlan squadrons, and 91 hussar squadrons. The artillery consisted of four foot artillery regiments and 10 horse artillery companies.[12]

The senior Prussian leadership was too old, the organisation and tactics were outmoded, and the '*savant* arms', the artillery and engineers, still suffered from

12 Clausewitz, *Catastrophe*, p.519

the neglect and ignorance of Frederick the Great. While the Prussians usually had more artillery than the French, they still employed battalion guns, which were attached to the infantry battalions, which diluted their artillery strength. They failed repeatedly to mass their superior numbers while the French employed their artillery according to their doctrine of infantry/artillery cooperation. The excellent French horse artillery continually used their superior mobility to strike at the decisive point and ranged across the battlefield when needed. While confident of victory against Napoleon and the Grande Armée, the Prussian army's performance in 1806 would be way out of line with expectations both from the French and the Prussians themselves. Scharnhorst made the comment that he knew what had to be done to be successful but that he was not sure it could be, given the situation with the Prussian army and its commanders.

The Prussians organised their available troops into four armies. The Principal Army commanded by the Duke of Brunswick was positioned near Weimar. *General der Infanterie* Rüchel's command was situated between Erfurt and Weimar. Prince Hohenlohe's command was near Kapellendorf and Jena. The Duke of Saxe-Weimar's command was marching on Illmenau.[13]

## Into the Fire

On 13 September Napoleon warned Prussia that an invasion of Saxony would be cause for war between the two countries. As a precautionary measure, Napoleon then ordered Berthier to concentrate the III, VI, VII Corps, the Cavalry Reserve and Dupont's infantry division at Würzburg as soon as he was informed that the French ambassador had departed from Berlin. Berthier had discovered that the Prussians had invaded Saxony on 19 September. The French ambassador in Berlin, however, did not write to Berthier until two days later, Berthier receiving the letter on 26 September.[14]

Napoleon did not immediately learn that Prussia was moving its army into Saxony. However, his early preparations for war with Prussia, as well as his order to concentrate the army for movement into Saxony and Prussia, indicated that Prussia's invasion of Saxony not unexpected. He further ordered the Imperial Guard to march eastward. When concentrating the Grande Armée for a campaign, Napoleon always made it a point to stay in Paris as long as possible in order to fool the enemy's intelligence. He also kept the Guard in Paris as long as possible to keep up the illusion of still attempting to keep the peace when it was obviously past the time when that was possible. When the Guard was finally ordered out on campaign, every effort was made to get them in-theatre in the shortest time

13 Clausewitz, *Catastrophe*, p.519.
14 Esposito/Elting *Atlas*, Map 58.

possible, even using wagons to transport the Guard infantry. That being said, if the campaign began before the Guard arrived, Napoleon did not wait for them and used line units for his escort.

Napoleon ordered Berthier to concentrate the III, V, and VII Corps along the Main River. Additionally, the I, IV, and VI Corps and the Cavalry Reserve were to concentrate between Amberg and Ansbach. Berthier sent a letter to Napoleon informing him that the Prussians had reached Hof. On 24 September Napoleon, still in Paris, received Berthier's letter of 19 September. Considering the overall situation deteriorating to such a degree that now war was unavoidable, Napoleon left Paris for the army the next day, 25 September, his first destination being Bamberg.

Prussia delivered an ultimatum to Napoleon demanding that all French troops were to withdraw over the Rhine; Prussia was to have a free hand in organising a 'league of north German states'; the French were to withdraw from several principalities in the Rhineland; any further differences were to be settled by negotiation. A reply from the Emperor was expected by 8 October.[15]

Napoleon arrived at Mayence on 28 September. He sent orders to Bernadotte and his I Corps to occupy Kronach. Additionally, orders were dispatched to all the leading corps to push forward cavalry reconnaissance aggressively. Further, the Cavalry Reserve was ordered to move forward and Murat was ordered to go to Würzburg. On 2 October Napoleon himself reached Würzburg.

On 5 October, Napoleon informed *Maréchal* Soult, who commanded the IV Corps, of his intentions when he invaded Saxony to face the Prussians. The Grande Armée would advance northward in three columns, with Soult leading the right column, followed by Ney's VI Corps. Bernadotte, commanding the I Corps, would lead the centre columns, followed by Davout's III Corps. The Cavalry Reserve, along with the Imperial Guard would follow the second, or middle, column. Lannes' V Corps would lead the left column, followed by Augereau's VII Corps. This compact massing of the army would allow it to manoeuvre and fight in any direction and its purpose was to find and fight the Prussian army wherever it was to be found.

On 7 October the previously-mentioned Prussian ultimatum reached Napoleon who was now in Bamberg. Everyone concerned knew that this meant war between France and Prussia and probably Russia as well. The Grande Armée was immediately ordered to advance northward toward Saxony and Prussia. At the same time, a single Prussian reconnaissance party reached Konigshofen. This single reconnaissance, authorised by Friedrich Wilhelm, was commanded by *Hauptmann* Müffling, who would in 1815 be the Prussian liaison officer with Wellington's Anglo-Dutch army in Belgium. Müffling was a skilled staff officer who would

15 Esposito/Elting, *Atlas*, Introduction to the Jena Campaign.

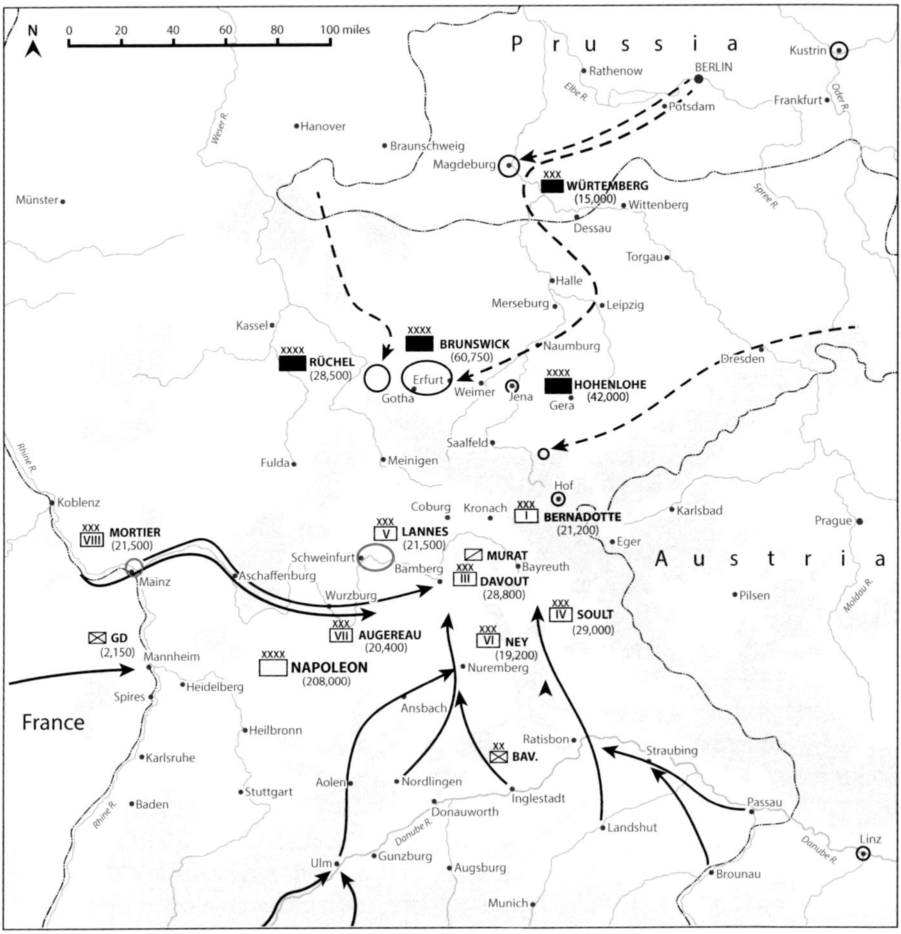


Operations prior to the Battles of Jena and Auerstadt. The French and Prussian armies are deployed and making their movement to contact from their initial deployments. Lestocq, who is not shown, is in East Prussia/Prussian Poland. (Map by George Anderson © Helion and Company)

later find himself assigned to Blücher's command during the retreat after Jena and Auerstadt.

The Grande Armée entered Prussian territory as well as crossing the Saxon frontier on 8 October. Compared with the tardiness of the Prussian army's movements and the obvious mental inflexibility of the senior Prussian leadership, the Grande Armée clearly demonstrated its training and professionalism by quickly and efficiently pulling out of its cantonments and moving northward to the Prussian frontier. The aforementioned Prussian reconnaissance party sent a report to Prussian headquarters that the French had left the Würzburg area and were advancing through Coburg and Kronach.

Napoleon at Jena, 14 October 1806. Lithograph after Horace Vernet.
(Anne S.K. Brown Collection)

Napoleon's plan of campaign was to manoeuvre against Berlin, forcing the Prussians to defend it. He believed that any Prussian offensive or movement southward would be slow, giving the French time to react. Napoleon concentrated the Grande Armée so that it would be able to manoeuvre in any direction to face the Prussians. Consequently, the III, V, and VII Corps would mass at the Main River with the I, IV, and VI Corps massing between Ansbach and Amberg. The Cavalry Reserve would be on the right flank of the army. They would then move northward both to pin the Prussian Army frontally and also manoeuvre against the Prussian rear.

The first serious action occurred on 10 October at Saalfeld between Lannes and Hohenlohe's advance guard commanded by Prince Louis Ferdinand of Prussia. The action was sharp and was a definite defeat for the Prussians. Prince Louis was killed in action, fighting hand to hand, by *Marechal des Logis Chef* Guindet of the 10e Hussards.[16] Both the defeat and Prince Louis' death greatly disheartened the Prussians.

On 14 October Napoleon met and defeated Hohenlohe's army, as well as Rüchel's independent command, at Jena. The Prussians were routed, and the Saxon contingent with Hohenlohe surrendered. The Saxon cavalry, however, cut its way out and escaped.

16 Charles Parquin, *Napoleon's Victories: From the Personal Memoirs of Captain Charles Parquin of the Imperial Guard, 1803-1814* (Chicago: The Werner Company, 1893), p.40.

The fall of the Duke of Brunswick at the Battle of Auerstadt, 14 October 1806. His mortal wounding left the main Prussian army essentially leaderless as Friedrich Wilhelm hesitated to assume command. Engraving by Wolff after Carle Vernet. (Anne S.K. Brown Collection)

> At the Webichtholz, before the gates of Weimar, a fierce charge of the French cavalry had dispersed the remnants of the Prussian army that had escaped from the field of Jena on the afternoon of the 14th of October 1806. Half dazed, Prince Hohenlohe, the general who for the first time had undergone decisive defeat, let himself be borne away in flight by his staff.[17]

The same day, *Maréchal* Davout met and defeated the main Prussian army at Auerstadt, northeast of Jena. Even though the Prussians outnumbered Davout's III Corps by over two-to-one, Davout's well-trained and -led command not only stopped the Prussian attacks, but executed a double envelopment of the Prussians. The Prussian commander, the Duke of Brunswick, was mortally wounded, being shot through both eyes. He later died after being led away from the battlefield to relative safety.

17 Von de Goltz, *Jena to Eylau*, p.1.

## Pursuit

The ideal situation for launching a pursuit against a defeated enemy is immediately after the enemy has been broken and is withdrawing. That is not always possible for a variety of factors, and it was not done after the battles of Jena and Auerstadt. Both battles were hard-fought, and at Jena's ending Napoleon realised that he had not fought the main Prussian army that he thought had been before him. He did know that a battle had been fought to the northeast of Jena and that he had definitely routed the two Prussian armies commanded by Hohenlohe and Rüchel. He did not know the outcome of the fighting to the northeast.

On 14 October at Jena, Hohenlohe's army was broken, defeated and leaving the field in disarray around 2:30 p.m. Into that rout marched *General der Infanterie* Rüchel and his small army, numbering not more than 15,000. He began by attacking the French, but the French aggressively came against him with a combined arms attack of infantry in open order supported by cavalry and artillery. His stand was broken and routed within an hour and the French cavalry pursued the Prussian fugitives for six miles, not allowing them any time for rallying and fighting on.

After marching and fighting all day, the exhausted French halted, Murat stopping at Weimar around 6:00 p.m. Some French cavalry continued the immediate pursuit for three miles more until stopping along the Erfurt road. Some French light cavalry continued beyond Weimar, but the French army halted just from being worn out.

At Jena Napoleon faced 48,000 Prussians and Saxons with an army of 96,000. However, around 40,000 of the French were not engaged. The French suffered over 5,000 casualties but they had inflicted 26,000 casualties on the Prussians and Saxons (15,000 of them prisoners), and captured 200 field pieces as well as 30 colours.[18] At Auerstadt after the Prussians either broke or retreated as best they could, some of them still in formed units, the French infantry halted at Eckartsberg around 4:30 p.m. Davout' corps cavalry brigade pursued the Prussians until 7:30 p.m. where they halted around Buttstadt. Davout had lost nearly 8,000 men in killed and wounded. The Prussians on the other hand, lost 15,000 (3,000 of them prisoners) as well as 115 field pieces.[19]

Napoleon did not issue any orders for the pursuit until 5:00 a.m. on 15 October. By that time, almost all contact with the Prussians had been broken. Murat and Ney would push past Weimar westward towards Erfurt, eventually to work northward towards the fortress city of Magdeburg. These orders reached the two

18 Esposito/Elting *Atlas*, Map 66. This source has been used for the numbers of casualties for the Jena and Auerstadt as it appears to be the most accurate.

19 Esposito/Elting *Atlas*, Map 66.

marshals at 7:00 a.m. on 15 October while the rest of the army remained in their bivouac areas.

There were two main reasons for this hesitation. There had been no word from Davout, and Napoleon did not know if he had been defeated. If that was the case, Napoleon might have to fight another battle on the 15th. Also, the avenues of retreat of the Prussian armies were unclear. They had been so thoroughly defeated that they had fragmented and there were crowds of fugitives and various detachments stretched all over the countryside.

Davout's first report to Napoleon reached him at 9:00 a.m. on 15 October. To be frank, Napoleon thought it unbelievable that Davout had defeated the main Prussian army on his own. Supposedly Napoleon remarked to the aide-de-camp that brought the dispatch those doubts. However, Davout sent a second dispatch which removed all doubt from Napoleon's mind as to the outcome at Auerstadt.

Davout was already in pursuit of the Prussians. *Chef d'Escadron* Meda, a squadron commander in the 7e Hussards, reported to his brigade commander, *Général de Brigade* Vialannes, that he was already 'in front of Leipzig' at 0300 on 15 October:

> I have taken several prisoners in the woods near the town; once my... scouts reported back, I proceeded through the town...I went half a league further on the road to Dresden... My arrival in this town created quite an impression...There was absolutely nothing at the post office, and I could find no mail. Leipzig and Dresden are terrorized...[20]

From Weimar the next day, 16 October, Napoleon sent the following message to Davout:

> I compliment you from the bottom of my heart on your wonderful conduct. I regret the men you have lost; but they died on the field of honor. Express my satisfaction to all your army corps and to your generals. They have forever earned the right to my respect and gratitude. Send me a report and have your army corps rest for a while in Naumburg.[21]

Davout and his III Corps would be given the signal honour of being the first French troops to enter Berlin as conquerors.[22] Davout's reply to Napoleon was succinct and to the point, pledging the continued valuable service of the III Corps to Napoleon.

20 Louis N. Davout (Trans. and Annotated by Scott Bowden), *Napoleon's Finest: Marshal Louis Davout and his 3d Corps: Combat Journal of Operations, 1805-1807* (Grand Rapids, Michigan: Military History Press, 2006), p.86.

21 Davout, *Combat Journal*, p.87.

22 Parquin, *Victories*, p.55.

After the receipt of Davout's second dispatch from Auerstadt, the overall situation was becoming much clearer. The overall plan for the pursuit of the Prussians was issued to the corps commanders at 2:00 a.m. on 16 October. Murat and Ney in particular were ordered to pursue the Prussians with their 'sword point at their kidneys'. Napoleon wanted a ruthless pursuit in order to not only complete the defeat of the Prussians, but to destroy them and their capacity to resist. Berthier and his assistants were busily writing and issuing orders for the pursuit of the Prussian army, both from Jena and Auerstadt. The marshal's aides-de-camp were galloping off in all directions delivering orders to hustle the designated units along.

The Cavalry Reserve, commanded by Murat with *Général de Division* Belliard as his chief of staff, was Napoleon's creation. It concentrated all of the heavy cavalry and dragoon divisions under one command, along with light cavalry divisions commanded by aggressive, talented general officers who had risen through the ranks of the French cavalry arm. There were also talented French junior officers at the squadron and regimental level who distinguished themselves during the pursuit. Among them were *Chef d'Escadron* Ameil, who commanded a squadron in the 5e Chasseurs à Cheval in Bernadotte's I Corps.[23] He would eventually reach regimental command of the 24e Chasseurs à Cheval and was brigaded with *Major* Marcellin Marbot's 23e Chasseurs à Cheval:

> With all his faults, the Emperor appreciated in him one quality, which he possessed to the highest degree: he was undoubtedly the best light cavalry officer in any European army. A finer tact or equal judgment in exploring a country with a glance was never seen. Before traversing a district he divined the obstacles which maps did not show, foresaw the points where streams, roads, or the smallest paths must come out, and could draw from the enemy's movements inferences which nearly always came true. Both in the details and in the general conception of war, he was a most remarkable officer.[24]

These hard-riding, aggressive commanders such as Ameil and Meda were the strength and heart of the pursuit of the defeated Prussians.

During the day of 15 October, Murat had 'coaxed' the fortress city of Erfurt into surrender, with the Prussian forces of Saxe-Weimar within supporting distance of the city. Saxe-Weimar panicked and withdrew, fearing that more French forces were nearby and would trap him. The surrender of Prussian forces to minimal

23 J. Leroy (ed.), 'Notes et Documents Provenant des Archives du General Baron Ameil' *Carnet de la Sabretache* No.15 (1907) 289-295, pp.289-295.

24 Marcellin Marbot (Trans. Arthur John Butler), *Memoirs of Baron Marbot* (London: Longmans, Greene and Co., 1892), Vol.II, p.233.

French commands was to become the norm during the pursuit, especially of Prussian-held fortresses.

Also on the 15th, Eugene of Wurttemberg, whose command was located at Halle, learned of the defeat of the Prussians at Jena and Auerstadt and the rout that ensued from both fields. He should have at least attempted to join with the king and attempt to organise units to resist the French pursuit. In point of fact Wurttemberg did little or nothing. Friedrich Wilhelm was still with the main army at this point and spent the night of the 14th/15th at Sommerda and remained there well into the day attempting to rally troops who were turning into fugitives and were not in formed units.

Of all the Prussian units engaged at Jena and Auerstadt, only the two divisions commanded by *Generalleutnant* Kalkreuth, which had been badly handled by the French at Auerstadt, were still intact. The commands of both Saxe-Weimar and Wurttemberg were still intact, but there were no attempts to join Kalkreuth's two divisions in order to continue resistance to the French.

The pursuit was to be pressed no matter what direction the Prussians chose in their retreat. Bernadotte, who had missed both Auerstadt and Jena, was to cut the road between Erfurt and Halle and drive on the fortress of Magdeburg, herding any Prussian units toward that city. There was now evidence that the Prussians were withdrawing in the direction of Erfurt as well as Magdeburg.

Mortier's provisional corps was ordered from Mayence to Fulda. Soult went to Sommerda and continued northwest, running into Kalkreuth at Greussen and capturing part of the Prussian trains. Friedrich Wilhelm found Hohenlohe at Nordhausen commanding about 15,000 men. He gave Hohenlohe over all command of the surviving Prussian units with orders to continue to Magdeburg in order to protect Berlin. If all else failed, and he could not stop the French from taking Berlin, Kalkreuth was to continue eastward and join the Russians as well as the Prussian corps under Lestocq. Friedrich Wilhelm requested an armistice from Napoleon, which Napoleon refused. Friedrich Wilhelm then decided to leave the army, even though he was the nominal commander-in-chief, and departed for Küstrin, effectively taking himself out of the campaign. His bravery under fire at Auerstadt had gained him both respect and admiration from the army,[25] but the King leaving the army suddenly was an additional blow to Prussian morale and will to fight.

The French pursuit was not without errors of omission and commission. Late in the day on 16 October, *Generaux* Lasalle and Klein had caught Prussian detachments commanded by or belonging to *Generalleutnant* Blücher and Kalkreuth. The two Prussians insisted that an armistice had been agreed to by Napoleon and Friedrich Wilhelm. Whether or not Blücher and Kalkreuth actually believed this as they knew one been requested, or it was merely energetic lying, is immaterial

25 Esposito/Elting, *Atlas*, Map 67.

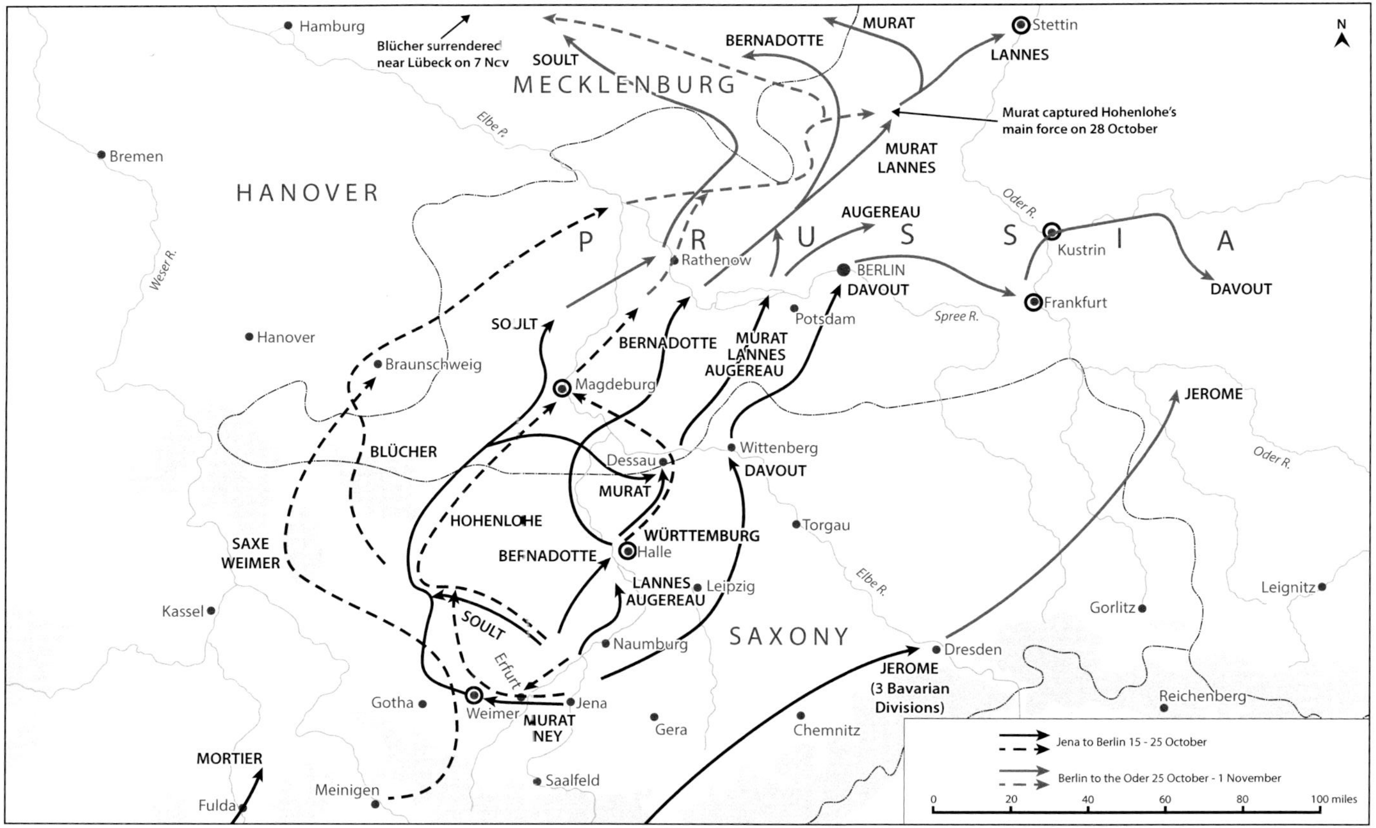


The Prussian retreat and French pursuit. The Pursuit of the defeated Prussian armies was concise and complete, whilst at the same time it was possible to redeploy Davout's corps to the east to face the Russians under Bennigsen. Both Lestocq, with the last organized Prussian field force, and Bennigsen are on the west bank of the Vistula (not shown). (Map by George Anderson © Helion and Company)

to the matter. The two French cavalry commanders believed the Prussians and let them pass uninterrupted and intact. When Napoleon found out about the incident, he was undoubtedly furious, or perhaps merely shook his head in disbelief. His displeasure was succinctly displayed in the Order of the Day of 19 October from the Imperial Headquarters at Merseberg.

> The Emperor expresses his displeasure with *Général de Division* Klein and *Général de Brigade* Lasalle, for having given free passage to two intercepted columns of the enemy, both having been so extremely simple as to believe the statement of General Blucher of the enemy's forces that an armistice of six weeks had been arranged. His Majesty orders that this mark of his displeasure be spread upon Army Orders...[26]

The order was signed by the chief of staff, *Maréchal* Berthier.

En route to his objective of Magdeburg, *General der Infanterie* Hohenlohe turned over his artillery in a separate column to Blücher and sent them towards Brunswick's command. Blücher saved the artillery in his charge until he re-joined Hohenlohe. He was then given command of the Prussian rear guard. One of the factors that was hampering the rallying of the Prussian army into at least a force capable of resistance was the available roads were also clogged with Prussian trains and artillery, which slowed the retreat of the Prussian units. This also greatly aided the ranging French cavalry, which was rapidly overrunning and capturing men, wagons, and artillery.

On 17 October, Bernadotte found Eugene of Wurttemberg's command and immediately attacked and routed it. Wurttemberg had established a position at the Saale River which was poor which undoubtedly aided Bernadotte. The latter was in trouble with Napoleon for his lack of performance on the 14th after having left Davout on his own to face the main Prussian army. In point of fact, Bernadotte had not contributed to the French effort in either battle on the 14th, having. marched between the two actions ignoring the smoke and roar of Davout's desperate fight behind him. This undoubtedly acted as a spur for Bernadotte to both behave himself and to better perform his duties.

Napoleon's objective, while still the destruction of the Prussian army, was now also Berlin. He believed that Magdeburg would fall of its own accord and directed Davout, Lannes, and Augereau to continue the advance on Berlin. The capture and occupation of the Prussian capital would consolidate the French hold on Prussia. It would also simplify the resupply of the Grande Armée both from the local population and from captured Prussian arsenals and depots.

26 Ernest Picard and Louis Tuetey (eds) (Trans. Louise Seymour Houghton) *The Unedited Correspondence of Napoleon I, 1804-1807* (New York: Duffield and Company, 1913), p.388.

Prussian Artillery c.1806. Watercolour by Gottlieb Doepler. (Anne S.K. Brown Collection)

In the Ulm and Austerlitz campaigns of the previous year, a significant portion of the French dragoon arm served dismounted as infantry until such time as remounts could be procured. At the end of that campaign there were not enough captured horses from the Austrians to mount the dismounted dragoon division. There were two provisional regiments that marched, not rode, into the 1806 campaign. As horses were captured, Napoleon addressed the problem of the dismounted dragoons in late October while the pursuit was still ongoing. He wrote to Berthier on 29 October regarding 4,000 remounts now available at Spandau. The dismounted dragoons were first on the list for remounts, but some were distributed to the Guard and Nansouty's cuirassier division.[27] More correspondence from the Emperor on this subject would follow during the remainder of the campaign and would also include saddles, horse harness, and other accoutrements.[28]

Not neglecting the resupply of the army for worn-out clothing, shoes, and uniforms, Napoleon issued instructions that captured material was to be distributed to the different corps as necessary.[29] Napoleon also ordered depots established for the use of the Grande Armée at Erfurt, Wittenberg, and Spandau.[30] Reinforcements for the units to be formed at a later time were also under consideration, as well as a new dragoon division to be commanded by *Général de Division* Beker, as were prisoners of war. The total number of prisoners taken during the campaign by the French, which to this point totalled approximately 140,000, were the subject of a dispatch on 18 November from Berlin.[31] Reinforcements and the formation of Beker's new dragoon division were the subject of a dispatch to *Général de Division* Dejean on 11 November, also from Berlin.[32]

Still retreating and not attempting a stand anywhere against the French, Hohenlohe finally reached the fortress city of Magdeburg with his remnants on 18 October. Napoleon had no definite word from Murat, Soult, and Ney – the army's left wing – for two days. Nevertheless, the advance on the Prussian capital was pressed. The roads were bad and the Harz Mountains were a definite obstacle, especially between Nordhausen and Halberstadt.

Davout crossed the Elbe between Dresden and Wittenberg on 19 October, after finding no Prussian units between Dresden and Wittenberg on the left bank of the Elbe. Bernadotte was ordered to advance on Aschersleben in order to establish contact with the Murat, Soult, and Ney.

On 20 October, Mortier's corps was ordered to occupy Hesse-Cassel. Prince Jerome, Napoleon's younger brother with one Bavarian and one Wurttemberg division (and with *Général de Division* Vandamme to do the actual commanding

27 Picard and Tuetey (eds), *Correspondence of Napoleon I,* p.390.
28 Picard and Tuetey (eds), *Correspondence of Napoleon I,* pp.393-393, 415-417, 427, 429,
29 Picard and Tuetey (eds), *Correspondence of Napoleon I,* p.396-397.
30 Picard and Tuetey (eds), *Correspondence of Napoleon I,* p.390.
31 Picard and Tuetey (eds), *Correspondence of Napoleon I,* p.424
32 Picard and Tuetey (eds), *Correspondence of Napoleon I,* pp.415-417.

and conduct operations), was ordered to Dresden. Jerome and Vandamme's mission was to clear Prussian Silesia of any Prussian opposition and to reduce the Silesian fortresses. The artillery captured from these fortresses would be sent to the Grande Armée to strengthen the French line of communications.

Reports from both Murat and Soult established that the Prussians were heading for Magdeburg. Napoleon again stressed the advance on Berlin. Napoleon believed that Magdeburg was an objective where the Prussians would attempt to assemble and sort out their disorganisation.[33]

Bernadotte was ordered to leave one division at Aschersleben and continue to the Elbe and establish a bridgehead at the mouth of the Saale River. Once that was accomplished he was to try and force his way across the Elbe.

Davout, having a bridge train, was to seize Wittenberg and cross the Elbe there. Lannes found that the bridge at Dessau on the Mulde River, close to where it joined with the Elbe, burned. As he had no pontoniers, he had to wait until a detachment was sent to him.

Murat and such of the Cavalry Reserve that was not employed elsewhere (the divisions of Sahuc and Klein), was ordered to move on Berlin. Before that, however, Napoleon ordered Murat to range over the countryside in the direction of Magdeburg. Napoleon's brother, Louis, was ordered to begin to move eastward from Holland with his available troops. Wurttemberg's defeated remnants arrived in Magdeburg, and although this gave Hohenlohe some reinforcements, dubious or not, it also indicated that Napoleon's objective might be Berlin. Hohenlohe deemed it impossible to cover Berlin, he immediately ordered a redirected retreat to the fortress of Stettin on the Oder River on the 21st.

On 21 October, the aggressive Lannes found the means to repair the Dessau bridge in preparation to cross the Elbe. Napoleon, being informed of Lannes' repair of the damaged bridge, then ordered the Guard, Augereau's VII Corps, and Grouchy's cavalry division to Dessau to cross the river. Later, as the situation changed somewhat, these three units were redirected to cross at Wittenberg which had been taken by Davout. His aggressive cavalry patrols (Davout had begun his military service as a cavalryman, which, apparently, was a family tradition) had surprised and taken the Torgau bridge intact.

Murat and Bernadotte were ordered to cross the river at Dessau, now that the three other commands had been ordered to Wittenberg to cross. Murat, on his own initiative and precluding Napoleon's orders, had massed the Cavalry Reserve at Egeln in preparation for the Elbe crossing. Davout had intercepted Prussian correspondence which indicated that Hohenlohe was not going to defend Berlin but was going to attempt to escape to the eastern side of the Oder.

In an operation as extensive and fast-moving as the pursuit of the Prussians, the gathering of intelligence was vital for the success of the operations. Knowing

33 Esposito/Elting, *Atlas*, Map 67.

where the enemy was as well as when, or as close to it as possible was an essential element of the pursuit. The French cavalry would aggressively question native civilians and would also seize the letters in the Prussian postal system for any usable intelligence. 'Cooperative' natives would also be employed as guides when necessary. The hard-riding light cavalry of both the Cavalry Reserve and the corps cavalry units constantly pushed not only to find the enemy, but to scour the villages and question the civilians in those towns and villages who might know something of interest such as the postmaster and the mayor. Civilians who knew the countryside and the best ways from village to town to village again would be pressed into service as guides.

Upon leaving Magdeburg, Hohenlohe marched in three columns, dividing his 40,000 men among them. Blücher would later re-join the main column and become the commander of the army's rear guard. Among other responsibilities, he was to collect stragglers and urge them to re-join their units if they could find them and continue the retreat with the arm. Scharnhorst, who had been Brunswick's chief of staff at Auerstadt, became Blücher's chief of staff for the remainder of the retreat.

On 23 October Soult was surprised by reports that Saxe-Weimar was advancing to intercept him south of Magdeburg. Soult reacted to these reports by advancing against where he believed Saxe-Weimar to be. He found out he had been fooled, took the wrong road, and missed any interception of the Prussian force. Apparently, Saxe-Weimar feinted an advance on Magdeburg in order to retreat to Sandau.

On 24 October Davout had reached Berlin while Lannes and Murat took up positions at Potsdam. The Grande Armée paraded through Berlin, led by Davout's III Corps.[34] Davout had received instructions for the entry into Berlin and how the III Corps would bivouac and occupy the Prussian capital, from Napoleon, via Berthier. They also ordered that *Général de Division* Hulin would be the French commandant of Berlin.[35] French light cavalry probing in the area of the Havel River apparently had found a Prussian north-bound column. Reports from Bernadotte, who was moving towards Brandenburg, seemed to confirm the intelligence from the light horsemen. Based on these reports, Napoleon ordered both Lannes and Murat to Spandau. Ney took up a blockade of Magdeburg and its garrison of 16,000.

On 25 October Napoleon, who knew that the Russians may well be marching against him to support their Prussian ally, ordered Davout and Augereau eastward across the Oder to act as a screen and early warning system against the Russians. Two Bavarian infantry divisions and one Wurttemberg infantry division were ordered northwest into Poland from Dresden. Jerome, Napoleon's younger brother, commanded two of them. The most experienced and talented of the Bavarian commanders, *Generalleutnant* Deroi, was with Jerome: hopefully to keep him to the task and not to do anything too foolish.

34 Charles Parquin, *Victories*, p.55.
35 Davout, *Combat Operations*, pp.90-91.

It was imperative to intercept Hohenlohe and not to allow him to get across the Oder. Bernadotte was ordered to follow Hohenlohe. Bernadotte had gathered considerable intelligence regarding Hohenlohe's march route. That being done, Murat and Lannes were ordered to Zehdenick as well as Templin to manoeuvre in order to head off Hohenlohe, trapping him between themselves and Bernadotte. Murat's command consisted of the divisions of Grouchy, Lasalle, Beaumont, and Milhaud.

The Imperial Guard as well as the two cuirassier divisions (commanded by *Généraux de Division* Nansouty and d'Hautpoul) were ordered to stay in Berlin. Ney was to remain in front of Mageburg and Soult was allowed to use his initiative and to go where needed. Soult found Saxe-Weimar's flank guard at Tangermunde and overwhelmed it, capturing it whole.

Napoleon entered Berlin on 28 October accompanied by the Imperial Guard who paraded into the city. *Sergent* Coignet noted that '…the Emperor moved proudly along in his plain dress, with his small hat and his one-sou cockade. His staff were in full uniform, and it was a curious site to see the worst-dressed man the master of such a splendid army.'[36] Jean-Baptiste Barres, another Imperial Guardsman, had the same impression of Napoleon's and his Guard's entrance into Berlin. He also remarked on the friendliness of the Berliners, and the general docility of the Prussian civilian population to the French victory: '…I said to myself, here's a Berliner who is hardly a Prussian! It looks as if it should have been easy to give his king and countrymen and all those who wear the Prussian uniform, such a sound thrashing!'[37]

The next day, 26 October, Lasalle and Grouchy ran into and destroyed Hohenlohe's flank guard at Zehdenick. Alerted, Hohenlohe turned to the north with his objective of reaching Stettin and Prenzlau. A cavalry detachment commanded by *Général de Division* Savary (one of Napoleon's imperial aides-de-camp: all general officers and specialists in their own branch of the service) was shadowing Hohenlohe, expertly informing the rest of the pursuit of Hohenlohe's location. Murat, reacting to the intelligence, finally caught up with Hohenlohe at Prenzlau on 28 October, forcing him to surrender his 16,000 remaining, exhausted troops.

One of the actions during this part of the pursuit was performed by the grenadier battalion of Prince August. One of the Prince's officers was Clausewitz, and the battalion as a whole had fought well at Auerstadt. In point of fact, this battalion was one of the few that had actually been trained in French combat methods. The Prince himself at Auerstadt had ended up commanding three battalions in the defeat, with command on his battalion devolving on Clausewitz himself. This would be the highest field command that Clausewitz would ever hold.[38]

36 Jean-Roche Coignet, *The Notebooks of Captain Coignet* (London: Greenhill Books, 1989), p.135.

37 Jean-Baptiste Barres (Trans.Bernard Miall), *Memoirs of a Napoleonic Officer* (New York: The Dial Press, 1925), pp.89-90.

38 Peter Paret, *Clausewitz and the State* (Princeton: Princeton University Press, 1985), p.125

The battalion performed well during the retreat, and when it was finally taken by the French the casualties incurred were heavy: that the battalion was part of Hohenlohe's rear guard is an indicator that it was intact and capable of fighting when necessary.

Further, on the 26th when 'Hohenlohe reached Furstenberg, Blücher Alt-Ruppin. The Duke of [Saxe]-Weimar crossed the Elbe at Sandau, and his rearguard, under the stern *Oberst* Yorck, bravely repulsed an attack of the French upon the ferry-the first encounter in this luckless campaign that was a Prussian victory'.[39] Hans David Yorck was a difficult subordinate and had been cashiered by Frederick the Great for insubordination.[40] He had been brought back to the army and reinstated before 1806 and had successfully rebuilt the Prussian light infantry, the Prussian *jägers* gaining a reputation as an elite unit under Yorck's 'inspired' leadership.[41]

In the rear-guard action at Altenzaum on the Elbe River on 26 October, Yorck commanded perhaps four or five light infantry battalions, consisting of his own *jägers* and the fusilier battalions. Yorck positioned his troops behind the town with his left flank anchored by the Elbe dam. At or about 4:00 p.m. he came into contact with Soult's corps cavalry, which he repulsed, using the terrain as well as his well-trained troops to defeat Soult's light horse. Soult then sent infantry against Yorck, which the Prussians held against and maintained their position. The cavalry were driven off 'in confusion' and the French infantry finally fell back on the town. Undefeated, Yorck withdrew after nightfall to Sandau. To maintain the semblance of being in place to renew the fighting in the morning, Yorck left his bivouac fires burning, an oft-used ruse, moved out and got his troops across the Elbe and away from the pursuing French. After successfully crossing the Elbe, Yorck then had the boats sunk to delay the French crossing. The French did pursue almost immediately and managed to inflict casualties on the withdrawing Prussians. Yorck got his most of his command out of danger by aggressive fighting and competent leadership.

On 29 October Murat approached the fortress city of Stettin on the Oder and found that Lasalle, with only his brigade of light cavalry, had bluffed the fortress into surrendering.

By 30 October Saxe-Weimar had turned over command of his corps to *Generalleutnant* Winning who then joined with Blücher's command, Blücher being senior taking over both commands. Winning wanted to escape the French pursuit by sea, planning to embark his troops at Rostock and then proceed to East Prussia. Blücher disagreed and cancelled the embarkation, wanting to begin his own private offensive against the French along the lower Elbe.

39 Von der Goltz, *Jena to Eylau*, p.43
40 John Elting, *Swords*, p.517
41 John Elting, *Swords*, p.517.

The ubiquitous Savary, with his small cavalry command, which consisted of the 1er Hussards and 7e Chasseurs à Cheval,[42] had kept track of Winning and was shadowing his movements. Making contact with Murat, Soult, and Bernadotte, Savary passed on the information that he had learned by following the Prussians, and those three marshals pursued Blücher and Winning without stopping for rest. They chased Blücher's united command to the northwest, Blücher making for the Hanseatic port of Lübeck . Savary was a skilled light cavalry officer and he avoided getting into trouble as well as not engaging the Prussians and therefore provided the larger combat units and commands with reliable information on the locations and movements of the main Prussian units allowing them to be hunted down and either cornered or destroyed.

Blücher reached Lübeck on 5 November, and prepared to defend the city against the French. Lübeck was only lightly fortified. Blücher promised the city government that he would not fight in the city, but demanded 'food and drink' after forcing his way into the city – thus exposing the inhabitants to French vengeance.[43] Blücher wanted to resupply his exhausted command and perhaps give the troops some rest before defending the city, but Murat, Soult, and Bernadotte arrived before the city the day after Blücher's arrival. Soult and Bernadotte stormed the neutral city out of hand on 6 November. There was desperate fighting in the streets of the city and the Prussian infantry occupied the houses in a desperate attempt to hold off the surging French. Part of Blücher's command escaped from the city as both the French and Prussians engaged in looting. Scharnhorst and most of Blücher's general staff were captured inside the city. The surviving Prussian infantry, those not killed or captured in the heavy fighting, continued fighting from the houses until either driven from them or killed where they stood.

Blücher, Müffling, and perhaps 10,000 of his original 21,000 men escaped from the fallen city and cross the Trave River, only to be pursued by the victorious French to the border of Denmark. There, the Danes sent troops under *Generalløjtnant* Johann Ewald to stop any encroachment of Danish territory by either the Prussians or the French.[44]

Napoleon sent his congratulations, signed by the chief of staff, to the three successful marshals in an Order of the Day, dated 9 November 1806:

> The Emperor expresses to the Grand Duke of Berg [Murat], the Prince of Ponte Corvo [Bernadotte], Marshal Soult, and to the infantry, cavalry,

42 Picard and Tuetey (eds), *Correspondence of Napoleon I*, p.410.

43 Michael Leggiere, *Blücher: The Scourge of Napoleon* (Norman: University of Oklahoma Press, 2014), p.109.

44 Leggiere, *Blücher*, p.110. This was the same Johann Ewald who had served with the British Army as part of the contingent from Hesse-Cassel that was sent to North America in the American Revolutionary War. Denied promotion, he subsequently accepted a commission from the Danish government and served until his death in 1813.

> artillery, and engineer corps under their orders, his satisfaction with their brilliant conduct at Lubeck, and the activity of their pursuit of the enemy...General Blucher's corps...was obliged to capitulate and surrender as prisoners of war with all its baggage and stores, to be taken to France. No other hostile troops remain on this side of the Vistula.[45]

On 7 November Blücher surrendered his command to Murat, Soult, and Bernadotte at Ratekau. Blücher lost at least 6,000 men in the fighting in and around Lübeck, French losses being reckoned at 1,500. These were the last Prussian units surrender to the French, leaving only the uncommitted units in East Prussia and Silesia active, undefeated, and not destroyed in the catastrophe. The Prussian Army, with the exception of the units in East Prussia under Lestocq, the Prussian garrisons in Silesia, and the garrison of Colberg, probably not more than 20,000 men total, was effectively destroyed.[46] As Murat accurately stated: 'The combat ends for lack of combatants'.[47]

Napoleon was concerned during the campaign with both straggling and looting by the French. Berthier wrote an Order of the Day from Imperial Headquarters in Berlin on 7 November addressing the subject:

> His Majesty is displeased to see that disorders are committed in the rear of the army, notably in the environs of Leipzig and Wittenberg. French commanders are all the less pardonable because, independently of the French forces under their command, they also have Saxon infantry and cavalry. They should establish patrols to arrest stragglers, being careful to put them under French officers or subalterns. The same dispositions should be made for Weimar, Erfurt, Gotha, Brunswick...French commanders should employ the local forces to see that property in the country is respected, and strenuously to repress all disorders which dishonor the army.[48]

## Conclusions

The French pursuit of the Prussian army after Jena and Auerstadt 'remains one of the greatest pursuits of history. In three weeks of unrelenting maneuver, battle, and marching, the French gathered 140,000 prisoners, 250 flags, and 800 field

45 Picard and Tuetey (eds), *Correspondence of Napoleon I*, p.412.
46 Leggiere, *Blücher*, 110.
47 Esposito/Elting, *Atlas*, Map 68.
48 Picard and Tuetey (eds), *Correspondence of Napoleon I*, p.410.

guns. Except for its units in East Prussia and Silesia, the long-feared Prussian Army was completely destroyed'.[49]

A comment by *Maréchal* Berthier succinctly described what was done during French operations from the Prussian ultimatum in September until the capitulation of Blücher in November:

> In warfare nothing is done, so long as anything remains to be done. No victory is complete so long as there is an enemy in the field...In our present situation there is but one order to be issued-to inflict as great a loss as possible upon the enemy and to exploit our victory in every way.[50]

What of the Prussians? Their army almost totally destroyed, the Prussian units in East Prussia would later fight well at the Battle of Eylau in February 1807, marching hard to intervene in the battle and undoubtedly saving the Russians from a decisive defeat. Gneisenau would hold the fortress of Colberg, in Pomerania, against the French until the Treaty of Tilsit. These overall minor actions can be considered to be the first instances of Prussian resurgence. Their country greatly shrunken in size by Tilsit, the Prussian reformers, supported by their king, began to reform and rebuild the Prussian Army based on the experience of being shattered by the Grande Armée. They undertook their task 'with vengeance very much in mind'.[51] While they never could match the Grande Armée in both numbers and tactical flexibility, the reforms to the army such as the introduction of the corps system and a greater use of light infantry, were lessons learned from 1806.

One of the most surprising occurrences during the campaign is that Prussian morale had been so shattered after Prince Louis' death and defeat and the complete defeat of Hohenlohe and Brunswick that the Prussian state, and most resistance to the French, completely collapsed. Fortresses throughout Prussia surrendered to small numbers of French, usually mostly cavalry. Erfurt surrendered with a garrison of 12,000; Hohenlohe surrendered 10,000 men and 64 field pieces at Prenzlau. At Pasewalk 4,000 Prussians surrendered to two brigades of light cavalry; Kustrin surrendered with 2,400 men and 92 guns; Magdeburg with a 25,000-man garrison surrendered to *Maréchal* Ney and the VI Corps, which the garrison actually outnumbered. Lastly, as already shown, Stettin with a 5,000 man garrison surrendered to Lasalle and a brigade of light cavalry.[52]

To sum up, the French pursuit after Jena and Auerstadt was the most relentless and complete pursuit of the Napoleonic period. The retreating and demoralised

49 Esposito/Elting, *Atlas*, Map 68.

50 Berthier to Soult, 3 December 1805 after Austerlitz, taken from *Le Maréchal Berthier* by Derrecagaix, cited in Peter Tsouras (ed.), *The Greenhill Dictionary of Military Quotations* (London: Greenhill Books, 2000), p.188.

51 Elting, *Swords*, p.517.

52 Leggiere, *Blücher*, p.108.

Prussian army was hunted down by the Grande Armée and either destroyed or captured. Prussian fortresses meekly surrendered to handfuls of French cavalry. Stettin surrendering to Lasalle's bluff was an outstanding example. The French captured 140,000 prisoners, 800 field guns, and 250 flags during the short campaign. In three weeks of campaigning, the Prussian army was all but destroyed. The army that Frederick the Great had inherited and maintained no longer existed.

French units were started eastward to face the Russians, as they were still marching westward and were not attempting to either negotiate or quit. Other units continued to pursue the Prussian units that had not capitulated. The last of Prussians, Blücher's, were finally cornered in the old Hanseatic city of Lübeck, and after attempting, and failing, to escape, surrendered. Further, the civil population succumbed to the French in an orderly and subservient manner. Towns and cities were easily occupied and order maintained by the French. The city fathers of Berlin met the leading French elements with the keys to the city. Old Prussia had been quickly and for the most part quietly occupied. The 'catastrophe' was complete, but the cost to Prussia in land and prestige would have to wait for the Treaty of Tilsit. Friedrich Wilhelm was lucky to keep at least some of Prussia intact and Napoleon had to be convinced of that course of action. The treaty would be harsh for the Prussians and that would feed their desire for vengeance.

Prussia was ill-prepared to fight a modern war. Her army was the shadow of Frederick the Great's triumphal army of the Seven Years War. Training standards were low, much of the army was on furlough for the majority of the year, and her generals were too old. What was worse, they scoffed at French fighting techniques and firmly believed that the Grande Armée was no match for the Prussian Army. Napoleon's comment on generals and generalship simply outline the problem with the majority of the Prussian generals in 1806: 'An army of lions commanded by a deer will never be an army of lions'.[53]

Years later while in exile on St Helena, Napoleon would give his professional judgment regarding Friedrich Wilhelm and Alexander, the two monarchs that he and the Grande Armée defeated decisively in the campaigns of 1806-1807:

> When I was at Tilsit with the Emperor Alexander and the King of Prussia, I was the most ignorant of the three in military affairs! These two sovereigns, especially the King of Prussia, were completely au fait as to the number of buttons there ought to be on the front of a jacket, how many behind, and the manner in which the skirts ought to be cut. Not a tailor in the army knew better than Frederick how many measures of cloth it took to make a jacket. In fact, I was nobody in comparison with them. They continually tormented me with questions about matters belonging to tailors, of which I was entirely ignorant, though, in order not to affront

53 Correspondence de Napoleon, Volume XXX as cited in Tsouras, *Dictionary*, p.97.

> them, I answered just as gravely as if the fate of an army depended on the cut of a jacket. The King of Prussia changed his fashion every day. He was a tall, dry looking fellow, and would give a good idea of Don Quixote. At Jena, his army performed the finest and most showy maneuvers possible, but I soon put a stop to their coglionerie, and taught them that to fight and to execute dazzling maneuvers and wear splendid uniforms were very different affairs. If the French army had been commanded by a tailor, the King of Prussia certainly would have gained the day, from his superior knowledge and art![54]

Lastly, Napoleon wrote to *Maréchal* Mortier in 1806 and the comment is pertinent to the Jena campaign: 'Intelligent and fearless generals assure the success of affairs'.[55] Napoleon believed in what he referred to as the '*feu sacre*', the sacred fire, which was the desire above all else to succeed or die in the attempt. The French commanders, with few exceptions had it; the Prussian commanders, with few exceptions, did not: 'But all that… he will learn will be of little use to him if he does not have the sacred fire in the depths of his heart, this driving ambition which alone can enable one to perform great deeds'.[56]

Napoleon may have been thinking of the Grande Armee of 1806 when he said the following to Gaspard Gourgaud in 1817:

> The ideal army would be the one in which every officer would know what he ought to do in every contingency; the best possible army is the one which comes closest to this. I give myself only half the credit for the battles I have won, and a general gets enough credit when he is named at all, for the fact is that a battle is won by the army[57].

Lastly, failures in war can usually, if not always, be laid at the feet of poor leadership. 'The worth of an army is entirely based on the generaux and leaders. A soldier always fights well; but his efforts will remain useless if the commander lacks knowledge.'[58] 'Having demonstrated that it was deficient in talent, the officer corps seemed intent upon proving itself bankrupt of valor as well.'[59]

54 Napoleon's comment while on St Helena in 1817, as cited in Tsouras, *Dictionary*, pp.244-245

55 *Correspondence de Napoleon*, Number XIII, to Mortier, 29 November 1806 as cited in Tsouras, *Dictionary*, p.216.

56 *Correspondence de Napoleon*, Number XXXII, as cited in Tsouras, *Dictionary*, p.38.

57 Napoleon to Gaspard Gourgaud, *St Helene: Journal Inedite de 1815 a 1818*, Vol.II, cited in Tsouras, *Dictionary*, p.39.

58 Pascal Bressonet (Trans. Scott Bowden), *Tactical Studies 1806: Saalfeld, Jena, and Auerstadt* (Grand Rapids, Michigan: Military History Press, 2009), p.342.

59 Craig, *Prussian Army*, p.35.

Scharnhorst, the erstwhile reformer and military educator as well as a skilled staff officer, remarked to his daughter Julie in three letters, 'The surrender of so many fortresses without cause shows the shameful conduct of our senior officers.'[60] Scharnhorst was very critical of the Prussian officer corps. Before hostilities he had remarked, in a statement that would prove to be prophetic, 'What ought to be done I know only too well. What is going to be done, only the gods know.'[61] Finally, 'Our officers do not know how to command. Only a few are of any use in their position.[62]

## Bibliography

Alger, John, and Griess, Thomas (eds.), *Definitions and Doctrine of the Military Art Past and Present* (West Point: Department of History: United States Military Academy, 1985).

Barres, Jean-Baptiste (Trans. Bernard Miall), *Memoirs of a Napoleonic Officer* (New York: The Dial Press, 1925).

Bressonet, Pascal (Trans. Scott Bowden), *Tactical Studies 1806: Saalfeld, Jena, and Auerstadt* (Grand Rapids: Michigan, Military History Press, 2009).

Clausewitz, Carl (Trans. Conrad Lanza), *Notes on Prussia During the Grand Catastrophe of 1806* (Fort Leavenworth Kansas: Command and General Service School, nd).

Coignet, Jean-Roche, *The Notebooks of Captain Coignet: Soldier of the Empire, 1799-1816* (London: Greenhill Books, 1989).

Craig, Gordon, *The Politics of the Prussian Army 1640-1945* (Oxford: Oxford University Press, 1956).

Davout, Louis N. (Trans. and Annotated by Scott Bowden), *Napoleon's Finest: Marshal Louis Davout and his 3d Corps: Combat Journal of Operations, 1805-1807* (Grand Rapids Michigan: Military History Press, 2006).

Elting, John R., *Swords Around A Throne: Napoleon's Grande Armée* (New York: The Free Press, 1988).

Esposito, Vincent J., and Elting, John R., *A Military History and Atlas of the Napoleonic Wars* (London: Greenhill, 1999).

Foucart, J.P., *Campagne de Prusse 1806* (Paris: Berger-Levrault et Cie, 1890).

Gallaher, John, *The Iron Marshal: A Biography of Louis N. Davout* (Carbondale and Edwardsville: Southern Illinois University Press, 1976).

60 Gerhard Scharnhorst, letter to his daughter Julie, found in *Scharnhorsts Briefe* dated 16 November 1806, as cited in Charles White, *The Enlightened Soldier* (New York: Praeger, 1989), p.128.

61 Gerhard Scharnhorst, *Scharnhorsts Briefe*, cited in White, *Enlightened Soldier*, p.127.

62 Gerhard Scharnhorst, *Scharnhorsts Briefe*, cited in White, *Enlightened Soldier*, p.128

Goltz, Colmar, Freiherr von der (Trans. C.F. Atkinson), *Jena to Eylau: The Disgrace and Redemption of the Old Prussian Army* (Naval and Military Press, Uckfield, East Sussex, nd).

Johnston, R.M. (ed.), *In the Words of Napoleon: The Emperor Day by Day* (London: Greenhill Books, 2002).

Johnston, R.M. (ed.), *The Corsican: The Virtual Diary of Napoleon Bonaparte* (Tucson: Fireship Press, 2010).

Kiley, Kevin F., *Once There Were Titans: Napoleon's Generals and Their Battles* (London: Greenhill, 2007).

Kiley, Kevin F., *Artillery of the Napoleonic Wars, 1792-1815: Field Artillery* (Barnsley: Frontline Books, 2015).

Leggiere, Michael, *Blücher: Scourge of Napoleon* (Norman: University of Oklahoma Press, 2014).

Leroy, J. (ed.), 'Quatre Lettres de Colonel Castex', *Carnet de la Sabretache*, Number 11 (1903), pp.179-181.

Leroy, J. (ed.), 'Guindey (Jean-Baptiste) 1785-1813', *Carnet de la Sabretache*, Number 12 (1904), pp.228-239.

Leroy, J. (ed.), 'Lettres et Rapports Extraits du Registre de Correspondence de 1806 du Marechal Ney, Duc d'Elchingen', *Carnet de la Sabretache*, Number 14 (1906), pp. 579-590.

Leroy, J. (ed.), 'Notes et Documents Provenant des Archives du General Baron Ameil', *Carnet de la Sabretache*, Number 15 (1907), pp. 289-295.

Marbot, Marcellin (Trans. Arthur John Butler), *Memoirs of Baron Marbot* (London: Longmans, Greene and Co., 1892).

Maude, F.N., *The Jena Campaign 1806* (London: Greenhill, 1998).

Mikaberidze, Alexander, *The Russian Officer Corps in the Revolutionary and Napoleonic Wars 1792-1815* (New York: Savas Beattie, 2005),

Nelson, Walter, *The Soldier Kings: The House of Hohenzollern* (New York: GP Putnam's Sons, 1970).

Paret, Peter, *Yorck and the Era of Prussian Reform 1807-1815* (Princeton: Princeton University Press, 1966).

Paret, Peter, *Clausewitz and the State: The Man, His Theories, and His Times* (Princeton: Princeton University Press, 1985).

Charles Parquin, *Napoleon's Victories: From the Personal Memoirs of Captain Charles Parquin of the Imperial Guard, 1803-1814* (Chicago, The Werner Company, 1893).

Petre, F. Loraine, *Napoleon's Conquest of Prussia, 1806* (London: Greenhill, 1993).

Picard, Ernest, and Tuetey, Louis (Trans. Louise Seymour Houghton) *The Unedited Correspondence of Napoleon I, 1804-1807* (New York: Duffield and Company, 1913).

Shanahan, William, *Prussian Military Reforms 1786-1813* (New York: AMS Press, 1966).

Simms, Brendan, *The Impact of Napoleon: Prussian High Politics, Foreign Policy, and the Crisis of the Executive, 1797-1806* (Cambridge: Cambridge University Press, 1997).

Tranie, Jean, and Carmigniani, Juan Carlos, *Napoleon et l'Allemagne: Prusse 1806* (Paris: Lavauzelle, 1984).

Tsouras, Peter (ed.) *The Greenhill Dictionary of Military Quotations* (London: Greenhill Books, 2000).

Van Creveld, Martin, *Command in War* (Cambridge, Massachusetts: Harvard University Press, 1985).

White, Charles, *The Enlightened Soldier:Scharnhorst and the Militarische Gesellshaft in Berlin, 1801-1805* (New York: Praeger, 1989).

5

# A Poor Place to Fight a War: Franco-Italian Operations in the Tyrol 1809

John H. Gill

Careful analysis of the principal campaigns, renowned personalities and great battles of the Napoleonic era continues to be a rewarding enterprise.[1] In focusing solely on the main armies and major engagements, however, we can lose sight of key operations on the fringes of the core events. These are often not only interesting in themselves but also provide essential context for the central forces and battles. The Franco-Austrian War of 1809, for example, is remembered for Napoleon's repulse at the Battle of Aspern-Essling and his later victory at the titanic Battle of Wagram. Some will also recall that Napoleon considered the opening actions around Regensburg as 'the most brilliant and most skilful manoeuvres' of his career.[2] At the same time, however, the French with their Bavarian and Italian allies fought a brutal war against a pertinacious insurgency in the mountains of the Tyrol, a war that opened simultaneously with the main campaign but dragged on for months after the armistice of Znaim on 12 July and even beyond the signing of the Treaty of Schönbrunn on 14 October. Popular accounts of the rebellion in the Tyrol in German abound and some aspects have been subjected to scholarly scrutiny. The complex socio-political circumstances, the colourful folk figures, and the conflict's resonance in memory, for example, have attracted considerable attention, especially from those interested in the issues of German nationalism. Likewise, the three Bavarian expeditions into the northern Tyrol have been examined in several English-language works as well as a host of studies in German.

1 An earlier version of the first portion of this study was published as 'This Wretched War' in *The Age of Napoleon*, 37, 2004.

2 Napoleon, 'Notes sur le manuscrit venu de Sainte-Hélène' in *Correspondance de Napoléon Ier* (Paris: Plon, 1858–70), Vol.XXXI, p.235.

Less well known are the operations conducted by French and Italian troops on the southern and eastern marches of the Tyrol in 1809. The activities of these French and Italian forces, however, deserve attention for at least two reasons. First, though long neglected, they are of interest in their own right as examples of the military challenges associated with confronting a tenacious enemy in forbidding terrain in a secondary theatre where resources of all sorts were slim. Second, they form an important part of the strategic picture Napoleon faced in 1809.[3] Outlining the principal military operations in the Tyrol thus leads to a greater clarity regarding the assets the French emperor committed to the region at different times and helps us achieve a deeper understanding of his generalship in this complex conflict. A brief book chapter cannot cover all the manifold facets of the complex war in the Tyrol in 1809 and issues such as the origins of the rebellion, Austro-Tyrolian frictions, disputes within the Tyrolian leadership, the numerous atrocities perpetrated by both sides, the mountain tactics of rebels and regulars, pacification efforts, and the re-introduction of civilian authority. These must await another opportunity.[4] With appropriate reference to the crucial Bavarian offensives, therefore, this chapter will focus on the little-known military operations of French and Italian troops along the Tyrol's southern and eastern borders during 1809, hoping thereby to illuminate a dark but important corner of this vast war and to connect these actions, minor and major, with the larger strategic perspective as viewed from French imperial headquarters. Readers will also gain a sense of the locations of units—to regimental and battalion level—when they were not engaged in the central theatre along the Danube,[5] as well as an appreciation for Napoleon's reliance on limited numbers of second-line forces to contain subordinate threats so he could concentrate his time, mental energy, and physical forces on the defeat of the principal enemy army.

When Austria decided to launch an offensive war against Napoleonic France in the spring of 1809, its plans called for simultaneous actions in multiple directions. The principal attack would be an invasion of Bavaria by the Main Army (Hauptarmee) under the personal command of the Archduke Charles, the Habsburg Empire's most renowned soldier at the time. Two of the Hauptarmee's corps (I and II) were to advance out of Bohemia, but the majority of Charles's force (III, IV, V, VI, I Reserve and II Reserve Corps) was to enter into Bavaria by crossing

3 For a study of the entire war, see the author's *1809: Thunder on the Danube* (London: Frontline, 2008–10).

4 There is a wealth of scholarship on the Tyrolian insurrection in German, but English-speakers seeking further information on the Bavarians may wish to consult the author's *With Eagles to Glory* (London: Greenhill, 2011) for military affairs and F. Gunter Eyck's *Loyal Rebels* (Lanham: University Press of America, 1986) for an overview of the socio-political background. Two entry points for the enormous literature in German are Josef Hirn, *Tirols Erhebung im Jahre 1809* (Innsbruck: Haymon, 1983) and Ferdinand Hirn, *Vorarlbergs Erhebung im Jahre 1809* (Bregenz: Teutsch, 1909).

5 This is in part an effort to mitigate the 'lost battalion' problem so common in military histories: where units pop in and out of the narrative without explanation.

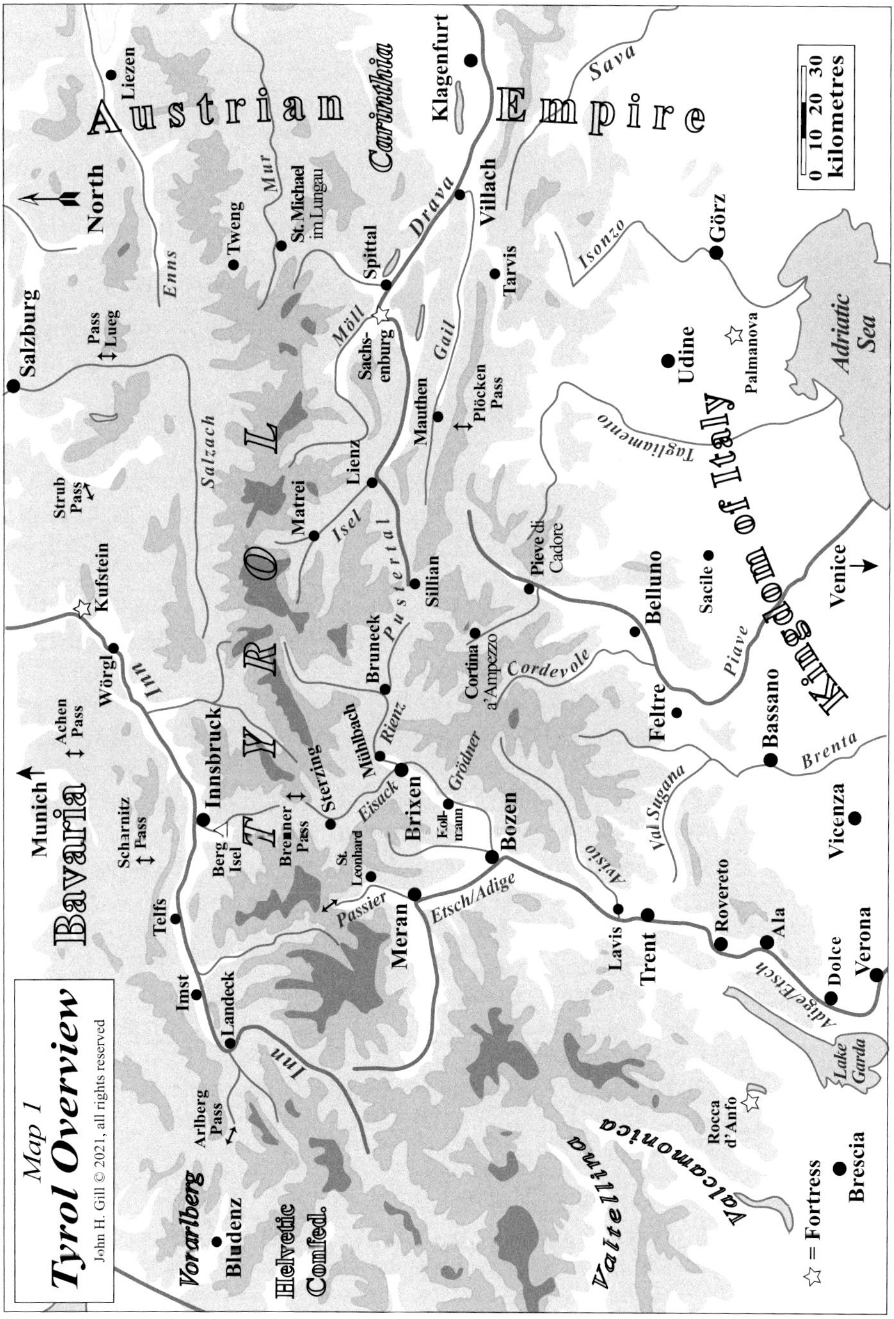
Map 1
Tyrol Overview
John H. Gill © 2021, all rights reserved
Austrian Empire
Bavaria
Munich
TYROL
Kingdom of Italy
Carinthia
Vorarlberg
Helvetic Confed.
Valtellina
Valcamonica
Salzburg
Liezen
North
Tweng
St. Michael im Lungau
Spittal
Villach
Klagenfurt
Tarvis
Görz
Udine
Palmanova
Adriatic Sea
Sachsenburg
Mauthen
Plöcken Pass
Lienz
Matrei
Sillian
Pieve di Cadore
Belluno
Sacile
Venice
Cortina d'Ampezzo
Bruneck
Feltre
Bassano
Mühlbach
Brixen
Sterzing
Brenner Pass
Innsbruck
Berg Isel
Kollmann
Bozen
St. Leonhard
Meran
Lavis
Trent
Rovereto
Ala
Dolce
Verona
Vicenza
Lake Garda
Rocca d'Anfo
Brescia
Kufstein
Wörgl
Strub Pass
Pass Lueg
Achen Pass
Scharnitz Pass
Telfs
Imst
Landeck
Arlberg Pass
Bludenz
Inn
Salzach
Enns
Mur
Drava
Möll
Gail
Isel
Pustertal
Rienz
Eisack
Grödner
Passier
Etsch/Adige
Avisio
Val Sugana
Brenta
Piave
Cordevole
Tagliamento
Isonzo
Sava
Adige/Etsch
0 10 20 30 kilometres
☆ = Fortress

the Inn River south of the Danube. Italy was the most important secondary theatre for the Austrian leadership and here the invasion was assigned to Archduke Johann and his Army of Inner Austria (VIII and IX Corps). Johann, Charles's younger brother, was also responsible for capturing the Tyrol in conjunction with local rebels. Further afield, the VII Corps would invade the Duchy of Warsaw (Poland) and an ad hoc force would push into French Dalmatia in the Balkans. These latter two operations were peripheral as far as the Tyrol was concerned, but actions in Italy and in the Danube valley would bear directly on the events under consideration here. Indeed, the Tyrol formed the critical connective link between these theatres of war and the fighting in the mountains would ebb and flow partly as a function of political–military developments north and south of the Alps.

## Opening Actions: April 1809

Napoleon had gifted the Tyrol to Bavaria's King Maximilian I Joseph as part of the Treaty of Pressburg in 1805 and one of Austria's central goals in 1809 was the return of the region to Habsburg sovereignty. This dynastic interest matched well with the desires of the Tyrolian population that chafed under Bavarian rule. Enthusiastic local patriots eagerly plotted with Austrian emissaries in advance of the war so the Tyrol was ripe for revolt when Habsburg troops marched up the valley of the River Drava on 9 April 1809. The Austrians were some 13,500 regulars and *Landwehr* (Austrian militia) of VIII Corps under the command of *Feldmarschall-Leutnant* Johann Gabriel Marquis Chasteler de Courcelles; a further 3,500 *Landwehr* were slated to join him. In addition to Chasteler, two small detachments from the Hauptarmee (totalling aproximately 1,500 men) entered the Tyrol from Salzburg and headed for Innsbruck, the region's capital.[6] Part of *Feldmarschall-Leutnant* Franz Freiherr Jellacic de Buzim's division of VI Corps, they were to protect the division's left flank as it marched to occupy Munich.

Combined with the invading Habsburg troops, the long prepared rebellion spread swiftly, engulfing the dispersed Bavarian garrisons (4,400 men), capturing Innsbruck, and bundling up a French replacement column of some 2,000 under *Général de Division* Baptiste Bisson, which had been marching north from Italy to join Marshal André Massena's IV Corps in Germany. By mid-April, the insurgents, with minimal assistance from Austrian regulars and *Landwehr*, had freed their homeland and were threatening to launch raids into neighbouring districts

6 Jellacic had left behind two small detachments. *Oberstleutnant* Paul Freiherr von Taxis had two companies of III/de Vaux Infanterie-Regiment, No. 45 joined with four companies of 2. Inner Austrian Volunteers, one company of 2. Salzburg Landwehr, a platoon of O'Reilly Chevaulegers-Regiment, No.3 and a company of Tyrolians (some 800 men). *Oberstleutnant* Samuel von Reissenfels commanded approximately 650 men in four companies of III/de Vaux Infanterie.

of Bavaria. Of the Bavarian garrisons, only the fortress of Kufstein, powerfully situated and commanded with energetic determination by *Major* Maximilian von Aicher, still held out against the exultant rebels.

Chasteler's lead troops reached Innsbruck on 14 April and he himself enjoyed an enthusiastic welcome the following day. Shortly thereafter, one of Jellacic's small detachments arrived from the opposite direction. Pleased with the success of the campaign thus far, Chasteler turned his attention to supporting Archduke Johann's invasion of Italy. Though a portion of his command had occupied Innsbruck and the surrounding area, the bulk of his troops had remained further south around Brixen (Bressanone) and he personally rode back over the Brenner Pass to arrive in Bozen (Bolzano) on the 21st. Here he encountered a collection of 12,000 insurgents and learned of Johann's 16 April victory at Sacile over the French Armée d'Italie under Napoleon's step-son, Viceroy Eugene de Beauharnais. Eugene was now retreating west towards Verona through torrents of rain and mud with Johann in pursuit. Ignorant of the Hauptarmee's situation and evidently quite confident, Chasteler marched south down the Etsch (Adige) valley towards Trent (Trento) and Verona hoping thereby to unhinge Eugene's left flank and support Johann's advance.

Meanwhile, a French force had been gathering at Dolce north of Verona to protect Eugene's alpine flank. This was based on a second replacement column of some 2,100 men under *Général de Division* Louis Lemoine. Like Bisson, Lemoine had been instructed to deliver his conscripts to IV Corps in Germany, but he had wisely retired to Trent on encountering masses of rebels at Brixen on 12 April. He now came under the orders of *Général de Division* Louis Baraguey d'Hilliers, sent to Trent by Eugene and charged with protecting the French left flank against threats from the Tyrol.[7] By 17 April, Baraguey d'Hilliers had a force of some 9,700 French and Italian soldiers at his disposal grouped in two divisions: *Général de Division* Honoré Vial's ad hoc French command consisting of Lemoine's column supplemented by the 112e Ligne and a squadron of the 7e Dragons; and *Général de Division* Achille Fontanelli's Italian division of nine Italian battalions, two squadrons of the Italian 2° Cacciatori and the remaining three squadrons of the French 7e Dragons (see Order of Battle 1).

Vial, who had fought in the region during the wars of the Revolution, was less than pleased with the assignment. 'I know from experience', he wrote to Eugene's chief of staff, 'that the Tyrol is a poor place to fight a war'.[8] Nonetheless, the steady arrival of these French reinforcements caused Chasteler's subordinates to fear a powerful enemy thrust into the Tyrol. Baraguey d'Hilliers, on the other hand,

7 Frédéric-François-Guillaume de Vaudoncourt, 'Mémoire sur la guerre soutenue par les insurgés tiroliens, en 1809 et 1810', *Journal des Sciences Militaires*, 1826, p.270.

8 Service Historique de la Défense (hereafter SHD), Correspondance du Général Vial, C4/80, Vial to Charpentier, 14 April 1809.

learning of the defeat at Sacile, did not feel secure at Trent and had no intention of advancing. With Eugene falling back and the Val Sugana providing an open avenue from the Brenta valley into that of the Adige, he worried that the position at Trent would be exposed to threats from the east. He thus withdrew to a position just north of Rovereto on the 21st but continued to worry that Eugene might suffer another defeat in the plains. In constant skirmishes with the Austrians and rebels, therefore, his French and Italian troops gradually dropped back to the south over the next seven days. By 28 April, he was established in a position at Dolce near the old Rivoli battlefield from 1797.

## Containing the Tyrol: May–June 1809

Eugene's fortunes, however, had improved dramatically by the end of April and, instead of withdrawing, he was preparing to advance. Johann's Italian offensive had stalled between Vicenza and Verona just as Eugene and his army recovered their poise. Moreover, Napoleon won a series of stunning victories against the Hauptarmee in Bavaria between 19 and 23 April, completely reversing the strategic situation. Withdrawal was now Johann's only option. Eugene, eager to pursue with his revived army, recalled Baraguey d'Hilliers and Fontanelli (five battalions and five squadrons) to participate in the chase.[9] Left behind at Dolce was French *Général de Division* Jean Rusca with Italian *Général de Brigade* Antonio Bertoletti and a mixed Franco–Italian division of some 5,200 infantry and cavalry (see Order of Battle 2).[10] For the next two and one half months, Rusca and his men would play a small but significant role in the Armée d'Italie's advance into Austria.

In conjunction with Eugene's counteroffensive, Rusca attacked an Austrian detachment at Ala, south of Rovereto, on 2 May. Rusca's advance benefited from the situation in Bavaria as Napoleon's defeat of Archduke Charles had forced Jellacic to retire from Salzburg thereby exposing the northern Tyrol to French attack. Learning of this peril on 28 April, Chasteler had hurried north to Innsbruck with the bulk of his small corps (10 battalions), leaving only five companies, half a squadron and two guns at Ala. Rusca thus encountered little difficulty in pushing the Austrians beyond Lavis. He then stormed into Trent on 4 May before marching east through the Val Sugana in accordance with his instructions to protect Eugene's alpine flank while simultaneously threatening Johann's.[11] With Rusca gone, however, the Austrians quickly reinforced their tiny detachment

9 The troops withdrawn were 112e Ligne, Italian 3° Linea and all of the cavalry with the exception of the 4th Squadron of the 7e Dragons.

10 Although there were seven Italian battalions, they were badly under strength.

11 Eugene to Napoleon, 6 May 1809 in Albert du Casse, *Mémoires et Correspondance Politique et Militaire du Prince Eugène* (Paris: Lévy, 1858-59), Vol.V, p.171.

and reoccupied Trent. In the process, they narrowly missed an opportunity of possibly destroying Rusca's little command. During his withdrawal, Archduke John had decided to shield his alpine right flank by strengthening the corps in the Tyrol. He thus detached a brigade under *General-Major* Josef von Schmidt from Bassano with instructions to join Chasteler at Trent via the Val Sugana.[12] At the same time, the Habsburg detachment that had just retaken Trent was to pursue Rusca from the west. Had both Austrian brigades complied with these instructions, Rusca would have been placed in an embarrassing situation indeed, trapped in the valley by strong regular forces supported by local rebels. Schmidt, however, turned north on learning of Rusca's presence in the Val Sugana and made his way to the Drava valley via Feltre. Rusca was thus free to continue with his task of protecting Eugene's left flank and unsettling the Austrians in the lowlands.[13]

Rusca, 'despite a cloud of peasants who crowned the heights and harassed his troops ceaselessly',[14] marched into Feltre on 8 May and proceeded northeast under instructions to gain Villach via the Gail valley.[15] He had a successful engagement with an Austrian detachment and some insurgents at Pieve di Cadore on the 10th, but found the mountain passes too difficult for his artillery and thus returned to the plains to cross the Alps at Tarvis in the wake of Eugene's main columns. As the Armée d'Italie drove north and east in pursuit of Archduke John, however, Eugene charged Rusca with protecting the army's line of communications to Italy and containing Chasteler in the Tyrol. In obedience to these orders, Rusca marched west up the Drava valley and occupied Spittal on 23 May, but his attempts to advance further and secure the fortress of Sachsenburg were blunted by insurgents and a handful of Austrian regulars in a series of skirmishes between 24 and 27 May.

While Rusca was marching through Tarvis to Spittal, a flanking column of two battalions (II/Reggimento Dalmato and four companies of the 3º Leggera) had pushed its way across the Plöcken Pass against considerable resistance on 27 May. These two battalions, numbering approximately 1,000 men under *Colonel* Angelo Moroni of the Reggimento Dalmato, arrived in Villach on the 29th, but Rusca was doubtless disappointed when the Dalmatian battalion left to join the Armée d'Italie on its march into Hungary. The Italians too soon departed, returning to their garrison station in the fortress of Palmanova.[16]

12 Schmidt's brigade consisted of the Johann Jellacic Infanterie-Regiment, No. 53, 2nd Banal Grenz-Regiment, No. 11 and four squadrons of Hohenzollern Chevaulegers-Regiment, No. 2.

13 Eberhard Mayerhoffer von Vedropolje, *Österreichs Krieg mit Napoleon I. 1809* (Vienna: Seidel & Sohn, 1904), p.130.

14 Du Casse, *Prince Eugène*, Vol.V, p.69.

15 'Ordre de mouvement pour le 8 mai', in SHD, Manuscript 734, Martin Vignolle, 'Journal Historique de la Campagne de 1809', May 1810.

16 Simone Addobbati, *Il Reggimento Reale Dalmata* (Zara: Artale, 1899), pp.14–8.

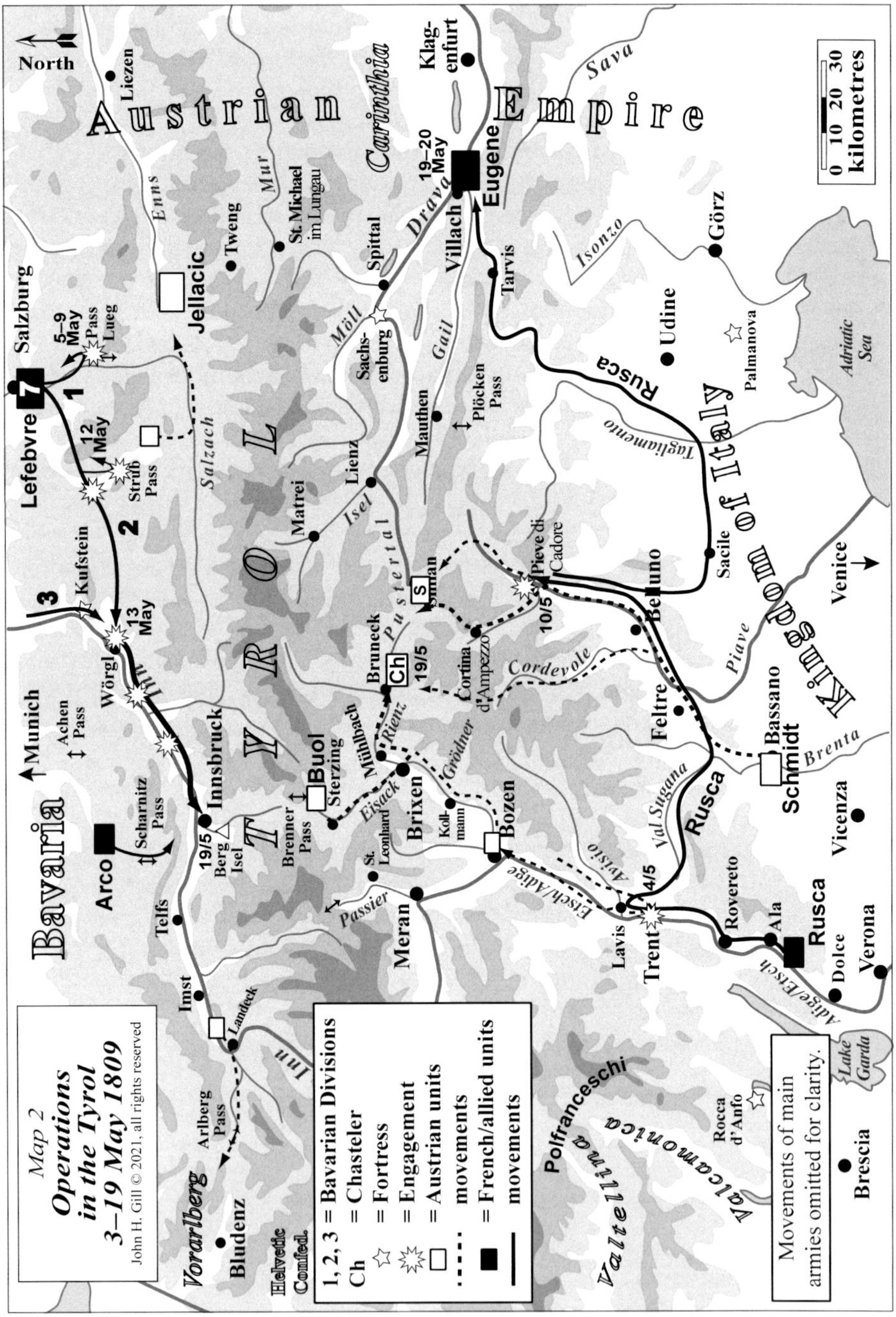
Map 2
Operations in the Tyrol 3–19 May 1809
John H. Gill © 2021, all rights reserved
1, 2, 3 = Bavarian Divisions
Ch = Chasteler
= Fortress
= Engagement
= Austrian units
movements
= French/allied units
movements
Movements of main armies omitted for clarity.
North
0 10 20 30 kilometres
Austrian Empire
Bavaria
TYROL
Kingdom of Italy
Carinthia
Vorarlberg
Helvetic Confed.
Munich
Salzburg
Liezen
Klagenfurt
Lefebvre
Jellacic
Eugene
Rusca
Schmidt
Buol
Arco
Polfranceschi
Innsbruck
Kufstein
Wörgl
Strub Pass
Pass Lueg
Achen Pass
Scharnitz Pass
Brenner Pass
Berg Isel
Telfs
Imst
Landeck
Arlberg Pass
Bludenz
Sterzing
Mühlbach
Bruneck
Brixen
Kollmann
Bozen
Meran
St. Leonhard
Lienz
Matrei
Sachsenburg
Spittal
Villach
Tarvis
Mauthen
Plöcken Pass
Tweng
St. Michael im Lungau
Cortina d'Ampezzo
Pieve di Cadore
Belluno
Feltre
Bassano
Vicenza
Verona
Dolce
Ala
Rovereto
Trent
Lavis
Sacile
Udine
Palmanova
Görz
Venice
Rocca d'Anfo
Brescia
Lake Garda
Adriatic Sea
Salzach
Enns
Mur
Drava
Möll
Gail
Isel
Inn
Eisack
Rienz
Grödner
Passier
Etsch/Adige
Avisio
Val Sugana
Brenta
Piave
Cordevole
Tagliamento
Isonzo
Sava
Valtellina
Valcamonica
Pustertal
5–9 May
12 May
13 May
19/5
19–20 May
10/5
4/5

Rusca did not remain long at Spittal. Learning that Chasteler was moving down the Drava valley from the west with the bulk of the Austrian troops from the Tyrol, the French general withdrew his isolated command to Villach on 1 June to avoid being outflanked. On the 4th, again concerned that Chasteler would edge around him, Rusca fell back to the walled town of Klagenfurt, enduring an indecisive skirmish and other 'outpost affairs' en route. Chasteler was indeed approaching, but he seems to have been in a desperate mental state after suffering a severe defeat at Wörgl on 13 May, quarrelling bitterly with his supposed Tyrolian allies, and learning that Napoleon had declared him an outlaw. Johann having granted him freedom to act as he thought best, Chasteler left a portion of his force in the Tyrol under *General-Major* Ignaz von Buol and marched east along the Drava in an effort to join the archduke in Hungary. Klagenfurt and Rusca blocked his path (see Order of Battle 3). Seeking only to escape, Chasteler hoped to mask the town with part of his command while slipping past with the rest. In the pre-dawn hours of 6 June, he set his plan in motion. Rusca, however, had no intention of being an idle spectator to the Austrian retreat. He had spent the 5th bolstering Klagenfurt's defences and had written to *Général de Division* Auguste Marmont requesting assistance. Marmont was marching north from Illyria with his small Army of Dalmatia to join Napoleon at Vienna and Rusca hoped they could co-operate to trap Chasteler between their two forces. As 6 June dawned, however, he had received no reply from Marmont. Nonetheless, he was determined to exploit his fleeting opportunity and sallied out of the town early that morning to open a lively and costly struggle that lasted until 7:00 p.m. Rusca initially enjoyed remarkable success as his swift attack in the morning caught the Austrians outside Klagenfurt's walls completely by surprise. At least four Austrian companies were destroyed (that is, over 100 men were killed or captured from each) in the opening onslaught and Rusca proceeded to press his advantage by attacking to the north-west. Fortunately for Chasteler, *Oberst* Anton von Volkmann of the Johann Jellacic Infanterie-Regiment No.53 held firm against the French and Italian assaults and the day concluded with Chasteler escaping to the east with most of his command. *General-Major* Schmidt, on the other hand, apparently overcome with confusion and panic, retired in the opposite direction, that is, back west into the Tyrol. With five companies, a weak half squadron of Hohenzollern Chevaulegers No.2 and two guns, he would remain there until the armistice in July.[17] Although Rusca had failed to prevent Chasteler's escape, he could be well pleased with the day's fight. In addition to preserving his small division, his prompt and vigorous action had inflicted heavy losses on the Austrians, including the capture of more than 650

17 Alexander Theimer, *Geschichte des k. k. siebenten Uhlanen-Regiments* (Vienna: Sommer, 1869), pp.248–52. Schmidt was to have been tried for his behaviour, but took his own life before his court martial was convened.

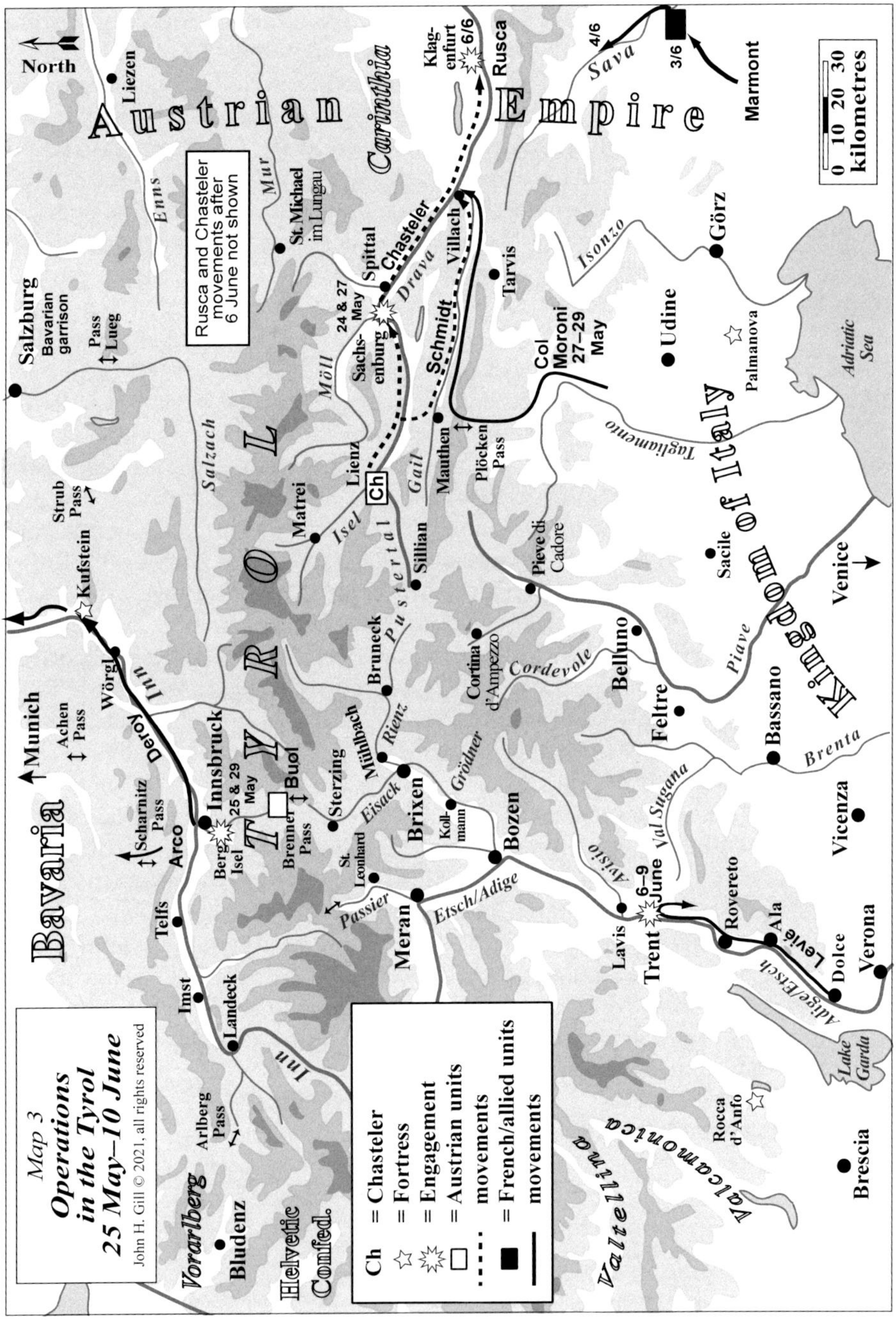
Map 3
Operations in the Tyrol 25 May–10 June
John H. Gill © 2021, all rights reserved
Ch = Chasteler
= Fortress
= Engagement
= Austrian units movements
= French/allied units movements
Rusca and Chasteler movements after 6 June not shown
North
Bavaria
Austrian Empire
Kingdom of Italy
TYROL
Carinthia
Vorarlberg
Helvetic Confed.
Valtellina
Valcamonica
Munich
Salzburg
Bavarian garrison
Pass Lueg
Strub Pass
Kufstein
Wörgl
Achen Pass
Scharnitz Pass
Innsbruck
25 & 29 May
Berg Isel
Arco
Telfs
Imst
Landeck
Arlberg Pass
Bludenz
Deroy
Inn
Enns
Salzach
Mur
Liezen
St. Michael im Lungau
Spittal
Chasteler
Drava
Villach
Klagenfurt
6/6
Rusca
Sava
4/6
3/6
Marmont
0 10 20 30 kilometres
Tarvis
Isonzo
Görz
Udine
Palmanova
Adriatic Sea
Col Moroni 27–29 May
Schmidt
Sachsenburg
24 & 27 May
Möll
Lienz
Ch
Gail
Mauthen
Plöcken Pass
Matrei
Isel
Pustertal
Sillian
Pieve di Cadore
Tagliamento
Sacile
Venice
Piave
Belluno
Cortina d'Ampezzo
Cordevole
Bruneck
Rienz
Mühlbach
Buol
Brenner Pass
Sterzing
Eisack
Brixen
Grödner
Kollmann
Bozen
St. Leonhard
Passier
Meran
Etsch/Adige
Avisio
Val Sugana
Feltre
Bassano
Brenta
Vicenza
Lavis
Trent
6–9 June
Rovereto
Ala
Levie
Dolce
Verona
Adige/Etsch
Lake Garda
Rocca d'Anfo
Brescia

prisoners.[18] Marmont diverted a portion of his army towards Klagenfurt, but was unable to arrive in time to snare and destroy Chasteler. He and his men were soon back on the road north to Graz and Vienna, leaving a disgusted Rusca in Carinthia (Kärnten).[19]

Rusca reoccupied Villach on 8 June and remained in the vicinity of these two towns with his little division for the next several weeks. Appointed military governor of Carinthia, he coped with small insurgent forays and, by his presence, held the Austrians troops in the Tyrol in check. Furthermore, he maintained the Armée d'Italie's line of communications from Hungary back across the Alps, securing a key portion of the long route and providing detachments to escort prisoners.

Far to Rusca's rear, Austrian agents had also instigated disturbances in the Valtellina and Valcamonica regions during mid-May. Prompt action by *Général de Brigade* Pietro Domenico Polfranceschi with a motley collection of some 1,200 depot soldiers, national guards, and gendarmes, however, quickly extinguished these sparks and small Austrian initiatives to support the nascent rebellion were withdrawn in the wake of Chasteler's defeat at Wörgl.[20]

## Repulses North and South: June 1809

This is a good point to catch up on events in the northern half of the Tyrol. In early May, at the same time that Rusca was heading east through the Val Sugana from Trent, *Maréchal* François Lefebvre arrived on Tyrol's borders with the three divisions of the Bavarian VII Corps, evicting Jellacic's division of Austrian regulars from Salzburg and occupying the city. Napoleon, driving rapidly on Vienna with the main army, was principally concerned that Jellacic might threaten the French right and rear in the Danube valley. He also wanted to quell the rebellion and open communications with Italy. He thus instructed Lefebvre to march on Innsbruck while keeping watch on Jellacic, optimistically hoping that VII Corps could quash the Tyrolian insurrection in four or five days.[21] Lefebvre duly marched into the Tyrol on 11 May with his 1st and 2nd Divisions from Salzburg and the 3rd from Kufstein supported by a column of reserve troops under *Oberst* Maximilian Graf

18 Frédéric-François-Guillaume de Vaudoncourt, *Histoire Politique et Militaire du Prince Eugène Napoléon* (Paris: Mongie, 1828), Vol.I, pp.375–7; Rusca's 10 June 1809 report in du Casse, *Prince Eugène*, Vol.V, pp.286–7; Alfons Freiherr von Wrede, *Geschichte des K. U. K. Infanterieregimentes Michael Grossfürst von Russland Nr. 26* (Györ: regimental, 1909), pp.307–8.

19 Gill, *Thunder*, Vol.III:129–33. Italian strength figure from Vaudoncourt, 'Mémoire sur la guerre', p.277.

20 For sources, see Gill, *Thunder*, Vol.III, pp.120–1.

21 Napoleon to Berthier, 9 May 1809, *Correspondance*, No. 15179, Vol.XVIII, pp.547–8; and Berthier to Lefebvre, 6 May and 9 May 1809, in Charles Saski, *Campagne de 1809* (Paris, 1899-1902), Vol.III, pp.175–6, 216.

Arco over the Scharnitz Pass. The Bavarians entered Innsbruck on the 19th after a series of vicious actions against the rebels and Austrian regulars in the Inn valley, the most notable being the crushing defeat of Chasteler's command at Wörgl on 13 May. The Wörgl catastrophe, the loss of Innsbruck, and the other struggles in the Inn valley left the Austro–Tyrolian leadership in disputatious disarray and the rebellion subsided into temporary torpor. A few quiet days in Innsbruck thus sufficed to persuade Lefebvre that the entire region had been pacified and he happily reported 'the complete submission of the Tyrol following our victories and the severe punishments which have been given.'[22] Although he had hardly begun to disarm the region, Lefebvre believed that Napoleon's orders required him to re-join the main army as rapidly as possible and he departed Innsbruck on 23 May, leaving behind *General-Leutnant* Erasmus von Deroy's 3rd Division of 5,000 men at the end of a tenuous line of communications.

Deroy was soon in grave danger. Only two days after Lefebvre's departure, the Bavarians found themselves involved in heavy skirmishing with the revived rebels and Austrian regulars. Following a major engagement against an Austro-Tyrolian force of some 13,000 on the 29th at Berg Isel outside the city, Deroy, badly outnumbered, nearly cut off, and mindful of the manner in which the previous Bavarian garrison had been eradicated, decided to withdraw.[23] On the night of 29 May, he skilfully evacuated his men and retreated back down the Inn valley.[24] Lefebvre, still in Salzburg, had decided to march to Deroy's rescue, but the needs of the main army intervened and he marched to the Danube valley in response to urgent orders from imperial headquarters. By 1 June, therefore, the Tyrol was again in the hands of the insurgents and Napoleon's hopes for a speedy elimination of this distraction were dashed.[25]

As on Rusca's front in Carinthia, an operational pause now ensued in the north. All through June and into late July, Deroy's men, supplemented by a hotchpotch host of depot troops and other newly-created Bavarian and French second line

22 Lefebvre to King Max Joseph, 21 May 1809 in Jean Sauzey, *Nos Alliés les Bavarois* (Paris: Terana, 1988), p.141.

23 See Gedeon Freiherr Maretich von Riv-Alpon, *Die zweite und dritte Berg Isel-Schlacht* (Innsbruck: Wagner, 1895).

24 The engagements at Innsbruck are generally known by the name of a prominent hill that dominates the level ground south of the city: Berg Isel. The fracas on 13 April that resulted in Bisson's surrender is widely considered the 'First Battle of Berg Isel', thereafter the numeration becomes confused. Some describe the skirmishing on 25 May as the second battle and the combat on the 29th as the third battle; others disregard the actions on the 25th, leaving a question over how to name the battles that took place on 13 August and 1 November. The easiest method is simply to refer to the battles by their dates.

25 Berthier to Lefebvre, 26 May 1809, *Correspondance*, No. 15259, Vol.XIX, p.46; Eduard Freiherr von Völderndorff und Waradein, *Kriegsgeschichte von Bayern unter König Maximilian Joseph I.* (Munich: unknown, 1826), Vol.II, p.179; and Edmond Buat, *1809 De Ratisbonne à Znaïm* (Paris: Chapelot, 1909), Vol.II, pp.5–7.

formations, fended off a series of bold, but largely ineffectual, Tyrolian raids into Bavaria proper.

South of the Alps, similar ad hoc collections of depot soldiers, national guards, and gendarmes tried to limit depredatory Tyrolian attacks on Bassano, Belluno, and other Italian towns. The only relatively 'major' action was an attempt by *Colonel* Joseph Levié with a small command built around the I and III/ 3° Linea (the only regular troops in the area) to recapture Trent. Leading some 1,400-2,000 infantry, 170 mounted gendarmes and three guns, Levié marched north up the Adige on 3 June, pushing back a tiny force of Austrian regulars under *Oberstleutnant* Christian Graf Leiningen.[26] On 6 June, the same day as the engagement at Klagenfurt, Levié succeeded in confining the tiny force of Austrian regulars in the Trent citadel. He could not, however, dislodge the determined Leiningen. Three days later, he was himself attacked by an overwhelming number of rebels and forced to withdraw to Ala south of Rovereto.[27]

## Wagram, Armistice, and Continued Fighting in the Tyrol: July–September 1809

The pause in the Tyrol ended in early July as Napoleon sought to gather every possible bayonet and sabre for his second attempt to cross the Danube. As a result, General Deroy's Bavarian 3rd Division left Bavaria for Linz on 6 and 7 July to replace *General-Leutnant* Carl Phillip Freiherr von Wrede's 2nd Division, which had departed on its legendary march to Vienna on 30 June. Likewise, Rusca was ordered to Bruck to help secure the French rear while Napoleon attacked the Austrian Main Army across the Danube.[28] In accordance with these instructions, Rusca left Bertoletti in Klagenfurt with three Italian battalions (approximately 900 men) and marched north with the rest of his small division on 3 July (approximately 2,400 men in six battalions with five guns).[29] The division, though moving in the army's rear, was by no means in a secure area and Rusca proceeded cautiously, probing towards Loeben on 5 July but retiring quickly to Knittelfeld

26 Leiningen had three companies each of Hohenlohe Infanterie and 9th Jägers along with one squadron of Hohenzollern Chevaulegers.

27 Details from Kasimir Freiherr von Lütgendorf, *Die Kämpfe in Südtirol* (Vienna: Seidel & Sohn, 1911), p.69; Wrede, *Geschichte*, pp.315–7; and Ludwig Freiherr von Welden, *Der Krieg von 1809 zwischen Oesterreich und Frankreich* (Vienna: Gerold, 1872), pp.263–6.

28 Napoleon to Eugene, 29 June 1809, *Correspondance*, No. 15467, Vol.XIX, pp.196–7.

29 Vaudoncourt, *Histoire Politique et Militaire*, Vol.I, p.427. Rusca's strength from SHD, C2/509, Armée d'Italie, *Situation Sommaire* for 25 June 1809; and SHD, C4/10, Rusca's *Situation* for 25 June 1809. Note that this assumes that the approximately 150 Italian chasseurs (from the 1° and 2° Cacciatori) accompanied Rusca and that Bertoletti was left with some artillery. It is not clear which Italian battalions stayed with Bertoletti and which went with Rusca.

on learning that *Feldmarschall-Leutnant* Ignaz Graf Gyulay was approaching from the south-east with Austrian IX Corps, a force several times larger than Rusca's miniature command. Before long, however, further intelligence revealed that although the Austrians had occupied Loeben, the garrison in the town was only a small advance guard under newly-promoted *General-Major* Ferdinand von Fellner. Rusca sensed an opportunity. Resolving to attack, he countermarched on 6 July and stormed into Loeben at 10:00 p.m., surprising and scattering the hapless Austrian force.[30] Rusca's attack cost the Austrians some 400 casualties, including Fellner who fell mortally wounded. Despite this satisfying little victory, the interrogation of prisoners and locals revealed that Gyulay's men had entered Judenburg in Rusca's rear and that superior forces were approaching from his front and right as well. The French general had no choice but to seek safety in retreat. Burning the Loeben bridge, Rusca withdrew from the town at 3:00 a.m. the following morning and marched via Liezen to Salzburg where he arrived on 13 July.[31]

In Salzburg, Rusca learned that Napoleon had agreed to an armistice with Archduke Charles at Znaim on 12 July. He also received the doubtless unwelcome news that his two French battalions (III/67e and III/93e Ligne originally from Lemoine's column) were to join their home regiments with the IV Corps in Moravia at the earliest opportunity. Though composed almost entirely of untrained conscripts, these two battalions had proven themselves over the past two months. Furthermore, the two French battalions totalled more than 1,100 men, so it was a much weaker 'division' that departed Salzburg on 17 July to return to the Klagenfurt area.[32] Insurgents planned to ambush Rusca's small force, but the cunning French general, marching at night and with few halts, outdistanced the rebels and returned safely to Spittal on the 21st.[33]

The terms of the 12 July armistice required *General-Major* Buol's Austrian troops to evacuate the Tyrol and give up the Sachsenburg fortress, which was accordingly turned over to Rusca on 1 August (see Order of Battle 4). The armistice also allowed Napoleon to redistribute the Armée d'Italie for occupation duties pending a final peace treaty. This included committing more forces to the

30 The Austrian force consisted of a battalion of Szuliner Grenzer, No. 4, one and one-half squadrons of Savoy Dragoner-Regiment, No. 5, and a detachment of Frimont Hussars, No. 9. See Karin Hummer, 'Eine Handschrift zum Franzosenjahr 1809 in Loeben', *Loebener Strauss* (1975), pp.71–5; Johann Baptist Schels, 'Der Feldzug 1809 in Italian', *Oesterreichische militärische Zeitschrift*, 1844; Friedrich von Seidel, 'Die Operationen des von dem Banus von Kroazien, Feldmarschall-Leutnant Grafen Ignaz Gyulai befehligten östreichischen neunten Armeekorps in Feldzuge 1809', *Oesterreichische militärische Zeitschrift* (1837), p.255–6; Welden, *Krieg von 1809*, p.232; Friedrich von der Wengen. *Geschichte des K. K. Oesterreichischen 13. Dragoner-Regiments Prinz Eugen von Savoyen* (Brandeis: regimental, 1879), pp.630–1; Hans von Zwiedineck-Südenhorst, 'Die Ostalpen in den Franzosenkriegen', *Zeitschrift des deutschen und österreichischen Alpenvereins* (1899), p.87.

31 SHD, C2/93, Rusca to Berthier, 11 July 1809; Vaudoncourt, Vol.I, pp.425–7.

32 SHD, manuscript, *67e Régiment d'Infanterie*, 1891, p.222.

33 See Maretich von Riv-Alpon, 'Struber'; and Welden, *Krieg von 1809*, p.282.

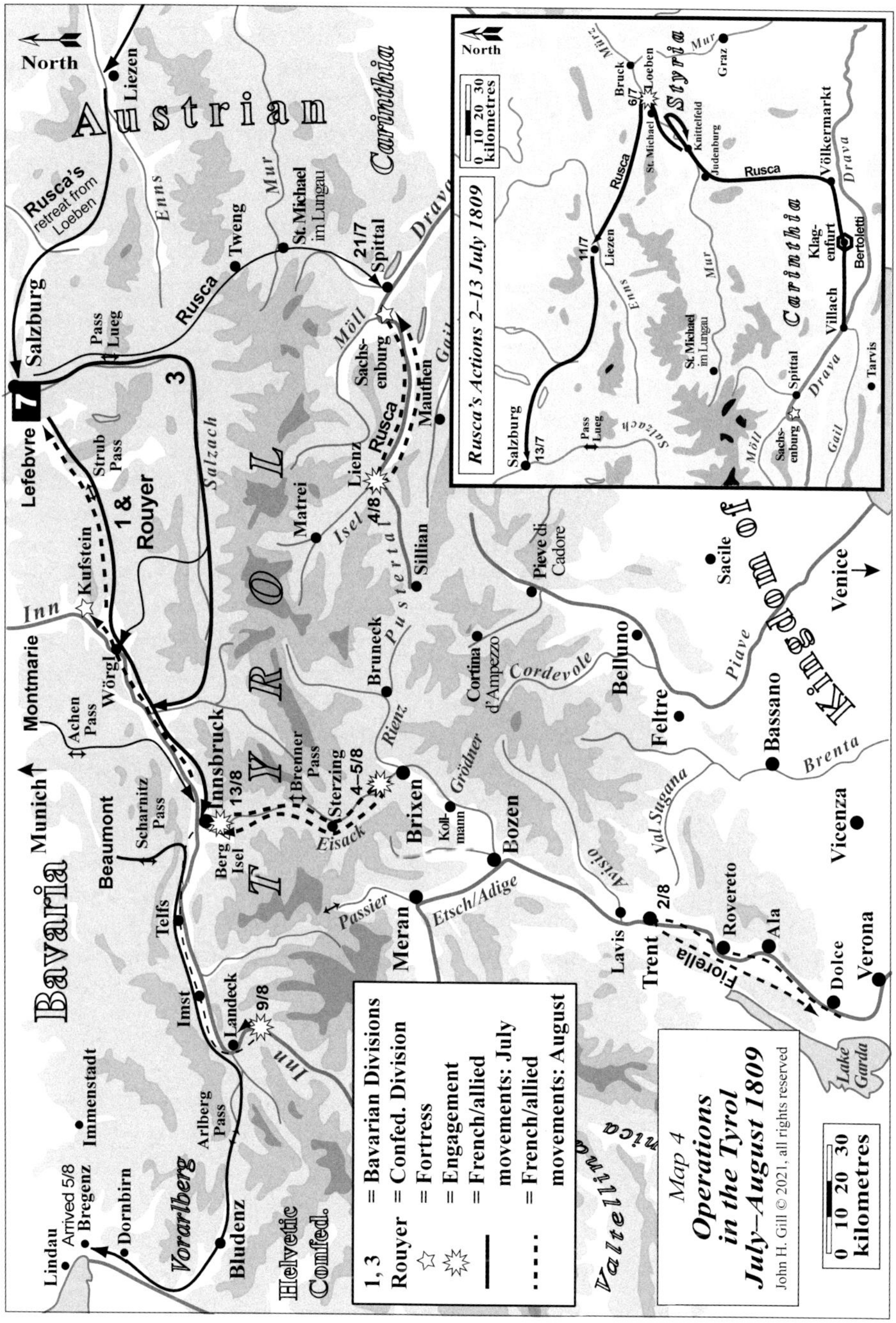
Map 4
Operations in the Tyrol July–August 1809
John H. Gill © 2021, all rights reserved
1, 3 = Bavarian Divisions
Rouyer = Confed. Division
= Fortress
= Engagement
= French/allied movements: July
= French/allied movements: August
Rusca's Actions 2–13 July 1809
North
0 10 20 30 kilometres

suppression of the rebellion. *Général de Division* Filippo Severoli's division from the Armée d'Italie thus moved from Hungary to Laybach (Ljubljana) in what is now Slovenia and detached several battalions to reinforce Rusca.[34] Bolstered by these reinforcements and believing that the departure of the Austrian regulars would lead the rebels to lay down their arms, Rusca left a battalion of the Italian 2° Leggera to garrison the fortress and advanced towards Lienz and Mauthen. After fighting his way into Lienz on 4 August, however, he was completely disabused of the notion that the Tyrolians had given up and quickly abandoned any attempt to disarm the neighbouring vales. Indeed, given the level of unrest, he was now in danger of being cut off in his exposed position and, on 11 August, Eugene ordered him to withdraw to Klagenfurt leaving strong detachments at Sachsenburg, Spittal, Villach, and Tarvis.[35]

Rusca's was not the only setback suffered by the French and their allies in August. In the Inn valley, Lefebvre's Bavarian VII Corps had undertaken a second march on Innsbruck in mid-July, shortly after Rusca had departed Salzburg. The Bavarian 1st and 3rd Divisions along with *Général de Division* Marie François Rouyer's small division of Confederation of the Rhine regiments thus advanced from Salzburg on 27 July supported by a Bavarian flanking column under French *Général de Brigade* Louis Pelletier, Comte de Montmarie, through the Achen Pass. At the same time, *Général de Division* Marc-Antoine Bonin de la Bonière, Comte de Beaumont, led a mixed French-German force across the Scharnitz Pass; he was to march through the Tyrol en route to suppressing the insurrection in the Vorarlberg. The Bavarians and Germans of VII Corps entered the Tyrolian capital on 30 July and sent a strong column across the Brenner Pass while a second force probed further up the Inn in the wake of Beaumont. Both met with disaster and recoiled back to Innsbruck under constant pressure from the insurgents. Attacked south of the city on 13 August, the Bavarians held their own in yet another Berg Isel battle, but Lefebvre was personally demoralised and facing an uncomfortable logistical situation. Seeing no alternative, the marshal ordered a retreat and, by 20 August, the men of the VII Corps were once again back at Kufstein and Salzburg.[36]

South of the Alps, *Général de Division* Pasquale Fiorella also ventured an advance, sending a small Italian force up the Adige valley on 1 August. This march

34 These were: Italian I, II, III/1° Linea with I and II/Reggimento Dalmato; French IV/22e Léger from Durutte's division may have been assigned to Rusca for a time as well. Additionally, one battalion (III) of the 4° Linea from Severoli's division was sent to garrison Fiume (Rijeka). SHD, C2/509, Armée d'Italie, *Situation Sommaire*, 10 August 1809 and *Situation*, 15 August 1809.

35 Du Casse, *Prince Eugène*, Vol.XVI, pp.144-46; Louis-François Lejeune, *The Memoirs of Baron Lejeune* (Felling: Worley reprint, 1987), Vol.I, pp.334-41; Josef Thonhauser *Osttirol im Jahre 1809* (Innsbruck: Wagner, 1968), pp.50–68; Vaudoncourt, *Histoire Politique et Militaire*, Vol.II, p.9; SHD, manuscript, Martin Vignolle, 'Historique de la Campagne du Tyrol en 1809', May 1810, pp.14–16.

36 See John H. Gill, *With Eagles to Glory* (London: Greenhill, 2011), Chapters 7 and 8 for detailed accounts of these operations.

toward Trent had not progressed very far, however, when he learned of Lefebvre's repulse and retired to Dolce.[37]

By late August, therefore, the Tyrol had once again freed itself from French and Bavarian occupation and another pause ensued as Napoleon concentrated his attention on concluding a favourable peace treaty with the Habsburgs. The Emperor, however, did not neglect the Tyrol. In an attempt to mollify the rebels, he instructed Berthier to have Rusca to send an officer to the insurgent commanders offering to restore peace and attend to local grievances if the Tyrolians would return to the Napoleonic fold.[38] This letter, however, was evidently intercepted by the rebels before it reached Rusca and the reconciliation initiative evaporated before it had a chance to develop.[39]

## From the Treaty of Schönbrunn to the End of the Rebellion: October–December 1809

Other than minor insurgent raids, late August and early September passed quietly for the French and their allies on the frontiers of the Tyrol. By mid-September, however, a force of approximately 3,200 men had assembled under *Général de Brigade* Peyri at Dolce (see Order of Battle 5). The experienced Peyri, using a plan devised in April by *Adjutant Commandant* Frédéric–François Guillaume de Vaudoncourt, advanced north on 26 September, capturing Trent on the 29th and reaching Lavis by 2 October.[40] Situated on the Avisio River approximately eight kilometres north of Trent, Lavis proved too exposed and Peyri was forced to withdraw to the Trent citadel on 6 October under heavy attack by the rebels. He received, however, a steady flow of reinforcements. When he returned to the attack on the 10th, he thus had approximately 5,900 effectives on hand and was able to throw the insurgents back north across the Avisio.

The French now paused to reorganise under a new leader, *Général de Division* Vial, who arrived from Venice to replace Peyri on 13 October, while the latter shifted to Belluno to command an ad hoc force of depot troops. Vial had some 4,600 French, Italians, and Neapolitans when he assumed command of the forces in the Adige valley, but he moved deliberately, waiting until the arrival of further reinforcements on the 20th to advance to Lavis (see Order of Battle 6).[41] He

37 The Italian troops were probably Leviè's. It is not clear whether Fiorella personally accompanied the advancing column or remained at his headquarters in Verona. Alessandro Zanoli, *Sulla Milizia Cisaplino-Italiana cenni Storico-Statistici dal 1796 al 1814* (Milan: no publisher given, 1845), Vol.II, p.100.

38 Napoleon to Berthier, 29 August 1809, *Correspondance*, No. 15725, Vol.XIX, pp.405–6.

39 Vaudoncourt, *Histoire Politique et Militaire*, Vol.II, pp.10–11; Hirn, *Tirols Erhebung*, p.700.

40 Vaudoncourt was promoted to *Général de Brigade* on 30 May 1809.

41 With the French and Italian components of the Armée d'Italie campaigning in Hungary and Austria, Napoleon had ordered French and Neapolitan troops from Naples to secure parts of northern and central

managed to occupy the town but, like Peyri, he could not clear the surrounding area sufficiently to hold it and soon returned to Trent. He launched another foray on 24 October and was making satisfactory progress when he received orders from Viceroy Eugene to suspend offensive operations. Leaving three battalions in the Val Sugana, Vial duly retired to Trent to await further instructions. If the net results of Peyri's and Vial's actions in the Adige valley seem at best modest, the two generals had nonetheless succeeded in clearing the rebels from the eastern shore of Lake Garda and in establishing firm control over both Trent and the western terminus of the Val Sugana. They thereby removed the threat of rebel raids against Verona and laid the foundation for further operations up the Adige into the heart of the Tyrol.

While Peyri and Vial were busy along the Adige, the French and their allies were also active in the eastern and northern portions of the Tyrol. In the east, Rusca had been principally concerned with supplying the fortress of Sachsenburg on the Drava, his efforts sparking repeated skirmishes with the numerous insurgents in the area. The rebels, however, were unable to force the garrison's surrender despite several attempts, and by 28 October, Rusca, with the reinforcements from Severoli's division, had relieved the fort and opened a secure line of communications. Furthermore, he sent a column north to St Michael im Lungau to establish contact with Bavarian cavalry probing south from Salzburg.

In the north, the Bavarian VII Corps had opened its third offensive into the Tyrol. Napoleon had relieved Lefebvre of command of the corps on 11 October, so the Bavarians were now under *Général de Division* Jean-Baptiste Drouet d'Erlon, the former corps chief of staff. Working closely with his Bavarian subordinates and local forestry officials, Drouet opened the offensive with a tactical masterpiece, overwhelming rebel outposts in a surprise attack southwest of Salzburg on the night of 16/17 October. The Bavarians entered Innsbruck once again on 28 October and fought a final battle at Berg Isel outside the city on 1 November, scattering the rebels and securing a firm hold on the middle stretch of the Inn.

The VII Corps offensive was part of Napoleon's grand plan to extinguish the Tyrolian rebellion now that the signing of the Treaty of Schönbrunn on 14 October freed him to concentrate his attention and his troops on the subjugation of the troublesome region. His strategy envisaged a French and allied force pushing into the region from three directions under the overall command of Viceroy Eugene: (1) the three Bavarian divisions from the north to Innsbruck as related above, (2) an ad hoc corps of three Franco-Italian divisions under Baraguey d'Hilliers up the Drava valley from the east to Brixen, and (3) Vial's division from the south to Bozen. In all, some 45,000 troops would be involved in the initial operations with more to be added later. As outlined in a set of 'Instructions for the Viceroy of Italy' written on the same day that the peace treaty was signed, Eugene was to exercise a

Italy.

combination of force and diplomacy to achieve his goal: 'disarm the countryside, subdue it, identify the principal agitators, listen to the grievances of the inhabitants and take steps to satisfy them.'[42] A thoughtful Bavarian artillery officer later observed: 'one must simultaneously flood the entire land in order to conquer it.'[43] Napoleon intended to do just that.

Although d'Erlon had initiated his attacks in mid-October, Baraguey d'Hilliers did not get his offensive underway until the end of the month (see Order of Battle 7). Severoli's division – which had absorbed Rusca's command – led the main body of the corps as it began moving up the Drava valley on 29 October, passing over into the Pustertal and reaching Bruneck on 4 November. *Général de Division* Gabriel Barbou followed Severoli, halting several kilometres east of Bruneck. *Général de Brigade* François-Antoine Teste, interim commander of *Général de Division* Jean-Baptiste Broussier's division (Broussier was in Graz recuperating from an illness), had the responsibility for garrisoning Sillian, Lienz, Sachsenburg, and Spittal, while holding most of his division at Villach and Klagenfurt. Rusca, a supernumerary now that his troops had been placed under Severoli's command, was entrusted with a small avantgarde of French troops that made its way through the Gail valley to take up a position slightly west of Bruneck. A detachment of several companies from the 13e Ligne provided flank protection to the north, marching through the valley of the Möll to re-join the main column at Lienz. Additionally, a small detachment of Dalmatian infantry and French chasseurs made its way to St Michael im Lungau to establish liaison with the VII Corps. By 4 November, therefore, Baraguey d'Hilliers was well ensconced in and around Bruneck with a fairly secure line of communications back to Villach and a link to Drouet d'Erlon.

In the south, Vial was to advance on Brixen and Eugene, expecting heavy resistance, directed Peyri to conduct a diversionary expedition from Belluno to distract the insurgents and ease Vial's march. The two generals were to coordinate their movements so that Peyri would reach the village of Kollmann between Brixen and Bozen no later than 4 November just as Vial was arriving in Bozen.[44] Vial was prepared to begin his advance on 31 October as ordered, but received new instructions to retard his movement so as to reach his objective on 6 November. He instructed Peyri to 'calculate your march in consequence,' but this missive apparently never reached its destination and Peyri proceeded to obey his original orders.[45]

Peyri faced a daunting mission. With some 900 men from ten different regimental depots and 18 Italian chasseurs, he was to cross the Dolomites at altitudes

42 Instructions for the Viceroy of Italy, 14 October 1809, *Correspondance*, No. 15945, Vol.XIX, pp.577–9.

43 Carl Baur, *Der Krieg in Tirol während des Feldzugs 1809* (Munich: Baur, 1812), p.150.

44 SHD, Correspondance du Général Vial, C4/80, Vial to Peyri, 29 October 1809.

45 SHD, Correspondance du Général Vial, C4/80, Vial to Peyri, 31 October 1809. Vaudoncourt states that Vial failed to communicate the change in orders to Peyri (*Histoire Politique et Militaire*, Vol.II, pp.26-27).

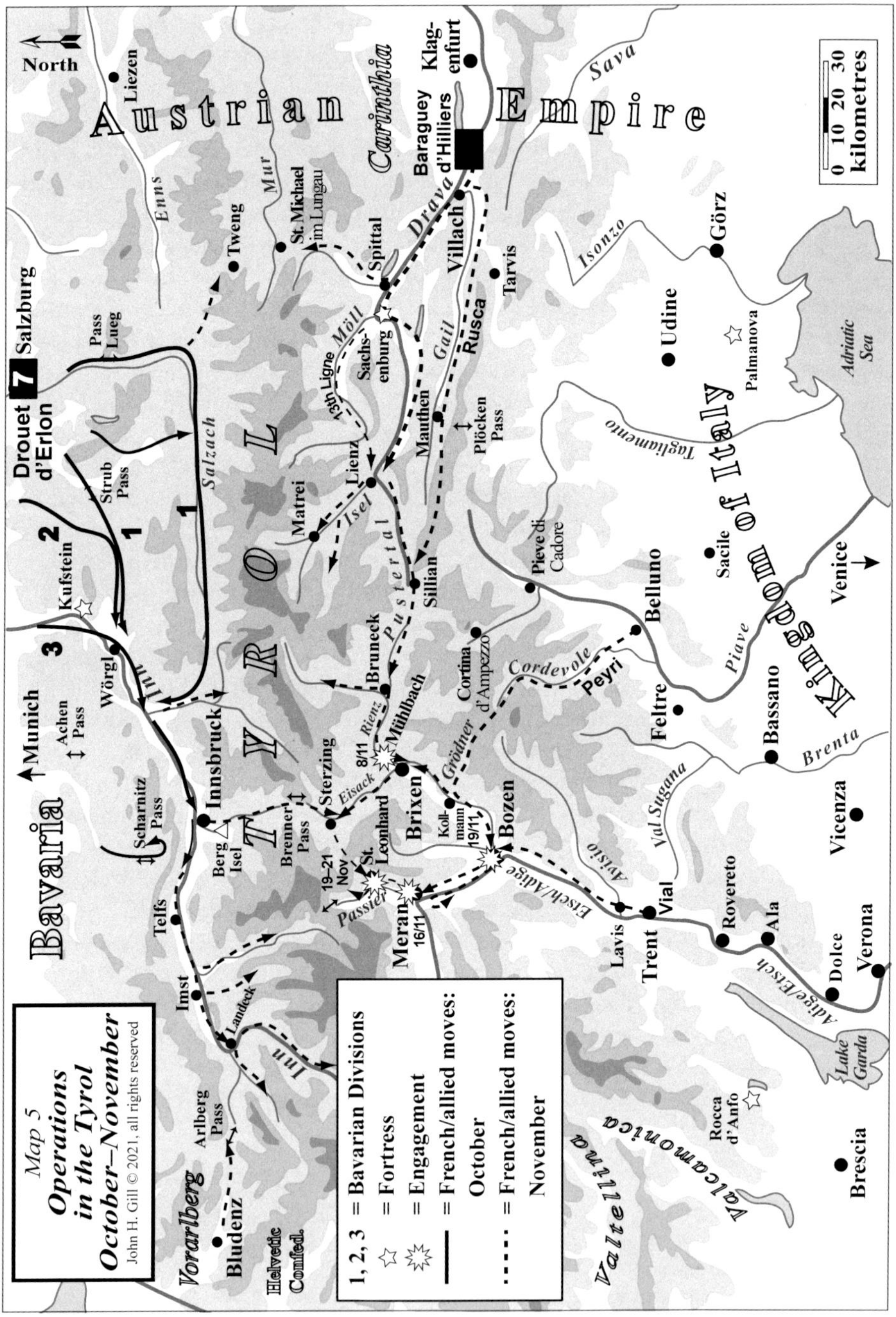
Map 5
Operations in the Tyrol October–November
John H. Gill © 2021, all rights reserved
1, 2, 3 = Bavarian Divisions
= Fortress
= Engagement
= French/allied moves: October
= French/allied moves: November
North
Bavaria
Austrian Empire
TYROL
Kingdom of Italy
Carinthia
Vorarlberg
Helvetic Confed.
Munich
Salzburg
Drouet d'Erlon
7
Baraguey d'Hilliers
Rusca
Peyri
13th Ligne
Kufstein
Wörgl
Innsbruck
Berg Isel
Scharnitz Pass
Achen Pass
Strub Pass
Pass Lueg
Telfs
Imst
Landeck
Arlberg Pass
Bludenz
Brenner Pass
Sterzing
St. Leonhard
19–21 Nov
Passier
Meran
16/11
Brixen
Mühlbach
8/11
Kollmann
19/11
Bozen
Bruneck
Pustertal
Rienz
Eisack
Grödner
Sillian
Lienz
Isel
Matrei
Sachsenburg
Möll
Spittal
Villach
Drava
Klagenfurt
Mauthen
Gail
Plöcken Pass
Tarvis
St. Michael im Lungau
Tweng
Mur
Enns
Liezen
Salzach
Inn
Cortina d'Ampezzo
Cordevole
Pieve di Cadore
Belluno
Feltre
Piave
Bassano
Brenta
Val Sugana
Avisio
Etsch/Adige
Lavis
Trent
Vial
Rovereto
Ala
Dolce
Verona
Adige/Etsch
Lake Garda
Vicenza
Sacile
Venice
Udine
Palmanova
Görz
Isonzo
Sava
Tagliamento
Adriatic Sea
Rocca d'Anfo
Brescia
Valcamonica
Valtellina
0 10 20 30 kilometres

up to 6,800 feet in unfavourable late-autumn weather against potential resistance from a skilful and tenacious foe.[46] Using deception to mislead local informers, he left Belluno on 1 November as ordered and marched up the Cordevole valley to reach the eastern/upper end of the Grödner (Gardena) valley with little difficulty, but was soon beset by insurgents. Employing a combination of prudence, audacity, and determination, however, he brought his little column safely to the Adige valley near Kollmann only to find himself surrounded by overwhelming numbers of rebels who blocked the road south to Bozen. His men were exhausted after having marched for the past several days with little food and less sleep, but Peyri rallied them for a desperate charge that overthrew the Tyrolians to their front and allowed the column to continue south, albeit under constant harassment. He and his weary men arrived in Bozen on the evening of 4 November as instructed, but were dismayed to see no sign of Vial. Fearing the worst, Peyri immediately set about preparing the town for defence while sending messengers in search of the other column. Luckily, Vial was not far distant. Nonetheless, after fending off rebels throughout the day, Peyri's men were almost out of ammunition when Vial's advance guard marched into Bozen in the late afternoon and evening of 5 November. Vial united his division at Bozen the following day, absorbed Peyri's men as an independent battalion and prepared for further operations. Peyri's march did divert the Tyrolians and open the way for Vial's advance, but the confusion in orders almost resulted in the loss of his entire column. In the event, it was a considerable tribute to his leadership, cunning, and drive that he successfully accomplished his mission with the loss of only 49 killed, 93 wounded and 19 missing. As Vial noted, under the circumstances, he had 'executed his movement perfectly.'[47]

As a consequence of these advances, by 5 November Eugene had completed the first critical step in conquering the Tyrol. The viceroy may have found 'this wretched war' thoroughly distasteful, but he had strong forces at Bozen in the south and Bruneck in the east, while d'Erlon in the north was moving towards the Brenner Pass from Innsbruck and had captured Telfs on the upper Inn.[48] The next phase would be to smother the rebellion in its heart—the triangular area between Brixen, Sterzing (Vipiteno) and Meran (Merano)—while simultaneously subduing the upper Inn valley. Eugene's lines of communication, however, especially the valleys connecting Bruneck and Villach, remained vulnerable to new outbreaks of unrest. Guarding these and pacifying the remoter corners of the region north

46 Depots of the 3e, 18e, and 28e Légère; the 13e, 29e, 56e, 60e, and 62e Ligne; a detachment from the Reggimento Dalmato, and eighteen chasseurs of the 1° Cacciatori. A number of Finance Guards voluntarily joined the column in Agordo.

47 Vaudoncourt, *Histoire Politique et Militaire*, Vol.II, pp.28–31; Rossi, "Il generale Peiri nel Trentino", *Rivista Militare Italiana* (1910); SHD, C4/80, Correspondance du Général Vial, Vial to Gavotti, 6 November 1809.

48 Eugene to his wife, 10 November 1809, Du Casse, *Prince Eugène*, Vol.XV, p.113.

of Lienz and west of Trent would consume a significant percentage of his troops through the end of the year.

From 5 to 12 November, the allies made great progress. Pushing carefully west from Bruneck on 6 November, Baraguey d'Hilliers found some 1,500 to 2,000 Tyrolians strongly posted with five guns at the Mühlbach defile (Mühlbacher Klause) where the main road passed over a bridge and through the gates of a sturdy old fort. After two days of thorough reconnaissance, the French and Italians advanced on the morning of 8 November. Rusca led the way, holding the 53e Ligne in a wood north of the Rienz River while Italian sappers cleared an abatis and a battery of four guns and a howitzer bombarded the little fort. At the same time, Baraguey d'Hilliers turned the battalion of the 2° Leggera around and sent it back upstream to crossing point over the swift, unfordable river. After about an hour, the Italian light infantry began to appear on southern side of the river, that is, on the right rear flank of the fort and its alarmed defenders. With the arrival of the Italians, the French generals ordered their men forward along the northern bank and infantry of the Italian 1° Leggera and 4° Linea launched a frontal assault while voltigeurs of the 53e clambered up the steep slopes north of the river. Against heavy fire from the spirited defenders, the Italians captured an outer lunette and the ditch but were frustrated to find the bridge destroyed and the fort's gate blocked by large rocks. By this time, however, the rebels, already unnerved by the appearance of the Italian 2° Leggera on their right, noticed the 53e Ligne's voltigeurs descending from the heights on their left. Abandoning their three remaining artillery pieces (the 1° Leggera had already captured the other two), the insurgents fled in all directions.[49] The French repaired the bridge, and by the evening of the 8th, Severoli's division was safely ensconced in Brixen.

After the victory at Mühlbach, events moved rapidly for several days. Bertoletti's brigade reached Bozen to complete the link between d'Hilliers and Vial on 10 November and the 53e Ligne met up with a Bavarian patrol in the Eisack valley between Sterzing and Brixen on the 11th. In the meantime, *Général de Brigade* Louis Gareau with the 92e Ligne of Broussier's division, had conducted an expedition from Lienz to Matrei to quell disturbances along the Isel River and its tributaries.[50]

Eugene, his army at last able to function as a cohesive entity, directed a reorganisation of his command on 12 November. The Bavarian corps continued unchanged, but all of the French, Neapolitan, and Italian units from the eastern and southern groups now came under Baraguey d'Hilliers, while Vial's troops

49 Max Gruber, *Bruneck und das westliche Pustertal im Jahre 1809* (Innsbruck: Wagner, 1952), pp.71–3; Vaudoncourt, *Histoire Politique et Militaire*, Vol.II, pp.34–6; : Vignolle, 'Campagne du Tyrol,' pp.93–7.

50 Although Broussier was ill in Graz, it is convenient to refer to the division by his name. As noted, it was temporarily commanded at first by *Général de Brigade* François-Antoine Teste and later (from 18 November) by *Général de Brigade* Louis Alméras. Broussier resumed command on 14 December. François-Antoine Teste, 'Souvenirs du Général Baron Teste', *Carnet de la Sabretache* (1911), pp.604–7.

were redistributed. Rusca, though lightly wounded on 8 November at Mühlbach, continued to lead a force called the 'avantgarde,' but this was now composed of five French regular battalions, the two Neapolitan regiments, and the Piave column from Vial's division. Vial retained three French and three Italian battalions as well as several infantry and cavalry detachments under Peyri and *Général de Brigade* Antoine Digonet.[51] Severoli's and Broussier's divisions remained the same, but the 53e Ligne returned to *Général de Brigade* Léonard Huard's brigade of Barbou's division. While the 53e marched for Sterzing on the 12th, however, its sister regiment, the 35e Ligne, remained behind in Bruneck. With his other battalions at Brixen under *Général de Brigade* Jean-Claude Moreau (three each of the 13e and 29e Ligne), Barbou thus became the northern anchor of d'Hilliers' sector.[52] Severoli and Rusca, on the other hand, would operate generally between Meran and Bozen along the Etsch, while Vial returned to Trent and the vales west of Lake Garda.[53] Broussier's three infantry regiments were responsible for the security of the valleys from Bruneck all the way back to Klagenfurt as well as the regions north thereof. Two cavalry regiments, 8e Chasseurs and 6e Hussards, also operated under d'Hilliers west of Klagenfurt, supplying detachments for courier, escort, and general security duties as well as occasional combat patrols. There was much coming and going in the following weeks, but this organisation and these areas of operation remained largely the same through late December (see Order of Battle 8).

French attention now focused on Meran and the valley north of the city: the Passeiertal. This was the home of Andreas Hofer, the innkeeper who had become chief of the insurgents. Rusca thus marched to Meran on 12 November with his new command, under orders to send detachments toward St Leonhard. The French and their allies, however, could not maintain themselves in the city, and the expedition up the valley by two battalions (one each of the 5e Ligne and the Neapolitan 1° Leggera under *Colonel* Louis Boy) was quickly repulsed.[54] Though reinforced by Bertoletti with two more battalions, Rusca's command came under heavy pressure on the 16th and, fearing he would be cut off from Bozen, the French general retired to the latter city during the night of 16/17 November.

In what was supposed to be a coordinated move with Rusca's approach from the south, two battalions (one each of the 13e and 53e Ligne) were sent across the mountains from the north with the intention of meeting Rusca's men in St Leonhard. This plan went badly awry. Departing Sterzing on 17 November under *Chef de Bataillon* Jean-Baptiste Doreille of I/13e, the Frenchmen made the

51 Digonet had joined Vial in mid-October.

52 One of these battalions was kept at Neidervintl on the road between Mühlbach and Bruneck.

53 The Reggimento Dalmato was an exception. It did not move a battalion to Bozen until 16 November; the other did not arrive until the 18th.

54 Boy, a Frenchman, was the commander of the Neapolitan 1° Leggera. He later returned to French service and became a general.

difficult crossing into the Passeiertal, but soon found themselves surrounded at St Leonhard. With Rusca gone from Meran, the insurgents were able to concentrate almost all of their available forces against Doreille's isolated troops. For three days, from 19 to 21 November, the two battalions held out as ammunition, food and water dwindled. Finally on the 22nd, with provisions exhausted, ammunition low and no ability to succour the wounded, Doreille surrendered his little command, and, much to the exaggerated delight of the Tyrolians, approximately 1,000 French regulars stumbled off into captivity.[55]

While Doreille and his men were besieged in St Leonhard, d'Hilliers, who was also short of food and ammunition, came under attack in Bozen on the 19 November. Although the rebel forays were easily repelled, his precarious logistical situation forced him to refrain from offensive action until a convoy of biscuit and cartridges arrived on the 22nd. Luckily for the French, d'Hilliers had already begun to draw Broussier's division toward Bruneck to free Barbou for operations north of Meran. As a result, all of Barbou's division was available when the corps resumed operations on 23 November. That day the avantgarde, under Huard in place of Rusca, returned to Meran.[56] Simultaneously, Barbou successfully marched the 13e Ligne (two battalions) and the 29e Ligne (three battalions) from Brixen to St Leonhard via Sterzing, increasing the size of his command by adding five elite companies of the 53e Ligne. He continued on to Meran on the 24th to join the avantgarde and most of Severoli's division in and around the city. Baraguey d'Hilliers kept this large force (some 18 battalions) between Meran and St Leonhard until 3 December, pacifying and disarming the region before turning back to Brixen, where the insurrection had been rekindled.[57]

The French in Meran were greatly encouraged by the arrival of 20 Bavarian chevaulegers from Landeck on 1 December. The Bavarian cavalrymen not only established another link, albeit somewhat tenuous, between VII Corps and d'Hilliers' command, they also brought news of the near-complete submission of the Inn valley. Vial could report similar progress. His small division had encountered almost no resistance since entering the region west of Lake Garda in mid-November. Thanks to these successes in the north and southwest, by 2 December, only the central and eastern reaches of the Tyrol remained to be subdued.

Troubles in those areas continued. Moreau's brigade in Brixen, for example, was more or less blockaded from 25 November until 6 December when Severoli's men, released by the submission of the Passeiertal, entered the city from Bozen. In the meantime, revolt had also broken out anew northeast of Bruneck.[58] The

55 Hirn, pp. 792–5; Vignolle, 'Campagne du Tyrol,' pp.117–22.

56 Rusca turned over command of the avantgarde to Huard on approximately 24 November and went to Milan to recuperate from the wound he had received on 8 November.

57 Bozen was garrisoned by the Reggimento Dalmato and the Neapolitan 1° Leggera (two battalions each).

58 Moreau had two battalions each of the 35e and 92e Ligne, the five elite companies of the 53e Ligne (returning to Sterzing from Meran), and two companies each of the Reggimento Dalmato and Neapolitan 1° Leggera.

rebels, numbering as many as six thousand, forced the French back into the town and besieged it, launching an unsuccessful attack on 2 December. The first French effort to reopen communications was made on 7 December from Brixen but failed owing to the 'weakness and indecision' of *Général de Brigade* Moreau. After receiving 'severe orders,' however, Moreau launched a second effort two days later with four battalions (two each of 35e and 92e Ligne) and succeeded in dispersing the insurgents into the hills.[59] With Bruneck relieved, *Général de Brigade* Louis Alméras of Broussier's division led three battalions (one of the 84e and two of the 92e Ligne) east on the 11th to re-establish secure communications with Lienz, which was threatened by revived rebellion in the Isel valley. Alméras entered Lienz on the 12th and the rebels in the southern stretches of the Isel valley capitulated the next day.[60]

From mid-December, therefore, the insurgency ceased to function in any co-ordinated fashion. Violent resistance continued to flare, but the various branches of the rebellion were isolated from one another as well as from external assistance. The principal areas of unrest were now the Bruneck–Lienz corridor and the northern Isel valley towards Matrei. To quell the latter, Broussier, now back in command, marched to Matrei from Lienz with seven battalions (92e Ligne and two battalions each of the 9e and 84e), almost his entire division, on 24 December. This imposing force and severe measures soon brought the region under French control, and Broussier returned to Lienz (9e and 84e Ligne) and Sillian (92e Ligne) on the 30th to prepare for a similar march up the Pustertal to Bruneck. On the first day of 1810, eight of Broussier's battalions moved into the towns between Sillian and Lienz to commence the process of disarming the locals and administering summary punishments. Proceeding methodically, the French slowly progressed west towards Bruneck, eventually allowing Moreau to shift to Brixen while Eugene ensured security in Broussier's rear by sending two battalions of the 23e Légère from *Général de Division* Pierre Durutte's division from Villach to Lienz and Sachsenburg.[61]

As Broussier edged westwards, Eugene felt sufficiently secure to begin withdrawing troops from the Tyrol. The two Neapolitan regiments, destined for Spain, had already departed on 2 December. Likewise, the Bavarians had begun moving units back home in mid-November, especially cavalry and artillery elements whose fodder-consuming horses were difficult to support in the resource-poor Tyrol. Major reductions, however, did not begin until early January 1810 with the gradual

59 Vaudoncourt, *Histoire Politique et Militaire*, Vol.II, p.47. Broussier referred to Moreau as an 'animal' and 'a timid rabbit'; see Broussier to Seras, 19 December 1809 in 'Une Lettre du Général Broussier,' *Carnet de la Sabretache* (1897), pp.166–7. Eugene and d'Hilliers lamented that he 'showed great weakness', Eugene to Clarke, 29 December 1809, Du Casse, *Prince Eugène*, Vol.XVI, pp.272–3.

60 Vignolle, 'Campagne du Tyrol,' pp.143–50; Vaudoncourt, *Histoire Politique et Militaire*, Vol.II, pp.45–8.

61 SHD, manuscript, Albert, *Historique du 98e Régiment d'Infanterie*, 1892. Based on Teste's memoirs and Broussier's letter mentioned above, the 23e Légère and the 62e Ligne arrived in Villach on 20 December.

departure of Severoli's division and the troops who had composed the avantgarde. By the end of January, the insurrection was finished and Baraguey d'Hilliers' corps was deployed on occupation duties according to a scheme that the Viceroy had outlined in late November: Barbou from Meran to Bozen and the Grödner valley; Broussier in Sterzing, Brixen and Bruneck; Durutte in the Pustertal from Lienz back to Villach and Klagenfurt; Vial from Trent to Rovereto and in the Val Sugana. Starting in late February, these remaining forces were gradually reduced as Napoleon re-established civil authority and redistributed the various districts of the Tyrol between Bavaria and the Kingdom of Italy.

## Observations

The campaign in the southern Tyrol was finally over after burning on for six months longer than the war it had accompanied and for three months beyond the signature of the peace treaty. Reviewing its long and meandering course through an operational lens, several interesting points emerge from the welter of marches, countermarches, ambushes, battles, and pacifications.

At the higher levels of planning and execution, the fighting in the Tyrol illuminates Napoleon's strategic thinking. First, 1809 is a splendid example of his clear operational vision and his unswerving focus on the crucial objective of the campaign, in this case the destruction of the Austrian Hauptarmee.[62] The insurrection in the Tyrol, though it endangered his communications and threatened to inspire unrest in Germany, was fundamentally secondary. Napoleon repeatedly drew on the troops engaged with the tenacious rebels to bolster his Army of Germany in its struggle with the Habsburg regular forces. Early July, when he withdrew Deroy's Bavarians and even Rusca's tiny division, was the most obvious instance of this strategic focus, but it recurred throughout the war and endured through the peace negotiations as Napoleon attempted to intimidate his Habsburg opponents.

Second, the war in the Tyrol shows Napoleon's ability to improvise; indeed, his reliance on improvisation to cope with secondary perils. While his regulars and the best of his allied troops confronted their Austrian counterparts, he was consistently able to conjure up second line formations, as *ersatz* as they might be, to oppose the insurgency. Though the emperor clearly desired the rapid eradication of the rebellion, his purposes were adequately served by containing it, and these units, their deficiencies and setbacks notwithstanding, sufficed to accomplish that task.

62 See John H. Gill, '1809: The Most Brilliant and Skilful Manoeuvres', in Michael V. Leggiere (ed.) *Napoleon and the Operational Art of War* (Leiden: Brill, 2016).

At the more tactical or operational levels, the suppression of the Tyrol highlights the enormous expenditure of troops, time, and attention required to overpower a determined though irregular foe in difficult terrain – even when that foe was outnumbered and isolated from any reasonable hope of external assistance. Some 45,000 French, Bavarian, Italian, and Neapolitan soldiers were committed for more than two months before the rebellion began to wane indisputably. Nevertheless, the ultimate French success showed that an insurgency could be quelled given enough resources, time, and commitment from the senior leadership, especially from Napoleon himself. The Tyrolian campaign of 1809 thus provides an instructive basis for comparison with the French experiences in places such as Spain and Calabria.

Filling in these military details of the war in the Tyrol thus broadens our understanding of French counter-insurgency operations at the height of the Empire. More important, however, an outline of this campaign is a necessary adjunct to the war of 1809. Though peripheral to the movements and combats of the regular forces, the actions in the Tyrol were part of the strategic context in which Napoleon operated. They were an integral element in his strategic calculus, and therefore demand a place in our analysis of his political and military decision-making during this last successful war.

# Annexe

A review of the Tyrolian campaign of 1809 highlights a number of interesting characteristics of Napoleonic mountain warfare in general and combat in the Tyrol in specific.

## *The Rebel Enemy*

Space does not permit detailed exploration of the enemies faced by the French, Italian, Bavarian, and German troops in the Tyrol during 1809, but a few comments may be employed to limn an outline image of their dogged foes. The rebels were a hardy, independent mountain people who had enjoyed a significant degree of local autonomy even though the region had been affiliated with the Habsburg crown since the fourteenth century. Politically and religiously conservative and loyal to the Austrian ruling family, they deeply resented the Tyrol's transfer to Bavaria through the Treaty of Pressburg in 1805. Especially galling were the imposition of Bavarian administrative procedures (often enforced with too much zeal and too little nuance), the introduction of conscription, and what the Tyrolians saw as interference in their religious practices by civil authorities from Munich. Transforming these grievances into rebellion was facilitated by the long-standing system of local defence in the Tyrol consisting of community-based *Schützen* (sharpshooter) companies usually numbering from 100 to 150 members. Although there was no real standing armed force, therefore, *Schützen* companies could be formed on short notice (usually by the sounding of village bells) to conduct an action and could assemble in thousands for brief periods of time before dispersing back to their homes. Skilled marksmen, these *Schützen*, inspired by religious fervour and a sense of injustice, knew their land and could rely on their neighbours for intelligence, provisions, and escape if necessary. Exploiting their mountaineering and shooting abilities, they would dominate the heights and often engage from ambush or attack and mutilate stragglers, couriers, and small parties. Among other mountain tactics, rebels, including women, would roll rocks and boulders on troops in the narrow valleys below, causing numerous, and often irremediable, casualties. The Bavarians saw them as little more than murderously dangerous bandits, revolting against their rightful monarch (the Bavarian king), and prosecuting an illegitimate form of warfare. The French and Italians likewise respected their foe's ferocity and local knowledge just as they were horrified by their atrocities. 'Fanatic' was commonly used to describe the enemy in the official reports and memoirs of the officers and men assigned to quell the rebellion. As in most insurgencies, brutality was heaped upon brutality by both sides with prisoners killed, villages burned, and churches desecrated as a matter of course (it was a matter of special note that one of the rebel leaders stepped in to save Doreille and his men when they were trapped in St Leonhard). The rebels, however, also had significant weaknesses. Among other things, they feared artillery and maintained an especial dread of cavalry. They were also often at odds with one another and with their Austrian allies. The most iconic leader, Andreas Hofer, an innkeeper from the Passier valley, for instance, could issue appeals for fighters, but he was not always answered in the first place or obeyed by those who chose to respond. Nourished by desperation, illusions, and lies (such as 'Vienna is restarting the war!' when in reality the Austrian Kaiser was preparing to give his daughter to Napoleon as a wife), the rebellion blazed on for weeks after the peace had been signed. As the French and their allies 'flooded the land with troops' (in the words of Bavarian *Hauptmann* Baur), however, the rebels gradually lost heart and returned to their homes. As for Hofer, he was betrayed and captured before being taken 'to Mantua in chains' to be tried and executed in February 1810.[63]

## The Regular Enemy

Austrian forces in the Tyrol consisted of both regular line units and newly-raised Landwehr (militia). Most of the regulars came from well-established regiments (and one of the new Jäger battalions) with a significant number of veterans; they generally proved resilient and courageous if not especially flexible. In addition to regular discipline and reliability, they brought cavalry and artillery. Even in small numbers, these arms were very valuable given that the rebels had no horse units and very few cannon. The *Landwehr*, on the other hand, were often problematic, lacking discipline, training, and equipment. Some units slowly melted away, particularly when they were near their home recruiting areas; Chasteler's battalions, for instance, largely disintegrated after the fight at Klagenfurt on 6 June.[64] An additional source of potential soldiers were '*Selbst-Ranzionierte*' or men who had been captured earlier in the war but had escaped the rather lax French prisoner of war system. Several thousand of such individuals seem to have made their way from Bavaria into the Tyrol and, though some simply went into hiding or turned to banditry, many found their way back to Austrian units or rebel militia companies. Although they could be integrated fairly rapidly, they were often in need of food, clothing, weapons, and ammunition, the latter being a special problem in the isolated Tyrol. None of these troops, however, regular or Landwehr, was familiar with the region or with mountain warfare as a specialized branch of combat, disadvantages that were compounded by their requirements for more regular supplies of victuals and munitions as compared to their rebel allies. Furthermore, they

63 'To Mantua in Chains' is the title of a patriotic song about Hofer and the rebellion.

64 Joseph von Anders, 'Geschichtliche Skizze der Kriegsereignisse in Tirol im Jahre 1809, *Oesterreichische militärische Zeitschrift*, 1834, pp.300–2.

were almost as alien to the region as the French, Italians, and Bavarians. Frictions over command, priorities, and supplies were not uncommon and violent incidents occurred between Austrians and Tyrolians when it became clear after Wörgl that Chasteler was planning to abandon the Tyrol.

## *Artillery*

Though 6-pounders were occasionally very useful (especially in battles in the Inn valley and around Innsbruck), the French and their allies generally considered such pieces too heavy and cumbersome, so they principally relied on lighter 3- or 4-pounders in the mountains. The regimental guns issued to the Armée d'Italie in September and October thus proved a boon to French and Italian commanders. Even these lighter weapons, however, were often too cumbersome and *Général de Division* Broussier, for one, expended considerable effort to create expedient mountain guns by crafting special light carriages. The Bavarians found that artillery of all types had a devastating psychological effect on the rebels (who seldom had any guns of their own). This benefit diminished as the war progressed (Vial wrote that he 'preferred bayonets' over a reinforcement of artillery), but always remained an important factor in deciding force composition.[65]

## *Howitzers*

The war generated a small debate on the utility of howitzers in the mountains. Some, such as *Général de Division* Broussier, believed them invaluable. 'This is a war of howitzers,' he wrote to his friend *Général de Division* Jean Mathieu Seras. Other qualified observers, such as Bavarian artillery *Hauptmann* Carl Baur, were more sceptical, claiming that the combat value of howitzers was limited owing to the terrain and the dispersion of possible targets.[66]

## *Snow*

By late November 1809, snow was a major factor in military operations. The French often found themselves village-bound and had to resort to *corvée* labour to clear the roads (increasing, of course, the resentment of the inhabitants). To cope with the snow and mountain terrain, some French and Bavarian commanders imitated

65 Broussier, 'Une Lettre du Général Broussier', pp.166–7; SHD, C4/80, Vial to Eugene, 18 October 1809. See also Bavarian unit histories cited in Gill, *Eagles*, Chapter 7.

66 Baur, 160–3, and Broussier, 'Une Lettre du Général Broussier', pp.166–7.

the local population by procuring crampons and mountain footwear (*espadrilles*) for their men (for the light troops as a minimum) in addition to modifying their artillery as outlined above.[67]

## French Allied Units

The Reggimento Dalmato and the Cacciatori d'Istria battalion of the Armée d'Italie seem to have enjoyed a formidable reputation in mountain, anti–partisan warfare. In part, this probably derived from the tactical and leadership skills of *Colonel* Moroni, the commander of the Reggimento Dalmato, but French and Italian commanders seem to have regarded them highly and repeatedly chose them for advance guard duties and other difficult, independent missions. The Tyrolians, on the other hand, attributed to the Dalmatian troops an especial degree of brutality.

## Italian Unit Strengths

The Italian units often had difficulty maintaining prescribed manpower levels. Although listed as having two battalions (III and IV), for example, the 1° Leggera only counted 476 officers and men as effectives in mid-July before heading for the Tyrol, that is, barely half of one fully–manned battalion (840). The 2° Leggera was in a similar situation with only 566 men in its two battalions (also III and IV) instead of the authorized 1,680. As a result, by mid-September the 4th battalions of these units were merged with the 3rd battalions so that each was able to field one battalion of at least 500 men. Many other Italian infantry units exhibited similar problems at different points during the campaign, the number of effectives generally fluctuating between 300 and 400 per battalion. The 1° Linea was unusual: by October, the strength of its three battalions was maintained at a respectable 500 to 550 each. French battalions in the Armée d'Italie were a different story. Though most had suffered grievous losses at Wagram on 5–6 July, they had begun to recover by early October and most entered the Tyrol campaign with nearly 600 officers and men 'present under arms.' In the French case, the 35e Ligne was the exception. Its first three battalions had been nearly wiped out at Sacile on 15–16 April and its October strength reports show each with only 100 to 200 effectives in their ranks; the only battalion near full strength was IV/35e (600 men) which had been on detached garrison duty and thus not present at Sacile.[68]

67 Teste to Vignolle, 5 December 1809 in Gabriel–Adrien Robinet de Cléry, *En Tyrol* (Paris: Ollendroff, 1897), pp.121–2; Teste, 'Souvenirs', pp.605–6; Broussier, 'Une Lettre du Général Broussier', p.167; Charles Pierre Lubin Griois, *Mémoires* (Paris: Plon–Nouritt, 1909), pp.392–3.

68 SHD, C2/509, Armée d'Italie, *Situations* and *Situations Sommaires*, 25 June to 10 October 1809.

## Orders of Battle

These order of battle snapshots only show French and Italian forces committed in the Tyrol. That is, they do not depict the French Armée d'Italie in its entirety. The forces dedicated to that region initially came under Prince Eugene's Armée d'Italie, but operated largely on their own from June until October when he was assigned overall responsibility for combatting the insurgency. Not shown here, for example, are significant forces from the Armée d'Italie on occupation duties in Hungary and Styria from August through December 1809 and the XI Corps (formerly the Army of Dalmatia) which came under Eugene starting in November. Likewise, these lists do not include the Bavarian VII Corps except at the aggregate level.

***Notes***:
All figures show effectives ('*présents sous les armes*') and do not include soldiers on detachment or in hospital.

All figures combine officers and men and, unless otherwise noted, all summary figures for divisions or brigades give only infantry and cavalry strengths (not artillery, train, others).

Battalions and squadrons are indicated by Roman numerals, thus III/67e Ligne is the 3rd Battalion of the 67e Ligne. 'Légère' indicates a French light infantry unit.

A *c.* indicates the figure is approximate. Estimated strength figures are annotated with *est.*

***1. Franco-Italian Forces on the Southern Front, 17–27 April 1809***[69]

*Général de Division* Baraguey d'Hilliers

*Général de Division* Vial's Division (*c.* 4,367 infantry and cavalry)

| | |
|---|---|
| 112e Ligne (I, II, III) | 2,104 |
| III/67e Ligne* | (see below) |
| III/93e Ligne* | (see below) |
| French March Battalion* | * *c.* 1,775 for all three Bns. |
| (Three companies each of 37e and 56e Ligne) | |
| Two French March Squadrons | *c.* 270 |
| (Replacements detachments from 19e, 23e and 24e Chasseurs-à-Cheval) | |
| IV/7e Dragons | 218 |
| (artillery?) | |

*Général de Division* Fontanelli's Division (5,352 infantry and cavalry)

*Général de Brigade* Julhien, *Général de Brigade* Bertoletti

| | |
|---|---|
| 1° Leggera (III, IV) | 705 |

69 Gill, *Thunder*, vol.II, p.361–2; Vignolle, 'Campagne du Tyrol,' p.8; strengths from Archives Nationales, Livrets des armées: Situations des troupes en Italie, AF*/IV/1377, Armée d'Italie, *Situation*, 1 May 1809.

| | |
|---|---|
| 2° Leggera (III, IV) | 814 |
| 3° Linea (II, IV) | 1,272 |
| 4° Linea (III, IV) | 927 |
| Cacciatori d'Istria | 685 |
| 2° Cacciatori a Cavallo *Principe Real* (III, IV) | 296 |
| 7e Dragons (I, II, III) | 653 |
| Artillery, train and sappers | 384 |
| 10 guns | |

Note: IV/2° Linea (727 officers and men) was apparently attached to Fontanelli for a few days (approximately 25–27 April), giving the division a total of over 6,000 men for a short time.

***2. Rusca's Division, late April to mid-May 1809***[70]

*Général de Division* Rusca (*c.* 5,290 infantry and cavalry)

| | |
|---|---|
| III/67e Ligne | 934 |
| III/93e Ligne | 786 |
| 1° Leggera (III, IV) | 852 |
| 2° Leggera (III, IV) | 1,101 |
| 4° Linea (III, IV) | 756 |
| Cacciatori d'Istria | *c.* 650 |
| IV/7e Dragons | 211 |
| Artillery, sappers, train troops | 417 |
| 10 guns | |

Notes: (1) the march companies of the 37e and 56e Ligne had been incorporated into the other two battalions; (2) the Cacciatori d'Istria did not arrive until early to mid-May.

***3. Forces at Klagenfurt, 6 June 1809***[71]

French forces under *Général de Division* Rusca, Governor of Carinthia (4,820 all arms)

*Général de Brigade* Julhien, *Général de Brigade* Bertoletti

| | |
|---|---|
| III/67e Ligne | 891 |
| III/93e Ligne | 729 |
| III/1° Leggera * | 650 |

70 Vignolle, 'Journal Historique, p.776; strengths from Archives Nationales, Livrets des armées: Situations des troupes en Italie, AF*/IV/1377, Armée d'Italie, *Situation*, 6 May 1809.

71 Gill, *Thunder*, Vol.II, pp.129–36. Rusca's strength from Armée d'Italie, *Situation Sommaire*, 25 May 1809 in Armée d'Allemagne, 'Livret de Situation', 1 June 1809, AG, C2/675; Chasteler's force is from Kriegsarchiv, Alte Feldakten, 8. Korps (Chasteler Tirol), Karton 1437, 'Aufstellung', *c.* 1 June 1809.

| | |
|---|---|
| III/2° Leggera * | 726 |
| III/4° Linea * | 662 |
| Cacciatori d'Istria | 627 |
| Detachment/1° Cacciatori a Cavallo *Real Italiano* | 85 |
| IV/2° Cacciatori a Cavallo *Principe Real* | 168 |
| Artillery, sappers, train troops | 282 |
| 10 guns | |

* The 4th battalions had been absorbed into the 3rd battalions by this time.

Part of Austrian VIII Corps, *Feldmarschall-Leutnant* Chasteler (*c.* 6,500–7,500)

| | |
|---|---|
| Advance Guard: *Major* Lachovsky | |
| 9. Jäger Battalion (one company) | 90 |
| 2. Banal Grenz-Regiment (three companies) | 469 |
| Hohenzollern Chevaulegers-Regiment No. 2 (one sq.) | *c.*70 |
| Klagenfurt Landwehr (detachment) | ? |
| Main Body: *General-Major* Fenner, *General-Major* Marcal, *Oberst* Mumb | |
| Hohenlohe-Bartenstein Inf-Regt No. 26 (one and 2/3 bns.) | *c.* 1,000–1,500 |
| Hohenzollern Chevaulegers-Regiment No. 2 (two sqs.) | *c.*140 |
| 1. Villach Landwehr (one battalion) | *est.* 500–600 |
| 2. Bruck Landwehr (one battalion) | 630 |
| 1., 2., 3. Klagenfurt Landwehr (three battalions) | *est.* 500–600 |
| 2 x 6-pounder, 2 x 3-pounder, 1 x howitzer | |
| *General-Major* Schmidt: | |
| I/Erzherzog Franz Karl Infanterie-Regiment No. 52 | *c.* 422 |
| 2. Banal Grenz-Regiment (four companies) | *c.* 620 |
| Hohenzollern Chevaulegers-Regiment No. 2 (half-sq.) | *c.*35 |
| Styrian Schützen (*Major* Lais) | *c.* 100 |
| 2 x 3-pounder | |
| *Oberst* Volkmann: | |
| Johann Jellacic Infanterie-Regiment No. 53 (two bns.) | 1,500 |
| Hohenzollern Chevaulegers-Regiment No. 2 (one sq.) | *c.*70 |
| 3 x 3-pounder | |
| Detached: | |
| Hohenlohe-Bartenstein Infanterie-Regiment No. 26 (two cos.) | *c.* 200–300 |
| 2. Banal Grenz-Regiment (two cos.) | *c.* 300 |

Roughly 5,800 Austrian regulars and Landwehr remained in the Tyrol under Buol following Chasteler's departure.

***4. Rusca's Division at Klagenfurt, 1 August 1809***[72]

*Général de Division* Rusca, Governor of Carinthia

*Général de Brigade* Bertoletti

| | |
|---|---|
| 1° Leggera (III, IV) | 462 |
| 2° Leggera (III, IV) | 490 |
| III/4° Linea | 478 |
| Cacciatori d'Istria | 322 |
| Detachment/1° Cacciatori a Cavallo *Real Italiano* | 65 |
| IV/2° Cacciatori a Cavallo *Principe Real* | 180 |
| Artillery, sappers, train troops | 79 |
| Reinforcements en route | |
| 1° Linea (I, II, III) | 1,210 |
| Reggimento Dalmato (I, II) | 882 |

***5. Franco-Italian Forces on the Southern Front, mid-September to mid-October 1809***[73]

*Général de Brigade* Peyri

| | |
|---|---|
| IV/14e Légère | 763 |
| IV/81e Ligne | 699 |
| 15e Demi-Brigade Provisoire (one battalion) | 485 |
| 3° Linea (I, III) | 682 |
| III/7° Linea | 434 |
| Detachment/2° Cacciatori a Cavallo *Principe Real* | 41 |
| Artillery, train, sappers | 174 |
| 9 guns | |

Two Neapolitan regiments, the 1° Leggera and the 1° Cacciatori a Cavallo, joined Peyri at Lavis on the night of 9/10 October. A detachment of the Italian 4° Linea joined Peyri by early November.

***6. Franco-Italian Division on the Southern Front, late October 1809***[74]

*Général de Division* Vial, *Général de Brigade* Digonet

| | |
|---|---|
| IV/14e Légère | 763 |
| 5e Ligne (III, IV) | 687 |
| 15e Demi-Brigade Provisoire (one battalion) | 505 |
| 3° Linea (I, III) | 720 |
| III/7° Linea | 434 |

72 SHD, C2/509, Armée d'Italie, *Situation*, 1 August 1809 and *Situation Sommaire*, 10 August 1809.

73 SHD, C4/3, Armée d'Italie, *Situation des troupes stationée dans le Tirol et commandée par M. le general Peyri*, 14 October 1809.

74 Vignolle, 'Campagne du Tyrol,' p.46.

| | |
|---|---|
| Detachment/2° Cacciatori a Cavallo *Principe Real* | 41 |
| 1° Leggera (Neapolitan) (I, II) | 1,005 |
| 1° Cacciatori a Cavallo (Neapolitan) (I, II) | 289 |
| Artillery, train, sappers | 175 |
| 3 x howitzers, 2 x 6-pounders, 4 x 3-pounders | |
| Joining Vial on 20 October: | |
| 81e Ligne (III, IV) | 1,241 |
| 101e Ligne (I, IV) | 982 |
| Detachment/4° Linea | 377 |
| Detachment/1er Ligne | 288 |

***7. Armée d'Italie, 'Troops of the Tyrolian Expedition', 1 November 1809***[75]

| | |
|---|---|
| Corps under Baraguey d'Hilliers | |
| Avantgarde, *Général de Division* Rusca | |
| 53e Ligne (I, II, III) | 1,872 |
| Detachment/8e Chasseurs-à-Cheval | *c.* 50 |
| Two guns | |
| Division, *Général de Division* Severoli | |
| Detachment/8e Chasseurs-à-Cheval | *c.* 150 |
| *Général de Brigade* Bertoletti | |
| III/1° Leggera | 645 |
| III/2° Leggera | 579 |
| Reggimento Dalmato (I, II) | 806 |
| IV/1° Cacciatori a Cavallo *Real Italiano* | 149 |
| Two guns | |
| *Colonel* Rossi (of 1° Linea) | |
| 1° Linea (I, II, III) | 1,617 |
| III/4° Linea | 477 |
| Detachment/2° Cacciatori a Cavallo *Principe Real* | 109 |
| Six guns | |
| Artillery, train, sappers | 507 |
| Division, *Général de Division* Barbou | |
| Detachment/8e Chasseurs-à-Cheval | *c.* 150 |
| *Général de Brigade* Moreau | |
| 13e Ligne (I, II, III) | 2,220 |
| 29e Ligne (I, II, III) | 1,785 |
| *Général de Brigade* Huard | |
| 35e Ligne (I, II, III, IV) | 1,262 |

75 SHD, C4/113, Armée d'Italie, *Situation*, 1 November 1809. Cannon allocation from Vaudoncourt, 'Mémoire sur la guerre', pp.495–6.

| | |
|---|---|
| Artillery and train | 319 |
| 10e Brigade de Cavalerie Légère, *Général de Brigade* Gauthier | |
| 8e Chasseurs-à-Cheval | *c.* 370* |
| 6e Hussards | 491 |

Under army command

| | |
|---|---|
| Reserve Division, *Général de Brigade* Teste (for Broussier, sick), *Général de Brigade* Gareau | |
| 9e Ligne (I, II, III) | 2,085 |
| 84e Ligne (I, II, III) | 1,923 |
| 92e Ligne (I, II, III) | 2,257 |
| Guardia Reale, *Général de Brigade* Lecchi, *Général de Brigade* Viani ** | |
| Guardia d'Onore | 286 |
| Veliti Reale (one battalion) | 625 |
| Guardia di Linea (two battalions) | 786 |
| Dragoni della Guardia (two squadrons) | 310 |
| Artillery and train | 194 |
| Vial's Division | |
| *Général de Brigade* Digonet | |
| IV/14e Légère | 717 |
| 5e Ligne (III, IV) | 660 |
| 81e Ligne (III, IV) | 963 |
| IV/101e Ligne | 520 |
| 15e Demi-brigade Provisoire | 496 |
| 3° Linea (I, III) | 683 |
| Detachment/2° Cacciatori a Cavallo *Principe Real* | 41 |
| 1° Leggera (Neapolitan) (I, II) | 869 |
| 1° Cacciatori a Cavallo (Neapolitan) (I, II) | 268 |
| Artillery and train | 217 |

Bavarian VII Corps under *Général de Division* Drouet d'Erlon 21,506 (as of 15 November)

* Approximately 350 detached from the 8e Chasseurs to other elements of Baraguey d'Hillers's command as shown.
** The Guard Division remained in Villach and did not participate in the active campaign.

Note: an additional 22,000 men from the Armée d'Italie were posted in Hungary and Styria under *Maréchal* MacDonald.

### 8. *Baraguey d'Hilliers' Corps, 1 December 1809*[76]

| Unit | Strength |
|---|---|
| Avantgarde, *Général de Division* Rusca | |
| IV/14e Légère | --[77] |
| 5e Ligne (III, IV) | 713 |
| 81e Ligne (III, IV) | 1,077 |
| 1° Leggera (Neapolitan) (I, II) | 1,034 |
| 1° Cacciatori a Cavallo (Neapolitan) (I, II) | 339 |
| | |
| Division, *Général de Division* Severoli | |
| 1er Brigade, *Général de Brigade* Bertoletti | |
| III/1° Leggera | 592 |
| III/2° Leggera | 601 |
| Reggimento Dalmato (I, II) | 887 |
| III/4° Linea | 395 |
| IV/1° Cacciatori a Cavallo *Real Italiano* | 163 |
| 2e Brigade, *Colonel* Rossi (1° Linea) | |
| 1° Linea (I, II, III) | 1,608 |
| Artillery, train, sappers | 280 |
| | |
| Division, *Général de Division* Barbou | |
| Det/8e Chasseurs-à-Cheval | |
| 1er Brigade, *Général de Brigade* Moreau | |
| 13e Ligne (I, II, III) | 2,263 |
| 29e Ligne (I, II, III) | 1,625 |
| 2e Brigade, *Général de Brigade* Huard | |
| 35e Ligne (I, II, III, IV) | 1,220 |
| 53e Ligne (I, II, III) | 1,645 |
| Artillery and train | 240 |
| | |
| Division, *Général de Brigade* Teste (interim for Broussier, sick) | |
| 1er Brigade, *Général de Brigade* Alméras | |
| 9e Ligne (I, II, III) | 2,183 |
| 84e Ligne (I, II, III) | 1,859 |
| 2e Brigade, *Général de Brigade* Teste | |
| 92e Ligne (I, II, III) | 2,270 |
| Artillery and train | 401 |

76 SHD, C4/113,Armée d'Italie, *Situations*, 1 and 15 December 1809. Note that Durutte's division was not listed as among the 'Troupes de l'expédition du Tyrol'.

77 The 14e Légère (662 officers and men) was also involved in the 'expedition to the Tyrol', but was apparently transferring from Vial's command to the advance guard on/about 1 December.

| | |
|---|---|
| *Général de Division* Vial's Division (3,800) | |
| *Général de Brigade* Digonet and *Général de Brigade* Peyri | |
| Detachment/1er Ligne | 293 |
| 101e Ligne (I, IV) | 978 |
| 15e Demi-Brigade Provisoire | 714 |
| 3° Linea (I, III) | 724 |
| IV/4° Linea | 376 |
| III/7° Linea | 410 |
| Detachment/2° Cacciatori a Cavallo *Principe Real* | 122 |
| Artillery and train | 140 |
| | |
| 10e Brigade de Cavalerie Légère, *Général de Brigade* Gauthier | |
| 8e Chasseurs-à-Cheval | 803 |
| 6e Hussards | 612 |
| | |
| *Général de Division* Durutte's Division (as of 15 December 1809) | |
| 1er Brigade, *Général de Brigade* Pastol | |
| 23e Léger (I, II, III) | 1,860 |
| 102e Ligne (I, II, III) | 2,057 |
| 2e Brigade, *Général de Brigade* Gareau | |
| 62e Ligne (I, II, III) | 2,287 |
| Artillery and train | 312 |
| | |
| Bavarian VII Corps under *Général de Division* Drouet d'Erlon | 21,958 |

6

# Maucune's Division at Salamanca

Garry David Wills

My book *Wellington at Bay: The Battle of Villamuriel 25 October 1812* features the 5e Division of the Armée de Portugal commanded by *Général de Division* Antoine-Louis Popon Baron de Maucune. During the research for this title, I was inevitably drawn to the performance of this division three months earlier at Salamanca, where they were broken by Major General James Leith's Anglo-Portuguese 5th Division, the division that they faced again at Villamuriel. Salamanca has been described as 'Wellington's Masterpiece' and although Assaye and Vitoria also have good claims to this title, there is no doubt that Salamanca was a spectacular victory for Wellington and a catastrophe for *Maréchal* Marmont and the French. The battle is often characterised as the 'beating of 40,000 men in 40 minutes' as reported by Napier, quoting an unidentified French officer.[1] However there are problems with this approach, especially with regard to what happened to Maucune's division. Rather than a blow-by-blow account of the battle, the purpose of this chapter is to highlight some of the potential anomalies in the accounts of the battle, with a particular focus on Maucune's division.

Antoine Louis Popon Baron de Maucune was born in Brive on 21 February 1772. Maucune joined the Corps des Pionniers in 1786 as a *sous lieutenant* and was promoted *lieutenant* in 1787. At the outbreak of the Revolution, he enlisted as a *grenadier* in the 1er Volontaires de Paris in July 1791. In May 1792 Maucune was wounded in the left chest at the taking of Menin, then in June became a *lieutenant* in the 23e Régiment d'Infanterie.[2] During the campaigns of the Grande Armée from 1805 to 1807 he served in the VI Corps under Ney, fighting at Elchingen, Jena

1 W.F.P. Napier, *History of the War in the Peninsula and in the South of France from the year 1807 to 1814* (London: Constable, 1993), Vol.V, p.209.

2 *Archives Nationale*, Paris, *Base de Données Léonore* (LEONORE) at <http://www2.culture.gouv.fr/documentation/leonore/recherche.htm>, dossier LH/2199/91.

Wellington at Salamanca; drawing after Small (Author's collection)

and Eylau. Maucune was promoted to *général de brigade* in March 1807 and fought at Friedland. Napoleon then made him a *Grand Officier* of the *Legion d'Honneur* and Baron. He then moved with the VI Corps to Spain in 1808. Maucune was subsequently wounded at Buçaco and twice more at Fuentes de Oñoro. Promoted to *Général de Division*, Maucune became the commander of the 5e Division, Armée de Portugal in May 1811. Maucune was wounded nine times in his 28-year career and he is one of the names inscribed under the *Arc de Triomphe*.

Oman and Fortescue both provide straightforward descriptions of Wellington's assault on Marmont's left and centre at Salamanca. In these accounts Wellington assaults and destroys each of the French divisions in turn, with their remaining soldiers fleeing to the bridge at Alba de Tormes, never to be seen again that day. For example Fortescue says that, after Packenham's and Leith's attacks, 'the [French] 5th and 7th Divisions were for all fighting purposes destroyed'.[3] Furthermore, the French counterattacks and the rearguard actions are described as being conducted entirely by the remaining divisions, specifically only Ferey's 3e Division in the case of the final rearguard on the El Barrero ridge at the head of the forest leading to Alba de Tormes.

While Napier described Maucune as 'maintaining a noble battle' during the withdrawal, he confused Maucune's 5e Division with both Bonnet's 8e and Ferey's

3 J.W. Fortescue, *A History of the British Army* (London: Macmillan, 1917), Vol.VIII, p.494.

3e Divisions at different times in the action.[4] However, there are other indications that Maucune had indeed fought 'a noble battle'. These indications are discussed in turn: Maucune's position when receiving Leith's attack; the fate of both his divisional artillery and his regimental eagles; the 'green flag' captured by the 11th Foot; the Salamanca eagles; and the account of Maucune's chief of staff, *Chef de Bataillon* Étienne-François Girard.

## Maucune's Position

At Salamanca, Maucune's division comprised two brigades each of two regiments. The first brigade was commanded by *Général de Brigade* Pierre-Louis d'Arnauld and comprised the 15e Régiment d'Infanterie de Ligne (15e Ligne) and the 66e Ligne. The regiments had, respectively, three and two battalions in the field, the 1/15e, 2/15e, 3/15e, 4/66e and the 5/66e. The second brigade was commanded by *Général de Brigade* Jacques Montfort and comprised the 82e Ligne and the 86e Ligne. Each regiment had two battalions in the field, 4/82e, 5/82e, 1/86e and the 2/86e.[5] Together the four regiments had 161 officers and 4,867 men, an average of 18 officers and 541 men per battalion.[6] The division's artillery comprised four officers and 212 men with 6 guns (three 8-pdrs, two 4-pdrs and one 6-inch howitzer).[7] Most of the men of the division will have been veterans of Fuentes de Oñoro and earlier campaigns.[8]

Following a campaign of marching and countermarching between Salamanca and Valladolid, on 22 July 1812, both Wellington and Marmont were marching south past Salamanca. Wellington ordered his assault when he saw the French over-extending their left wing. Oman's map shows Thomières' 7e Division separated by more than three-quarters of a mile from Maucune and the French centre. Oman bases part of his account on Marmont's memoirs, specifically stating that Maucune had pressed his advance too close on the village of Arapiles, two-thirds of a mile to his front. However, Oman also states that only Maucune's skirmishers approached the village.[9] Significantly, Oman also shows Maucune's division one-and-a-quarter miles from the Greater Arapile. Similarly, while Fortescue has Maucune sending only skirmishers towards the village of Arapiles, he has

4 Napier, *History*, Vol.V, p.178.
5 *Service Historique de la Défense* (SHD), Paris, C8 466, *Situation* Armée d'Espagne, 15 August 1812, Armée de Portugal *situation* dated 15 June 1812.
6 C. Oman, *History of the Peninsular War* (London: Greenhill, 1996), Vol.V, p.602.
7 SHD C8 466, *Situation* Armée d'Espagne,15 August 1812, return for Armée de Portugal dated 15 June 1812.
8 G.D. Wills, *Wellington at Bay: The Battle of Villamuriel, 25 October 1812* (Warwick: Helion and Company, 2020), p.77.
9 Oman, *History*, Vol.V, pp.435–437.

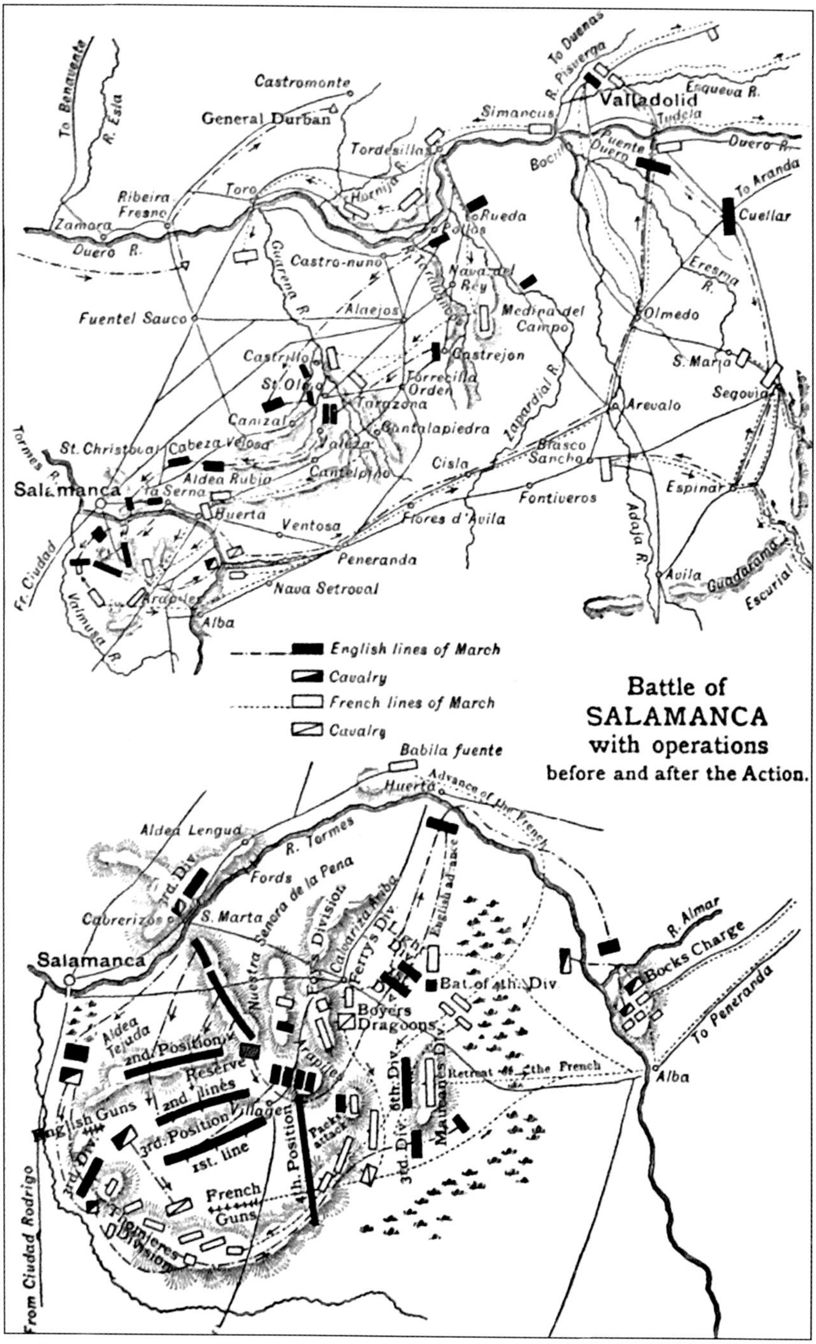


Napier's maps of the campaign and battle. (Author's collection)

Maucune and Thomières both advancing along Monte de Azan towards Miranda de Azan with his map showing Maucune half a mile beyond Arapiles and with Clausel opposite Arapiles and Leith.[10] These accounts have created the impression that Maucune rashly advanced too far along the plateau.

In fact, Maucune's initial deployment conformed to his orders, as Marmont himself reported to King Joseph immediately after the action, 25 July 1812.

> I caused it [the table land] to be occupied by the *5e Division* and the reserve of horse artillery, with strict orders to confine themselves to the taking of the table-land… General Maucune broke and drove off the English detachment which occupied the heights… I thought it necessary to bring up fresh troops to act with vigour in support of General Maucune… so that General Maucune, notwithstanding the brilliant success which he had obtained, was forced by superior numbers to retire…[11]

Marmont started the journey towards blaming Maucune on 31 July 1812, in his letter to the Minister of War:

> Accordingly, I gave orders to the 5e Division [Maucune] to take a position on the extreme right of this plateau, the fire from which was perfectly connected with that from Arapiles; … The 5e Division, after taking the indicated post, extended to the left without any motive nor reason.[12]

In his memoirs, published in 1857 five years after the author's death, Marmont went a step further:

> At that moment, General Maucune warned me that the enemy was withdrawing. He was asking to attack them. I could see better than him what was going on, and I could judge that, since the movement of the enemy was only preparatory, we had not yet arrived at the moment to attack them with advantage. Consequently, I told him to keep calm. But General Maucune, a man of little capacity, though a very brave soldier, could not contain himself when he was in the presence of the enemy. He was the same general, who, at the passage of the Duero five days before, would have so seriously compromised the army by his disobedience if the enemy had been in position, as might have been expected. This inevitably meant that,

10 Fortescue, *History*, Vol.VIII, p.486.

11 Anon., *The confidential correspondence of Napoleon Bonaparte with his brother Joseph sometime King of Spain* (New York: Appleton, 1856), Vol.II, pp.232–233.

12 A. Du Casse, *Mémoires et correspondance politique et militaire du roi Joseph* (Paris: Perrotin, 1854), Vol. VIII, p.204.

> contrary to my resolution never to place him at the head of the column, he found himself, by chance, by the natural arrangement of the troops, in this position. General Maucune did much more: he came down from the plateau and went closer to the enemy, without any orders. I noticed it and sent him the order to retire up there [onto the plateau]. Having had little regard for his obedience, I determined to go there myself, and, after taking a last look, from the top of the [Greater] Arapile, on the whole movements of the English army, I had just folded my telescope and set off to join my horse, when a single cannon shot, fired from the English army, from the two-piece battery which the enemy had placed on the other Arapile, broke my arm, and gave me two broad and deep wounds to my ribs and kidneys, and thus put me out of action.[13]

Maucune's misdemeanour on 17 July 1812 during the approach to Nava del Rey had been to advance half a league (approximately one and a half miles) further than ordered towards Rueda, which the British had left 15 hours earlier. It may have upset Marmont but was not deemed worthy of mention by Oman; nor is it included in Marmont's report to the minister of war on 31 July 1812. Maucune's chief of staff, Girard, reported that it was him whom Marmont reproached and that neither Maucune nor *Général de Brigade* Thomas Mignot, Baron de Lamartinière, Marmont's chief of staff, agreed with Marmont.[14]

Earlier French accounts of the battle blame only Thomières for exceeding his orders.[15] Oman described how 'Foy insinuates that Maucune's advance, at least in its early stages, was consonant with Marmont's intentions'.[16] However the phrase 'at least in its early stages' is Oman's not Foy's and the key point is that Foy does not criticise Maucune at all. This is the key phrase from Foy;

> *Quand on vit les Anglais se développer, on fit appuyer à droite les têtes de colonne afin de occuper des mamelons qui dominaient la pleine et se succédaient les uns aux autres; l'occupation de un mamelon donnait la tentation de occuper un autre. On fut ainsi conduit, d'attaque en attaque, jusqu'au village des Arapiles, que la 5e Division tint pendant quelques instant.*[17]

13 A.F.L.V. de Marmont, *Memoires du Maréchal Marmont, Duc De Ragusa* Third Edition (Paris: Perrotin, 1857), Vol.IV 1811–12, pp.238–239.

14 Marmont, *Memoires*, Vol.IV, pp.228–229; Du Casse, *Roi Joseph*, Vol.VIII, p.204; Oman, *History*, Vol.V, pp.399–400; P. Desachy, *Les Cahiers du Colonel Girard, 1766–1846* (Paris: Plon, 1951), p.199.

15 C-T. Beauvais de Préau (ed.), *Victoires, conquêtes, désastres, revers et guerres civiles des ...* (Paris: C.L.F. Panckoucke, 1820), Vol.XXI, p.46; Jacques-Vital Belmas, *Journaux des sièges faits ou soutenus par les Français dans la Péninsule* (Paris: Firmin Didot, 1836), Vol.I, p.233.

16 Oman, *History*, Vol.V, p.438.

17 M. Girod de l'Ain, *La Vie Militaire du Général Foy* (Paris: Plon Nourrit, 1900), p.175.

Oman translated this as;

> He [Marmont] had made his arrangements for a decisive blow: when the English were seen to take up their position, the heads of the columns were turned to the left, so as to occupy the elevations which dominate the plain, and swell up one after another. The occupation of one led to the temptation to seize the next, and so by advance after advance the village of Arapiles was at last reached. Maucune's division actually held it for some minutes.[18]

Note that Foy is here referring to the advance to Arapiles village rather than the advance beyond the village towards Miranda de Azan.

The evidence for Maucune advancing along the plateau until he was one-and-a-quarter miles away from the Greater Arapile and directly south of the village of Arapiles, appears to rest on Marmont's memoirs together with a belief that it was consistent with Maucune's behaviour as a general.[19] The key phrases in Marmont's memoirs are the repeated claim that after 'taking the post indicated, the fifth division extended [*s'étendit*] to its left without motive and without reason' and the statement that Maucune 'came down from the plateau and went closer to the enemy, without any orders'.[20] It is hard to tally these statements with the maps of Oman and Fortescue. Neither statement justifies placing Maucune's division one-and-a-quarter miles to the west of the Greater Arapile: indeed, Oman's positioning of Maucune at the summit of the Monte de Azan is the exact opposite of 'came down from the plateau and went closer to the enemy' or, to employ the description offered by *Capitaine* Pierre Castel, aide de camp to Clausel, (also published in the 1850s) 'driven by the ardour of the battle, it [Maucune's division] rushed blindly towards the enemy columns, four times stronger than its own'.[21]

Other eyewitness accounts confirm that Maucune's men were still formed on Monte de Azan with only his skirmishers pushed ahead towards the village, when they were attacked by Leith.[22] Furthermore, while Marmont accused Maucune of *extending* rather than *moving* to the left, it is clear from other eyewitness accounts that Maucune deployed his division with the brigades deployed in two lines rather than extended in a single line.[23]At Villamuriel in October 1812 Maucune deployed up to half of his division as skirmishers: unfortunately we can only speculate as to whether he fought like this at Salamanca, although this may have been the

18 Oman, *History*, Vol.V, p.438.
19 Oman, *History*, Vol.V, p.430; R. Muir, *Salamanca 1812* (New Haven: Yale University, 2001), p.60.
20 Marmont, *Mémoires*, pp.238–239.
21 P. Castel, *Relation de la bataille et retraite des Arapiles*... (Toulouse: Caseaux, 1854), p.18.
22 Muir, *Salamanca*, pp.109–110.
23 Muir, *Salamanca*, p.111.

source of Marmont's '*s'étendit*' remark. However, the allied accounts suggest that Maucune's skirmishers withdrew to the main position as Leith's men advanced.

This raises the question that if Marmont in later life can be considered an unreliable witness with regard to Maucune, what can we say about Maucune's actual movement and deployment?

Presuming that he followed standard practise, Maucune would have deployed his division of two brigades in two lines of battalion columns, one brigade in the front line and the other behind. Within the brigades, the regiments were positioned based on their seniority, with the more senior regiments – that is to say, those with the lower numbers – on the right.[24] The deployment of the division with d'Arnauld's brigade in the front line is perhaps supported by the respective casualties of the two brigades:[25]

| | Casualties | | | Relative to total infantry losses of the division | Losses relative to original strength |
|---|---|---|---|---|---|
| Unit | Officers | Men | Total | | |
| D'Arnauld | | | | | |
| 15e Ligne | 17 | 590 | 607 | 34.9% | 36% |
| 66e Ligne | 10 | 578 | 588 | 33.9% | 50% |
| Montfort | | | | | |
| 82e Ligne | 10 | 262 | 272 | 15.7% | 27% |
| 86e Ligne | 5 | 265 | 270 | 15.5% | 23% |
| | | | 1,737 | | 35% |

Thus, d'Arnauld's brigade suffered 69 percent of the casualties reported by the division.[26]

It also tempting to believe that Corporal John Douglas (3/1st Foot) was referring to d'Arnauld in his account of Leith's advance on the French line, from his position on the right of Lieutenant Colonel Charles Greville's Brigade:[27]

> At this moment a French officer mounted on a white horse seemed to be very busy endeavouring to keep his men to their work, when a corporal of the name of Joffrey and I got leave to try if he was ball proof; and running out a few yards in front kneeled down and fired together, but which of us

24 P. Foucart, *Campagne de Prusse (1806) d'Après les Archives de la Guerre, Tome Iena* (Paris: Berger-Levrault, 1887), pp.703–704; Anon., *Réglement Concernant l'Exercice et les Manoeuvres de l'Infanterie, du 1er Août 1791* (Paris: Journal Militaire et Chez Belin, 1792), p.1.

25 SHD C8 467, *Situation* Armée d'Espagne, 1 November 1812, *État des pertes éprouvées par l'Armée de Portugal depuis le 18 Juilliet jusqu'au 8 Août 1812*; these losses combine those killed or prisoner of war, wounded and missing.

26 Muir, *Salamanca*, pp.253–258; although it is likely that this return underestimated the true losses, this does not affect this comparison.

27 Greville (1/38th Foot) commanded the first brigade in place of Major General Andrew Hay.

> struck him must still remain a mystery, but down he went. Poor Joffrey, while in the act of rising off his knee, received a ball in the breast which numbered him with the dead also.[28]

*Général de Brigade* d'Arnauld had a horse killed under him and was taken prisoner, but he managed to escape overnight and re-join the army.[29] However five senior regimental officers from the division also became casualties and are alternative targets for Douglas and Joffrey. These officers were *Chef de Bataillon* Jacques Villemant (3/15e Ligne, killed in action), *Major en 2e* Pierre Louis Ducheyron du Pavillion (commanded 66e Ligne, wounded and died 3 October 1812 in Bayonne),[30] *Chef de Bataillon* Jean Vivarès (4/66e Ligne, wounded and prisoner of war), *Capitaine* Jean Baptiste Marie Demay (commanded 5/66e Ligne, wounded) and *Chef de Bataillon* Joseph Ninon (5/82e Ligne, died of wounds). Whoever Douglas saw fall, Maucune then had to lead his division without the commander of his leading brigade, one of whose regiments was reduced to being commanded by a company commander.[31]

Map One is based on the geography as reflected in the first edition of Spain's *Mapa Topográfico Nacional*,[32] overlayed with Oman's positioning of the divisions of Leith and Maucune. The individual battalions are shown as if deployed in line, given their strength on the day. Thus, the French battalion columns are represented as separated by their full deployment distance (N.B. the depths of the units are exaggerated). The artillery must have been posted to the right of Maucune's division.[33]

Oman's map presents some challenges when matching it to the eyewitness accounts that we have. Leith's division is positioned in front of the village of Arapiles with the whole of both Greville's Brigade and Spry's Brigade in front of the village. However, Lieutenant Peter Le Mesurier described how the 1/9th Foot advanced through the village at the beginning of the attack while the other battalions in Greville's Brigade did not:

28 S. Monick (ed.), *Douglas's Tale of the Peninsular War and Waterloo, 1808–1815* (London: Leo Cooper, 1997), p.46.

29 J. Courcelles, *Dictionnaire historique et biographique des généraux Français: depuis le onzième siecle jusqu'en 1820* (Paris: Author, Arthus Bertrand and Treuttel and Wurtz, 1822), Vol.V, p.150.

30 A. Liévyns, J.M. Verdot and P. Bégat, *Fastes de la légion-d'honneur: biographie de tous les décorés accompagnée de l'histoire législative et réglementaire de l'ordre* (Paris: Bureau d'Administration, 1847), Vol.V, p.240.

31 A.Martinien, *Tableaux, par corps et par batailles, des officiers tués et blessés pendant les guerres de l'Empire (1805–1815)* (Paris: Charles-Lavauzelle, 1899), pp.152, 271, 293; SHD 2Yb 157, *Contrôles des Officiers* 15e Ligne; SHD 2Yb 349, *CdO* 66e Ligne; SHD 2Yb 397, *CdO* 82e Ligne; SHD C8 466, *Situation* Armée d'Espagne, 15 August 1812; unit allocations as of 15 June 1812. With all three senior officers of the 66e Ligne casualties, *Capitaine* Antoine Salles took command of both battalions (LEONORE, dossier LH/2448/44).

32 Available online at < http://signa.ign.es/signa/Pege.aspx>.

33 Oman, *History*, Vol.V, p.431; Desachy, *Girard*, pp.201; Oman has two batteries from the army reserve while Girard mentions only one.

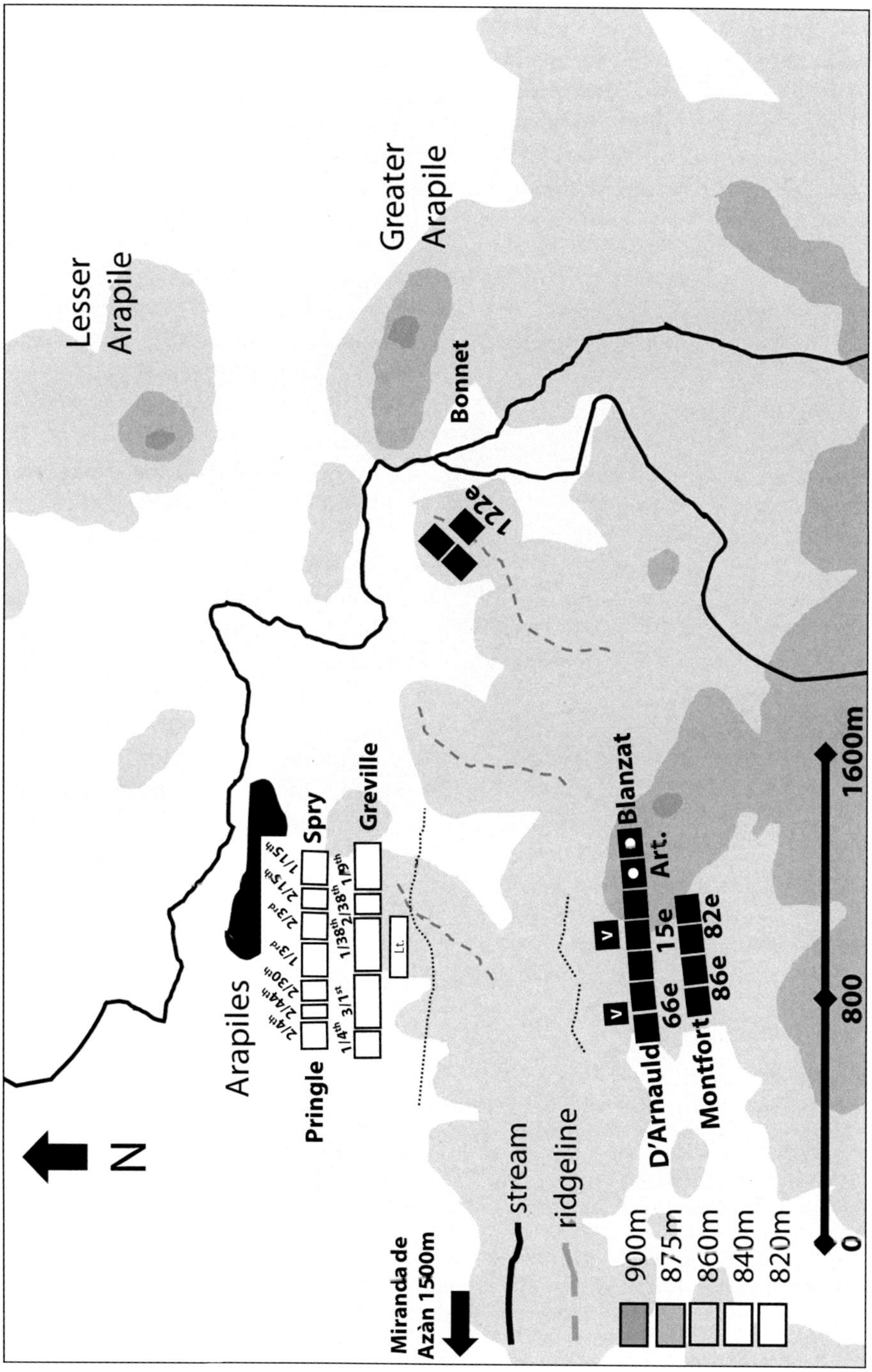


Map One – Oman's positioning of Leith and Maucune. (© Garry D. Wills)

> At four we were ordered to advance in line. A village lay between the two lines, in consequence of which we broke in column of sections and advanced in double quick time, shot and shell pouring on us. When we had passed the village, we formed line and moved on in the same order as a regiment would do on l'Hyvreuse, that is to say admirably well. Here the 9th pushed forward before the brigade, the enemy about two hundred yards in front.[34]

Sir James Leith after a portrait by John Wright. (Author's collection)

Muir points to an anomaly provided by the then unidentified soldier of the 1/38th Foot, who were in the centre of Greville's Brigade, but who also described passing through 'a village'.[35] However Gareth Glover's recent identification of this man as Private James Cooley,[36] identifies him also as a member of Willshire's light company, who would therefore have been detached from the regiment during the advance.[37]

Le Mesurier's statement that the French, presumably their skirmishers, were within 200 paces of the regiment once it had passed the village is also inconsistent with Oman's map, which shows Maucune's division deployed 1,500 paces or 1,100 metres from Arapiles village. While Maucune would deploy his skirmishers forward from his position, they

34 A. Greenwood (ed.), *Through Spain with Wellington: The letters of Lieutenant Peter Le Mesurier of the fighting Ninth* (Stroud: Amberley, 2016), p.118; compare with Monick, *Douglas*, pp.44–46; l'Hyvreuse is in St. Peter Port, Guernsey, where Le Mesurier's family lived.

35 Muir, *Salamanca*, p.118, citing National Army Museum, London, Accession No. 1979-12-21, *Manuscript memoirs of an unidentified soldier of 38th (1st Staffordshire) Regiment of Foot, of his career in the Army 1808 (c)-1815.*

36 Waterloo Association Archive; *The Story of Private Joseph Cooley? 38th Foot*, available at <https://archives.waterlooassociation.org.uk/wordpress/search-detail/?modes_query=%7BWord%20search%7D%3D%2A%7Bcooley%7D&start_archive_docs=4>, accessed 10 October 2020.

37 The National Archives, Kew (TNA), WO25/1742, Casualty return 1/38th Foot, 24 October to 24 November 1812.

would normally be expected to be within 300 paces of the first line battalions.[38] Lieutenant Colonel William Warre (aide de camp to Marshal Beresford) also has Maucune's skirmishers in the village of Arapiles sometime after 4:00 p.m.[39]

Furthermore, if Oman's map is correct then the observation of Captain Andrew Leith Hay (aide de camp to Leith) that Maucune's artillery was 'further back' relative to the infantry would have put them on the reverse slope.[40]

A final concern about Oman's map is that the line of Leith's advance, with Major General John Gaspard Le Marchant's brigade of heavy cavalry on his right, would inevitably drive Maucune's men more to the south, across the front of Pakenham's advance, towards Azan Alqueria, rather than southeast towards Alba de Tormes. Lieutenant William Grattan (88th Foot, Wallace's Brigade, 3rd Division) mentions that there was contact between Pakenham's 3rd Division and Leith's 5th Division but this only involved a few men; 'some men of the 5th division got intermingled with ours'.[41] Thus Grattan, whose regiment formed the centre of Wallace's line, the leading brigade of Pakenham's 3rd Division, is not describing the 5th Division crossing the line of advance of the 3rd Division, as implied by Oman's map.[42]

It seems more likely that, having emerged from behind the Greater Arapile, Maucune would have taken a more direct route towards the village of Arapiles across the extreme right end of the Monte de Azan as ordered by Marmont. Moving northwest past the Greater Arapile, the hill slopes down from over 870 metres to the village of Arapiles at approximately 840 metres. The slope is not even but undulates creating a succession of small ridgelines or crests, which are consistent with those that feature in the accounts of both Douglas and Le Mesurier.[43]

Given the available evidence, we must at least consider the scenario that Leith attacked Maucune along a northwest to southeast axis, as shown in Map Two, rather than Oman's north to south axis. This map positions Maucune some 550 metres from the village with his skirmishers 300 metres closer, reflecting Le Mesurier's account. It is possible that Maucune positioned d'Arnauld's brigade on an alternative line, further forward, just 150m from the village, when his

38 Morand's instructions for skirmishers, 1811, at <http://www.demi-brigade.org/tirdaven.htm>, accessed 4 June 2017, citing V.I. Charkevitscha, *Materials from the Military (Training) Archives of the General Staff. The 1812 Patriotic War. Part II: Documents Seized from the Enemy. Vol.I: Outgoing Correspondence of Marshal Davout (from 14 October to 31 December 1811)* (St. Petersburg: Publisher Unknown, 1903), pp.6–11.

39 W. Warre, *Letters from the Peninsula, 1808–12* (London: John Murray, 1909), p.287; Warre was a brevet major in the 23rd Light Dragoons, a lieutenant colonel in the Portuguese service.

40 A. Leith Hay, *A Narrative of the Peninsular War* (Edinburgh: Daniel Lizars, 1831), Vol.II, p.55.

41 Grattan, *Adventures*, p.248.

42 Lieutenant Colonel John Alexander Wallace (1/88th Foot) was in command of the 1st Brigade of the 3rd Division due to his seniority, but his regiment formed the centre of the brigade because it was the junior regiment in the brigade.

43 Monick, *Douglas*, p.45; Greenwood, *Le Mesurier*, p.118.

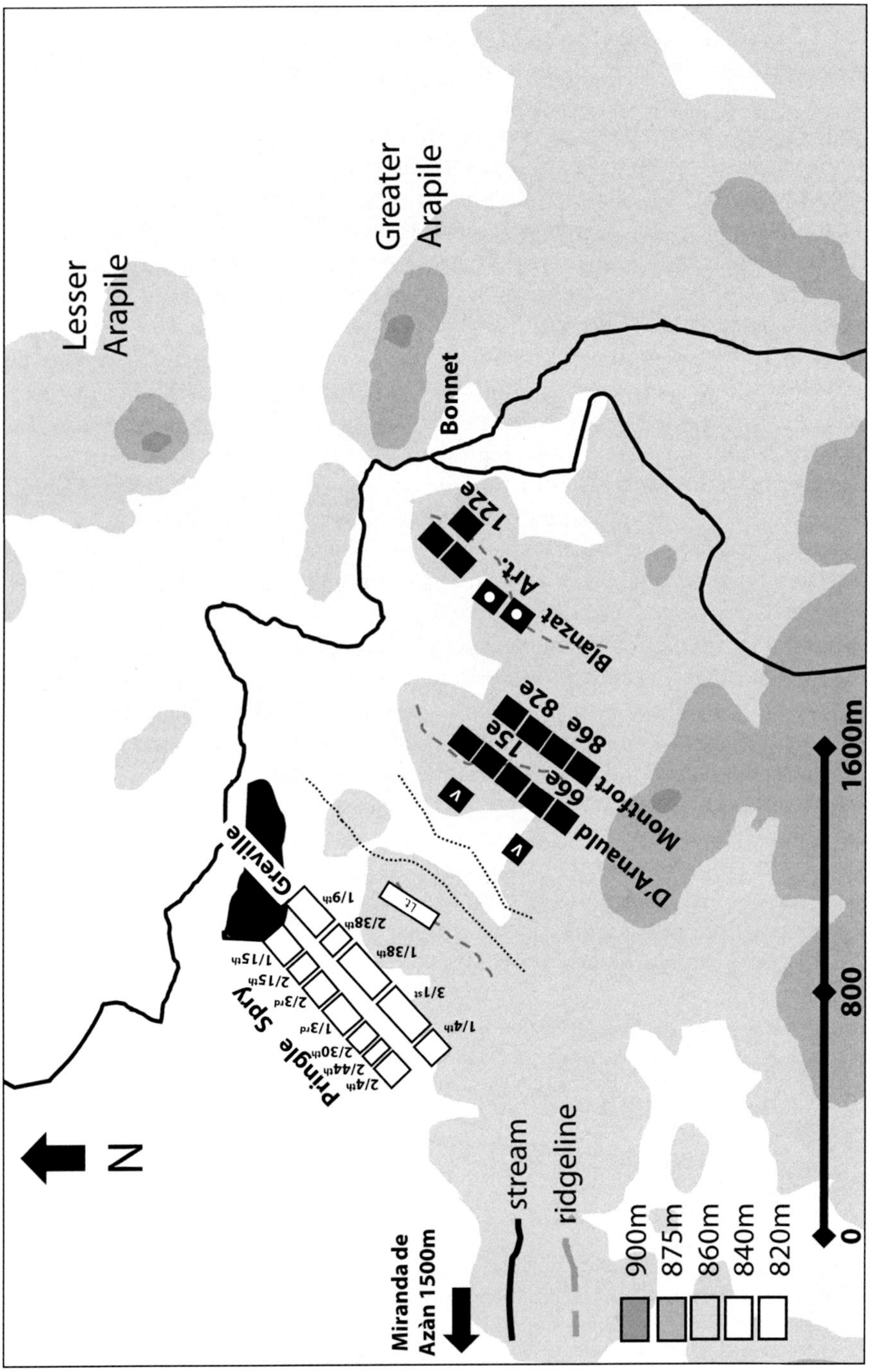


Map Two – Alternative disposition of Leith and Maucune. (© Garry D. Wills)

View looking west from the Greater Arapile. (Author's Photograph)

skirmishers managed to get into the village temporarily.[44] It may even be the position that Marmont referred to in his memoirs. However, the evidence we have suggests otherwise, for example, Warre described how:

> [W]e remained quiet till a little before four in the evening, when the enemy opened a most tremendous cannonade upon our whole position from, I should guess, upwards of 50 pieces of cannon, and soon after pushed forward a crowd of sharpshooters, it should appear, however, only to insult our army, as they were not supported, and the heavy columns they had on the hills did not move forward.[45]

This is also reflected in the other allied accounts.[46]

The other alternative is that Maucune deployed his division 400 metres further up the slope alongside both the possible site for his artillery and the 122e Ligne from Bonnet's 8e Division, which was deployed on 'an intermediate hillock … between the large plateau and the hill of Arapile [i.e. the Greater Arapile], which protected the exit from the village'.[47] This position seems less likely as Leith Hay

44 Oman, *History*, Vol.V, p.435.
45 Warre, *Letters*, p.287.
46 Leith Hay, *Narrative*, Vol.II, p.55; Monick, *Douglas*, p.45; Greenwood, *Le Mesurier*, p.118.
47 Marmont, *Mémoires*, p.238.

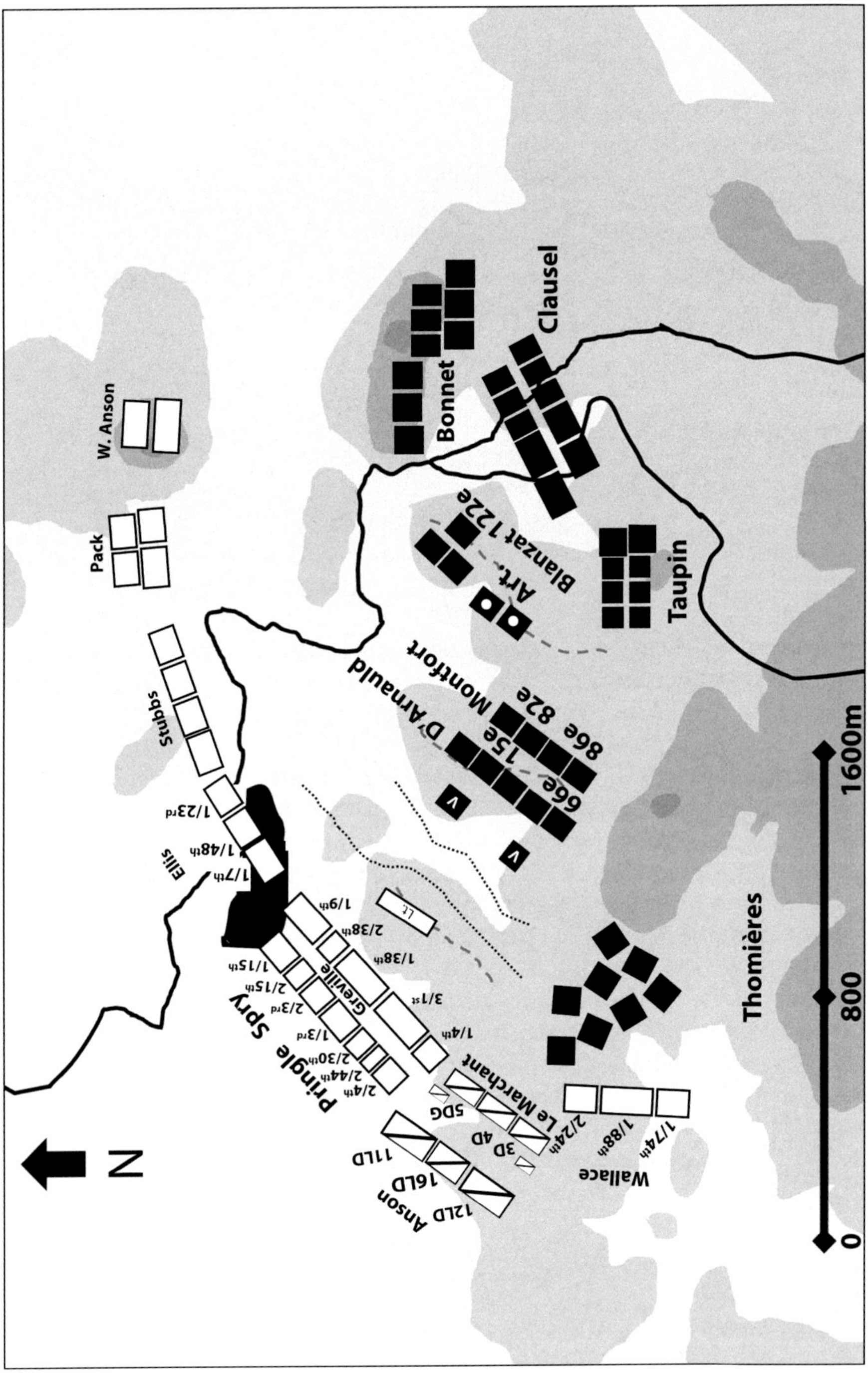


Map Three – The Divisions Around Maucune. (© Garry D. Wills)

has Maucune's artillery to the rear of his infantry.[48] On the other hand this higher position is perhaps supported by its proximity to the stream which Douglas mentions as the position of the French second line.[49]

Map Three is an attempt to place the other divisions into the context of an attack by Leith using a northwest to southeast axis.[50] Douglas has the British cavalry advancing alongside the 5th Division and making contact after the first clash between the infantry.[51] The overall disposition is consistent with the capture of the drum major's staff of the 66e Ligne by the 5th Dragoon Guards.[52] The map follows Muir with regard to the arrangements of the regiments within Le Marchant's brigade, although normal precedence would have the 5th Dragoon Guards on the right and the 3rd Dragoons on the left.[53] Girard also stated that the cavalry 'turned our left and beset us from behind'.[54] At the moment of contact, Leith Hay described the French infantry in squares or columns in his different editions (we should note that it would have been difficult to tell the difference, from distance, between a battalion in column or square, especially if the square was formed by closing the intervals in the column).[55] Douglas has Maucune's infantry in a mixture of lines and squares, when they were assailed by Leith and Le Marchant.[56] Le Mesurier also reported that Maucune's battalions to his front, began to retire once Leith's men got to within 100 yards:

> When we came within 100 yards they [the 15e Ligne would have been directly to Le Mesurier's front] faced to the right about and moved off in ordinary time, which, however, they quickened as we advanced on them till such a time that, finding us too close, they ran as fast as they could, put leg to the ground, and we following them, cheering.[57]

Having begun the action formed in battalion columns, beset simultaneously by Leith and Le Marchant, we can suppose that some of Maucune's battalions formed line, some retired in column and some formed square, dependent on their

48 Leith Hay, *Narrative*, Vol.II, p.55.

49 Monick, *Douglas*, p.46; however, it is not clear whether Douglas refers to Maucune's second line or a following division.

50 Muir, *Salamanca*, pp.101, 124–128.

51 Monick, *Douglas*, p.46.

52 R. Cannon, *Historical Records of the Fifth or Queen Charlotte's Regiment of Dragoon Guards* (London: William Clowes, 1839), p.59.

53 Muir, *Salamanca*, pp.125, 139; R. Muir, R. Burnham, H. Muir, R. McGuigan, *Inside Wellington's Peninsular Army, 1808–1814* (Barnsley: Pen and Sword, 2006), p.99.

54 Desachy, *Girard*, p.200.

55 Muir, *Salamanca*, p.122; T.E. Crowdy, *Napoleon's Infantry Handbook* (Barnsley: Pen and Sword Military, 2015), p.187.

56 Muir, *Salamanca*, pp.120–121; Monick, *Douglas*, p.46.

57 Greenwood, *Le Mesurier*, p.118.

View looking south south west from the Greater Arapile. (Author's Photograph)

individual circumstances, with varying levels of success. Thus, the unsuccessful attempts to seize the eagles of the 66e Ligne and 82e Ligne suggests that the 4/82e Ligne was caught by Le Marchant's heavy cavalry, before it formed square and the 4/66e Ligne after they it had been broken by Leith. On the other hand, it seems that the more exposed 1/86e Ligne had time to form square as the cavalry approached.

Another advantage of the repositioning of the Leith—Maucune contest on a northwest to southeast axis is that Leith's division is then much better placed to support Cole during Clausel's counterattack when Marshal Beresford redirected Spry's Brigade to attack the flank of the attacking French units. Indeed, Spry's after action report states that his infantry had only to turn left to engage the French.[58] If Leith had attacked Maucune on Oman's north-south axis, Spry's Brigade would have been approximately 900 metres away from the Fusilier Brigade of the 4th Division as it advanced.[59]

58 R. Burnham, personal communication.

59 Muir, *Salamanca*, p.147.

## Maucune's Divisional Artillery

Unlike the divisions around him, Maucune got away from the battlefield with his divisional artillery intact (Clausel lost one 4-pounder, Ferey one 8-pounder and three 4-pounder, Sarrut one 6-inch howitzer, Taupin one 8-pounder,[60] Thomières three 8-pounders and one 4-pounder, Bonnet one 8-pounder).[61] Girard has *Chef de Bataillon* Charles Blanzat, Maucune's artillery commander, forming a battery of 12 guns at the beginning of the action, Maucune's six divisional guns and six from the army reserve. Girard further records that Blanzat was reduced to 10 guns during the retreat, the missing guns presumably from the reserve guns. Although Maucune's artillery was reduced by one 8-pounder by 15 September 1812, this is not untypical of the army. The *situation* of that date shows that an additional 15 guns to be missing from the army's order of battle.[62]

## Maucune's Regimental Eagles

Maucune's division retired from Leith's and Le Marchant's assault in sufficient order to retain the four eagles they carried.[63] In his history Oman stated that:

> A regiment whose 1st battalion was elsewhere carried not an eagle but a simple standard per battalion instead. Of such regiments, wanting their senior battalion and therefore their eagle, there were with Marmont three. Two, the 66th and 82nd, were in Maucune's division, one, the 26th, in Ferey's. The colours probably belonged to some of these, of which several were much cut up, especially the 66th.[64]

However, eagles were carried by the 1/15e, 4/66e, 4/82e and 1/86e, the two fourth battalions being the senior battalions in their respective regiments, both regiments having lost their first three battalions in the West Indies.[65] The history of the 66e Ligne records how '[the 66e Ligne's] eagle, when compromised in the midst of

60 *Général de Brigade* Eloi Champagne Taupin commanded the 6e Division, while *Général de Division* Antoine François Brenier de Montmorand was absent sick in Valladolid as reported in the *Situation* of 15 June 1812 (SHD C8 466).

61 Muir, *Salamanca*, p.211; citing Lamartinière's return (*Archives Historique de la Guerre* C7–15).

62 Desachy, *Girard*, pp.201-2; SHD C8 466; c.f. SHD C8 467; 15 September— two 8 pounders, two 4 pounders plus one 6-inch howitzer.

63 SHD C8 467; the Armée de Portugal *situation* includes a statement of losses including eagles for the period covering Salamanca, 18 July to 8 August 1812.

64 Oman, *History*, Vol.V, p.470, footnote 1.

65 P. Charrié, *Drapeaux et étendards de la Révolution et de l'Empire* (Paris: Copernic, 1982), pp.205, 210, 211.

View looking west from the Greater Arapile (Author's Photograph)

an English cavalry charge, was saved by Lieutenant Balthazard'.[66] This officer was *Sous Lieutenant* Jean Baptiste Fulgence Baltazard who was born in Grandpré, 1 January 1775 and had joined the army as a *soldat* in August 1793. He was promoted to *sous-lieutenant* and *porte-aigle* in 1811 having joined the 66e Ligne as *serjeant* in 1805. In defending his eagle (that of the 4/66e), he was trampled by the horses of the British cavalry, which resulted in a 'very significant hernia'. For this action Baltazard was rewarded with the *Légion d'Honneur*.[67]

Similarly, the history of the 82e Ligne records 'Captain Mottier defended, against a platoon of British cavalry, the eagle guard [of the 82e Ligne] that had been entrusted to him, and managed to bring back the pole, broken by the bullets and the sabre cuts of the enemy'.[68] This officer was *Lieutenant* and *1er Porte-Aigle* Jean Julien Mottier who was born in Les Loges-Marchis, 16 June 1773 and joined the army as a *soldat* in June 1793. He joined the 82e Ligne as *sous lieutenant* in 1807. He was promoted to *capitaine* on 4 September 1812.[69]

66 A-H, Dumay, *Historique du 66e régiment d'infanterie, 1672–1900* (Tours: E.Arnault, 1900), p.59.

67 SHD 2Yb349, *Contrôle des Officiers* 66e Ligne, p.26; LEONORE, dossier LH/100/78.

68 P. Arvers and C.F. Brecht, *Historique du 82e Régiment d'Infanterie* (Paris: Lahure, 1876), p.127.

69 LEONORE, dossier LH/1947/3; SHD 2Yb397, *Contrôle des Officiers* 82e Ligne, p.98; neither of these sources contain the story in the history.

It is without doubt that Maucune's division was defeated and broken by Leith's division and Le Marchant's heavy cavalry, so the question is how did Maucune manage to escape with both his guns and his eagles? There are two possible reasons. Firstly, if Maucune was positioned at the eastern end of the Monte de Azan, the divisions of Clausel, Taupin and Bonnet could have provided some sanctuary for his broken battalions. Secondly, the British cavalry of Le Marchant's and Anson's Brigades, comprising some 2,000 sabres, were attacking three French divisions with over 14,000 men in various states of order and disorder, spread over twice their own frontage, and although plenty of damage was done by the charge, in the chaos, smoke and dust there would have been ample opportunity for others to get away to relative safety.

## Timescale

The timescale offers another window onto Maucune's battle, which has received relatively little attention. Oman's timetable has Maucune being attacked by Leith at around 05:00 p.m. and the contest did not last long, traditionally less than 40 minutes.[70] At a march pace of 2½ miles per hour the broken division would have been expected to have covered the 7¼ miles to Alba de Tormes by 08:30 p.m. Meanwhile the French counterattack was in turn defeated and the final rearguard was formed on the El Barrero ridge. Oman has Clinton leading the assault on the French rearguard when he was worried that it was getting dark, and Douglas has the French subsequently in full retreat through the woods 'a little after sunset'.[71] Captain Henry Ross-Lewin (32nd Foot, Hinde's Brigade, Clinton's 6th Division) has the order for the last attack being received at 07:30 p.m.[72] Grattan has the final action taking place between 08:30 p.m. and 10:00 p.m.[73] Corporal James Hale (9th Foot, Leith's 5th Division) has the action finishing 'a little after' 10:00 p.m.[74] On this day sunset was at 08:47 p.m. and civil twilight, the point at which artificial light is required out of doors, was at 09:17 p.m. with full dark occurring only at 11:00 p.m. This suggests that the final combat took place sometime between 08:30 p.m. and 10:30 p.m. The timescale thus allows up to three hours for Maucune to rally the 5e Division in time to join Clausel's rearguard. That he was able to do this seems far from unlikely given the level of casualties especially in Montfort's brigade, and is consistent with the account of Maucune's chief of staff, Girard. To emphasise this

70 Oman, *History*, Vol.V, pp.448–450.

71 Oman, *History*, Vol.V, p.463; Monick, *Douglas*, p.47.

72 H. Ross-Lewin, *With the 32nd in the Peninsular and other Campaigns* (Dublin: Hodges, Figgis and Company, 1904), p.184.

73 Grattan, *Adventures*, pp.252–253.

74 J. Hale, *Journal of James Hale, late Sergeant in the Ninth Regiment of Foot* (Cirencester: Philip Watkins, 1826), p.87.

point *Capitaine* Lemonnier-Delafosse (31e Légère, Ferey's 3e Division) wrote that the action ended in full night: that is, approximately 11:00 p.m.[75]

## The Rearguard

Although Lemonnier-Delafosse's account gives the impression that Ferey's 3e Division alone manned the position at El Barrero, he was only a captain at the time and other accounts provide a different picture. Castel described how;

> Indeed, the troops of the three left-wing divisions, which, as we have just seen, had recently been repelled, were being jumbled to the left of the second line and offering the spectacle of the disorder that always follows a forced retreat. Some of these divisions were spread over a woody mound, located to the left rear. The army was thus in a very critical position…[76]

The woody mound he refers to is on the El Barrero position, and significantly, he does not describe the beaten divisions as streaming away to Alba de Tormes. French histories also suggest that Clausel managed to rally the broken French left wing, for example:

> Clausel re-established the order of battle, rallied the left and the centre on the right. Bringing together Bonnet's division with some regiments, he placed them in position on the heights of Arriba, and had them supported by a battery of fifteen pieces of cannon: this learned and bold manoeuvre, carried out in the presence of an already victorious army… thus saved the army of Portugal from a complete destruction.[77]

And:

> Already the army was routed when General Clausel took command. He rallied left and centre on the right, took up position on the heights behind Arriba, and by this clever manoeuvre he saved the army. The enemy continued his attacks, but he was repulsed; the night ended the fight.[78]

75 J-B. Lemonnier-Delafosse, *Campagnes de 1810 en Portugal, 11, 12, 13 en Espagne, 14 en France, 1815 en Belgique ou Souvenirs Militaires* (Havre: Lemale, 1850), p.163.
76 Castel, *Relation*, p.20.
77 Beauvais, *Victoires*, p.47.
78 Belmas, *Journaux*, Vol.I, pp.233–234.

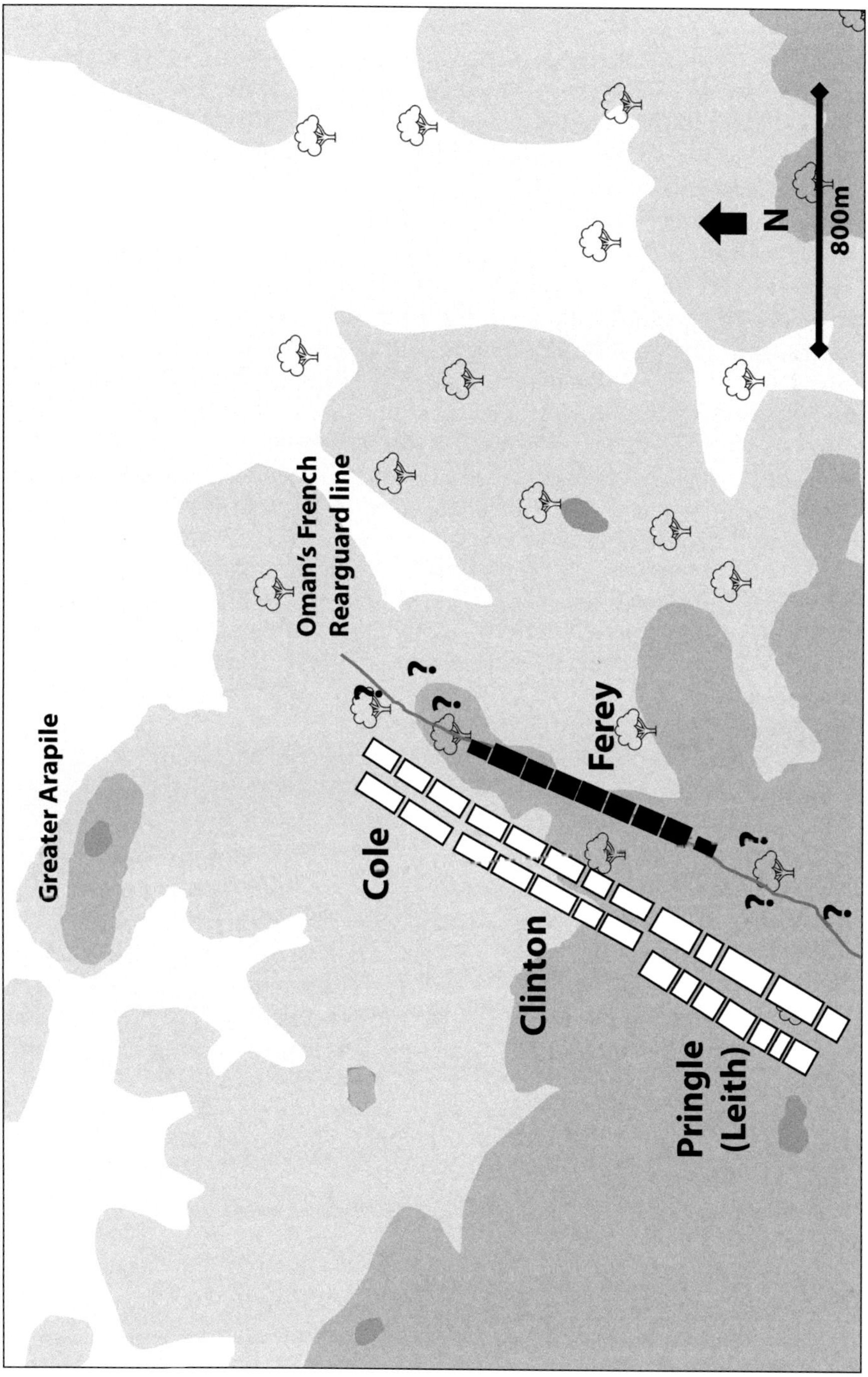


Map Fou- – Ferey's Rearguard. (© Garry D. Wills)

Similarly, the regimental histories of the 15e and 66e Ligne regiments in Maucune's division both mention that the troops fought until nightfall; '...At night, our troops withdrew in good order by the *Route de Alba de Tormes*',[79] and 'one of the first engaged, the 66e bravely did their duty by fighting until night'.[80]

Furthermore, Oman having detailed the destruction of the divisions of Thomières, Maucune, Clausel and Bonnet, describes how, during the final assault, 'there was much resistance: on Sarrut's intact battalions many of the broken regiments had rallied. These men, besmeared with blood, dust, and clay, half naked, and some carrying only broken weapons, fought with a fury not to be surpassed'.[81]

Oman has the final assault on the French rearguard led by Clinton's 6th Division supported by the Fusilier Brigade of the 4th Division on his left and the 5th Division on his right. Douglas describes how the 5th Division flanked the hill, causing the French to retire.[82] Together these units would have a frontage of 1,800 metres even with the divisions arrayed in the customary two lines. Oman has Ferey's division deployed in one line with the outer battalions deployed in square, this would enable them to cover a frontage of only 850 metres. The disparity in frontage is not consistent with the intensity of the ensuing firefight or the casualties suffered by the British and Portuguese. This suggests that Clausel had indeed managed to rally and re-form other previously broken battalions to extend the line on the left and right flanks.

## The Green Flag

A green flag was captured by the 11th Foot, which was part of Clinton's 6th Division, in the closing assault on the French rearguard. A drawing of this captured flag was published by Edward Orme, in August 1812, and shown to be devoid of any markings as described in the history of the 11th Foot.[83] Similarly a green flag devoid of markings is illustrated in a collection of drawings of flags in Chapel of the Royal Hospital Chelsea. This is marked as an 'east indian flag', but may have been the 11th Foot's prize from Salamanca.[84] This flag is consistent with the 1811 decree, and the February 1812 order of the day, for the new *fanions* of the French infantry.[85] The battalions that did not carry eagles, were intended to have carried simple

79 M.L.A. de Tarragon, *Historique du 15e Régiment d'Infanterie* (Paris: Charles-Lavauzelle, 1895), p.219.

80 Dumay, *Historique du 66e régiment d'infanterie*, p.59.

81 Oman, *History*, Vol.V, p.461; taken, in part, from Grattan, *Adventures*, p.253.

82 Monick, *Douglas*, p.47.

83 The Royal Collection Trust, RCIN 750679, *Battle of Salamanca: trophies taken from French. 22 July 1812*; the drawing is by William Thomas Fitzgerald and is dated August 1812.

84 National Army Museum, Accession 1974-05-77, *War flags and co at Chelsea Hospital, 1883; drawn by John Ford in 1841, compiled by John Dowling in 1883.*

85 Charrié, *Drapeaux*, p.210-211.

ensigns or *fanions*, with no markings, on a staff with a simple spearhead. Although Charrié doubts that any of the official flags went to Spain in 1812, he also concludes that the regimental colonels were able to manufacture their own.

The most likely explanation of 'the green flag' is therefore that it was a *fanion* of the fifth battalion of a French infantry regiment. The alternative suggestion, included in the history of the 11th Foot, is that the flag belonged to a foreign unit in French service. However, the only such unit present was the small detachment of the Régiment de Prusse or 4e Régiment d'Étranger, which, if it had a flag, would have had one of the standard French pattern. Finally, it is unlikely that any flag other than a *fanion* would have been without markings of any kind. The history of the 11th Foot states that the regiment was opposed to the French 122e Ligne, Bonnet's 8e Division, but this would have earlier in the day and the 122e had only its first, second and third battalions present.[86]

There were only three fifth battalions present at Salamanca, two in Maucune's division, the 5/66e (d'Arnauld's brigade) and the 5/82e Ligne (Montfort's brigade) and the third in Ferey's division, the 5/26e Ligne. Of these battalions, the 5/26e Ligne would be the obvious candidate as owner of the green flag captured by the 11th Foot. However, the casualties of the two battalions of the 26e Ligne were only 29 percent, whereas the 66e Ligne lost 50 percent, while the 82e Ligne lost 27 percent.[87] Fortescue gives the strength of these battalions based on the same 1 August 1812 *situation* that Oman used, although he gives the battalions of the 26e Ligne as the first and second. The following table includes Fortescue's numbers for the 2/26e Ligne, assuming a clerical error on his part:[88]

| **Unit** | **Present under arms (officers/men)** | | | | **Losses** |
|---|---|---|---|---|---|
| | **15 June** | **15 July** | **1 August** | **15 September** | |
| 5/26e Ligne | | 18/556 (2/26e?) | 17/510 (2/26e?) | | 8% |
| | 18/553 | | | 11/328 | 40% |
| 5/66e Ligne | | 19/593 | 17/270 | | 53% |
| 5/82e Ligne | | 20/502 | 19/396 | | 23% |

Of these three battalions, the 5/66e Ligne was the only one disbanded after the battle and its cadre sent back to France, therefore the 5/66e Ligne should at least be seen as a candidate for the owner of the 11th Foot's 'green flag'. It is also noteworthy that, given normal precedence, we would expect the 11th Foot to be deployed at the opposite end of Ferey's line from the 5/26e Ligne.

86 R. Cannon, *Historical Record of the Eleventh or North Devon Regiment of Foot* (London: Parker, Furnivall and Parker, 1845), pp.65, 68.

87 Muir, *Salamanca*, p.259.

88 SHD C8 466, C8 467, *Situation* Armée de Portugal 15 June and 15 September; Fortescue, Vol.VIII, pp.663–664.

## Girard's Account

Girard's account (written after 1831) is particularly self-serving and has been discounted by some, however his account is worthy of consideration in this context. Initially Girard described an exchange with *Capitaine* Fabvier, one of Marmont's aides de camp, in which he claims to have predicted the impending disaster. He then describes the results of Leith's and Le Marchant's assault on Maucune's division as follows;

> Wellington sent all his forces against our three divisions which, despite their courage, could not resist beyond an hour. Perhaps they would have held longer if a large force of cavalry had not turned our left and beset us from behind at the moment our front line was hardly containing masses of infantry. Courage was useless; it was necessary to abandon the field and the cavalry completed our disarray. General Taupin's division on the extreme left [i.e. behind the line from Maucune to Thomières] was badly abused. General Thomières who was on his right was killed and his division gave way, sweeping along General Maucune and all others. The disorder became so great that the enemy cavalry was confused with us and only thought to withdraw. The superior officers wanted to take the opportunity to try to rally their men, but all their efforts were in vain.
>
> As Chief of Staff, I particularly took care of the artillery. I sought them where I had myself positioned them early in the fight and found *chef de bataillon* Blanzat [the division's artillery commander] who I had positioned with a battery of twelve pieces ordering him to hold the position to the last extremity. He told me that he had fired his last volley at thirty paces and that having no time to reload, he had withdrawn, while already two of his horses had been bayonetted. He had left his guns at the bottom of the position and was looking for the general or myself to receive new orders. We could make out the first piece in the middle of the dust and smoke, soon others followed, most of the men and animals injured.
>
> I then noticed a great movement to our rear, and I thought that the cavalry was coming at us. I formed a square with the caissons and double-shotted all our guns; I gathered as many of the scattered infantry as I could and formed them in the intervals of the pieces. We were not well formed in this order when English squadrons, believing we were an easy target arrived at the gallop. Their charge though impetuously directed on two sides of the square was foiled, but so close to us that Major Blanzat was stunned by an enemy cavalryman that disengaged himself from the servant who fought at his side.
>
> The withdrawal of the cavalry allowed us to join a group of our infantry near where … Clausel … gathered some thousands of men he put in line along a dry stone retaining wall that the cavalry could not cross.…

The Battle of Salamanca from Maxwell's Life of Wellington. Artist George Bryant Campion; Engraver James Tillits Wilmore (Author's collection)

Wellington sent significant forces to compel him [Clausel] to abandon the position which he had to take, without success. He began the assault with yet more but with no more success. We were fighting so closely that the wads of the muskets reached the chests of the men of the first rank. We were going to charge with the bayonet when the enemy withdrew, abandoning on the field several thousands of dead or wounded.

We ourselves were almost all *hors de combat* and in a much more critical situation such that our only chance of retirement was the passage of the Tormes at the little town of Alba. The enemy could easily have taken this bridge. Fortunately, he used the night to rally and to prepare for the next day's pursuit. General Clausel took the opportunity to move his troops to the other side, but as this crossing could not be accomplished without confusion, it was ensured by General Maucune, who took up a position at the head of the bridge and remained there until the army gained the other bank.

To cover this passage, General Maucune and I — almost the only remaining senior officers! — had with difficulty gathered together a thousand to twelve hundred men and Chief de battalion Blanzat's battery, reduced to ten pieces. My outposts were so close to the enemy's that we could hear the talk between them.[89]

89 Desachy, *Girard*, pp.201-202.

Obviously, anyone brought up with Oman's and Fortescue's view of Salamanca may find Girard's account incredible: however, if we look at it from his perspective it becomes more credible. He does not underplay the initial chaos and confusion caused by the British assault. However, he makes no mention of d'Arnauld's capture and this significant omission demonstrates his focus, amid the chaos, on the divisional artillery resources. The fact that Maucune and Blanzat did retain the divisional artillery endorses Girard's account although he probably exaggerated his own role.

## The Salamanca Eagles and other trophies

The two eagles captured at Salamanca were those of the 22e Ligne (Taupin's 6e Division) and the 62e Ligne (Thomières's 7e Division). Tradition has it that the eagle of the 22e Ligne was taken by Ensign John Pratt of the 30th Foot. The eagle of the 62e Ligne was taken by Lieutenant William Pearce of the 2/44th Foot in Leith's 5th Division, as described by his brigade commander Lieutenant Colonel Francis Brooke (4th Foot) in his report written on 23 July 1812 (When Leith was wounded during the attack, Major General William Henry Pringle took command of the 5th Division and Brooke took command of Pringle's Brigade based on seniority):

> Sir,
> I have the honour to report to you the conduct of the 2nd Brigade, 5th Division in the action of the 22nd Inst.
>
> It must be in your recollection of the very steady manner in which it advanced under a very heavy fire of round[shot] and grape to within twenty paces of the enemy's columns which had for some time opened a heavy fire of musketry. The brigade reserved its fire until this moment when pouring in a well-directed fire along the line, instantly advanced to the charge in double quick time, broke the enemy's columns in every direction and pursued them at the point of the bayonet for some distance until ordered to halt. During the whole of this time I cannot too much praise the conduct of the officers, non-commissioned officers and privates of this brigade for their gallant and steady conduct. I particularly wish to mention Major Piper comr 1st Battn 4th Regt and Lt. Col. Hamilton 30th, Lt. Col. Harding of the 44th Regt and Capn Anwyl[l] 4th Regt as Brigade Major. I also wish you to notice the gallant conduct of Major Faunce with the light companies which were detached during the day.
>
> I also beg to notice that the 4th Regt has taken the colour of the 62nd Ligne this being the second time in four months it has taken the colours of two different regts. The 44th have also taken an eagle of, the 30th Regt the left colour of the 62nd Ligne.
>
> The light regts always carry small flags.

> I have the honour to be,
> yr ob[edien]t servant
> F. Brooke
> Lt. Col. 4th Regt
> Comng 2nd Brigade
> 5th Division
>
> I beg to state that in the names of officers I have forgot to mention Major Williamson 4th Regt 2nd Battn.[90]

Interestingly Brooke prioritised the lesser achievement of his own regiment over the capture of a French eagle by another regiment in the brigade. Obviously the 62e Ligne was not a light regiment.

Lieutenant William Pearce was specifically named by his commanding officer, Lieutenant Colonel George Harding, 44th Foot, in his report to Pringle:

> Camp near Alba de Tormes
> 23rd July 1812
>
> Sir
> I beg of you to present to His Excellency the Commander of the Forces an Eagle taken from the enemy by the 44th Regiment in the vigorous charge we made upon them yesterday at the same time I have to mention that it was the good fortune of the Light Company commanded by Captain Ballard to secure it and he assures me that it was first seized upon by his subaltern Lt. Pearce.
>
> In reporting to you the gallant conduct of the 44th Regt under my command I have to say that it called forth the most flattering marks of your approbation on the field of battle to this I have only to add that their conduct excited my admiration as it did your applause and I am sure you will mention them as they deserve.
>
> Sir, I have the honour to be
> Your most obedient servant
> George Harding Major,
> Lt. Col. Com[mandin]g 2nd Bn 44th Regt.[91]

Furthermore, Captain Thomas Ballard, who commanded the light companies of Pringle's Brigade, also named Pearce:

90 University of Manchester Library (UML) GB 133 Eng MSS 1273; Letter 16, Brooke's report, 23 July 1812.
91 UML GB 133 Eng MSS 1273; Letter 18, Harding's letter to Pringle, 23 July 1812.

Sir
24th July 1812

I beg to mention to you that I commanded the light companies of the 2nd Bn 4th, 30th and 44th Regts which formed the right of the first line when we advanced and drove the enemy from their position and my own company being on the right of all took an eagle which is in the possession of my subaltern Lt Pearce. Your favourable report of this circumstance will do me much service and forward my views in the army.

Brigade Major Anwyll communicated your orders to me in the field and I trust that I conducted myself to your satisfaction.

Sir I have the honour to be
Your most obedient servant,
Thomas Ballard Captn 44th Regt.[92]

It also noteworthy that for this attack, the 1/4th Foot from Pringle's brigade were deployed with Greville's Brigade, and Ballard's report suggests that the light company of the 1/4th Foot was deployed with the light companies of Greville's Brigade.

Orme's drawing of the Salamanca trophies also shows the *banderoles* (streamers or pennants) carried by the 2e and 3e *porte-aigles* for both the 22e and 62e Ligne as the four smaller flags captured. These were created by Imperial Decree in 1809.[93]

Thus it would appear that the reports of Ballard and Harding are referring to the actions of the merged light companies of the brigade, which comprised the light companies of the 2/4th, 2/30th and 2/44th Foot. They clearly captured the intact eagle guard of the 1/62e Ligne, This in turn suggests that Ensign John Pratt of the 2/30th Foot's light company captured the 62e Ligne's *3e porte-aigle*'s white *banderole* rather than the eagle of the 22e Ligne, while the 4th Foot took the *2e porte-aigle*'s red *banderole* (or vice versa depending on what Brooke meant by 'left colour'). This has the ring of a fair division of spoils, between the three regiments involved, after the event. Although Pratt is not named in the reports of Brooke, Harding or Ballard, he is named in this context in the history of the 44th Foot, which also includes a spirited description of the combat for the trophies.[94] However a letter published in 1844 by 'one of Greville's brigade' claimed that the eagle was merely 'picked up' by Lieutenant Pearce.[95] Furthermore, Ensign John Pratt's own state-

92 UML, GB 133 Eng MSS 1273; Letter 19, Ballard's letter to Pringle, 24 July 1812.

93 Charrié, *Drapeaux*, p.194.

94 UML, GB 133 Eng MSS 1273, items 18, 19; T. Carter, Historical *Record of the Forty-Fourth or East Essex Regiment of Foot* (Chatham: Gale and Polden, 1887), p.66.

95 *Naval & Military Gazette and Weekly Chronicle of the United Service*, Saturday 25 May 1844, p.322.

ment of service does not include any claims to have taken an eagle.[96] It is unlikely that he would have excluded this, as he, for example, claimed to be at the Battle of Villamuriel, 25 October 1812, when the October Monthly return, recorded on that day, shows that he was 'on command with the sick at Salamanca'.[97] The idea that Pratt was somehow attached to the Portuguese Caçadores N.12 is not supported by either Hall, Halliday or Challis.[98]

This leaves the capture of the eagle of the 22e Ligne to the Portuguese officer, as described by Lieutenant Colonel Chichester William Crookshank of the 38th Foot, then commanding the Caçadores N.12:

> At the Battle of Salamanca commanded the same battalion [Caçadores N.12] which took the eagle of the 22nd French regiment, had two horses shot under me and received a severe contusion.[99]

The eagle of the 22e Ligne was taken by *Capitão* Jerónimo Pereira de Vasconcelos of the Caçadores N.12 in the 3rd Division, who was subsequently mentioned in Beresford's order of the day, 25 August 1812.[100]

Leith Hay reported that a Major Birmingham of the Regimento de Infantaria N.15 from the 5th Division was seen carrying an eagle.[101] However this officer would have been *Tenente Coronel* Walter Birmingham of the Regimento de Infantaria N.21 in Power's Brigade of Pakenham's 3rd Division, to which Caçadores N.12 also belonged.[102] This confusion may also have resulted in Douglas claiming that 'a little before sunset a Portuguese soldier of our Division picked up an eagle'.[103]

The return compiled by *Général de Brigade* Thomas Mignot, Baron de Lamartinière, mentions that the eagle of the 101e Ligne was taken instead of that of the 62e.[104] Charrié's source for the 101e Ligne's eagle having been captured, was the prisoner of war Alphonse Henri d'Hautpol, who was twice wounded and captured at Salamanca, while serving as a *capitaine* in the 59e Ligne as part of Clausel's 2e

96 TNA, WO25/790/93, 1829 Statement of service when he was serving in the 27th Foot.

97 TNA, WO17/138, 30th Foot, October monthly return.

98 J.A. Hall, *A History of the Peninsular War, Vol.VIII; the Biographical Dictionary of British Officers Killed and Wounded, 1808–1814* (London: Greenhill, 1998), p.476; A. Halliday, *The present state of Portugal, and of the Portuguese Army* (Edinburgh: G.R. Clarke, 1812), pp.224–5; Challis's Peninsular Roll Call (CHALLIS), at < https://www.napoleon-series.org/research/biographies/GreatBritain/Challis/c_ChallisIntro.html>.

99 Arquivo Municipal de Mafra (AMM), PT/AMM/CFLLTV/TT-MNE/091; Halliday, *Portugal*, p.202.

100 D. Cruickshank on Carole Divall's blog at <http://www.caroledivall.co.uk/2009/03/31/first-article/ >; see the first response; A.N. dos Santos, *Collecçao das Ordens do Dia do... Guilherme Carr Beresford...* (Lisbon: Quartel General, 1812), p.147.

101 Leith Hay, *Narrative*, Vol.II, p.59.

102 CHALLIS.

103 Monick, *Douglas*, p.47.

104 Muir, *Salamanca*, p.144.

Division.[105] In his memoirs, d'Hautpol wrote that during a visit to London in 1814: 'My heart sank when, visiting Westminster, I saw, hung in the vault, many French flags. I recognized the eagle of the 39e, taken in the retreat from Portugal and that of the 101e taken at the Battle of the Arapiles'.[106]

D'Hautpol's identification of the eagle of the 101e Ligne is not supported by Orme's illustration of the Salamanca trophies, which shows that neither eagle carried its flag and only the 22e Ligne's eagle carried its number, the other is bare (in fact today the *caisson* which would have carried the number is missing altogether), so without the flag d'Hautpol could not have identified the unit.[107] It seems more likely that Lamartinière's return is misleading; in this return, the losses of the 62e Ligne appear just above those of the 101e Ligne, so a clerical error is not unlikely.[108]

Orme's drawing also shows an unmarked white ensign captured at Salamanca and this is most likely to be the *fanion* of a second battalion. The regiments that lost more than 50 percent casualties at Salamanca were the 66e Ligne (4e and 5e Battalions; 5e Division), the 22e Ligne (1er, 2e and 3e; 6e Division), the 62e Ligne (1er, 2e and 3e; 7e Division) and the 101e Ligne (1er, 2e and 3e; 7e Division).[109] Of these the 62e and 101e Ligne lost more than 75 percent. Of these second battalions, only the 2/101e is not in the order of battle in September.[110] Thus it much more likely that the 101e Ligne lost its second battalion's *fanion*, as well as the 'Jingling Johnny' from its regimental band.[111]

These conclusions lead to an obvious question, how did Ensign Pratt become accepted as the traditional captor of the eagle of the 22e Ligne? Divall's account suggests that Lieutenant and Adjutant John Garland of the 2/30th Foot was crucial in making Pratt's case when he wrote in 1844:

> Seeing in your *Gazette* of the 15th instant a letter from one of Colonel Greville's brigade assuring you that only one Eagle was taken or picked up at the Battle of Salamanca by the 44th is quite correct, but I beg also to inform you (to the best of my recollection, so long a period having now elapsed) that another Eagle came into the possession of an Officer of the 30th in the same Brigade and who accompanied the Officer of the 44th to Head Quarters of the British army where they deposited the two eagles.

105 Charrié, *Drapeaux*, p.212; he only states that the eagle of the 101e Ligne was 'perhaps lost at Salamanca'.

106 A.H. d'Hautpol, *Memoires de Général Alphonse Henri d'Hautpol pair de France, 1789–1865* (Paris: Librairie académique Didier, Perrin, 1906), pp.62, 89.

107 RCIN 750679, *Battle of Salamanca: trophies taken from French. 22 July 1812.*

108 SHD C8 467, *Situation* Armée d'Espagne, 1 November 1812.

109 Muir, *Salamanca*, p.259–260.

110 SHD C8 467, *Situation* Armée d'Espagne, 1 November 1812.

111 P. Griffith, *A History of the Peninsular War: Modern Studies of the War in Spain and Portugal, 1808-14* (London: Greenhill Books, 1999), p.35.

> The Officers' names are Lieut.-Colonel Wm Pearce, K.H., late Lieut 44th, and Major John Pratt, late 30th Reg., now deceased.[112]

Given the first-hand accounts of Ballard and Harding reproduced above, it is reasonable to conclude that Garland misremembered the capture of the eagle and two *banderoles* of the eagle guard of the 62e Ligne. The eagle of the 22e Ligne is now on display in the museum of Ensign Pratt's regiment, the Lancashire Infantry museum, after it was moved from the Royal Hospital Chelsea in 1947.

What does the story of the 'Salamanca Eagles' tell us about the story of Maucune's 5e Division at Salamanca? The capture of the eagle of the 62e Ligne, rather than one of Maucune's eagles, by the skirmishers of Leith's division may suggest that Maucune's division was forced out of the path of Leith's division by the assault of Le Marchant's cavalry, thus enabling him to salvage part of his division to fight again later in the day.

## Conclusions

Muir remarked that the movements of Maucune's division at Salamanca are 'impossible to reconstruct precisely'.[113] Any attempt to review Maucune's place in the history of Salamanca will inevitably be based on the interpretation of a collection of weak signals. In his memoirs Marmont accused Maucune of two mistakes, firstly that he extended to his left and secondly that he advanced too close to the village of Arapiles. Oman interpreted this to mean that Maucune marched along the Monte de Azan following Thomières, but this is not consistent with Marmont's actual words. Maucune could have extended his division by deploying Montfort's brigade to the left of d'Arnauld's but this would have placed Montfort's men in the way of the British cavalry charge. The evidence for Maucune's further advance along the Monte de Azan rests on Marmont's memoirs, but his correspondence immediately after the battle gives no evidence of Maucune moving from his position at the eastern end of Monte de Azan. In this position Maucune would have been covering the further deployment of the French divisions onto the Monte de Azan. Therefore, it is at least possible that it was here that he was assailed by Leith, attacking along a northwest to southeast axis rather than Oman's north to south axis. The march of Thomières's 7e Division left Maucune's own left flank and rear unprotected when Leith and Le Marchant attacked and, in this sense, Marmont's and Castel's accusation that Maucune advanced too close to the village may be closer to the truth. Maucune's division would have been better supported if it had

112 C. Divall, *Redcoats against Napoleon* (Barnsley: Pen and Sword, 2009), pp.102–103, refering to *Naval & Military Gazette and Weekly Chronicle of the United Service*, 22 June 1844.

113 Muir, *Salamanca*, p.118.

remained closer to the position of the 122e Ligne, while covering the deployment of the other French divisions. Certainly, Oman's placing of Maucune's division 1100 metres away from the village, on the peak of the Monte de Azan, fits neither with French tactical practise nor the British eyewitness accounts.

Furthermore, there is evidence to suggest that Maucune's division did not simply disperse after this assault, but that Maucune managed to rally his men, at least in part, and continue the fight alongside Ferey and Clausel in the final rearguard action on the El Barrero ridge, until broken again by Wellington's final assault. Indeed, Girard's account places Maucune in the '*Maréchal* Ney' role at the bridge of Alba de Tormes. This is interesting since, although he described Maucune as 'a man of outstanding bravery', Girard also described him as having a reputation for being 'unbearable' to his subordinates and was clearly not a champion of his.[114]

Taken together, Orme's illustration of the Salamanca trophies and Pringle's correspondence gives sufficient insight to understand how Ensign Pratt was involved in the capture of the Salamanca trophies, and that this did not involve the eagle of the 22e Ligne. Orme's illustration demonstrates clearly that the *fanions* for the French battalions that did not carry eagles, were, contrary to Charrié's belief, used in the Peninsular, perhaps made locally.

Maucune may have been unfairly cast as a villain by Marmont and most histories of the battle of Salamanca, but this forms only a small part of Maucune's overall record. Maucune was an aggressive and successful regimental officer. However, his record as a brigade and division commander is somewhat chequered. In May 1809, Maucune was defeated and wounded when he tried to defend Santiago by advancing against superior numbers of Spanish regulars and partisans, led by *Brigadier* Martin de la Carrera.[115] However in November of the same year at the battle of Alba de Tormes, he particularly distinguished himself in the pursuit of the fugitives and the capture of the defended bridge over the Tormes. During the retreat from Burgos later in 1812, it was Maucune who led Souham's advanced guard harrying Wellington's army to the Duero and beyond. In June 1813, his troops were surprised by the Light Division at San Millán de la Cogolla, although he lost his baggage, he managed to extract his infantry through his 'presence of mind'.[116] Maucune's division missed the Battle of Vitoria but helped delay the Allied pursuit at Tolosa.[117] His division was again scattered at 2nd Sorauren in late July 1813 and at the Bidassoa in October. After these defeats, *Maréchal* Soult replaced him with Jean François Leval. Assigned to command the right wing of the Armée d'Italie, Maucune was defeated by Murat at the Taro River in April 1814

114 Desachy, *Girard*, pp.194, 215.
115 Oman, *History*, Vol.2, p.385.
116 Oman, *History*, Vol.6, pp.375-376.
117 D. Smith, *The Greenhill Napoleonic Wars Data Book* (London: Greenhill, 1998), p.432.

while defending against three-to-one odds.[118] Maucune left active service during the First Restoration.

It is interesting to compare Marmont's views of Maucune, with those of Souham, who only three months after Salamanca, in the aftermath of Villamuriel, wrote the following endorsement; 'General Maucune in all actions in which he takes part, manages to inspire the troops that he commands with the enthusiasm and dedication of which he has already given so much evidence'.[119]

Maucune's performance as a general was perhaps best summarised by one of his regimental commanders *Colonel* Jean Béchaud, 'this general said that he prefers to observe the movements of the enemy closely with his own eyes, rather than from a distance, which increases and multiplies the objects; he still places himself between the line of skirmishers and the heads of his columns'.[120] Béchaud also described Maucune charging with the chasseurs à cheval at Monasterio de Rodilla on 13 October 1812, when he was effectively a corps commander, leading two infantry divisions and a brigade of light cavalry.[121]

'Glory is fleeting', but it is more so when your commander-in-chief casts you as the 'fall guy' 33 years after your death. However, *Général de Division* Antoine-Louis Popon Baron de Maucune's bravery, nine wounds, and 28 years' service to France, if not his skill as a general, will be remembered so long as the Arc de Triomphe stands.

## Acknowledgements

I would like to thank the following people who have contributed to the research for this chapter; Rory Muir provided a copy of Lamartinière's return for the 26e Ligne, Christophe Pénichon, who provided photographs of the *Situations*, Jorge Planas Campos for generously providing his photographs of the *contrôles des officiers* and his help in identifying *Major* Ducheyron, and Hans-Karl Weiss for directing me to an important source via the Napoleon Series Discussion Forum. Finally, I would like to thank the staff of the archives, museums and libraries listed in the bibliography.

118 Smith, *Data Book*, p.522.

119 2nd Duke of Wellington (ed.), *Supplementary Despatches, Correspondence and Memoranda of Field Marshal Arthur, Duke of Wellington, K. G.* (London: John Murray, 1860), Vol.XIV, p.151.

120 J. Colin, 'Journal du Colonel Béchaud de l'Armée de Portugal Octobre 1812', *Revue des études napoléoniennes*, Vol.II, 1912, p.403.

121 Colin, *Béchaud*, p.392.

# Bibliography


***Archives***

Arquivo Municipal de Mafra (AMM)
PT/AMM/CFLLTV/TT-MNE/091, Crookshank's statement of service.

Service Historique de la Défense, Paris (SHD)
C8 466, *Situation* Armée d'Espagne, 15 August 1812.
C8 467, *Situation* Armée d'Espagne, 1 November 1812.
2Yb 157, *Contrôle des Officiers*, 15e Ligne.
2Yb 349, *Contrôle des Officiers*, 66e Ligne.
2Yb 397, *Contrôle des Officiers*, 82e Ligne.

National Army Museum, London
Accession 1974-05-77, War flags and co at Chelsea Hospital, 1883;drawn by John Ford in 1841, compiled by John Dowling in 1883.

The National Archives, Kew
WO17/138, 30th Foot, October monthly return.
WO25/790/93, John Pratt's 1829 Statement of service.
WO25/1742, Casualty return 1/38th Foot, 24 October to 24 November 1812.

The Royal Collection Trust, Windsor;
RCIN 750679, *Battle of Salamanca: trophies taken from French. 22 July 1812.*

University of Manchester Library;
GB 133 Eng MSS 1273, Pringle's Correspondence.

***Books***

Anon., *Réglement Concernant l'Exercice et les Manoeuvres de l'Infanterie, du 1er Août 1791* (Paris: Journal Militaire et Chez Belin, 1792).

Anon., *The confidential correspondence of Napoleon Bonaparte with his brother Joseph sometime King of Spain* (New York: Appleton, 1856).

Arvers, Paul and Brecht, Charles Frédéric, *Historique du 82e Régiment d'Infanterie* (Paris: Lahure, 1876).

Beauvais de Préau, Charles-Théodore (ed.), *Victoires, conquêtes, désastres, revers et guerres civiles des …* (Paris: C.L.F. Panckoucke, 1820).

Belmas, Jacques-Vital, *Journaux des sièges faits ou soutenus par les Français dans la Péninsule* (Paris: Firmin Didot, 1836).

Cannon, Richard, *Historical Record of the Eleventh or North Devon Regiment of Foot* (London: Parker, Furnivall and Parker, 1845).

Cannon, Richard, *Historical Record of the Fifth or Princess Charlotte of Wales's Dragoon Guards* (London: William Clowes, 1839).

Casse, Albert du, *Mémoires et correspondance politique et militaire du roi Joseph* (Paris: Perrotin, 1854).

Castel, Pierre, *Relation de la bataille et retraite des Arapiles…* (Toulouse: Caseaux, 1854).

Carter, Thomas, Historical *Record of the Forty-Fourth or East Essex Regiment of Foot* (Chatham: Gale and Polden, 1887).

Charrié, Pierre, *Drapeaux et étendards de la Révolution et de l'Empire* (Paris: Copernic, 1982).

Courcelles, Jean Baptiste Pierre Jullien de, *Dictionnaire historique et biographique des generaux Francais: depuis le onzième siècle jusqu'en 1820* (Paris: Author, Arthus Bertrand and Treuttel and Wurtz, 1822).

Crowdy, Terry E., *Napoleon's Infantry Handbook* (Barnsley: Pen and Sword Military, 2015).

Desachy, Paul, *Les Cahiers du Colonel Girard, 1766–1846* (Paris: Plon, 1951).

Divall, Carole, *Redcoats against Napoleon* (Barnsley: Pen and Sword, 2009).

Dumay, Alfred-Hippolyte, *Historique du 66e régiment d'infanterie, 1672–1900* (Tours: E. Arnault, 1900).

Fortescue, John William, *A History of the British Army* (London: Macmillan, 1917).

Foucart, Paul, *Campagne de Prusse (1806) d'Après les Archives de la Guerre, Tome Iena* (Paris: Berger-Levrault, 1887).

Girod de l'Ain, Maurice, *La Vie Militaire du Général Foy* (Paris: Plon Nourrit, 1900).

Grattan, William, *Adventures with the Connaught Rangers, 1809–14* (London: Greenhill, 1989).

Greenwood (ed.), Adrian, *Through Spain with Wellington: The letters of Lieutenant Peter Le Mesurier of the Fighting Ninth* (Stroud: Amberley, 2016).

Griffith, Paddy (ed.), *A History of the Peninsular War: Modern Studies of the War in Spain and Portugal, 1808-14* (London: Greenhill, 1999).

Hale, James, *Journal of James Hale, late Sergeant in the Ninth Regiment of Foot* (Cirencester: Philip Watkins, 1826).

Hall, John Alexander, *A History of the Peninsular War, Vol.VIII; the Biographical Dictionary of British Officers Killed and Wounded, 1808–1814* (London: Greenhill, 1998).

Halliday, Andrew, *The present state of Portugal, and of the Portuguese Army* (Edinburgh: G.R. Clarke, 1812).

d'Hautpol, Alphonse Henri, *Memoires de Général Alphonse Henri d'Hautpol, pair de France, 1789–1865* (Paris: Librairie académique Didier, Perrin, 1906).

Hay, Andrew Leith, *A Narrative of the Peninsular War* (Edinburgh: Daniel Lizars, 1831).

Lemonnier-Delafosse, Jean Baptiste, *Campagnes de 1810 en Portugal, 11, 12, 13 en Espagne, 14 en France, 1815 en Belgique ou Souvenirs Militaires* (Havre: Lemale, 1850).

Liévyns, A. and Verdot, Jean Maurice and Bégat, Pierre, *Fastes de la légion-d'honneur: biographie de tous les décorés accompagnée de l'histoire législative et réglementaire de l'ordre* (Paris: Bureau d'Administration, 1847).

Marmont, Auguste Frederic Louis Viesse de, *Memoires du Maréchal Marmont, Duc De Ragusa* (Paris: Perrotin, 1857, Third Edition).

Martinien, Aristide, *Tableaux, par corps et par batailles, des officiers tués et blessés pendant les guerres de l'Empire (1805–1815)* (Paris: Charles-Lavauzelle, 1899).

Monick, Stanley (ed.), *Douglas's Tale of the Peninsular War and Waterloo, 1808–1815* (London: Leo Cooper, 1997).

Muir, Rory, *Salamanca 1812* (New Haven: Yale University Press, 2001).

Muir, Rory and Burnham, Robert and Muir, Howie and McGuigan, Ron, *Inside Wellington's Peninsular Army, 1808–1814* (Barnsley: Pen and Sword, 2006).

Napier, William Francis Patrick, *History of the War in the Peninsula and in the South of France from the year 1807 to 1814* (London: Constable, 1993).

Oman, Charles, *History of the Peninsular War* (London: Greenhill, 1995, 1996).

Santos, António Nunes dos, *Collecçao das Ordens do Dia do... Guilherme Carr Beresford...* (Lisbon: Quartel General, 1812).

Ross-Lewin, Henry, *With the 32nd in the Peninsular and other Campaigns* (Dublin: Hodges, Figgis and Company, 1904).

Smith, Digby, *The Greenhill Napoleonic Wars Data Book* (London: Greenhill, 1998).

Tarragon, Marie Louis Adrien de, *Historique du 15e Régiment d'Infanterie* (Paris: Charles-Lavauzelle, 1895).

Warre, William, *Letters from the Peninsula, 1808–12* (London: John Murray, 1909).

Wellington, 2nd Duke of (ed.), *Supplementary Despatches, Correspondence and Memoranda of Field Marshal Arthur, Duke of Wellington, K.G.* (London: John Murray, 1860).

Wills, Garry David, *Wellington at Bay: The Battle of Villamuriel, 25 October 1812* (Warwick: Helion and Company, 2020).

### *Journals*

Colin, Lieutenant Colonel Jean, (ed.) 'Journal du Colonel Béchaud de l'Armée de Portugal Octobre 1812', *Revue des études napoléoniennes*, 1912, vol.II, pp.385–411; 1913, vol.I, pp.89–114.

*Naval & Military Gazette and Weekly Chronicle of the United Service*, 25 May 1844.

### *On-line Sources*

*Archives Nationale*, Paris, *Base de Données Léonore* (LEONORE), at <http://www2.culture.gouv.fr/documentation/leonore/recherche.htm>

Carole Divall's blog, at <http://www.caroledivall.co.uk/2009/03/31/first-article/ >

Challis's Peninsular Roll Call (CHALLIS), at < https://www.napoleon-series.org/research/biographies/GreatBritain/Challis/c_ChallisIntro.html>.

*Mapa Topográfico Nacional*, < http://signa.ign.es/signa/Pege.aspx>.

Waterloo Association Archive; *The Story of Private Joseph Cooley? 38th Foot*, available at <https://archives.waterlooassociation.org.uk/wordpress/search-detail/?modes_query=%7BWord%20search%7D%3D%2A%7Bcooley%7D&start_archive_docs=4>.

7

# Rockets at Leipzig – The British Contribution to the 'Battle of Nations' October 1813

Guy Dempsey

Great Britain, the 'paymaster of Europe', spent vast amounts of money to help bring about a rendezvous of Prussian, Russian, Austrian and Swedish armies on the plains of Saxony in October of 1813 where they combined to win a decisive victory over Napoleon and his forces at the Battle of Leipzig.[1] It is less well known that it also made a unique military contribution to the battle in the form of a small, rocket-armed unit of the Royal Horse Artillery under the command of Captain Richard Bogue. Fighting as part of the Army of the North under the command of Prince Charles Jean of Sweden (the former *Maréchal* Jean-Baptiste Jules Bernadotte of France, who had been selected as the successor to the Swedish throne 1810), the so-called Rocket Brigade

Captain Bogue from a watercolour by Slattery 1812. (Public Domain)

1 John Sherwig, *Guineas and Gunpowder – British Foreign Aid in the Wars with France 1793-1815* (Cambridge, MA: Harvard University Press 1969), p.309.

played a small but significant role in the success of the allied armies on 18 October, the third day of the multi-day 'Battle of Nations'.

The story of the Rocket Brigade starts with musings of a self-taught English engineer named William Congreve. He was not the inventor of rockets, but in 1804 (at the age of 32) he became intrigued with the possibility that rockets 'might be successfully employed, both afloat and ashore, as a military engine'.[2] The first thing that had to be done, however, was to improve and standardise the design, construction and performance of the ancient weapons. As Congreve himself described his contribution:

> To claim the invention of the rocket [is] indeed absurd, for this belongs to some of the heroes of Chinese antiquity—to claim the application of it to the purposes of war [is] equally absurd, for this was the invention of the remote ages of the mogul empire. The only merit I claim, therefore, as the author of the rocket system in this country, is that I have obtained from this principle of power, by a just combination of parts, the result of much thought and experiment, and certainly by the introduction of a new principle of internal construction, ranges, and the power of carrying weights infinitely beyond any thing ever before conceived in this country, or known in India…[3]

Since the Napoleonic wars were not a fertile time for military innovation, with inventions like Austria's air rifles, France's military balloons, and Robert Fulton's submarine achieving little or no success, Congreve's musings might not have led to any practical result except for two crucial, unusual circumstances. First, his father, William Congreve the elder, was an artillery officer who had for many years been in charge of the Royal Laboratory at Woolwich with responsibility for much technological innovation in British artillery and, in 1803, he became the sixth officer to reached the rank of Colonel Commandant of the Royal Artillery.[4] Second, the younger Congreve was a friend of George Augustus Frederick, the Prince of Wales (and Prince Regent from the onset of the final illness of King George III in 1811),

2 William Congreve, *A Concise Account of the Origin and Progress of the Rocket System* (London: J. Whiting, 1810), p.1. A detailed account of the early efforts of Congreve to turn rockets into an effective weapon of war can be found in Simon Werrett, 'William Congreve's Rational Rockets,' *Notes and Records of the Royal Society of London*, v. 63, No. 1 (March 2009), pp.35-56.

3 William Congreve, *Postscript to the Concise Account of the Origin and Progress of the Rocket System* (London: J. Whiting, 1808), p.14.

4 Donald E. Graves, *Sir William Congreve and the Rocket's Red Glare* (Alexandria Bay, NY and Bloomfield, Ontario: Museum Restoration Service, 1989), p.5. Congreve the elder became a lieutenant general in 1808 and a baronet in 1812. See also James Earle, *Commodore Squib: The Life, Times and Secretive Wars of England's First Rocket Man, Sir William Congreve, 1772-1828* (Newcastle upon Tyne: Cambridge Scholars Publishing, 2010).

so he was the beneficiary of powerful royal patronage. This unique combination of nepotism and royal patronage meant that Congreve enjoyed enormous technical and monetary support for his rocket endeavours even though Congreve never held any military rank in the British army.

Much of Congreve's initial work concerned improvement of the rockets themselves. The body of each rocket was a cylinder formed of sheet iron that contained the explosive mixture of saltpetre, sulphur and brimstone that provided the propulsive force for the weapon. The payload was mounted at the front of the cylinder. To stabilise the flight of the rocket, a long stick was attached to the side of each rocket by means of three reinforcing bands.[5] To make the sticks easier to handle, they were sometimes issued in 3-1/2' lengths so that multiple sticks could be joined together by way of iron ferrules to create a single stabiliser. Congreve standardised the sizes of the rockets. The largest rockets, which carried an explosive incendiary payload, were identified by their diameters – six, seven and eight inches. They could weigh up to 50 pounds, needed a 14-foot stabiliser and had ranges from 2,000 to 2,500 yards. The medium rockets were 42-, 32-, and 24-pounders and the light ones were 18-, 12-, and 9-pounders. There were four different types of payload – incendiary material, explosive shells, round shot, and case shot. He also designed equipment for launching rockets from ships and wagons and frames for doing the same on land.

Congreve's work was validated by the successful use of his explosive rockets in a naval bombardment of Boulogne in 1806, the siege of Copenhagen in 1807, and the siege of Flushing in 1809. Despite that success, however, no rocket forces were included in the British armies fighting in the Peninsula despite the theoretical advantages offered by a shock weapon that could be deployed against enemy forces on the battlefield more easily and efficiently than traditional artillery but had, in the best case, a similar anti-personnel effect.[6] Rockets continued to be used in sporadically in naval and amphibious operations and some field tests, but it would take several more years of work for Congreve to improve his 'Rocket System' sufficiently to create a practical battlefield asset.

In 1811, the Board of Ordnance placed a detachment of 30 men and one non-commissioned officer from the Royal Horse Artillery at the disposal of Congreve to assist him in development of equipment and tactics for the land use of rockets.[7] It is probably not a coincidence that command of the detachment was given

5 Comprehensive details of rocket construction are revealed by the technical drawings in C.E. Franklin, *British Rockets of the Napoleonic and Colonial Wars 1805-1901* (Staplehurst, Kent: Spellmount 2005).

6 An artillery lieutenant named Lindsay was sent to Portugal in 1810 to test some rockets, but the experiment not successful. A.D. McCain, "The Soul of Artillery:' Congreve's Rockets and Their Effectiveness in Combat,' *Journal of the Society for Army Historical Research* (2000), Vol.78, pp.252-263 at pp.257-259.

7 H.B. Latham, 'The Rocket Service and the Award of the Swedish Decorations for Leipzig,' *Journal of the Royal Artillery* Vol. LVI (1929-30), pp.419-432 at 421.

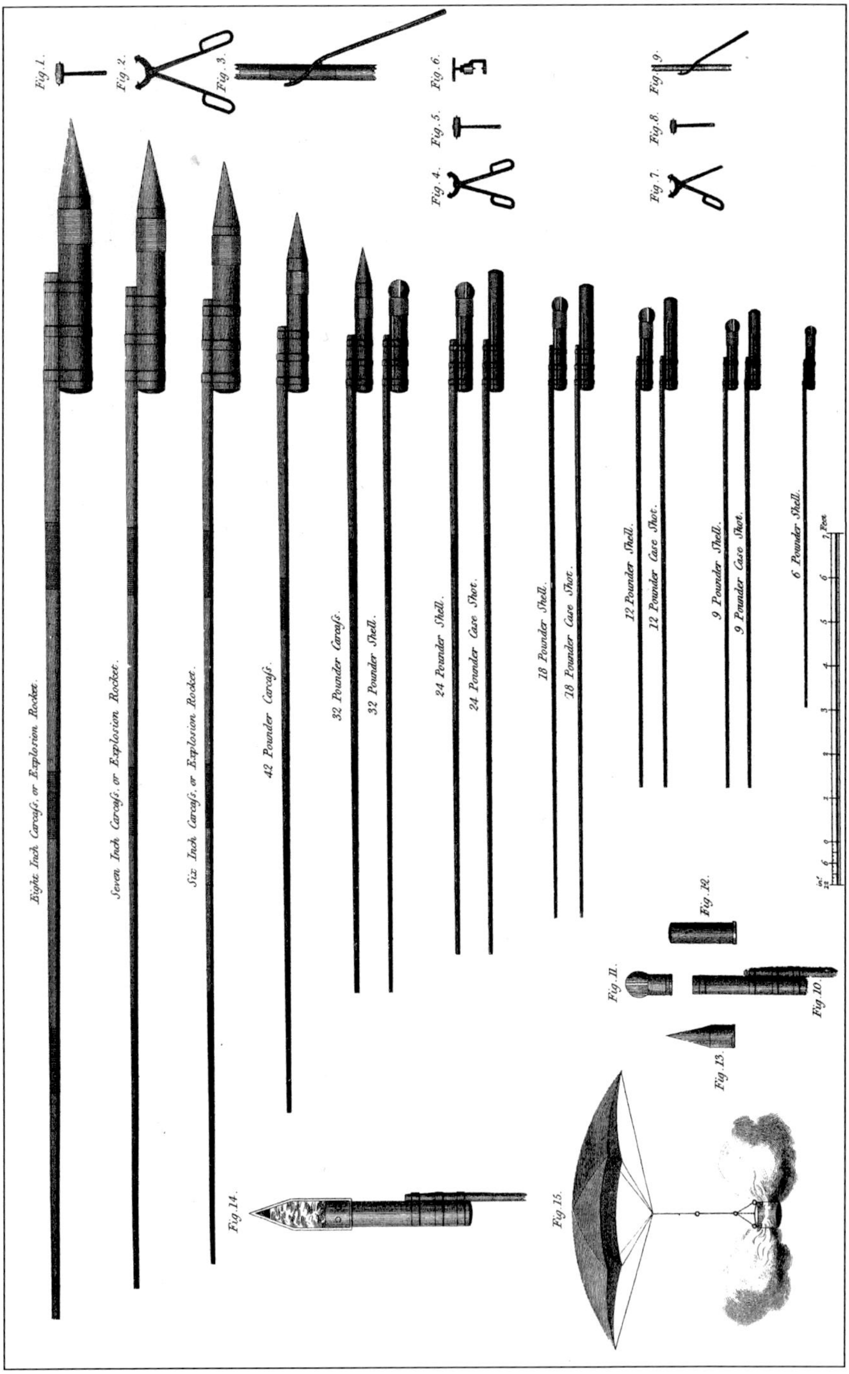


Chart of Congreve Rockets Sizes from *Details of the Rocket System* (1814). (Anne S.K. Brown Collection)

to Captain Richard Bogue, another good friend of the Prince Regent.[8] Bogue, born in 1782, was an experienced officer who had joined the RHA in 1798, been promoted to the rank of second captain in 1806 and had commanded a Horse Artillery battery during the Corunna campaign of 1808. Bogue kept a diary of his Peninsular service in Moore's march to Corunna in 1808-09 and the entries evidence the fact that he was an educated and observant man interested in art, architecture and foreign customs.[9] His habit of journal writing continued in 1813 but, unfortunately, the whereabouts of the journal from that year is currently unknown to this author.[10]

The rocket cavalry operated in sub-divisions, with two sub-divisions making a single division and three divisions making a full troop. The personnel of each sub-division consisted of one non-commissioned officer, 17 men and 21 horses at full strength. The troopers were further divided into five sections of three mounted rocketmen, each carrying four rockets plus their sticks. The sub-division also included two additional mounted men each leading two horses that each carried 18 additional rockets. The centre man in each section also carried a V-shaped iron trough for firing rockets on the ground. This device (sometimes called a '*bouche a feu*' by Congreve even thought that means 'gun' in French) was one foot and six inches in length and had four spikes on the bottom so that it could be fixed to ground. The firing trough weighed six pounds and was carried behind the saddle in a small leather case on top of the soldier valise.[11] Congreve envisioned that a full rocket troop would have a strength of approximately 180 officers and men, the same as a troop of horse artillery.

Although mobility was a key attribute of the rocket artillery, each troop still needed wheeled transport to carry its reserve ammunition and to provide firing frames used to launch heavy rockets at high angles for long range bombardments. Consequently, one heavy and one light rocket 'car' was assigned to each division. The former carried four men with 40 rounds of 24-pounder rockets and the latter two men with 60 rounds of 12-pounder ammunition. Each car had a limber and two wooden launch frames and was drawn by four horses with two mounted drivers. Each sub-division had a 'curricle ammunition cart, or tumbril,' drawn by

8 James Alex Brown, *England's Artillerymen – An Historical Narrative of the Services of the Royal Artillery* (London: Hall, Smart, and Allen, 1865), p.123. Bogue married in 1807, but this source reports that Bogue's handsome appearance earned him the sobriquet 'Look and Die' from the female followers of the Prince.

9 The diary, along with a summary biography of Bogue (and a portrait), can be found in John H. Leslie, *The Services of the Royal Regiment of Artillery in the Peninsular War 1808-1814* (London: Hugh Rees Limited, 1908), pp.38-39.

10 Bogue's journal for 1813 was offered for sale along with some related items at Bonhams auction house in Lot 85 of the Waterloo Sale – Wellington, Waterloo and the Napoleonic Wars, 1 April, 2015. There are some excerpts from the journal in the lot description.

11 William Congreve, *Details of the Rocket System* (London: J. Whiting, 1814, reprint London nd), text opposite Plate 3.

Trooper of Mounted Rocket Corps 1812 by Charles Hamilton Smith. (Anne S.K. Brown Collection)

Rocket Brigade firing from cart from *Details of the Rocket System* (1814). (Anne S.K. Brown Collection)

two horses with a single driver. To spare the horses of the rocket troopers, many of the rockets they carried in action were transported in the curricle when the unit was travelling long distances.[12]

The new weapon required a new type of artilleryman to handle it:

> The Rocket trooper has no heavy weights to lift—no guns to spunge [sic], or to limber up and unlimber. He is required merely to be light and active for mounting and dismounting, and for moving nimbly on foot with a single Rocket, when in action: so that, whereas an artilleryman cannot average less than 13 stone, the Rocket trooper need not exceed 10 stone, a difference amounting to within a few pounds to the whole weight of ammunition carried by the men, even in action. It is needless to add that the difference in the men must also give great facility in recruiting for a Rocket corps.[13]

12 Congreve, *Rocket System*, 'Constitution and Strength of a Troop of Rocket Horse Artillery'.

13 Congreve, *Rocket System*, text opposite Plate 3.

Transporting rockets on foot rather than on horseback was not just part of the established drill for firing rockets. It was an expedient that could be employed in difficult terrain:

> The holsters… slip on and off from the pummel [sic] with great facility, which is an object of some importance, as part of the service of the Rocket trooper is, when from some impassible obstacle, he can no longer advance on horseback, to dismount and pass over such obstacle, with his ammunition holsters and chamber, on foot.[14]

One British officer noted such behaviour in field: 'I left the rocket men, each with one rocket ready in his hand, and three on his back in a case, with three poles on his shoulder, just going to cross [the river]'.[15]

The rocket solders wore the basic Royal Horse Artillery uniform, complete with a so-called 'Tarleton' helmet with bearskin roach, but their weaponry and equipment were customised by Congreve:

> The men are armed with a sabre, which is in action suspended to the saddle, that they may not be incumbered [sic] in mounting and dismounting. Each man has besides a pistol in his cross belt, and a spear head in his holster, which may occasionally be fixed at the end of one of the Rocket sticks, so as to give the further aid of a very formidable lance. Instead of carrying a slow match, which would be dangerous as well as inconvenient, the portfire is lighted in action by a flash of powder obtained from a pistol lock and pan, mounted on a small stock; and a light portfire stick for discharging the Rocket, about three feet in length, is constructed of a thin iron tube, which shuts up, and is carried in the holster…[16]

The horse equipment consisted of a saddle and large holsters for the rockets, and '[e]very part of this equipment except for the sticks, is so completely concealed by the shabracque [sic], that the Rocket trooper has the appearance of merely being a lancer'. There is an illustration of a member of the 'Mounted Rocket Corps' in the series of prints of British soldiers based on artwork by Charles Hamilton Smith which shows some, but not all, of these features. More accurate, if less polished, depictions of mounted rocket soldiers appear in Congreve's *Details of the Rocket System*. Congreve explained in his text that these represent 'the mode of equipment for carrying Rockets on horseback, as it was arranged during the course of

14 Congreve, *Rocket System*, text opposite Plate 1.

15 F. Seymour Larpent, *The Private Journal of F. Seymour Larpent* (2nd revised ed., London: Richard Bentley, 1853), Vol.2, p.164, Journal Entry for 24 February, 1814.

16 Congreve, *Rocket System*, text opposite Plate 1.

experiments, which were carried on, under my direction, at Bagshot, in 1811; [and] as it was subsequently carried into actual service, under Captain Bogue, with the allied armies in Germany, in the ever memorable campaign of 1813…' The recollections of Captain E.C. Whinyates, who commanded rocket forces at Waterloo, help to complete the description of the appearance of rocket soldiers:

> With respect to the costume and equipment of the Rocket Troop at the Battle of Waterloo, the men were dressed like the Horse Artillery, viz.: with a laced jacket (having three rows of buttons in front) and helmet. Their appointments (both of horse and man), however, differed from those of the Horse Artillery. They had a pouch belt, which the Horse Artillery had not. Each mounted man carried a fasces [bundle] of three or four rocket sticks in a bucket in a manner similar to the mode lances and Dragoon carbines are carried. These sticks were carried on the right side of the horse. Besides these the centre of Threes carried a small trough on his saddle bag, in which the rocket was laid when fired, and every man in the Rocket Sections carried rockets in his holsters. Should you entertain any intention of representing the costume of the troops the small flag attached to the rocket stick should not be introduced. It was added by the Captain as an ornament, and was discontinued, and not part of the real equipment. The Horse appointments were those of the Light Cavalry, and the N.C. Officers and gunners had blue shabraques laced with yellow.[17]

The men who would fire the rockets needed special training, which had to be developed from scratch because the way the weapons were handled and deployed in combat was so different from the handling and deployment of traditional artillery. In combat, the centre man of each section would remain mounted and hold the horses of the other two men, who would dismount. One man would move forward 15 or 20 paces to place the firing trough in position and light the portfire, while the other two men prepared rockets for firing by withdrawing them from the holsters and affixing their sticks, an awkward process under any circumstance but particularly so under enemy fire. Then the first man was ready, the second dismounted man would run forward with the first, ungainly assembled rocket and place it in the trough to be fired.[18] Firing a rocket certainly required more fortitude than firing a cannon because of the risk of an explosion if the weapon was improperly handled: '… great care, however, must be taken to fix the stick securely, as everything depends upon it; the vent also must be carefully uncovered, as, if

17 E.C. Whinyates to William Siborne, 20 November 1842, H.T. Siborne (ed.), *Waterloo Letters* (London: Parker & Son, 1891), No. 84, pp.207-208. The best and most comprehensive modern study of the uniforms and equipment of the rocket troops is Franklin, *British Rockets*.

18 Congreve, *Rocket System*, text opposite Plate 3.

Trooper, Rocket Brigade, right profile, from *Details of the Rocket System* (1814). The colour of the trooper's collar is shown here as black, but should be red. (Anne S.K. Brown Collection)

Rocket Brigade, left profile, from *Details of the Rocket System* (1814). The colour of the trooper's collar is shown here as black, but should be red. (Anne S.K. Brown Collection)

not perfectly so, the Rocket is liable to burst; and in the firing the portfire must not be thrust too far into the Rocket, for the same reason'.[19] The fiery backwash and noise of the weapons was also a significant concern: 'The very flight of the Congreve rocket is startling; it springs from the ground in a volume of flame, and then rushes along with a continued roar, with its large head blazing…'[20]

Moreover, Congreve rockets were well known to be somewhat erratic weapons so a rocket soldier was in danger even if the weapon was successfully launched:

> They certainly made a most tremendous noise, and were formidable spitfires; no cavalry could stand if they came near them, but in that seemed the difficulty, for none went within half a mile of the intended object, and the direction seemed extremely uncertain. The ground was very bad, and on a flat, or along a road, where they would ricochet or bound along straight they might do very well, but in the present experiment they went bang into the ground, sometimes within two hundred yards, and sometimes one way and sometimes another. Some of them, instead of going fourteen hundred yards, as intended, were off in a hundred, and some pieces of the shell came back even amongst us spectators, one very near Dr. N and me, whilst we were standing on one side, out of the way as we thought. The fire, however, seemed very strong, as one got into a green hedge, and set it in a blaze directly; the furze and heath were on fire, and only put out by the rain.[21]

Captain Cavalié Mercer had a similar experience with rockets during the retreat from Quatre Bras in June of 1815 during the Waterloo campaign:

> Meanwhile the rocketeers had placed a little iron triangle in the road with a rocket lying on it. The order to fire is given—portfire applied— the fidgety missile begins to sputter out sparks and wriggle its tail for a second or so, and then darts forth straight up the chaussee. Our rocketeers kept shooting off rockets, none of which ever followed the course of the first; most of them, on arriving about the middle of the ascent, took a vertical direction, whilst some actually turned back upon ourselves—and one of these, following me like a squib until its shell exploded, actually put me in more danger than all the fire of the enemy throughout the day.[22]

19 Congreve, *Rocket System*, text opposite Plate 3.

20 Anon., *Tales of the Wars; or, A Naval and Military Chronicle* (London: William Mark Clark, 1838), Vol.III, p.344.

21 Journal entry for 20 January, 1814, Larpent, *Journal*, Vol. 2, pp.113-114.

22 Cavalié Mercer, *Journal of the Waterloo Campaign* (London: Blackwood & Sons, 1870), Vol..1, pp.279-280.

Congreve himself conceded that, in terms of accuracy, the firing of 'a single rocket is not to be compared with a single gun shot, by firing it at a target'. He realised, however, that the way to compensate for this erratic behaviour of the individual rocket was to fire as many rockets as possible at once, so firing en masse was the preferred tactic he adopted: 'An officer, therefore, having the use of this weapon under his direction, must ever bear this maxim in mind – and his first consideration must be—to make his discharges against the enemy in as powerful vollies as he can'.[23] Congreve estimated that a single sub-division could 'without any extraordinary effort... discharge 80 rounds of 6-pounder ammunition in three minutes'.[24]

By the start of 1813, the training of the men, the improvement of rocket technology, and the production of an inventory of rockets were all well advanced and Congreve was keen to see what his men and his weapons could achieve under combat conditions.[25] Surprisingly, however, he wanted the first rocket unit to join the Russian armies in northern Europe and not the British army in the Peninsula. He revealed his motivation for this unusual preference in a 22 January, 1813 letter to Colonel Henry Bunbury: '... it [the rocket detachment] is now completely equipped [and] ready for service and will be able to distinguish itself [in Europe] without having to worry about the prejudice which, I am sorry to say, too much prevails against everything new in our service...'[26] He may have been thinking specifically of the Duke of Wellington when he wrote this, because the Duke was known to have a negative view of the new weapon: 'I assure you that I am no partisan of Congreve's rockets, of which I entertain but a bad opinion, from what I recollect of the rockets in the East Indies, of which I believe those of Congreve are an imitation'.[27]

Congreve's lobbying eventually succeeded in May 1813, when a committee of Royal Artillery officers inspected the experimental rocket unit and recommended that it be tried in combat.[28] On 7 June, the unit was denominated by Royal Warrant as the 'Rocket Brigade' and was detached for active service in Germany under Captain Bogue.[29] The Rocket Brigade then marched from Woolwich to join a small British force sailing to Swedish Pomerania under the command of

23 Congreve, *Rocket System*, 'General Instructions for the Use of Rockets'.

24 Congreve, *Rocket System*, text opposite Plate 3.

25 There were rocket units deployed in 1813 to the war in North America between Great Britain and the United States, but they were part of the Royal Marine Artillery, not the Royal Artillery. In 1814, their weapons created the 'rocket's red glare' mentioned in the national anthem of the United States. See Graves, *Sir William Congreve and the Rocket's Red Glare*, p.4.

26 Congreve to Bunbury, 22 January, 1813, The National Archives, Kew (TNA), WO 1/427, p.475.

27 Wellington to Vice Admiral George Berkeley, 6 November 1810, Lt Col Gurwood (ed.), *The Despatches of Field Marshal the Duke of Wellington* (London: John Murray, 1836), Vol.6, p.564.

28 Description of Lot 85, Bonhams 1 April, 2015.

29 Latham, 'Rocket Service', p.421.

Major General Samuel Gibbs.[30] The primary task of the force was to garrison the fortress of Stralsund in Swedish Pomerania in order to free up Swedish forces to join the so-called Army of the North operating under the command of Sweden's Crown Prince in conjunction with the main allied armies of Russian, Prussian and Austrian troops fighting Napoleon in the heart of Germany. A Swedish report dated 8 August indicates that the strength of the Rocket Brigade upon its arrival in Germany was noticeably below the troop establishment envisioned by Congreve:

| | |
|---|---|
| Officers | 5 |
| Non-Commissioned Officers | 3 |
| Privates | 127 |
| Riding horses | 63 |
| Other horses | 40 |
| Ammunition | 3,440 rockets[31] |

Two of the officers in addition to Bogue were Lieutenants Thomas Fox Strangways and Amherst Wright.[32] The identity of the other two officers is unknown. Wright had served at the siege of Copenhagen in 1807, so he probably was familiar with rockets from that campaign. Strangways was only 23 in 1813 and there is no record of prior active service for him prior to his arrival in Germany.

When the general armistice ended in August 1813, Gibbs's brigade remain in garrison, but on 22 August, the 2/73rd Foot and half the Rocket Brigade were detached for service in northern Germany with the allied force opposing the French XIII Corps of *Maréchal* Louis-Nicolas Davout that was based in Hamburg and supported by a Danish Auxiliary Corps under General Prince Friedrich von Hessen.[33] This force was a polyglot corps composed of Swedish, Prussian, Russian, and Hanoverian troops as well as the infantry, cavalry and artillery forces of the Russo-German Legion and even some units of the Kings German Legion. The whole allied force was under the command of Lieutenant General Count Ludwig von Wallmoden-Gimborn while the detached portion of the Rocket Brigade was commanded by Lieutenant Strangways.

After a month of careful manoeuvring, the Rocket Brigade detachment finally experienced combat on 16 September, 1813, when Wallmoden's men

30 The date of Bogue's departure is provided in Description of Lot 85, Bonhams 1 April, 2015. The force commanded by Gibbs consisted of one battalion each of the 1st, 25th, 33rd, 73rd and 91st Regiments. John W. Fortescue, *History of the British Army* (London: Macmillan & Co., 1920), Vol. IX, p.237.

31 Royal Artillery Institution, Woolwich, England (RAI), MD/383, 'The British Mounted Rocket Battery Under Swedish Command,' p.2. This document is a compilation of information from the Swedish archives that has been collected and translated into English.

32 According to the Army List, Strangways and Wright were both promoted to the rank of lieutenant on 1 February, 1808, but Wright nevertheless seems to have been the senior officer.

33 RAI, MD/383, 'Rocket Battery under Swedish Command,' p.2.

encountered an inferior French force under *Général de Division* Marc Nicolas Louis Pécheux near the town of Göhrde. An allied success was never in doubt, but Pécheux put up a stout resistance and even managed to save a majority of his men. Strangways' detachment was part of cavalry force consisting of the 3rd Hussars of the King's German Legion, the Hanoverian Estorff Hussars and a battery of horse artillery. The rocketeers suffered no casualties except for two horses wounded and one missing,[34] but did make a contribution to the victory that was noted by fellow countryman Thomas Morris of the 2/73rd Foot: 'The square of French infantry on the left... were still firm; but there happened to be two or three of the rocket brigade in the field, and the first rocket fell directly in the square, putting them in the greatest confusion...'[35] The fact that the rockets caused consternation as much or more than casualties was a distinctive feature of the weapons which was also noted by a British officer who observed some Congreve rockets in France in 1814:

> We had with us, in place of artillery, a Brigade of Congreve Rockets, newly arrived from England ... the foe came on, capering and shouting in high expectation ... They were yet advancing, with huzzas when the first rockets were let off and rushed straight in amongst them with a terrible roar. For a moment, they were still, not a shout was heard, and in the next moment they were in full retreat, and the firing soon ceased... the effect of our rockets were most decisive, and nothing can be better calculated as a substitute for cannon in similar circumstances. It was just dark enough too, to display their fiery train and to add to the real dangers they carry in the display of their fuses. I can give you no idea of their appearance, but they appeared to me to realize all Mother Bunch's stories of fiery dragons and serpents.[36]

Meanwhile, in the aftermath of the Battles of Grossbeeeren and Dennewitz, the Swedish Crown Prince summoned Bogue and the rest of the Rocket Brigade to join the Army of the North. This was not a simple exercise because there was a shortage of horses to pull the rocket carts, but Charles Jean was able to provide the necessary replacements. At the same time, Prince Charles Jean issued orders for Strangways' detachment to rejoin its unit. Lieutenant Charles Poten of the 7th Line Battalion of the King's German Legion was assigned to conduct the detachment

34 Dispatch from General Wallmoden, 20 September 1813, in Anon., *Bulletins of the Campaign of 1813 [Compiled from the London Gazette]* (nl [London]: np, nd), p.714-720.

35 Thomas Morris, *Recollections of Military Service, in 1813, 1814, & 1815* (London: J. Madden, 1845), p.30.

36 G.K. Blackman, Letter of Thomas Maynard, Surgeon, Coldstream Guards, to George Blackman, 11 August 1814, reproduced in Notes and Documents 1604, *Journal of the Society of Army Historical Research*, Vol.79, No. 319 (Autumn 2001), pp.257-258.

back to join the Army of the North (presumably because he could speak German fluently).[37]

The Prince was clearly intrigued by these novel weapons and wanted to learn more about them. The result was a special order for Bogue dated 18 September:

> His Royal Highness the Crown Prince of Sweden being informed of your arrival at Reetz with the Rocket Battery under your commands [sic], desires you to come tomorrow at this town with some select men, in order to try the rockets under the eyes of His Royal Highness. The remaining part of the Battery is to remain in Reetz until you receive further directions.[38]

That demonstration must have impressed the Crown Prince, since he thereafter took a particular interest in the Rocket Brigade. He also assigned the Rocket Brigade to participate in the bombardment of the fortress of Wittenberg on the Elbe River held by the French, a development that was noted in one of the official Swedish bulletins of the campaign (and printed in translation in *The Times*):

> Wittenberg continues to be strongly bombarded. In the night of the 27th and 28th [of September] the town was on fire in several places; a tower of the castle was on fire and fell in. Exclusive of the bombs, rockets were also used, under the very able direction of the English Captain Bogue.[39]

Strangways' detachment re-joined Bogue sometime after 28 September, and the full unit then travelled to Roslau, where it arrived on 2 October. Bogue himself, however, was probably visiting with the Crown Prince, as is evidenced by the following 1 October letter (in somewhat fractured English) to Bogue from *Generalleutnant* Friedrich Wilhelm Freiherr von Bülow:

> His Highness the Crown Prince desires, Sir, that you may send in the course of the day your battery to Roslau and that you may come yourself to his General Quarter at Zerbst. I received in that very moment the order to inform you of his intention, and I prevail with great pleasure on the opportunity to pay you my thanks for the good will & strength with which you sustained our common task: may I be so happy as to see once

37 N. Ludlow Beamish, *The History of the King's German Legion* (London: Thomas and William Boone, 1837), Vol.2, p.203. Poten accompanied the Rocket Brigade at Leipzig but did not obtain any recognition of that service.

38 RAI, MD/383, 'Rocket Battery under Swedish Command,' p.4. The orders for Bogue were probably issued in French, the one language that most of the allied troops had in common.

39 *The Times*, 20 October 1813, p.3.

> the effect of your rakets in a ranged battle, and beated [sic] our enemies with united force.[40]

The tone of the letter suggests that Bogue was known to, and had cordial relations with, Bülow, who commanded the Prussian contingent of the Crown Prince's army. Shortly thereafter, the Crown Prince ordered the Rocket Brigade 'to join the Headquarters brigade, thus coming under the command of Colonel Arfvedsson [Arfwedson]'.[41]

For Bogue, service at headquarters involved reviews of troops ('the Russian & Prussian Cavalry are beautiful') and rounds of dinners with generals and diplomats ('Dined with the Minister – We have now been joined by General Blucher'). It also involved an unfortunate personal mishap which is recorded in his last journal entry dated 11 October: 'rec.d a dreadful kick on the ankle yesterday for a troop horse, which give me great pain -- & I am unable to put my foot to the ground'.[42] While he was recuperating he had time to start a letter to an unnamed friend (possibly Major Ayde) dated Bemburg on the Saale, 12 October 1813.[43] The letter says that Bogue 'has been pretty constantly on the move' since he last wrote on 30 August and starts with a brief summary of Wallmoden's campaign against Davout: 'We followed Marshal Davout to [undecipherable], but always halted most respectfully when he did and when he advanced, we fell back. The fact was that Count Wallmoden had not a sufficient number to attack him'. He then mentions joining Bülow for the attack on Wittenberg ('I did so & threw in rockets three different times'). Bogue also analyzes the immediate strategic situation with surprising awareness of the identity of Napoleon's commanders: 'He has with him Ney, Berthier, Marmont, Victor, Poniatowksi, etc., but we have now got into his rear, & he in ours'. The letter is unfinished and ends with the sentence: 'A battle is hourly expected, when I shall write more'.

Due to the behaviour of the Crown Prince, however, the chances of the Rocket Brigade's participation in such a battle were uncertain even as the other allied armies began to engage the French at Leipzig on 16 October.

The first half of October featured complex manoeuvres by all the armies in Germany as Napoleon sought to isolate and defeat some portion of the allied forces while the allies sought to avoid that result and force Napoleon to face battle against the combined armies of the coalition, but during this entire period Prince Charles Jean was markedly reluctant to commit the Army of the North irrevocably to a battle with the French Grande Armée. The Crown Prince's primary motivation for this stance was most likely a desire to preserve his Swedish troops for his priority

40 Bülow to Bogue, 1 October 1813, Lot No. 85, Bonhams 1 April, 2015.

41 RAI, MD/383, 'Rocket Battery under Swedish Command,' p.8.

42 Description of Lot No. 85, Bonhams 1 April, 2015, Item (i).

43 Description of Lot No. 85, Bonhams 1 April, 2015, Item (vii), image provided by Bonhams.

Rocket Brigade on the march from *Details of the Rocket System* (1814). (Anne S.K. Brown Collection)

objective of defeating Denmark and obtaining possession of Norway, but he may also have had some trepidation about a direct confrontation with Napoleon. The job of convincing Charles Jean to take a more active role fell in large part to Lieutenant General Sir Charles Stewart, an official envoy of the British government. Stewart was an experienced soldier whose career had veered towards diplomacy due to physical handicaps: 'General Stewart is a very gallant and a very able officer of cavalry... He labours, however, under two bodily defects, the want of sight and of hearing... and the defect in his sight having been occasioned by a wound, it cannot be remedied by the assistance of glasses'.[44]

Frustrated with the Crown Prince's dilatory behaviour and inspired by the impending attacks on Napoleon by the allied Armies of Silesia and Bohemia, Stewart took the unorthodox approach on the morning of 16 October of sending Charles Jean a letter that, despite a smokescreen of polite phrases, in effect questioned the courage of the Swedish leader. Stewart used the Rocket Brigade to achieve this result by 'begging' the Prince to release the Bogue and his 'rocketeers' to participate in the coming battle even if Charles Jean preferred to stay 'in the second line'. A second letter sent by Stewart on the evening of the 16th attempted to pique the jealousy of the Prince by describing the success of Blücher during the

44 Wellington to the Duke of York, 25 June, 1811, 2nd Duke of Wellington (ed.), *Supplementary Despatches, Correspondence and Memoranda of... Wellington* (London: Longmans, Green, Reader, and Dyer, 1865), Vol.7, p.165.

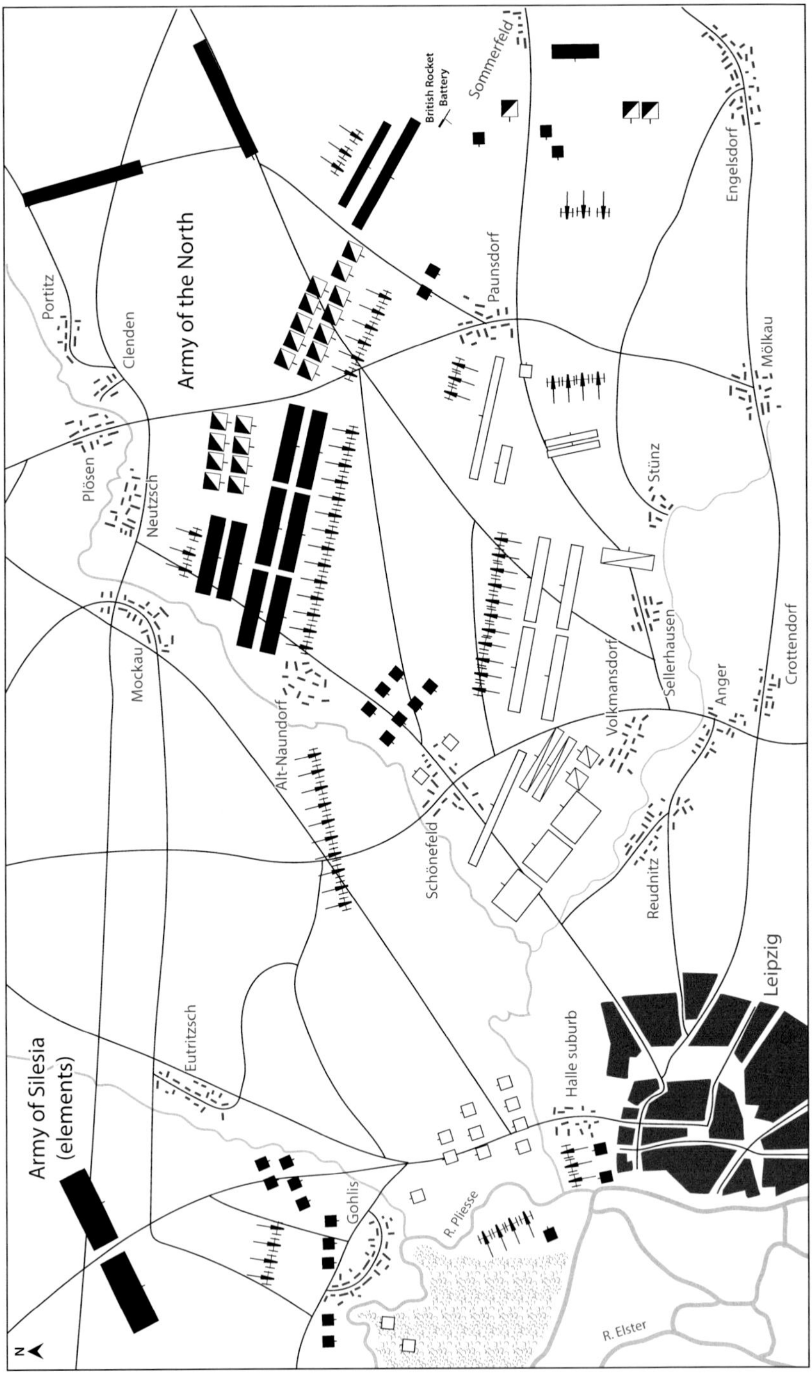


The northern sector of the Leipzig battlefield, 18 October 1813 Troop dispositions, taken from George Nafziger, *Napoleon at Leipzig* (Chicago: Emperor's Press, 1996), p.224, are representative only, and are included to indicate the approximate lines held by the two sides and their relative strengths. (Map by George Anderson © Helion and Company)

day and ended with a challenge calculated to inspire the Prince to action. Taking the liberty of speaking a one soldier to another, Stewart predicted that 'if you do not commence your march, you will always regret that decision'. Charles Jean was angered by Stewart's impertinence, but he also responded as hoped and ordered the Army of the North (and the Rocket Brigade) to join the battles at Leipzig on the 18th (albeit with Bülow's Prussian corps leading the way rather than his own Swedes).[45]

On the afternoon of 18 October, the Army of the North approached Leipzig from the northeast and found itself facing the sector of the French defensive perimeter held by the VII Corps commanded by *Général de Division* Jean Reynier which was composed of both French and Saxon troops. The perimeter had contracted somewhat during the day as a result of earlier fighting, but the French still held the village of Paunsdorf despite the disturbing defection of a Saxon cavalry brigade. Reynier had commanded his Saxon troops since the start of the Russian campaign, so they had an established relationship but he was undoubtedly aware that the Saxons had served in 1809 under the command of Charles Jean when he was still French *Maréchal* Bernadotte and that the Crown Prince had issued a number of proclamations in September urging the Saxons to abandon Napoleon's cause. He therefore took the precaution of moving the French division of *Général de Division* Pierre Durutte into his front line and leaving his Saxons in reserve. It was shortly thereafter (3:00 pm by one estimate) that the French were introduced to Bogue and his rockets in an encounter described by Stewart:

> Some Prussian battalions of General Bulow's corps were warmly engaged also at Pounsdorf [sic], and the enemy were retiring from it, when the Prince Royal directed the rocket brigade, under Captain Bogue, to form on the left of a Russian battery, and open upon the retiring columns. Congreve's formidable weapon had scarce accomplished the point of paralysing a solid square of infantry, which, after our fire, delivered themselves up (as if panic struck), when that gallant and deserving officer, Captain Bogue, alike an ornament to his profession and a loss to his friends and country, received a shot in the head, which deprived the army of services. Lieutenant Strangeways [sic], who succeeded in the command of the brigade, received the Prince Royal's thanks for the important assistance they had rendered.[46]

45 Stewart changed his surname to 'Vane' in 1819 and used it when he wrote his memoirs of the last campaigns against Napoleon which contain his communications with the Crown Prince. Charles William Vane [Marquess of Londonderry], *Narrative of the War in Germany and France in 1813 and 1814* (London: Henry Colburn & Richard Bentley, 1830), pp.163-166.

46 Stewart to Castlereagh, 19 October 1813, printed in *The Times*, 4 November 1813.

In his later memoir of the campaign, Stewart acknowledged that his report was not completely accurate in all details because of the haste in which it was written: 'I wrote it . . . on a stone in the field of battle, when the fire had ceased, without correction or amendment'.[47] Also in his memoir, he recollected being aware that the successful use of Congreve rockets in these circumstances was a noteworthy event in itself: 'I felt great satisfaction at witnessing, during this day, a species of improved warfare, the effects of which were truly astonishing; and produced an impression upon the enemy of something supernatural'.[48] Stewart's own conduct was praised in one of the official bulletins of the Crown Prince: 'During the fighting on the 18th, Lt. General Sir Charles Stewart himself positioned the battery of English rocketeers under the hottest enemy fire, and he voluntarily undertook the performance of several orders from the Prince Royal, which were executed to the particular satisfaction of His Royal Highness'.[49]

More, and perhaps more accurate, details of this episode are provided by Mr. John James, a cousin of General Stewart who served as a volunteer civilian attaché to Stewart's mission and was present at Leipzig on the 18th.[50] In the aftermath of the battle, he wrote a personal letter of condolence to Bogue's father-in-law, John Hanson, describing the events of the day:

> The Rocket Brigade, under the command of Captain Bogue, had been attached, in its general movements, to the body guard of the Crown Prince of Sweden, under the command of Colonel Lievitson [Arfwedson?], with, however, the understanding, that on days of action it was to be more at liberty than that corps, and subjected only to the direction of Captain Bogue. Conformably with this arrangement, at the commencement of the action on the morning of the 18th, Captain Bogue addressed himself to General Winzingerode, commanding the advance of the Crown Prince, expressing his desire to see the enemy, with permission to engage. The General, much struck with the gallantry and spirit of the address, granted, as guard, a squadron of dragoons, and requested Captain Bogue to follow his own plans and judgment. Captain Bogue lost no time in approaching to the attack of the village of Paunsdorff, then in possession of five enemy's battalions, upon whom he opened, in advance of the whole, a most destructive fire. This was returned by musketry, and for some time a very hot combat ensued; when the enemy, unable to withstand the

47 Vane, *Narrative of the War*, p.175.

48 Vane, *Narrative of the War*, p.172.

49 Bulletin of 18 October 1813, Coupé de St.-Donat and B. de Roquefort, *Mémoires pour Servir a l'Histoire de Charles-XIV-Jean, Roi de Suède et de Norwège* (Paris:Plancher, 1820), Vol.2, p.104.

50 Most sources assume that James was a soldier and some even give him the rank of lieutenant, but that was not the case. He had already distinguished himself in combat before Leipzig. Vane, *Narrative of the War*, p.38 and p.174.

Rocket Brigade ground firing technique from *Details of the Rocket System* (1814). (Anne S.K. Brown Collection)

> well-directed fire of Captain Bogue's Brigade, fell in confusion, and began to retreat. Captain Bogue seizing this moment, charged at the head of the squadron of cavalry; and the enemy, terrified at his approach, turned round, and taking off their caps, gave three huzzas; and every man, to the number of between two and three thousand, surrendered to the Rocket Brigade, not, I believe, exceeding two hundred men. The intelligence of this success being communicated to the Crown Prince, he sent his thanks to Captain Bogue for such eminent services, requesting, at the same time, that he would continue his exertions; and the Brigade proceeded, in consequence, to the attack of (I believe) the village of Sommerfeldt, still further in advance. Sir C. Stewart accompanied the Brigade, and I was of the party. The situation taken up in flank of the village was exposed to a most heavy fire, both of cannonball and grape shot, from the enemy's line, and from the riflemen in the village: a ball from the latter soon deprived us of the exertions of poor Bogue; it entered below the eye, and passing through the head, caused instantaneous death.[51]

The status of James an eyewitness to these events is confirmed by another anonymous Englishman present at the battle: 'I had the opportunity, although but for a few minutes, of seeing Mr. James; he was with Captain Bogue during the action, [and] at his side at the moment of his fall...'[52]

51 John James to John Hanson, 11 November, 1813, in William Hanson, *Short Journal of a Visit to Sicily, 1810* (London: J. Darling, 1814), Exhibits. This letter is reproduced in many sources. This was a difficult time for the Hanson family since Hanson's son (and therefore Bogue's brother-in-law), an officer in the 20th Light Dragoons, was killed in action on the east Coast of Spain on 13 September.

52 'Extract of a private letter,' E. Gifford, *Memoirs of the Life and Campaigns of Napoleon Bonaparte* (London: J. & J. Cundee, nd), Vol.2, p.327.

The official report of the battle (dated 24 October, 1813) sent by Amherst Wright to Lieutenant General Sir John McLeod of the Royal Artillery does not provide any additional details and, indeed, seems to echo some other sources, which is reasonable since Wright himself was not a participant in the action. Wright, who identifies himself as 'Lieut. and Cmndt. of the Rocket Battery Employed with the Army of the North of Germany,' says the battery was first employed along with some cavalry against Saxon troops and then moved to the flank of the allies:

> A heavy firing commenced from the Rocket Battery on the right of the enemy's line which had the desired effect and threw the enemy into great confusion. The cavalry immediately charged and the whole of the enemy's five battalions laid down their arms. An immense number of the enemy were killed by the rockets, and several bodies were found burning after the action.

Wright's report of Bogue's demise is similar to that of Hanson: '...Captain Bogue received a rifle ball in his head near the temple which caused instantaneous death'.[53] Wright also included a mention of the services of Assistant Surgeon Baird tending to the unit's wounded.

Astonishingly, we may actually know the name of the Frenchman who killed Bogue – Nicolas Louis Pascal Perot. Perot, born in 1785, had entered the French Army in 1806 as a member of the *Gendarmes d'Ordonnance*, an elite unit formed that year by Napoleon to attract young men from noble and wealthy families into his service. When the unit was disbanded in 1807, the men, including Perot, were assigned to other units as junior officers. He fought with distinction in Spain, but it was his conduct at Lutzen and Bautzen in the spring of 1813 that earned him the cross of the Legion of Honour on 3 August.[54] His biography offers the following account of his interaction with the Rocket Brigade:

> During the campaign of 1813 in Saxony, Perot repeated the type of accomplishments by which he had acquired one of the most impressive military reputations during the war in Spain. His conduct at Leipzig on 18 October was remarked by the entire army – with 20 men of the 42e Ligne, in which he was serving as adjutant-major, within the sight of a squadron of enemy cavalry, he charged a battery of Congreve rockets, killed its commanding officer with his own hand and destroyed its equipment after his men had bayoneted the artillerymen who were firing those infernal weapons.

53 Lt Amherst Wright to Lt Gen. McLeod, 24 October 1813, TNA WO 55/1129, pp.124-126.

54 Dossier LH/2104/7 in the Legion of Honour Database: <http://www2.culture.gouv.fr/LH/LH178/PG/FRDAFAN83_OL2104007V002.htm> (accessed 28 April, 2019).

> The attack on the rocket battery was still underway when the nearby enemy squadron advanced at the gallop to saber the French soldiers. Perot had his men face the cavalrymen but did not give the order to fire until the enemy cavalry was only four paces away. The resulting volley emptied many saddles and the survivors fled swiftly to avoid suffering the same fate.[55]

This description Perot's success is certainly exaggerated given what we know of the relatively few casualties suffered by the Rocket Brigade. Nevertheless, it is inherently plausible that the unique experience of encountering rockets in combat would have caused Perot to have a particularly vivid recollection that such an event occurred, although the specific claim that Perot caused the death of Bogue is impossible to verify. The regimental history of the French 42e Ligne notes that during the fall campaign in 1813 the 4th battalion of the regiment was assigned to the 12e Demi-Brigade Provisoire then serving in the 13e Division of Reynier's VII Corps under the command of *Général de Division* Guilleminot, but that same source indicates that this unit was part of the garrison of Torgau on 18 October, and not fighting at Leipzig.[56] Nevertheless, given the fluid nature of provisional units like the 12e Demi-Brigade, the possibility that Perot might have remained with the VII Corps for the battle cannot be dismissed. A German author using some primary sources provides modest additional support for the Perot position: 'During the advance of the Horse Artillery Battery No. 6 against Sellerhausen, the also advancing English Rocket Battery deployed in its line of fire, preventing it from firing. The tirailleurs which had been fired upon immediately took advantage of this to push forward, shooting the commander of the Rocket Battery…'[57]

The most noteworthy point of all these accounts is the astonishing level of success apparently achieved by the Rocket Brigade in terms of the number of enemy soldiers killed, wounded, dispersed or captured. There is no matching account from French sources that confirms such results, but the French records for the battle are necessarily incomplete due to the magnitude of the defeat. However, at least two German accounts provide some substantiation of the damage caused by Congreve's rockets. The first was written by a soldier in one of Bülow's regiments:

> It was at this juncture that I realized the terrible effects of the Congreve rockets… each time a rocket was fired and went hissing and shooting forth fire into an enemy column and exploded, one saw whole files hurled down.

55 Entry for Nicolas Louis Pascal Perot in 'Une Société d'hommes de Lettres et de Militaires' [Pierre François Tissot], *Les Fastes de la Gloire, ou les braves recommandés à la postérité* (Paris: Tissot, 1822), Vol.4, pp.96-97.

56 Francis Louis Picard, *Histoire du 42e Régiment d'Infanterie* (Montbéliard: H. Barbier, 1875), p.337.

57 *Generallieutenant* von Strotha, *Die Königlich Preussische Reitende Artillerie vom Jahre 1759 bis 1816* (Berlin: Vossische Buchhandlung, 1868), p.416-417. Translated from the German by Geert van Uythoven.

> The scorched and battered bodies lay in great piles where they fell. At first the French did not seem familiar with the new weapon of death and stood up against it; but when they saw what fearful destruction it wrought and in what a ghastly manner the victims dies, even if only a drop of fuel came too near, there was no holding them. Whenever they saw a rocket coming, whole columns ran away and abandoned everything. [58]

The other observer was *Oberst* Hermann von Boyen, a Prussian staff officer:

> [T]he rockets produced a most unusual effect near where they were ignited. The French column, which hitherto had been advancing in very good order... was utterly dispersed just as one breaks up an ant heap with a blow, and it ran in total disorder... amidst our almost universal laughter. When we marched next day across the scene of the French advance, we convinced ourselves of the important effects of the rockets. A considerable number of corpses lay there, but in addition several of them were completely burnt on their faces and uniforms in a most uncommon way, so that one could readily understand how the enemy's morale had been shaken by this extraordinary operation.[59]

It also may be the case that some of the soldiers apparently 'panicked' by the rockets were actually Saxon troops defecting to the allies. The timing of the two incidents lends some credibility to this interpretation of events since it was the retreat of Durutte's men from Paunsdorf that opened the way for the Saxons to leave their positions and join the allies. The following note in Gneisenau's biography of Blücher, which is attributed to 'an eye-witness', specifically identifies one of the units targeted by the rockets as Saxon:

> On the 18th, at Paunsdorf, one of Congreve's rockets fell before the front of a battalion of Saxons; but the fusee [sic] burning out by accident, before it burst, it produced no effect.
>
> Some of the men, on examining it, and discovering it to be one of the English rockets, of which they had heard such a terrible description, began to crack their jokes on this new-created harmless messenger; but in the midst of their merriment, a second happening to fall in the ranks, spreading destruction and dismay all around, the whole battalion, as if seized with a sudden panic, broke and dispersed itself instantaneously,

58 Wenzel Krimer, *Errinerugen eines alten Lützower Jägers, 1795-1819* (Stuttgart: Verlag von Robert Lutz, 1913), p.66. Translated from the German by Antony Brett-James.

59 Hermann von Boyen, *Denkwürdigkeiten und Erinnerungen 1771-1813* (Stuttgart: Verlag von Robert Lutz, 1899), pp.383-384. Translated from the German by Antony Brett-James.

> nor could the officers, with all their authority and threats, collect and rally the men again, to bring them into the line.[60]

After Bogue's death, the Rocket Brigade stayed in action, but no record of the additional combat results it may have achieved has been found. The unit was, however, observed later in the day by the Count de Rochechouart, a French émigré officer serving as aide-de-camp to Emperor Alexander of Russia. The sole surviving British officer noticed by Rochechouart must have been Lieutenant Strangways:

> The Prince of Sweden had moved far in advance of his entourage to provide personal encouragement to a company of English 'artificiers-artillereurs' firing Congreve rockets. Because the English artillerymen were obliged to move within half-range of formidable French artillery batteries in order to have their weapons take effect, half the company had been rendered hors de combat in the blink of an eye (so to speak), and when Bernadotte saw that development, he went to encourage the men still standing. It was thus that we found him, in a hail of shot, surrounded by the dead and dying. Mounted on a tall white horse, he was clad in a violet-colored velvet pelisse adorned with gold braid, wore a cocked hat with gold lace and white plume surmounted by an immense plume in the Swedish colours [yellow and blue], and held a baton covered with violet velvet and decorated with a gold crown at each end. Nothing could be more impressive than the martial appearance of this illustrious military leader as he urged on the brave English captain, the only remaining officer, in the midst of his mutilated men.[61]

Despite the scene described by Rochechouart and the prominent role played by the Rocket Brigade in the action, its reported casualties were remarkably light. Only Driver James Jenkins was killed in addition to Captain Bogue and just six other troop members were wounded:

> Bombardier Duncan
> Acting Bombardier Grey
> Gunner Royal
> Gunner Currel
> Gunner Rogers
> Gunner Palmer

60 August von Gneisenau (Translated with considerable additions by J.E. Marston), *The Life and Campaigns of Field Marshal Prince Blucher of Wahlstatt* (London: Sherwood, Neely & Jones, 1815), p.254.

61 Comte de Rochechouart, *Souvenirs sur la Révolution, l'Empire et la Restauration* (Paris: Librairie Plon, 1933), p.304.

A casual observer may have assumed a greater level of carnage, however, because the unit also had 26 horses killed or wounded.[62]

Although there was still plenty of fighting around Leipzig on the 19th as the allies stormed the city and snuffed out the rear guard left by Napoleon to cover his retreat, the Rocket Brigade was not involved. Instead, the men attended to the funeral of their late commander: '...the body was... decently interred the next morning at the town of Taucha, about two miles from Leipsic [sic]; all the brigade attending with the deepest regret this melancholy ceremony'.[63] Late in the day, Emperor Alexander and the British ambassador, Lord Cathcart, received a special request from Prince Charles Jean to review his Swedish troops. As reported by Cathcart: 'We found the Swedish army formed in line to the number of about 20,000 men, seemingly in good order, and certainly not much the worse for the military service they had endured. The Emperor also inspected the English rocket-brigade attached to that army, and under the command of Lieutenant Strangways'.[64] Some sources say that during this inspection Alexander spontaneously removed his own decoration of the Order of Saint Anne and presented it to Strangways. He was certainly was awarded that decoration, but verification of the manner in which it was bestowed is lacking.

Bogue received a prominent posthumous mention in the Crown Prince's report: 'Colonel Diederichs, commanding the Russian artillery attached to General Bülow's corps, rendered great service on this occasion. Captain Bogue, commanding the English rocket company, signalised himself in like manner. This brave officer was killed, and is universally regretted. The rockets produced the most decisive result'.[65] The British press continued to report assiduously on the activities of the Rocket Brigade. Stewart's 19 October account of the battle (with its favorable mention of Bogue) was published in the Times on 4 November due to the efforts of a civilian businessman named Edward Solly who carried a copy across Germany and the North Sea to England faster than the official courier.[66] A brief obituary of Bogue appeared in *The Times* on 8 November and that was followed on 12 November by a fuller account quoting the letter of Mr. James to Bogue's in-laws. According to a senior officer in the Peninsula, the cause of this publicity was easily (if somewhat cynically) explained: 'General --- [sic], who is very wise and knowing in the secret views and springs of everything (or at least would be thought so), says, that all that fuss of the Crown Prince and Sir Charles Stewart, as to the effect of the

62 Lt Amherst Wright to Lt Gen. McLeod, 24 October 1813, TNA WO 55/1129, pp.124-126.

63 John James to John Hanson, 11 November, 1813, in Hanson, *Short Journal*, Exhibits.

64 George Cathcart, *Commentaries on the War in Russia and Germany in 1812 and 1813* (London: J. Murray, 1850), p.355.

65 Bulletin of 21 October 1813, J. Philippart (ed.), *Memoirs and Campaigns of Charles Jean, Prince Royal of Sweden* (Baltimore: Neal, Wills, & Cole and Coale & Maxwell, 1815), p.381.

66 *The Biographer* (March 1884), pp.90-91.

rockets in the North, was to please the Prince Regent in England, the great patron of the rockets'.[67]

The Rocket Brigade spent a brief time in Leipzig following the battle, primarily to make good its loss of horses. To expedite this process, the Crown Prince ordered Bülow and Winzingerode to give first choice of captured mounts to Strangways and his men, with the horses being paid for by Lieutenant General Stewart. Ironically, Stewart himself also needed a new horse because both his orderly and the horse he rode in the battle ('a grey, docked stallion') disappeared from in front of the King of Prussia's residence.[68]

One private of the Rocket Brigade made good use of this time with a bit of sharp dealing: 'A British private who was attached to the rocket brigade, and who had picked up a little broken French and German, went to the largest hotel in Leipzic [sic] and displaying an English shilling to the landlord, enquired if this piece of coin was current there. 'Oh yes,' replied he, 'you may have whatever the house affords for that money, it passes current here at present'. Having eaten a full meal, the soldier presented the same single shilling as full settlement for the bill. The innkeeper realised he had been tricked, but he also realised that he would be unlikely to obtain any further payment. He then conceived the plan of paying the soldier to play the same trick on a rival innkeeper, but after the money changed hands, the rocketeer revealed that the innkeeper had been twice fooled:

> Sir, I deem myself in honour bound to use my utmost endeavour to put your wishes into execution, I shall certainly do all that I can, but, must candidly inform you, that I fear I shall not succeed, since I played the very same trick on that gentleman yesterday, and it is to his particular advice alone, that you are indebted for the honour of my company to-day.[69]

After this brief respite, the Rocket Brigade found itself headed west as the Crown Prince launched the Army of the North in a campaign against *Maréchal* Davout and Napoleon's Danish allies. There was no immediate fighting, but there was cold and discomfort. On 1 November, the Crown Prince granted a cash reward of 20 shillings to every noncommissioned officer and 10 shillings to every private of the Rocket Brigade because of its good conduct at Leipzig. Swedish records reveal that the Brigade mustered 12 NCOs and 157 men on that date.[70] On 6 November, the Crown Prince (and, presumably, the Rocket Brigade) arrived at Hanover.[71]

67 Larpent, *Journal*, Vol.2, p.114.

68 RAI, MD/383, 'Rocket Battery under Swedish Command,' pp.8-9.

69 Anon., *The Soldier's Companion, or Martial Recorder* (London: Edward Cock, 1824), Vol.1, pp.428-429.

70 RAI, MD/383, 'Rocket Battery under Swedish Command,' p.9.

71 Philippart (ed.), *Memoirs of Charles Jean*, p.419.

There was still some additional praise and rewards to be handed out for Leipzig. On 25 November, *Fältmarskalk* Curt von Stedingk, the commander of the Swedish army, received from Lieutenant Wright a list of the members of the Brigade who had most distinguished themselves in the fighting at Leipzig and as a result, on 8 December, ten members of the Brigade were awarded the Swedish decoration for 'brave conduct in the field' ['*För Tapperhet i Falt*'].[72] The recipients were Lieutenant Strangways (who received a gold medal) and the following soldiers: Sergeant-Major James Wright, Sergeant Daniel Dunnet, Bombardier Thomas Lloyd, Gunners John Thimmonds, John Eaves and George Munro, and Drivers George Fox, John Paltculls, and John Bates, all of whom received silver medals.[73] The medal was suspended from a blue and yellow ribbon.

There was sporadic fighting between the Army of the North and the French and Danes during November and the first half of December, but none that involved the Rocket Brigade, which was still attached to the headquarters of the Swedish army. On the verge of invading Denmark, the Crown Prince agreed to a cease-fire requested by the Danes for the period from 15-29 December, but the important fortress of Glückstadt on the Elbe in the Duchy of Holstein was excluded from armistice.[74] By order of 15 December, the Rocket Brigade was re-assigned the reserve artillery and on the 16th, half the unit was assigned to participate in the siege of Glückstadt.[75] The Crown Prince was aware effect of incendiary rockets on towns composed mainly of wooden buildings and hoped to achieve the same results in this new siege. He also may have hoped that the Danes would still have a vivid memory of the fires started by rockets during the British siege of Copenhagen in 1807.

The armistice was extended to 5 January, 1814, but the siege of Glückstadt continued unabated, with the besiegers fortified with special distributions of aquavit twice a day.[76] The bombardments had their desired effect and the fortress surrendered the day the general cease-fire expired: 'The Swedish and English artillery, and the detached corps of Count Woronzoff, have eminently distinguished themselves'.[77] The Crown Prince took this occasion to bestow yet another honour on the senior officers of the Brigade:

72 Latham, 'Rocket Service', pp.448-449. This was a medal of valour and not an order of knighthood. Nicholas Carlisle, *A Concise Account of the Several Foreign Orders of Knighthood and Other Marks of Honourable Distinction, Especially of Such as Have Been Conferred upon British Subjects* (London: John Hearns, 1829), p.468. Since Leipzig was not a British battle honour, there was no clasp for the battle when the Military General Service Medal was awarded to surviving British soldiers of the Napoleonic wars in 1848.

73 RAI, MD/383, 'Rocket Battery under Swedish Command,' pp.10-11.

74 Bulletin of 16 December 1813, Philippart (ed.), *Memoirs of Charles Jean*, p.445.

75 RAI, MD/383, 'Rocket Battery under Swedish Command,' pp.11.

76 RAI, MD/383, 'Rocket Battery under Swedish Command,' pp.12.

77 Bulletin of 6 January, 1814, Philippart (ed.), *Memoir of Charles Jean*, p.466. Surprisingly, the men of the Rocket Brigade were not the only Englishmen thanked for their service in the siege. The Bulletin also

> His Royal Highness the Prince Royal orders that, in view of the zeal, activity and intelligence demonstrated by Messrs. Wright and Strangways, lieutenants of the Brigade of Mounted Rocketeers, they are to receive the rations prescribed for officers of the rank of captain, and that they should be considered during their service [with the Swedish army] as having that same rank.[78]

On 18 January, Wright received the same gold medal for valour that had previously been awarded to Strangways. Both officers also eventually received knighthoods in the Swedish Order of the Sword.

On 14 January, 1814, Denmark, Sweden and England signed the Treaty of Kiel which ended the fighting between Denmark and Sweden. The cornerstone of the peace was an exchange of territory whereby Sweden acquired sovereignty over Norway while Swedish Pomerania was ceded to Denmark as compensation. The end of hostilities eliminated the need for the Rocket Brigade to be attached to the Swedish army and the unit was accordingly re-assigned to Wallmoden's corps on 16 January. On 18 January, the Rocket Brigade received orders to join the British expeditionary force in Holland under the command of Sir Thomas Graham. Accompanied by two horse artillery batteries of the King's German Legion, the Rocket Brigade reach Holland in March of 1814 and remained there until the Waterloo campaign.[79]

The successes of the Rocket Brigade contributed to a decision to give a more permanent establishment to the rocket forces serving in the field, but the exact way in which this was accomplished was somewhat surprising. While the Rocket Brigade had been in Germany, a second rocket force had been created using men of the 5th Battalion of the Royal Artillery and had been deployed to join Wellington's army in the Peninsula in September 1813 under the command of Second Captain H.B. Lane. Next, another small detachment from the 5th Battalion was formed under the command of Captain W.G. Eliot for service in the Netherlands. When General Orders were issued in late December 1813 to add two rocket troops to the official establishment of the Royal Horse Artillery, the Horse Guards specified that '[t]he detachment going out [to Holland] under Captain Eliot and that serving in the Peninsula under Captain Lane are to be formed into one troop [under the command of Eliot] and the detachment under Lieuts. Wright and Strangways are to be considered the other'.[80] So far so good, but when Captain E.C Whinyates was designated to take command of Bogue's old force, the issue of seniority came

reports that a Royal Navy flotilla under the command of Captain Farquhar 'took an active and honourable part in the attack of the place, and greatly contributed to its surrender'.

78 RAI, MD/383, 'Rocket Battery under Swedish Command,' pp.12.

79 Latham, 'Rocket Service', p.429.

80 TNA, WO55/642, p.317, quoted in Latham, 'Rocket Service', p.432.

into play. Because Whinyates was junior in rank to Eliot, the Rocket Brigade in Germany became the 2nd Rocket Troop despite its greater length of service.[81]

It is satisfying to report that the late Captain Bogue was not forgotten by either the Swedish Crown Prince or his own patron, the Prince Regent. Prince Charles Jean made a posthumous award of the Swedish Military Order of the Sword, 4th Class (Knight), to Bogue's widow, along with an undoubtedly welcome present of 10,000 thalers. The gift was accompanied by the following personal letter:

> Kiel, 6 January, 1814
>
> Madam,
> The King, my sovereign, has deigned to authorise me to confer the Cross of his Military Order of the Sword not alone on the Swedish officers, but on those also of the Allied Troops who distinguished themselves in fighting for the common cause.
>
> The manner in which your husband has conducted himself during the campaign, has well merited this reward of the brave.
>
> He died on the field of honour; and the plains of Leipzig, the last witnesses of his courage and of his intrepidity, saw him perish before I could confer on him this order of Knighthood.
>
> I conform myself, Madam, to the customs of the English nation, of which Sweden is the faithful ally; and I transmit to you the Decoration of the Order of which your husband rendered himself so worthy. May it be in your hands a consolatory remembrance of his loss, as it is a testimony to his valour, and of the personal esteem with which he had inspired me! I pray God, Madam, to bless and to keep you in his holy protection.
>
> /s/ Charles Jean[82]

Not to be outdone, the Prince Regent granted a pension to Bogue's widow and two children on 22 July, 1814.[83]

In October of 1814, two English merchants named G. Holy and J. Drabble visited Bogue's grave and conceived the plan of erecting a monument to commemorate his services. With the help of other contributors and a Leipzig merchant named Wagner, they put their plan into action and the work was complete by August of 1815. The finished monument was a large cube of stone with marble inserts on all four sides carved with the following inscription in both English and German:

81 Latham, 'Rocket Service', pp.431-432.

82 This letter appears in both the original French and the English translation quoted here in Hanson, *Short Journal*, Exhibits. Blücher also paid his respects to Bogue's widow by letter when he visited London in the summer of 1814. Description of Lot 85, Bonhams 1 April, 2015, Item (ii).

83 Description of Lot 85, Bonhams April 1, 2015, Item (v).

> 'Let those journeying hither behold this stone.
> The memorial alike of private worth and military glory'.
> Sacred to
> Richard Bogue, Esq.
> A native of Hampshire in England
> and Captain in his Britannic Majesty's Regiment of Royal Horse Artillery
> who fell in the 31st year of his age
> gloriously fighting for the combined cause of Germany and her allies,
> at the battle of Leipsic, on the 18th of October, 1813,
> while commanding the Congreve Rocket brigade,
> having by distinguished services as the village of Paunsdorf
> borne a most conspicuous part
> in the victory of that memorable day.
> As a soldier,
> he united professional science with the most ardent valour,
> and in private life,
> as a husband and father,
> (leaving a widow with two infant children)
> he afforded a model of for every domestic virtue.
> That this distinguished officer therefore
> may live beyond the grave,
> his countrymen who have since visited this spot
> where his remains were interred,
> have at their own voluntary expense
> dedicated this monument to his respected name.[84]

The monument was restored in 1896 by members of Bogue's family and some officers of the Royal Artillery.

In 1820, Charles Jean, now King of Sweden, awarded the Swedish medal for bravery to five more Leipzig veterans of the Rocket Brigade:

> Upon a humbly made representation His Majesty has graciously deigned to confer the silver medal for brave conduct in the field on the following Royal British Non-commissioned Officers, who when serving in the British Rocket Brigade, distinguished themselves at the battle of Leipzig:
> Serjeant Michael Taylor;
> Serjeant Robert Chalkley;

84 F.A. Whinyates, 'Captain Bogue and the Rocket Brigade,' *Minutes of Proceedings of the Royal Artillery Institution*, Vol.XXIV (1897), pp 131-136, at p.131. This article contains a drawing of the monument. A recent photo of the monument can be found at <http://napoleon-monuments.eu/EnNap/Bogue.htm> (viewed 2 May, 2019). It appears that only half the inscription remains.

Corporal Edward Marks;
Corporal William Wareham; and
Bombardier John Guy.[85]

This additional award was inspired by the discovery that Wright's original recommendation of soldiers to receive the medal had mistakenly listed only the longest serving rocketeers, not those who were most distinguished at Leipzig.[86]

The success of the Rocket Brigade at the Battle of Leipzig ensured that rockets would be a battlefield weapon for the British army for many years to come, with the Congreve rocket soon being replaced by the Hale rocket.[87] It also ensured that other nations would adopt the technology for their own armies, with countries that had been on the receiving end of rocket fire being the first to act. The French starting investigating rockets after the attack on Boulogne while Danish experimentation with rockets began after the siege of Copenhagen. *Maréchal* Davout actually tested rocket weapons during the siege of Hamburg in 1813-14. The Austrian and Prussians followed along after the Napoleonic Wars had ended.[88] The problem of rocket accuracy was never fully solved, however, so the military significance of rockets was always minor. One Prussian soldier who had witnessed the rockets at Leipzig would have said that was a good thing: 'Haven't we enough instruments of death without needing to resort to these diabolical things…'[89]

## Bibliography


### *Archival Sources*

Legion of Honour Database
Dossier LH/2104/7: <http://www2.culture.gouv.fr/LH/LH178/PG/FRDAFAN83_OL2104007V002.htm>
Royal Artillery Institution, Woolwich, England,
MD/383, 'The British Mounted Rocket Battery Under Swedish Command'
The National Archives, Kew
WO 1/427: Foreign Troops on British Pay. German levies and armies. Departmental (Transport Office and Miscellaneous).
WO55/642: General Orders, Artillery (Series 2).


85 J.H. Leslie, 'Swedish Medals Granted to the Rocket Brigade, R.H.A., For the Battle of Leipzig, October 16-18, 1813,' *Journal of the Royal Artillery*, Vol. XL (1913-14), p.327.
86 Latham, 'Rocket Service', p.451.
87 See generally, Franklin, *British Rockets*.
88 Frank Winter, *The First Golden Age of Rocketry* (Washington and London: Smithsonian Institution Press, 1990), pp.82-110.
89 Krimer, *Errinerugen eines alten Lützower Jägers*, p.66. Translated from the German by Antony Brett-James.

WO 55/1129: Artillery Letters and Letter Books (Woolwich) From Officers. Home.

***Published Sources***


Anon., *Bulletins of the Campaign of 1813 [Compiled from the London Gazette]* (nl [London]: np, nd).

Anon., *Tales of the Wars; or, A Naval and Military Chronicle* (London: William Mark Clark, 1838).

Anon., *The Soldier's Companion, or Martial Recorder* (London: Edward Cock, 1824).

Boyen, Hermann von, *Denkwürdigkeiten und Erinnerungen 1771-1813* (Stuttgart: Verlag von Robert Lutz, 1899).

Brown, James Alex, *England's Artillerymen – An Historical Narrative of the Services of the Royal Artillery* (London: Hall, Smart, and Allen, 1865).

Beamish, N. Ludlow, *The History of the King's German Legion* (London: Thomas and William Boone, 1837).

Blackman, G.K., Letter of Thomas Maynard, Surgeon, Coldstream Guards, to George Blackman, 11 August 1814, reproduced in Notes and Documents 1604, *Journal of the Society of Army Historical Research*, Vol.79, No. 319 (Autumn 2001), pp.257-258.

Carlisle, Nicholas, *A Concise Account of the Several Foreign Orders of Knighthood and Other Marks of Honourable Distinction, Especially of Such as Have Been Conferred upon British Subjects* (London: John Hearns, 1829).

Cathcart, George, *Commentaries on the War in Russia and Germany in 1812 and 1813* (London: J. Murray, 1850).

Congreve, William, *A Concise Account of the Origin and Progress of the Rocket System* (London: J. Whiting, 1810).

Congreve, William, *Details of the Rocket System* (London: J. Whiting, 1814, reprint London nd).

Congreve, William, *Postscript to the Concise Account of the Origin and Progress of the Rocket System* (London: J. Whiting, 1808).

Earle, James, *Commodore Squib: The Life, Times and Secretive Wars of England's First Rocket Man, Sir William Congreve, 1772-1828* (Newcastle upon Tyne: Cambridge Scholars Publishing, 2010).

Fortescue, John W., *History of the British Army* (London: Macmillan & Co., 1920).

Franklin, C.E., *British Rockets of the Napoleonic and Colonial Wars 1805-1901* (Staplehurst, Kent: Spellmount 2005).

Gifford, E., *Memoirs of the Life and Campaigns of Napoleon Bonaparte* (London: J. & J. Cundee, nd).

Gneisenau, August von (Translated with considerable additions by J.E. Marston), *The Life and Campaigns of Field Marshal Prince Blucher of Wahlstatt* (London: Sherwood, Neely & Jones, 1815).

Graves, Donald E., *Sir William Congreve and the Rocket's Red Glare* (Alexandria Bay, NY and Bloomfield, Ontario: Museum Restoration Service, 1989).

Gurwood, Lt Col (ed.), *The Despatches of Field Marshal the Duke of Wellington* (London: John Murray, 1836).

Hanson, William, *Short Journal of a Visit to Sicily, 1810* (London: J. Darling, 1814).

Krimer, Wenzel, *Errinerugen eines alten Lützower Jägers, 1795-1819* (Stuttgart: Verlag von Robert Lutz, 1913).

Larpent, F. Seymour, *The Private Journal of F. Seymour Larpent* (2nd revised ed., London: Richard Bentley, 1853).

Latham, H.B., 'The Rocket Service and the Award of the Swedish Decorations for Leipzig,' *Journal of the Royal Artillery* Vol. LVI (1929-30), pp.419-432.

Leslie, J.H., 'Swedish Medals Granted to the Rocket Brigade, R.H.A., For the Battle of Leipzig, October 16-18, 1813,' *Journal of the Royal Artillery*, Vol. XL (1913-14), p.327.

Leslie, John H., *The Services of the Royal Regiment of Artillery in the Peninsular War 1808-1814* (London: Hugh Rees Limited, 1908), pp.38-39.

McCain, A.D., "The Soul of Artillery:' Congreve's Rockets and Their Effectiveness in Combat,' *Journal of the Society for Army Historical Research* (2000), Vol.78, pp.252-263.

Mercer, Cavalié, *Journal of the Waterloo Campaign* (London: Blackwood & Sons, 1870).

Morris, Thomas, *Recollections of Military Service, in 1813, 1814, & 1815* (London: J. Madden, 1845).

Nafziger, George, *Napoleon at Leipzig* (Chicago: Emperor's Press, 1996).

Philippart, J. (ed.), *Memoirs and Campaigns of Charles Jean, Prince Royal of Sweden* (Baltimore: Neal, Wills, & Cole and Coale & Maxwell, 1815).

Picard, Francis Louis, *Histoire du 42e Régiment d'Infanterie* (Montbéliard: H. Barbier, 1875).

Rochechouart, Comte de, *Souvenirs sur la Révolution, l'Empire et la Restauration* (Paris: Librairie Plon, 1933).

St.-Donat, Coupé de and B. de Roquefort, *Mémoires pour Servir a l'Histoire de Charles-XIV-Jean, Roi de Suède et de Norwège* (Paris:Plancher, 1820).

Sherwig, John, *Guineas and Gunpowder – British Foreign Aid in the Wars with France 1793-1815* (Cambridge, MA: Harvard University Press 1969).

Siborne, H.T. (ed.), *Waterloo Letters* (London: Parker & Son, 1891).

Strotha, *Generallieutenant* von, *Die Königlich Preussische Reitende Artillerie vom Jahre 1759 bis 1816* (Berlin: Vossische Buchhandlung, 1868).

'Une Société d'hommes de Lettres et de Militaires' [Pierre François Tissot], *Les Fastes de la Gloire, ou les braves recommandés à la postérité* (Paris: Tissot, 1822).

Vane, Charles William [Marquess of Londonderry], *Narrative of the War in Germany and France in 1813 and 1814* (London: Henry Colburn & Richard Bentley, 1830).

Wellington, 2nd Duke of (ed.), *Supplementary Despatches, Correspondence and Memoranda of . . . Wellington* (London: Longmans, Green, Reader, and Dyer, 1865).

Werrett, Simon, 'William Congreve's Rational Rockets,' *Notes and Records of the Royal Society of London*, v. 63, No. 1 (March 2009), pp.35-56.

Winter, Frank, *The First Golden Age of Rocketry* (Washington and London: Smithsonian Institution Press, 1990), pp.82-110.

Whinyates, F.A., 'Captain Bogue and the Rocket Brigade,' *Minutes of Proceedings of the Royal Artillery Institution*, Vol.XXIV (1897), pp 131-136.

# Index

## *From Reason to Revolution series – Warfare 1721-1815*

http://www.helion.co.uk/series/from-reason-to-revolution-1721-1815.php

The 'From Reason to Revolution' series covers the period of military history 1721–1815, an era in which fortress-based strategy and linear battles gave way to the nation-in-arms and the beginnings of total war.

This era saw the evolution and growth of light troops of all arms, and of increasingly flexible command systems to cope with the growing armies fielded by nations able to mobilise far greater proportions of their manpower than ever before. Many of these developments were fired by the great political upheavals of the era, with revolutions in America and France bringing about social change which in turn fed back into the military sphere as whole nations readied themselves for war. Only in the closing years of the period, as the reactionary powers began to regain the upper hand, did a military synthesis of the best of the old and the new become possible.

The series will examine the military and naval history of the period in a greater degree of detail than has hitherto been attempted, and has a very wide brief, with the intention of covering all aspects from the battles, campaigns, logistics, and tactics, to the personalities, armies, uniforms, and equipment.

### Submissions

The publishers would be pleased to receive submissions for this series. Please contact series editor Andrew Bamford via email (andrewbamford@helion.co.uk), or in writing to Helion & Company Limited, Unit 8 Amherst Business Centre, Budbrooke Road, Warwick, CV34 5WE

### Titles

No 1 *Lobositz to Leuthen: Horace St Paul and the Campaigns of the Austrian Army in the Seven Years War 1756-57* (Neil Cogswell)

No 2 *Glories to Useless Heroism: The Seven Years War in North America from the French journals of Comte Maurés de Malartic, 1755-1760* (William Raffle (ed.))

No 3 *Reminiscences 1808-1815 Under Wellington: The Peninsular and Waterloo Memoirs of William Hay* (Andrew Bamford (ed.))

No 4 *Far Distant Ships: The Royal Navy and the Blockade of Brest 1793-1815* (Quintin Barry)

No 5 *Godoy's Army: Spanish Regiments and Uniforms from the Estado Militar of 1800* (Charles Esdaile and Alan Perry)

No 6 *On Gladsmuir Shall the Battle Be! The Battle of Prestonpans 1745* (Arran Johnston)

No 7 *The French Army of the Orient 1798-1801: Napoleon's Beloved 'Egyptians'* (Yves Martin)

No 8 *The Autobiography, or Narrative of a Soldier: The Peninsular War Memoirs of William Brown of the 45th Foot* (Steve Brown (ed.))

No 9 *Recollections from the Ranks: Three Russian Soldiers' Autobiographies from the Napoleonic Wars* (Darrin Boland)

No 10 *By Fire and Bayonet: Grey's West Indies Campaign of 1794* (Steve Brown)

No 11 *Olmütz to Torgau: Horace St Paul and the Campaigns of the Austrian Army in the Seven Years War 1758-60* (Neil Cogswell)

No 12 *Murat's Army: The Army of the Kingdom of Naples 1806-1815* (Digby Smith)

No 13 *The Veteran or 40 Years' Service in the British Army: The Scurrilous Recollections of Paymaster John Harley 47th Foot – 1798-1838* (Gareth Glover (ed.))

No 14 *Narrative of the Eventful Life of Thomas Jackson: Militiaman and Coldstream Sergeant, 1803-15* (Eamonn O'Keeffe (ed.))

No.15 *For Orange and the States: The Army of the Dutch Republic 1713-1772 Part I: Infantry* (Marc Geerdinck-Schaftenaar)

No 16 *Men Who Are Determined to be Free: The American Assault on Stony Point, 15 July 1779* (David C. Bonk)

No 17 *Next to Wellington: General Sir George Murray: The Story of a Scottish Soldier and Statesman, Wellington's Quartermaster General* (John Harding-Edgar)

No 18 *Between Scylla and Charybdis: The Army of Elector Friedrich August of Saxony 1733-1763 Part I: Staff and Cavalry* (Marco Pagan)

No 19 *The Secret Expedition: The Anglo-Russian Invasion of Holland 1799* (Geert van Uythoven)

No 20 *'We Are Accustomed to do our Duty': German Auxiliaries with the British Army 1793-95* (Paul Demet)

No 21 *With the Guards in Flanders: The Diary of Captain Roger Morris 1793-95* (Peter Harington (ed.))

No 22 *The British Army in Egypt 1801: An Underrated Army Comes of Age* (Carole Divall)

No 23 *Better is the Proud Plaid: The Clothing, Weapons, and Accoutrements of the Jacobites in the '45* (Jenn Scott)

No 24 *The Lilies and the Thistle: French Troops in the Jacobite '45* (Andrew Bamford)

No 25 *A Light Infantryman With Wellington: The Letters of Captain George Ulrich Barlow 52nd and 69th Foot 1808-15* (Gareth Glover (ed.))

No 26 *Swiss Regiments in the Service of France 1798-1815: Uniforms, Organisation, Campaigns* (Stephen Ede-Borrett)

No 27 *For Orange and the States! The Army of the Dutch Republic 1713-1772: Part II: Cavalry and Specialist Troops* (Marc Geerdinck-Schaftenaar)

No 28 *Fashioning Regulation, Regulating Fashion: Uniforms and Dress of the British Army 1800-1815 Volume I* (Ben Townsend)

No 29 *Riflemen: The History of the 5th Battalion 60th (Royal American) Regiment, 1797-1818* (Robert Griffith)

No 30 *The Key to Lisbon: The Third French Invasion of Portugal, 1810-11* (Kenton White)

No 31 *Command and Leadership: Proceedings of the 2018 Helion & Company 'From Reason to Revolution' Conference* (Andrew Bamford (ed.))

No 32 *Waterloo After the Glory: Hospital Sketches and Reports on the Wounded After the Battle* (Michael Crumplin and Gareth Glover)

No 33 *Fluxes, Fevers, and Fighting Men: War and Disease in Ancien Regime Europe 1648-1789* (Pádraig Lenihan)

No 34 *'They Were Good Soldiers': African-Americans Serving in the Continental Army, 1775-1783* (John U. Rees)

No 35 *A Redcoat in America: The Diaries of Lieutenant William Bamford, 1757-1765 and 1776* (John B. Hattendorf (ed.))

No 36 *Between Scylla and Charybdis: The Army of Friedrich August II of Saxony, 1733-1763: Part II: Infantry and Artillery* (Marco Pagan)

No 37 *Québec Under Siege: French Eye-Witness Accounts from the Campaign of 1759* (Charles A. Mayhood (ed.))

No 38 *King George's Hangman: Henry Hawley and the Battle of Falkirk 1746* (Jonathan D. Oates)

No 39 *Zweybrücken in Command: The Reichsarmee in the Campaign of 1758* (Neil Cogswell)

No 40 *So Bloody a Day: The 16th Light Dragoons in the Waterloo Campaign* (David J. Blackmore)

No 41 *Northern Tars in Southern Waters: The Russian Fleet in the Mediterranean 1806-1810* (Vladimir Bogdanovich Bronevskiy / Darrin Boland)

No 42 *Royal Navy Officers of the Seven Years War: A Biographical Dictionary of Commissioned Officers 1748-1763* (Cy Harrison)

No 43 *All at Sea: Naval Support for the British Army During the American Revolutionary War* (John Dillon)

No 44 *Glory is Fleeting: New Scholarship on the Napoleonic Wars* (Andrew Bamford (ed.))

No 45 *Fashioning Regulation, Regulating Fashion: Uniforms and Dress of the British Army 1800-1815 Vol. II* (Ben Townsend)

No 46 *Revenge in the Name of Honour: The Royal Navy's Quest for Vengeance in the Single Ship Actions of the War of 1812* (Nicholas James Kaizer)

No 47 *They Fought With Extraordinary Bravery: The III German (Saxon) Army Corps in the Southern Netherlands 1814* (Geert van Uythoven)

No 48 *The Danish Army of the Napoleonic Wars 1801-1814, Organisation, Uniforms & Equipment: Volume 1: High Command, Line and Light Infantry* (David Wilson)

No 49 *Neither Up Nor Down: The British Army and the Flanders Campaign 1793-1895* (Phillip Ball)

No 50 *Guerra Fantástica: The Portuguese Army and the Seven Years War* (António Barrento)

No 51 *From Across the Sea: North Americans in Nelson's Navy* (Sean M. Heuvel and John A. Rodgaard)

No 52 *Rebellious Scots to Crush: The Military Response to the Jacobite '45* (Andrew Bamford (ed.))

No 53 *The Army of George II 1727-1760: The Soldiers who Forged an Empire* (Peter Brown)

No 54 *Wellington at Bay: The Battle of Villamuriel, 25 October 1812* (Garry David Wills)

No 55 *Life in the Red Coat: The British Soldier 1721-1815* (Andrew Bamford (ed.))

No 56 *Wellington's Favourite Engineer. John Burgoyne: Operations, Engineering, and the Making of a Field Marshal* (Mark S. Thompson)

No 57 *Scharnhorst: The Formative Years, 1755-1801* (Charles Edward White)

No 58 *At the Point of the Bayonet: The Peninsular War Battles of Arroyomolinos and Almaraz 1811-1812* (Robert Griffith)

No 59 *Sieges of the '45: Siege Warfare during the Jacobite Rebellion of 1745-1746* (Jonathan D. Oates)

No 60 *Austrian Cavalry of the Revolutionary and Napoleonic Wars, 1792–1815* (Enrico Acerbi, András K. Molnár)

No 61 *The Danish Army of the Napoleonic Wars 1801-1814, Organisation, Uniforms & Equipment: Volume 2: Cavalry and Artillery* (David Wilson)

No 62 *Napoleon's Stolen Army: How the Royal Navy Rescued a Spanish Army in the Baltic* (John Marsden)

No 63 *The Battle of the Chesapeake 1781: The Royal Navy and the Battle that Lost America* (Quintin Barry)

No 64 *Bullocks, Grain, and Good Madeira: The Maratha and Jat Campaigns 1803-1806 and the emergence of the Indian Army* (Joshua Provan)

No 65 *Sir James McGrigor: The Adventurous Life of Wellington's Chief Medical Officer* (Tom Scotland)

Following the annexation of the Punjab in 1849, the British Raj acknowledged the fighting prowess of the proud Sikh nation by recruiting Sikh warriors for military service. This respected military tradition continued into the first decade of the 20th century. Thus Sikhs were in high demand at the outbreak of the First World War. They came forward in their thousands and enlisted in numbers disproportionate to the population. Representing approximately 1 to 2 percent of the Indian population, they contributed 20 percent of the British Indian Army manpower strength in 1914. The resultant conflict was a truly global one for the Sikhs who fought in far-flung campaigns on the Western Front, Gallipoli, Mesopotamia, Persia, Africa, Palestine and the Far East. Their manpower contribution reached over 100,000 men by the time of the Armistice. In this, his first book, Sukwinder Bassi seeks to address the largely forgotten Sikh effort by examination of their wartime collective experience. Their voices are thematically arranged and chronologically ordered to allow reader comprehension of changing personal attitudes and perspectives towards the ongoing conflict. Moreover, this volume explores the myriad reasons why Sikhs rose to the challenge of 1914-18, and how this is linked to cumulative psyche, martial tradition, coercion and the contemporary political situation in the Punjab. Utilising research from hundreds of unpublished correspondence to and from Sikh servicemen, testimonies, contemporary newspaper articles, archives and wide range of other sources, this volume explores the Sikh experience during the First World War, a conflict the effects of which are still with us today.

"This book offers an inimitable insight into the experiences, motivation, hopes and fears of the Sikh, a martial race unique within the Imperial troops who fought for King and Empire. The contribution of these fearless warriors is hugely underrepresented in the popular history of the First World War where Christian, Hindu, Muslim and Sikh lived, fought and died together in the cause of freedom and peace. In our modern, multicultural United Kingdom we must understand more of that which binds us rather than divides us and this contemporary narrative shines a light on the selfless contribution of heroes, descendants of whom now call these shores their home."

Brigadier Peter S Rafferty MBE DL; Former Colonel, the Duke of Lancaster's Regiment, successor regiment to the Manchester Regiment of the Jullundur Brigade

"'Thousands of heroes have arisen' … and will continue to rise in the defence of all that is just and sacred. Sukwinder Bassi's book is a haunting account of 'Sikh Voices of the Great War 1914-18' and a very valuable addition to the available literature. The 47th Sikhs, now 5th Battalion Sikh Regiment, were a component part of the Jullundur Brigade and their incredible action at Neuve Chapelle on 28 October 1914 is just one example of the Sikh soldier's 'josh' which is recalled with awe over a century later."

Pushpindar Singh Chopra, son of the late Major General Mohinder Singh Chopra who commanded the crossing between India and Pakistan during the 1947 partition

Sukwinder Singh Bassi is the British-born son of Sikh parents who emigrated to England from the Punjab. He has had a long career developing his research and analytical experience in the field of health informatics, and works for England's health and social care regulator. He has a passionate interest in military and social history, with a special interest in both world wars and, in particular, Sikh heritage. His motivation for compiling this book was created on the back of a tour of the Great War battlefields of northern France and Belgium in 2014. Accompanied by his eleven-year-old son, Sukwinder was transfixed by the rows and rows of Sikh names at the Indian Memorial in Neuve Chapelle and on the Menin Gate in Ypres. He decided then and there that he would find out as much as possible about the people who had come thousands of miles to fight in Europe. Sukwinder's first book, Thousands Of Heroes Have Arisen, is the result of more than five years of painstaking research and endeavour, immersing the reader in the Sikh experience of the Great War years.